The Big Summer Cookbook

The Big Summer Cookbook

300 FRESH, FLAVORFUL RECIPES FOR THOSE LAZY, HAZY DAYS

Jeff Cox

JOHN WILEY & SONS, INC.

For Allison, Elizabeth, Isis, and Sean

Published by John Wiley & Sons, Inc., Hoboken, New Jersey
Published simultaneously in Canada

Library of Congress Cataloging-in-Publication Data
Cox, Jeff, 1940-
  The big summer cookbook: 300 fresh, flavorful recipes for those lazy, hazy days / Jeff Cox.
     p. cm.
  Includes index.
  ISBN 978-0-470-11427-8 (pbk)
1. Cookery, American. I. Title.
  TX715.C8697 2009
  641.5—dc22
                        2009023910

Book design by Debbie Glasserman
Printed in the United States of America
10 9 8 7 6 5 4 3 2 1

Acknowledgments

Thanks to Bob Engel at Gourmet Mushrooms, Paula Downing of Sebastopol, and recipe testers Ali Holmes, Wriston Jones, Archie Hughes, Allene Donato, Debbie Keating, David Woodruff, Jason Ecklund, Tomomi Hasimoto, Monique Egli, Mary Marincik, and Nancy Sieck. Special thanks to Betsy Fischer, instructor and coordinator for the Center for Culinary, Wine, and Hospitality Careers, at Santa Rosa Junior College in the heart of northern California's wine country. Heartfelt thanks to my editors, Linda Ingroia and Charleen Barila, and those copy editors and proofreaders who smoothed and corrected my copy. And thanks to my wife, Susanna, for her support and cogent critiques as she tasted these recipes as I made them.

Contents

Introduction

The cymbal clashes and fireworks of May thunderstorms herald the approaching summer. The days lengthen as the weeks pass into June. The mad rush of spring's green growth begins to slow. The kids get out of school. The lawn needs mowing. And summer settles in.

Summer releases us from the physical and psychological confinement of the cold months into an expansive communion with nature. Summer's presence is familiar, like the return of our loving, caring mother who lays a feast all around us.

Now the days are a riot of bright sun and hot fun, the evenings only slowly fade into night, and the magical, fragrant, sensual nights relax us. We feel alive. Our senses heighten and our horizons expand. Outdoors, in the sunlight and fresh air, it's possible to feel at home in the world, a part of grand nature rather than a bundled figure huddled away from the dark, killing cold.

When it's here, summer seems eternal, as if it will never end. Summer's warmth generates thousands of aromas that don't exist in the cold months—we can smell the clean earthiness of the forest floor, the scent of roses, the sweet tang of newly mown grass, and the salt of the ocean miles before we reach it.

We hear more, too: insects buzz and crickets chirp. Birds hoot and call. Leaves rustle in the wind. We might catch the sound of an outdoor band, children's laughter, or the roar from the baseball park when a slugger sends a ball arcing into the stands.

We get to see glorious summer sights: huge thunderheads lit from within by flickers of lightning, moving away across the sea; lightning bugs that look like stars floating up from the grass to join those in the sky; rainbows; and the myriad colors of flowers in gardens.

We feel more: ocean water warm enough for swimming, soft earth and grass under our bare feet, warm sunlight on our bare skin.

And not least, we taste more: in summer, food is most delicious. Peaches come sun warm and ripe from the tree. Tomatoes come ripe from the vine.

If the progress of the year encapsulates a human life in miniature, with spring being childhood and young adulthood, fall being middle age, and winter being old age, then summer is life at the height of its powers. The flowers of spring become the fruits and seeds of summer, gathering sugar, ripening toward the harvest. Spring courtships become summer's children. Now is when creativity abounds. Now is when the work gets done. Life is a miracle, and summer gives us the miraculous in full display. We celebrate the season as we always do—with feasts of food and drink, companionship, laughter. The food is so good, so fresh, and so tasty that it's a celebration in itself.

This book, then, is a guide to getting the most out of the wonderful foods of summer. And a hymn of praise for the season that makes all the others worthwhile.

JEFF COX

How to Use This Book

The chief elements of eating well in the summertime are fruits, vegetables, and fresh herbs. Summer presents us with a smorgasbord of plant-based foods available only at this most luxuriantly fertile of seasons. After all, meats, dairy, eggs, fish, oils, and such are available year-round with minor variations.

In the following chapters you'll find a basketful of recipes for using summer's profusion of goodies. There are hearty but simple breakfast treats, like homemade French Toast (page 29) and Summer Vegetable Quiche (page 32); and tasty party foods for your next get-together, including Tomato Chutney (page 45), Stuffed Squash Blossoms (page 54), and Maryland Crab Cakes (page 58).

Looking for a light lunch? Try a sandwich like the summer classic Lobster Roll (page 74), or a nutritious salad such as Caprese Salad (page 96) or Grilled

Peach and Fig Salad (page 109). Comforting soups are a welcome treat, no matter what season. Make a refreshing Sweet-and-Tart Gazpacho (page 135) or New England Clam Chowder (page 141).

You'll be inspired by the variety of main dish ideas in the book, including classic burgers, grilled seafood, and delicious steaks and ribs. But don't forget the fixin's; you'll find nutritious sides like Ratatouille (page 215) and Grilled Eggplant and Tomato Caponata (page 210).

No meal would be complete without dessert. Try a cool, crisp sorbet or homemade ice cream on those long, hot days. Or for a special treat, bake a Summer Stone Fruit Cobbler (page 260) or Strawberry Shortcake (page 246). There are a number of inspiring drink ideas, like homemade Lemonade (page 266) and Fruity Agua Fresca (page 265).

What you won't find in this book are premade, processed foods from the big corporations—full of sugar, salt, and fat, and ready to be microwaved, baked, or boiled. These recipes use fresh, whole foods, and if you're wise, they'll be organic—grown without agricultural chemicals, without genetic modifications, and in fields fertilized with the very stuff that they will use to build their healthy tissues.

One of the best ways to utilize the fresh ingredients of summer is to make your own homemade staples, like Heirloom Tomato Pasta Sauce (page 293) or Homemade Barbecue Sauce (294). Make enough to keep for the months ahead, so you'll always have the refreshing taste of summer, even as the weather starts to cool.

The recipes are marked with icons to help identify quick-cooking recipes, ones that can be made ahead, and ones that require no cooking time at all (a big help when it's too hot to even think about cooking). Throughout the book, you'll find helpful hints, informative sidebars, and even some summer stories of my own. Fresh, seasonal summer produce is highlighted in individual Summer Spotlight sidebars throughout the book to give you buying and storing tips and information on the many ways you can utilize the ingredient in your summer recipes.

I will only add this note of encouragement: when you're at the summer table, do as the French do. Slow down, relax, eat slowly and moderately, and enjoy everything the food has to offer in the way of sensuous pleasure.

Summer
The Most Delicious Season

Summer is about great food. And great food is about delicious flavors and aromas. And delicious flavors and especially aromas are about memories. And fond memories have a lot to do with summer.

Summer evenings we spent as kids with grandparents or parents who may now be gone live on in our memories along with the foods we ate then. I remember my grandfather Hardebeck, my mom's dad, who always wore a bow tie, visiting us at our home in the Pocono Mountains of Pennsylvania. I can see my dad in the backyard cooking steak on the grill during one of Grandpa's visits, with my mom standing by (ready with criticism if the meat wasn't done to the absolute turn). Her station was in the kitchen, making the best darn hash browns anyone ever tasted. Dad's steaks always turned out great, to me—with a smoky aroma and a crusty char-grilled exterior and pink juicy interior. The smell of the browned potatoes and onions, and the bacon grease used to make the hash browns, mingled with the steak. I loved grandpa, and memories of my family flood back easily when prompted by memories of the aromas of grilled sirloin steak and hash browns. Without the food associations, what would I remember of those long-ago days when I made sure my dog, Debbie (named after the grade school cutie I had a crush on), got a piece of the steak?

But I digress—in a way I'm sure all of us can digress: back to the summers of our youth, the swimming holes and swimming pools, the skinned knees, the trips to the beach and the mouthfuls of saltwater, the camping out in the mountains, the soda pop and ice cream, the wild fruits, and all the rest of the goodness life showers on us when we are new and unsuspecting.

American summer cooking is as exotic and important as the cuisines of cultures we may think of as exotic. I'll put a dish of Southern fried chicken up against a salmon *coulibiac* any day. Our American cuisine reflects the ever-growing melting pot we have become. Once upon a summer afternoon, we drank Cuban frozen daiquiris on the veranda. A decade later, we downed British gin and tonics on the patio. And today, we're back to Cuba for *mojitos* on the deck. Where once we nibbled on clams casino (mmm—rich with bacon) and later ate spicy Buffalo wings, now we bite into steak *satay* dipped in *chimichurri* sauce.

No matter where our summer recipes are from, they all come back to darn good eatin'—that's what summer means now. These sunny days and balmy nights not only improve our own spirits, but they also call forth nature's version of a broad smile: summer-luscious fruits and vegetables. And these fruits and vegetables never taste better than when they're grown close to home, because they're fresher and because local farmers can plant varieties with the best taste rather than ones that are hard and ship well.

Using Summer's Incredible Bounty

The three months of summer ride in on waves of fresh vegetables and fruits, especially the summer staples. Fresh ears of corn, of course, and tomatoes, but also summer squash, green beans, okra, local peppers sweet and hot (like a first summer love), cucumbers, beets, and eggplant. And the summer fruits! Apricots, cherries, peaches, nectarines, melons . . . and now is when you can find all this bounty grown locally and organically, with incomparable flavor and freshness. One can just imagine how our ancestors felt when the cold, lean days of the off-seasons faded into the time of sun-warmed days and shirtsleeve evenings, and the wonderful staples of summer appeared. We can feel something of that same thrill enjoying nature's gifts from our local gardens and farms.

There was a time in America when summer meant work—and lots of it. Planting crops, cultivating them, harvesting them, drying and baling hay, cutting corn and turning it into silage, putting up food for the cold months, and taking the harvest to town to sell. It wasn't that long ago, in the scheme of things, that most Americans were farmers.

Today, most Americans are no longer farmers, but 30 percent of us are gardeners—even if we just grow a few tomato plants. Or roses. Or herbs. Gardening, even a little of it, is grounding and relaxing. I knew an L.A. cop, a young woman, assigned to South Central L.A., a high-crime area. She told me that when she got home, her first 45 minutes were always spent alone in her garden. Only then had the reservoir of tension from her job drained away enough for her to be inside with her family.

Summer is the season of fecundity. I strongly encourage you to take advantage of the season by growing something to eat. If that's impossible, visit one of the pick-your-own farms where you can gather strawberries, blueberries, and brambleberries right from the plants. It puts you in touch with that strong, vibrant force of summer and the positive and valuable regenerative effects it has on a person.

Most of the vegetables grown in the temperate parts of America are either tropical plants like tomatoes and peppers, or annual plants that spend the winter as seeds, such as corn and beans. That means they can only be grown in most of America during the frost-free summer months. So when the weather turns warm, that's the time to take advantage of the rich diversity and high quality of our foodstuffs. Do that by following the recipes that fill this book, and also by preserving the great flavors of summer by freezing, canning, and drying.

And because summer is the time when we're active and spending more time out of doors, which affords us less time in the kitchen, we need recipes that are quick and easy to make. You'll find them here as well.

Locally grown summer fruits and vegetables are easy to find these days. They're in supermarkets, specialty stores, farmers' markets, roadside stands, and available directly from the farm and pick-your-own operations. And we're growing them ourselves: remember that 30 percent of American families grow some type of vegetable garden, about a third of all meals eaten in this country are provided by restaurants, and more and more chefs—and even some fast food outlets—are using locally grown ingredients in season. The very best chefs may spend their mornings at the farmers' markets selecting ingredients for that evening's meals.

Besides the huge variety of vegetables that come to our markets in summer, the best varieties of our favorite fruits appear in summer, too: Sparkle strawberries, Bing cherries, Santa Rosa plums, Royal Blenheim apricots, Red Haven peaches, Northland blueberries. They're there for a few weeks at most—and then, sadly, they're gone. Oh, but when they're "in," what a time we can have! Prices plunge as the crop swamps our local markets, even as the quality is hitting its seasonal highs.

We wait all year for those big, fat, juicy Bings to show up in the stores, refusing to buy the expensive substitutes from the southern hemisphere, refusing to buy the inferior early varieties, biding our time. Then, suddenly, there they are. We buy a bag for fresh eating. "Life is just a bowl of cherries" runs through our minds as we set a sumptuous bowl of them on our kitchen counter. What else can we do with them? What can we make out of them? How can we preserve their goodness for the off-season?

Hence this book.

Summer is a time when we can capture peak flavor and nutrition, not just in fruits and vegetables, but also in other foods. For instance, summer is the season when pastures are green and lush, and the cows and sheep are grazing and the goats browsing. This verdancy has a profound effect on their milk, and cheesemakers know that summertime is when milk is at its best. It's also when grass-fed beef is at its best, for the meat animals are enjoying the benefits of fresh, green pasture—exactly the food that nature has designed their digestive systems to eat. In summer, chickens—at least those raised as free-range birds—can eat their natural diet, which includes worms and insects, and lay the finest eggs. And the hot, hard light of the summer sun calls forth the most aromatic esters and volatile oils from fresh herbs.

The greatest variety of fruits and vegetables is available to us during the height of the growing season. Foods in season taste best and can be vine-ripe, meaning they contain more flavor components and nutrients than out-of-season foods picked green. Far from being a new idea, eating seasonally is the way most people on earth have eaten since time immemorial, out of necessity not choice.

There are many good reasons to look for locally produced food during the summer. It's not hard to find, no matter where you shop. Then, the supply line from the farm to your table is as short as possible, ensuring that the food is at its peak of quality and nutrition. Supporting local agriculture means preserving local farmland, and that strengthens local communities.

There is an important environmental ethic that develops on family farms. Family farmers care not only about the bottom line, but also about the life on the farm: the human beings and their pets, farm animals, the life in the soil, and the wildlife that lives there or passes through. There may be some foods that are literally only available locally at some time during the summer. Here in Sonoma County, that would be the Crane melon. Long ago, a family named Crane discovered a choice melon on their farm that came true to seed—that is, planting the seed of a Crane melon produces more Crane melons. The melons are light yellow and extremely sweet and aromatic, and we locals look forward to them every year. They appear at the end of the summer season and are sold in selected stores and at the Crane Melon Barn on a side road between Petaluma and Santa Rosa. You won't find them anywhere else. But many areas of the country have such local gems. Look for them in your region and you're very likely to find them.

If you can find it and afford it, choose organically grown food. Organic agriculture is clean agriculture, using no toxic chemicals or other agricultural products or medicines that endanger the soil, the local ground water and streams, the local wildlife, the farmer and his family, or the people who eat the food.

Many of the foods of summer these days, whether found at a supermarket or farmers' market, are artisanal—that is, they are grown or produced by someone who cares about the craft of creating the best possible foods from the ground up. I recently saw a summer vegetable stand with a display of zucchini—one of the most common of vegetables. The display was beautiful: each squash a perfectly formed, unblemished cylinder the same length as the others. I didn't measure them with a ruler; they may have been four to four and a half inches long. Each still had its rich yellow-orange flower attached to the blossom end. That indicated the zucchinis were picked that day and were as fresh as they could be. Some of the cylinders were green and some yellow, and the colors alternated in the display. I couldn't resist and bought eight squashes. At home, I made Zucchini Quiche. (See the recipe on page 33.)

In other words, what looks really good at the market will probably be really good on the plate, if you have good techniques and recipes for preparing it. That's what this book is for.

What's in Season?

The United States is a large country with many climates—the U.S. Department of Agriculture lists 11 climate zones ranging from Zone 1, where winter lows are 30 to 40 degrees below zero Fahrenheit (Alaska), to Zone 11, which never experiences frost (Hawaii). And so you may find local, fresh corn and green beans in Florida at times of the year when the ground is frozen solid in Minnesota. Summer fruits and vegetables show up about a month earlier in northern California than they do in New York.

The following list of what's in season in the summer months represents a median—accurate for the broad swath of the country that falls into Zones 6 and 7. In colder areas, the local, fresh foods will show up later and disappear earlier. In warmer regions, they'll arrive earlier and stay later.

Be aware that most fruits and some vegetables have early-, mid-, and late-season varieties. Mid-season varieties tend to be the highest quality because they are original or heirloom types that were the proven standard of quality years ago, before breeding programs developed early and late varieties to extend the season. The fruits, vegetables, and herbs listed on pages 10–12 are what you can expect to find at your markets during the summer months.

calling all iphone users

If you're like me, you think you'll never download all those apps for your iPhone. But you might consider downloading Locavore. This application handily pulls together lots of information on what's in season in your area, where to find farmers' markets (that information could come in handy if you're traveling), and has links to the Epicurious Web site for recipes that use the foods you'll find at the markets.

And Zeer (www.zeer.com), a leading supplier of consumer information about groceries and ingredients, has launched a "Food Reviews" app for the iPhone. The app lists product reviews as well as complete nutrition facts, ingredient information, and allergy warnings for more than 110,000 grocery items.

	JUNE	JULY	AUGUST	SEPTEMBER
FRUITS				
Apples			●	●
Apricots	●	●		
Blackberries	●	●		
Blueberries	●	●		
Boysenberries		●		
Cherries	●	●		
Figs		●	●	
Grapes			●	●
Loquats	●			
Marionberries		●		
Melons		●	●	●
Nectarines	●	●	●	
Peaches	●	●	●	●
Pears			●	●
Plums	●	●	●	●
Pluots	●		●	●
Raspberries	●	●		
Strawberries	●	●		
VEGETABLES				
Arugula	●	●		
Beets	●	●		
Bok choy	●			
Broccoli	●			●
Cabbage	●	●		●
Carrots	●	●		
Chard	●	●		

SUMMER SEASONALITY CHART
continued

	JUNE	JULY	AUGUST	SEPTEMBER
Collards				●
Corn			●	●
Cucumber	●	●	●	●
Eggplant			●	●
Endive	●	●		
Fava beans	●			
Fennel	●	●		
Garlic	●	●		
Green beans	●	●		
Kale	●			
Kohlrabi	●			
Leeks			●	
Lettuce	●	●		
Mesclun	●	●		
Mizuna	●			
Okra			●	
Onions		●		
Onions, green			●	
Onions, red			●	
Onions, sweet			●	
Peas	●			
Pepper cress	●			
Peppers			●	
Potatoes		●	●	●
Radishes	●			
Spinach	●	●		●
Summer squash	●	●	●	●
Tat-soi	●			

SUMMER SEASONALITY CHART				
continued				
	JUNE	JULY	AUGUST	SEPTEMBER
Tomatillos				●
Tomatoes		●		●
Tomatoes, heirloom			●	
HERBS				
Basil	●	●	●	●
Cilantro	●	●		
French tarragon			●	●
Marjoram			●	
Mint	●	●	●	
Oregano	●	●	●	●
Parsley	●	●		
Rosemary	●			
Sage	●			
Savory		●	●	●
Summer & winter savory	●	●	●	●
Thyme	●	●	●	●

Stocking Your Summer Kitchen

PANTRY POWER

One of the most important elements of your kitchen is the pantry. When you're short on time (or energy!), what you need is a low-fuss meal. The only way to achieve that is to have a fully stocked pantry at the ready so you can pull together a quick, delicious meal in no time flat.

Be sure to properly store your ingredients, and be mindful of expiration dates on perishables. You'll find a variety of homemade summer staples on page 278.

IN THE PANTRY

Arborio rice

Balsamic vinegar

Basmati rice

Beef stock

Cannellini beans

Canola oil

Chicken stock

Extra virgin olive oil, for
    cooking

High-quality extra virgin
    olive oil, for dipping or
    salads

Honey

Kosher salt

Molasses

Orzo

Quinoa

Red kidney beans

Rice wine vinegar

Sea salt

Sesame oil

Sherry vinegar

Small pasta (farfalle,
    rigatoni, fusilli, penne)

Soy sauce

Whole black pepper in a
    pepper mill

PERISHABLES

Capers

Dijon-style mustard

Dill pickles

Garlic

Ketchup

Lemon juice

Mayonnaise

Olives (green and black)

Onions

Shallots

Whole grain brown mustard

Worcestershire sauce

IN THE FRIDGE

Crème fraiche or sour cream

Eggs

Greek yogurt or plain yogurt

Milk

Parmesan cheese

HERBS AND SPICES

Basil

Chili powder

Chives

Dry mustard

Fennel seeds

Herbes de Provence

Mustard seeds

Oregano

Parsley

Red pepper flakes

Rosemary

Sage

Savory

Sesame seeds

Tarragon

Thyme

Equipment at the Ready

A well-equipped summer kitchen doesn't require a cook's catalog full of doohickeys, but the equipment you do have should be high quality, with features that make it a pleasure to use. Whenever something can be done better by hand, or with simpler equipment, that's the direction I choose.

WASHING AND SCRUBBING—For scrubbing I use a natural-bristle vegetable brush with a wooden head and handle. It cleans up root vegetables that have accumulated dirt on their journey from farm to your kitchen. Farm workers', wholesalers', and retailers' hands have touched them all along the way. I'm not a germophobe. In fact, there's good evidence that exposure to microorganisms in the environment helps our immune systems to develop properly. But human hands are vectors for a variety of diseases, and a good scrubbing of carrots, turnips, rutabagas, parsnips, and such under cold running water simply makes sense.

CHOPPING, DICING, AND MINCING—You'll need what's called a chef's knife. These come in different sizes—because chefs' hands come in different sizes—and you need one that will fit comfortably in your hand. They have a wide blade and a slight curve to the sharp edge.

Look for a knife with a full tang, that is, the blade and extension to which the handle is attached are all one piece. Stainless steel knives are hard to sharpen. High-carbon steel is a much better material, and just a few swipes on the steel, as the sharpening rod is called, returns the blade to razor sharpness. Incidentally, the proper way to sharpen a knife on a steel is to hold the knife so that the sharp edge is against the steel and the top of the blade leans out about 5 degrees, then draw the knife swiftly down the steel so the sharp edge is swiped from the tang end toward the tip. Now repeat on the other side of the steel with the other side of the blade, swiping down one side and then the other five or six times each.

Here in Kenwood, a little town of just a few hundred people, the Fourth of July is all about community and ritual and food.

The day starts with 3K and 10K foot races—the latter quite a feat given the area's hilly terrain. After the race, there's a pancake breakfast down at the nondenominational church, where we get to see people we haven't seen since the last Fourth of July. Most of the town turns out and there's a big mash-up in front of the church: sweaty runners cooling down after their exertions and those who came straight from bed. After the breakfast, everyone lines both sides of Warm Springs Road—Kenwood's unofficial Main Street—for what must be the nation's cutest Fourth of July parade. It consists of a handful of VFW and American Legionnaires who receive the dutiful applause of the crowd, kids in carts, cute and snappy little dogs on leashes, a few classic cars like the Studebaker Sky Hawk and the behemoth 1959 Cadillac, and a couple of local fire trucks. Tom Smothers, who lives nearby, often sits on the reviewing stand and does some of his fancy yoyo tricks. And that's about it.

Then, a beer truck shows up in the town park, along with all sorts of stands selling barbecued chicken, pork and beef ribs, corn dogs, cold soft drinks, ice creams, and home-made cookies and cakes. The real culinary star of the Fourth of July party in Kenwood is the chili con carne stand in the park. It's deeply flavored, rich, meaty, smoky, and just what those runners need to replenish their energy.

Adults paint children's faces, and kids have a climbing tower and air-inflated jumping room.

There's a bandstand where a local blues-and-rock band covers popular hits much too loudly and some of the folks who've had enough beer to loosen up get up in front of the bandstand and dance solo.

In the evening, when it turns dark, thoughts turn to the fireworks displays. Kenwood is too small for fireworks, so Kenwoodians go into the town of Sonoma for a solid hour of rockets that explode into gorgeous varieties of colorful blossoms, often punctuated by booms that make the town's dogs slink under their front porches and quiver.

All across America, towns small and large are having similar celebrations, sometimes with surprising results. About a century or more ago, Charles Ives, a youngster in Connecticut, sat in the Danbury town square, listening to his father's marching band, but also to other bands on other sides of the square simultaneously. Instead of producing a cacaphony in young Ives, it enthralled him and led him to compose some of his most famous music, combining disparate melodies into one piece. And it's for these compositions that he's remembered today.

Country kids in the Midwest and East mark the Fourth of July as the very day when the wild black raspberries turn ripe.

And many years ago, one of my mother's friends told me about the quality of being intimate when you're older. "It's less like the Fourth of July and more like Thanksgiving," she laughed.

BLENDING AND PUREEING—Food processors are fine if you have a lot of blending or pureeing to do, but for most home kitchen work, a simple blender is enough. Get one with several buttons that pulse as long as you hold them down, but stop when you release pressure. That saves you from having to flip each button off and on. Ignore the labels that say things like whip, chop, grate, puree. The blender simply whizzes more or less slowly—if you grate long enough, you'll be pureeing. Just know what texture you're after and stop when you get there.

MARINATING AND CHILLING—Many recipes call for marinating and chilling meats and other ingredients for an hour or so, or overnight. Gallon-size food storage bags are useful, but I prefer sturdy plastic containers with lids. The big advantage is that they are stiff and stack, and if your fridge is like mine, stackability is essential. There are glass and ceramic dishes, but usually these have lids with knobs on top as handles, and that prevents stacking. Also, plastic doesn't break when the dish slips out of your hand and crashes to the floor.

FREEZING—The most useful pieces of equipment for freezing in my home are a roll of masking tape and a permanent marker. That's because when I make broth from leftover chicken bones, or freeze demi-glace cubes, or store anything else of a perishable nature in the upright freezer in the garage, I slap a piece of masking tape on the freezer container or bag and write the contents and the date on the tape. Otherwise, you end up with a freezer full of mystery containers and a thousand questions: "Is this pie from last blackberry season or the one before?" "What *is* the stuff in this plastic bag, anyway?" "When did I freeze this sausage— and what kind of sausage is it?"

Some things don't need this treatment—that bottle of Stoli will be long gone before it ever goes bad. I keep the tape and marker right on top of the freezer and am religious about marking every container. Who has time to memorize the contents and provenance of everything in the freezer?

Other than a load of ice cube trays and freezer bags, the only other piece of freezer equipment I use frequently is the Krups Glaciere ice-cream maker. I keep the bowl of the unit in the deep freeze until needed. Then it sits up on a platform that turns it, covered with a top that has a projection that turns the mixture the way a moldboard plow turns the earth. I fill the bowl with the ice cream or sorbet mixture, turn it on, and in about 25 minutes or so, I have soft ice cream. I turn this into a freezer container and immediately put it into the deep freeze to harden. The bowl cleans up quickly.

Once upon a time I had a hand-cranked ice-cream maker, but soon decided that using it to make ice cream is a version of purgatory I don't want to revisit. There are versions with electric motors to turn the dashers, but I'm satisfied with the Glaciere unit.

GRILLING—I'm sure I'm not the only one whose first attempt at using a charcoal grill resulted in chickens aflame, burnt black on the outside and bloody at the bone. We learn to tame the intensity of our Webers by letting the charcoal burn down to white ash before putting on the meat, and by adjusting the air holes on the lid and in the bottom of the unit, but only after much trial and error have resulted in imperfect results.

The biggest improvement in my grilling technique on a charcoal-burning grill came when I put aside the charcoal lighter fluid and started using a canister-style charcoal starter. Put the briquettes in the top of the can, stuff two sheets of crunched up newspaper in the bottom, light the newspaper, and soon the can is shooting red fire out the top. The briquettes have started to burn and are ready to be spread across the steel rods in the bottom of the grill's bowl, where their ferocious heat subsides into a steady, white-ashed burn. Once I moved to the can, no longer did my chicken and steaks taste and look like burnt petroleum waste.

But the biggest improvement of all came when my wife bought me a gas grill for my birthday. This unit allowed me to adjust the heat with the turn of a dial— or several dials, since it has four dials, one for each of four gas tubes. With the heat on low and the top up, meat and vegetables will grill slowly and gently.

With the top down, the food will grill but also bake. The grill includes an electric motor that turns a spit in the top, for rotisserie meats. I turn the two outside burners to high, center a drip pan between them, and place the skewered and tied chicken onto the spit over the drip pan, which revolves as it cooks; then I close the top. In an hour and a quarter, I have a perfect spit-roasted chicken, basted all the while in its own juices.

Other essential equipment for the grill is a stiff steel brush for cleaning up the grill surfaces. Grill baskets are useful—they allow you to flip them over to grill both sides of the food without having to pry the food off the grill bars. However, whether for meat or fish, they have long handles that prevent the grill's lid from closing all the way. I've stopped using them because they stop me from adjusting the heat exactly as I want it.

I have found other grill matrices are useful. Some have closer spacing of their grill bars or perforations in a stainless steel plate for the heat to come through. These prevent small items like shrimp or zucchini slices from falling through.

The best grilling advice I ever got was to let the burners blast away on high for a full 10 minutes before using the steel brush on the grill bars and placing food on them. This keeps the bars free of grease—it burns away—and also makes the grill extremely hot, which prevents meats from sticking. The worst thing you can do is to place cold meat on cold, greasy grill bars and then turn on the heat. That process literally welds the meat to the bars and when you go to pry it off, all the browned, flavorful goodies stick to the bars and are left behind.

I used to do the annual full cleaning of the grill by hand, but it was a long, slow, tedious, and dirty job that I resented. That all changed when I got a power washer that fires thin jets of water with such force that crud like grease and discoloration are lifted off and washed away. It's still a tedious, dirty job, but it takes far less time than it used to. For daily grill cleaning, I use a simple hand tool called the Grilldaddy that has both steel brushes and a water reservoir for creating steam on the hot grills.

SERVING DISHES AND PLATTERS—Someone once told me that it's wise to spend money on quality for the things we use and live with every day. So it's good to have serving platters we really love. Big colorful Italian bowls for salads, a Limoges platter, a really good paella pan, big wooden cutting boards for cheeses and appetizers—they add an artistic touch to even ordinary meals and are a pleasure to use.

PICNICKING—The equipment can be as simple as a paper bag or as elaborate as a picnic basket with its own silver, dishes, glassware, and compartments for wine and food. Whatever it is, you need a cloth to lay on the ground or over a picnic table. My favorite way to have everything on hand for a picnic is to get out my German Army–issue rucksack, or backpack as we call it here in the United States. There's plenty of room for the cloth, the food and drink, napkins, plates, and utensils.

If you use a backpack, adjust the straps so the weight rides high on your back, even up on your shoulders. You want the weight pressing down on your shoulders, not pulling back on them by having the pack halfway down your back. You'll be much more comfortable for a longer hike that way. I learned that little trick on 20-mile hikes in basic training. I can't envision a picnic extending to a 20-mile hike, but packing in five miles to a pristine spot for lunch is within reason.

The strongest appetite stimulant I know is swimming. After a morning or afternoon of playing in the water, hunger turns ravenous. Swimming, because it uses just about every muscle in the body, quickly drains one's fuel tank.

I learned to swim at Pop Pierce's Day Camp in Manhasset, Long Island—about as suburban a place as you'll find—when I was six. And I practiced my technique at the Village Bath Club at the east end of town during the next two summers. The venues were, as they sound, safe and very suburban, and I was just one of the gaggle of kids who frolicked there. Because it was close to home, I wasn't far from the food I needed to recharge. Peanut butter and jelly sandwiches were prime refuelers then, and they still are. They take no cooking—a plus in the summer. Even a kid can make them, or maybe especially a kid can make them, and they are just as delicious now as when I came home from swimming.

Except that while the idea of the peanut butter and jelly sandwich is the same, the actual sandwich these days is far different from the ones that slaked the swimming hunger in my childhood. Then it was sliced white bread, hydrogenated peanut butter from a jar that became a milk glass after it was empty, and supermarket grape jelly made from Concord grapes.

Now, the bread is whole grain, from Nancy Silverton's La Brea Bakery in Los Angeles—bread packed with flavor and a variety of seeds and grains, the kind of bread one would have had to go to Europe to find back in the days of Wonder Bread. The peanut butter I grind myself from a machine in my local Whole Foods. The tub is warm from the heat of crushing and pulverizing the organic peanuts into butter. No salt. No hydrogenation. No nothin' but peanuts. And the jelly? Red raspberry or strawberry jam from Kozlowski Farms here in Sonoma County, made from their own stands of brambleberries or strawberry beds.

When I was eight years old, my life changed—drastically. Dad quit his job as art director of a company in Manhattan and moved us to the wilds of the Pocono Mountains of eastern Pennsylvania. And it *was* wild in those days.

One fall, someone shot a 700-pound black bear about 12 miles from my house. I could look out our back window and see deer, bobcat, pheasant, wild turkey, and ruffed grouse—all game I would learn to hunt and eat with relish in future years.

But summer was still for swimming. A creek meandered through pastures in the valley below our house. The creek banks were made of clay, riddled with holes where muskrats made their dens. We kids carried rocks to one end of a wide area in the creek to make a low dam so we could swim behind it. We smeared clay on our bodies and faces, thinking we looked like Indians. I had another swimming hole about two miles away, in the hemlock-draped hills, where a clean stream coursed down through a series of five waterfalls before flowing away through meadows of wildflowers and grasses. This was my secret place. The water was spring-fed, ice cold, and so pure and clear you could drink it.

There were no peanut butter and jelly sandwiches in the woods. But the woods and fields were bursting with food. Wild berries grew everywhere. Wild grapes hung from the sassafras trees in the fence rows. By the time I was in my early teens, my friends and I knew all about fishing and cooking trout over a small campfire. We all had .22s and shot the occasional rabbit, gutted and skinned it, split it in half, and cooked it on green branches set over and above a small fire.

Now that I look back on my early years and the places I swam, I realize that the sunny, chlorinated pools of the suburbs and the wild, natural pools of my country swimming holes were a universe apart. From the suburban pools I learned about relationships with other kids. From the country swimming holes, I learned about my relationship with the natural world.

And my relationship with nature was as hunter and gatherer to nature's abundance. I was much better fed—nutritionally and spiritually—after working up a great hunger in nature's swimming holes than I ever was in suburbia.

"If music be the food of love, play on," Duke Orsino famously said in Shakespeare's *Twelfth Night*. And he was right, in that sharing an outdoor musical experience with someone and something edible you care about can strengthen the bonds of love.

It helps if the music is romantic and the food and drink summery. It was only a few years ago that the Russian National Symphony played Rimsky-Korsakov's *Scheherazade* at Chalk Hill Winery in Sonoma County and had everyone swooning as we ate hors d'oeuvres and drank chilled Chalk Hill Chardonnay.

How romantic it gets depends mostly on whom you're with. There was one unforgettable event that took place on the lawn outside Packer Chapel on the campus of Lehigh University one summery day many years ago. Each year, the Bethlehem Bach Choir—a dedicated group of very talented townspeople—sings Bach's *Mass in B Minor* in the chapel. Tickets are expensive, and we were impoverished college students, but the day was warm and the stained glass windows of the chapel were thrown open so air could circulate. And so I and several friends—including student nurses from the nearby nurses' training program at St. Luke's Hospital—opened a blanket on the lawn and sat ourselves down with a basket full of cherries and chicken sandwiches, and a cooler of daiquiris.

I still remember the warmth of the sun, the smell of the grass, the filling sandwiches and tangy daiquiris, the contentment of lying back with my head on my girlfriend's lap, and the heavenly feeling when the choir's hundred voices, accompanied by the chapel's thunderous tracker organ, swelled and spilled through the windows to surround us. We ate and drank and sat transfixed by the music. We were wrapped in pleasure for a good hour and a half.

Speaking of outdoor concerts and good summer food, there's a band shell in Healdsburg here in northern California where a local band that specializes in Sousa marches happened to be playing early one afternoon while I was in that town. I ducked into the Downtown Bakery and Creamery for some of its homemade gelato and a cinnamon twist. The counterperson and I were talking and I asked if the twists were a new item. She said the *San Francisco Chronicle* had written about the bakery and mentioned how good the cinnamon twists were. "But we didn't make cinnamon twists," she laughed. "So many people were asking for them that we came up with a recipe and here they are."

Outdoor concerts are even better, if that's possible, when they're under the summer stars. New York City has been providing free classical concerts at the Naumburg Bandshell in Central Park for a hundred years. If you live in Southern California, the Hollywood Bowl and its natural hillside amphitheater makes for a dreamy evening of music al fresco. And all across this land, cities and towns are home to concerts of every kind of music you can think of, where food stores and carts sell local specialty foods. Beignets in New Orleans. Cheese steaks and hoagies in Philadelphia. Loose meat sandwiches in the Midwest. Oyster po'boys in Seattle. Lobster rolls in Maine.

If music be the food of love, let's eat!

BREAKFAST & BRUNCH

Nothing says summer like a lazy weekend brunch on the patio. It's the perfect time to enjoy the early morning breeze. The recipes that follow all invoke fond memories of breakfasts at home with my family and friends, so why not share them with your loved ones?

apricot-lemon preserves

MAKES 6 HALF-PINTS

Apricots have an affinity for lemons that will surprise you. These preserves exalt an English muffin or some homemade sandwich bread (page 76). They also make a wonderful sweet-sour glaze for boneless, skinless chicken breasts. Look for apricots with a blush on their cheeks and a sweet ripeness yet firmness of texture.

Six ½-pint canning jars with lids
Canning pot with rack
5 pounds unpeeled ripe apricots
6 cups sugar
⅓ cup freshly squeezed lemon juice

1. Pull the apricots apart at their seam line and discard the pits. In a bowl, stir the fruit halves and the sugar until well mixed and the sugar has dissolved. Cover the bowl and set aside for 4 hours (or place it covered in the fridge overnight).

2. When you're ready to cook, place a stack of saucers in the freezer. Place a large stock pot over medium-high heat and add the fruit and the lemon juice. Mix well, stirring frequently to prevent scorching, until the fruit reaches a jellylike texture.*

3. Remove the pot from the heat and pour into a large baking dish. Set aside until cool, then cover the dish with foil and refrigerate overnight.

4. The next day, sterilize the jars and lids in boiling water. Place a large stock pot over medium-high heat and add the apricot mixture. Cook until it comes to a boil.

5. Remove from heat and ladle the preserves into the jars, leaving about ½-inch headspace. Put on the lids finger tight and process in a boiling water bath for 10 minutes. Be sure the jars don't touch each other or the bottom of the pot, and that there are at least 2 inches of rapidly boiling water covering most of the jars.

6. Remove the jars from water and set aside to cool. Keep in a cool dry place unopened, for up to a year.

*Drop some of the preserves on a freezing cold saucer. After the drop chills, swipe a finger through it. The finger mark should remain and the surface of the preserves should wrinkle a little. Do this several times—hence the several cold saucers—as the mixture boils, because if the fruit is overcooked and scorches, it will be too thick and acquire an acrid taste.

☀ Apricots

One of the best things about apricots is their ability to enhance the flavors of so many other foods. This delicious stone fruit tastes best when the weather is hot and dry, so wait for the fruits that appear in July and August, when apricots hit their peak.

Look for apricots that are soft to the touch, but not mushy. At their peak, apricots' flesh is juicy and sweet, with a very succulent texture. They will only keep for a few days at room temperature, so store your extras in the freezer for better preservation. Simply cut the apricots in half and remove the pits. Add a little orange juice to the storage bags—just enough juice to keep the apricots covered.

brioche

MAKES 2 DOZEN ROLLS

These cute little breads, with their brown topknots, make great dinner or breakfast rolls. They're also fun to make, allowing you to whap away your frustrations on the dough—the more whapping, the better the brioche.

2 packets active dry yeast
⅓ cup warm (110°F) water
2 tablespoons sugar
3½ cups all-purpose flour
1 teaspoon kosher salt
¾ cup (1½ sticks) unsalted butter
3 large eggs
3 tablespoons olive oil
½ cup milk

1. In a large bowl, add the yeast, warm water, and 1 tablespoon of the sugar and stir to mix and soften the yeast. Add ¾ cup of the flour and stir. Cover the bowl with a damp dish towel and place in a warm spot for about 1 hour, or until the dough has doubled in size.

2. In a large bowl, mix together the remaining 1 tablespoon sugar, the remaining 2¾ cups flour, and the salt. Add the butter and, using two knives, cut it into the dry ingredients until the butter pieces are the size of small peas. Beat in 2 of the eggs. Add the yeasted flour mixture to the butter and flour mixture and mix it in.

3. Flour a board, take the dough in your throwing hand, and slam it down on the board. Pick it up, quickly form it into a ball, and slam it down again. Repeat for 8 to 10 minutes.

4. Brush a large bowl with oil and add the dough. Cover the bowl with a damp dish towel and place in a warm spot for about 1 hour, or until it doubles in size.

5. Divide the dough: Take three-quarters of dough and halve it. Continue to divide the dough portions in half until you have 24 similar-sized portions in total. Shape each into a ball and place them in a greased 24-cup muffin tin.

6. Shape the remaining one-quarter portion of dough into 24 smaller balls, using the same dividing technique. Using your pinkie, make a depression in the top of each of the large balls in the muffin tin. Place a small ball into the depression. Gently cover the tin with a piece of wax paper and place in a warm spot for about 1 hour, or until the dough doubles in size.

7. When ready to bake, preheat the oven to 400°F. Using small, sharp scissors, make 4 equally-spaced cuts in the dough of the large ball close to and around the topknot. In a small bowl, whisk together the remaining 1 egg and the milk until well combined. Using a pastry brush, brush the topknot with some of the egg mixture. Bake for 12 minutes, or until golden brown.

✱ BRIOCHE LOAF
To make a loaf instead of rolls, let the dough rise again for 1 hour after the first rise. Punch down this twice-risen dough and place it in an oiled 5 x 9-loaf pan, letting it rise for a third hour. Make 3 diagonal slices in the top, then brush lightly with the egg-milk mixture and bake for 20 minutes at 400°F.

brioche french toast

MAKES 4 SERVINGS

Brioche soaks up eggy, creamy batter beautifully and makes a sunny start to the day. While you can use store-bought bread, nothing tastes better than the homemade version made with your own hands. Make homemade brioche at least one day in advance of making the French toast, so the bread has time to set.

Eight ½-inch-thick slices of brioche (p. 28)
1 cup half-and-half or buttermilk, or ½ cup
    of either + ½ cup light sour cream
3 large eggs
2 tablespoons orange juice
1 ounce Cointreau
Dash vanilla extract
¼ teaspoon salt
4 tablespoons butter
1 cup maple syrup, warmed

   1. Prepare the brioche loaf as directed on page 28. Cut it into 8 slices.
   2. In a medium bowl, whisk together the half-and-half, eggs, orange juice, Cointreau, vanilla, and salt until smooth.
   3. Preheat the oven to 350°F. Soak the brioche slices in the egg mixture for 30 seconds on each side.
   4. Place a large skillet over medium-low heat and melt 1 tablespoon of the butter. Place 2 slices of soaked brioche in the pan (as space allows) and cook 2 to 3 minutes, or until golden brown. Gently turn the bread over with a spatula and cook until the other side is golden brown.
   5. Place finished slices on a rack (like a wire mesh pizza pan) in the oven for 5 minutes.

   6. Repeat steps 4 and 5 until all slices are cooked. Serve with warm maple syrup.

lemon pancakes

MAKES 4 SERVINGS

This light and airy breakfast dish full of lemon flavors is just right for a sunny morning out on the patio or deck.

4 eggs, separated
3 tablespoons granulated sugar
Pinch salt
1 organic (or well-washed) lemon, zest
    removed and juiced
¼ cup milk
¼ cup tepid water
½ cup cornstarch
4 egg whites
3 tablespoons butter
1 tablespoon lemon juice
Powdered sugar

   1. Preheat the oven to 400°F.
   2. In a medium bowl, whisk together the yolks, sugar, and salt until the yolks are bright yellow in color.
   3. Add the zest, milk, and water to the yolks. Whisk in the cornstarch until the mixture is smooth.
   4. Beat the egg whites until they form stiff peaks. Fold the whites into the yolk mixture until the mixture is foamy and smooth, but don't whip the whites in, or they will deflate too much.
   5. Place a 10-inch iron skillet over medium heat and add the butter. When the butter stops bubbling, pour all the batter into the skillet and cook for about 2 minutes.

6. Using a spatula, lift an edge of the pancake to make sure the bottom is set and is a light golden brown. Place the skillet in the oven and bake for about 5 minutes, or until the top has set.

7. Remove from the oven and slide the pancake onto a warmed serving platter. Sprinkle with lemon juice and sprinkle a little powdered sugar over the top. Serve while puffed and hot.

A VARIETY OF PANCAKES

One of the best things about pancakes is the endless combination of toppings and add-ins. Try some of these delicious combinations or get creative by making your own using fresh, seasonal fruit.

- APRICOT-LEMON PRESERVES (PAGE 27)
- POPPY SEEDS AND LEMON ZEST
- FRESH RASPBERRIES, BLACKBERRIES, OR BLUEBERRIES
- SLICED PEACHES AND TOASTED WALNUTS

corn muffins

MAKES 8 MUFFINS

Barbecued ribs hot off the grill. Southern fried chicken. What do they have in common? The need for some fresh-baked corn muffins, steaming hot so the butter melts on them. Delicious! This recipe adds the taste of fresh summer corn to the usual cornmeal.

2 ears fresh corn
1 cup cornmeal
1 cup all-purpose flour
2 tablespoons sugar
1 ½ tablespoons baking powder
½ teaspoon salt
1 egg
¼ cup melted butter or butter substitute

1. Slice open the rows of corn kernels from the bottom of the ear to the tip, working around the ear until all the rows are sliced open.

2. Place the ear of corn in a large bowl. Using the back of a knife, press into the kernels, scraping down the ear so that the milk and soft kernel contents—no skin—fall into the bowl. With the right amount of pressure, the tough kernel skins will be left behind. Set aside.

3. Preheat the oven to 425°F. Grease or spray an 8-cup muffin tin or line with paper muffin cups. In a large mixing bowl, combine the cornmeal, flour, sugar, baking powder, and salt. Set aside. In a small bowl, whisk the egg until light yellow, then slowly beat in the melted butter. Stir in the corn. Pour into the cornmeal-flour mixture and beat until smooth.

4. Pour the batter into the muffin tin. Bake for 20 minutes, or until a toothpick inserted into the top of a muffin comes out clean.

✳ SPICY CORN MUFFINS
Grease the muffin tin with bacon drippings for added flavor. Add 1 teaspoon of minced chipotle peppers to the batter for more spice.

carrot-currant muffins

MAKES 12 MUFFINS

If friends are staying over, they'll be delighted if you serve these spicy, moist muffins hot from the oven in the morning. Rather than launching into the recipe in the morning, spend some time the night before doing some prep work. The morning result will be worth it.

DRY INGREDIENTS

1 ½ cups pastry flour
2 teaspoons baking powder
1 teaspoon cinnamon
½ teaspoon salt
½ teaspoon nutmeg
¼ teaspoon cloves
¼ teaspoon allspice

CARROT MIXTURE

2 eggs
¾ cup sugar
1 ½ cups peeled and grated carrots (about 2 large carrots)

FILLING

5 tablespoons canola oil or unsalted butter
¼ cup orange juice
½ cup chopped walnuts
½ cup currants

1. In a large bowl, mix the dry ingredients. Set aside.
2. In a large bowl, whisk the eggs and sugar until well mixed. Add the carrots. Mix in and set aside.
3. Preheat the oven to 400°F. Grease or spray a 12-cup muffin tin or line with paper muffin cups.

4. If using butter, place a medium saucepan over medium-low heat and add the butter. Stir periodically until the butter melts, but don't let it brown.
5. Add the butter or oil, orange juice, nuts, and currants to the carrot mixture. Mix until well combined. Add the carrot mixture to the flour mixture and fold until the dry ingredients are moistened. Some lumps will remain.
6. On a sheet of wax paper, divide the batter into 2 equal parts, then divide each part into 2 more equal parts. Each of these parts will fill three muffin cups. Add the batter to the muffin tin.
7. Bake for 15 to 18 minutes, or until a toothpick inserted into the top of a muffin comes out clean. Allow the muffins to rest in the tin for a few minutes, then place them in a basket lined with a clean cloth napkin or dish towel. Serve warm.

easy tomato tarts

MAKES 4 SERVINGS

These little tarts, with their combined flavors of tomato, basil, and olive oil, are very Italian. They're at their best when the tomatoes are ripest and the basil the freshest. Perfect for a casual weekend brunch, they also make easy appetizers for a summer night's cocktail party.

WINE SUGGESTION: SERVE WITH PROSECCO FOR BRUNCH

2 teaspoons dry yeast
3 tablespoons warm water
1 cup all-purpose flour
½ teaspoon kosher salt

3 tablespoons cold unsalted butter

1 egg, well beaten

2 large ripe tomatoes, thinly sliced

4 tablespoons thinly sliced (into threads) basil

Fleur de sel

4 tablespoons extra virgin olive oil

1. In a small cup, add the yeast and the warm water (no hotter than body temperature). Set aside.

2. In a large bowl, mix together the flour and kosher salt. Add the butter and, using 2 knives, cut it into the flour until the flour has the consistency of coarse meal. Add the yeast and egg to the flour.

3. Flour your hands and knead the dough until it reaches a smooth consistency. Cut the dough in half, then cut those halves into 2 equal pieces. Roll each of the 4 pieces into a ball. Cover with paper toweling and set in a warm spot for about 2 hours, or until the dough doubles in size.

4. Place a baking sheet or oven stone in the oven and preheat to 500°F. Using a floured rolling pin or the floured heel of your hand, shape each dough ball into a circle about 5 inches in diameter.

5. Top each circle of dough with 1 or 2 slices of tomato and a tablespoon of the basil threads. Sprinkle each with a pinch of fleur de sel and drizzle each with a tablespoon of oil.

6. Place the tarts on the baking sheet or stone and cook for about 10 minutes, or until the edges are brown and puffed, but not black. Serve immediately.

summer vegetable quiche

MAKES 6 SERVINGS

A great thing about quiche is that it's equally delicious when served hot from the oven, or the next day at room temperature—saving you the trouble of cooking. This recipe combines hearty summer vegetables with the cheese and eggs that make quiche so delectable.

WINE SUGGESTION: ALSATIAN RIESLING

1 homemade Flaky Pie Crust (see page 251) or store-bought

2 cups thinly sliced summer squash

1 cup diced eggplant

2 tablespoons kosher salt

2 tablespoons butter

2 tablespoons canola oil

1 cup diced onion

1 teaspoon minced garlic

2 eggs

1 cup seeded and diced fresh plum tomatoes

1½ cups grated Gruyère cheese

¼ cup crumbled blue cheese

¼ cup crumbled feta cheese

¼ cup chopped parsley

1 tablespoon fresh lemon juice

Freshly ground black pepper to taste

1. Preheat the oven to 350°F. Line a 9-inch pie pan with the crust and add beans or pie weights. Par-bake the crust for 10 to 12 minutes, or until light brown.

2. Place the squash and eggplant in a colander and toss them with the kosher salt. Set in the sink to drain, about 20 to 30 minutes. Rinse quickly and pat dry.

3. Place a skillet over medium heat and

add the butter and oil. When the butter stops foaming, add the onion and, stirring occasionally, cook for about 5 minutes, until clear and golden. Add the garlic and continue cooking for 30 seconds.

4. Lower the heat to medium-low and add the squash and eggplant. Sauté for about 4 to 5 minutes, stirring, until lightly browned.

5. While the vegetables cook, in a medium bowl, beat the eggs thoroughly and stir in the tomatoes, cheeses, and parsley.

6. Add the vegetables, the lemon juice, and black pepper, and mix well. If using a store-bought pastry shell, crimp the edges if you like with your fingers or a fork. Pour the mixture into it.

7. Bake the quiche for 20 to 25 minutes, or until the top is golden and a toothpick inserted in the center comes out clean. Remove from the oven, set the quiche on a trivet or heat-resistant surface, and allow to cool for 15 minutes before serving.

* PARMESAN-SWISS QUICHE WITH
  SUMMER VEGETABLES

Omit the blue cheese and substitute grated Parmesan. Substitute any Swiss cheese for the Gruyère.

zucchini quiche

MAKES 4 SERVINGS

Zucchini has a mild flavor, but it adds a lovely texture and color to this quiche. The Homemade Biscuit Mix adds a nice flaky texture to the quiche crust.

WINE SUGGESTION: ALSATIAN GEWURZTRAMINER

GOOD TO KNOW: PAR-BAKING

Par-baking involves partially cooking or baking bread or dough, then rapidly freezing it. This is a great technique to utilize when baking, especially in the summer when you don't want to work in a hot kitchen more than necessary. Simply bake once and freeze what you don't use.

Partially baking dough helps preserve its internal structure and keeps it stable. When you're ready to bake a pie, tart, quiche, or fresh loaf of bread, simply remove the frozen par-baked dough from the freezer, allow it to thaw, and follow your recipe accordingly.

1 homemade Flaky Pie Crust (see page 251) or store-bought
3 cups green and yellow zucchini, thinly sliced
3 zucchini blossoms torn into 2-inch pieces (optional)
1 ½ cups of grated Gruyère cheese
1 cup Homemade Biscuit Mix (see page 34) or store-bought
4 eggs, lightly beaten
½ cup canola oil
½ cup chopped onion
1 clove garlic, minced
1 teaspoon chopped fresh oregano
2 teaspoons chopped parsley
½ teaspoon freshly ground black pepper

1. Preheat the oven to 350°F. Line a 9-inch pie pan with the crust and add beans or pie weights. Par-bake the crust for 10 to 12 minutes, or until light brown.

2. In a large bowl, mix all the other ingredients, reserving ½ cup of the cheese. Remove par-baked crust and pie pan from

Summer Squash and Zucchini

Unlike its more robust winter cousins, summer squash is mild in flavor and works in a variety of summer dishes. Zucchini is perhaps the most popular or well-known summer squash. It comes in both green and yellow varieties.

Look for small, brightly colored squash with ends that look freshly cut. The skin should nick easily if you scrape a piece with your thumbnail. The smaller the squash, the better: larger vegetables have more water and seeds, lending a more diluted flavor.

Squash blossoms, or zucchini blossoms, may look like decorations but they are indeed edible. Try stuffing and baking them, or dipping them in batter and frying them for a delectable bite-sized appetizer (see page 54, Stuffed Squash Blossoms).

the oven and fill it with the quiche mixture.* Sprinkle the reserved cheese evenly on top.

3. Bake for 35 to 45 minutes, or until golden brown and a toothpick inserted in the center comes out clean.

*If you have filling left over, bake it in a greased ramekin along with the quiche.

HOMEMADE BISCUIT MIX
1 cup pastry flour
1 ½ teaspoons baking powder
¼ teaspoon salt
1 tablespoon cold unsalted butter

In a small bowl, mix together the flour, baking powder, and salt. Add the butter and, using 2 knives, cut it into the dry ingredients, until the butter pieces are small.

sour cream breakfast cake

MAKES 12 SERVINGS

It's a lazy summer morning, you sleep in, then stumble into the kitchen looking for some breakfast. Imagine your pleasant surprise when you remember that you had made this simple sour cream coffee cake the night before. Have a slice out on the deck with a pot of good coffee, some fresh fruit, and a copy of the morning paper. Why can't all mornings be like this?

CAKE
2 cups pastry flour
1 teaspoon baking soda
1 teaspoon baking powder
¼ teaspoon salt
½ cup sweet butter at room temperature
1 cup sugar
2 eggs
1 teaspoon vanilla
8 ounces sour cream

TOPPING
¼ cup pastry flour
¾ cup dark brown sugar, packed
Pinch salt
1 teaspoon ground cinnamon
½ cup chopped pecans
¼ cup butter at room temperature

1. Preheat the oven to 350°F. Grease a 9 x 13-inch baking pan.

2. Make the cake: In a large bowl, sift together the flour, baking soda, baking powder, and salt.

3. In another large bowl, cream the butter and sugar together until they are light and fluffy. Beat in the eggs, vanilla, and sour cream until well combined. Add the wet ingredients to the dry ingredients and stir well to combine.

4. Make the topping: In a third large bowl, add all the ingredients. Using your hands, mix until well combined.

5. Pour half the cake batter into the prepared pan. Sprinkle half the topping over the batter. Pour the rest of the batter over the topping, followed by the remainder of the topping. Bake for 40 minutes, or until a knife inserted in the center comes out clean. Allow the cake to cool in the pan.

SUMMER MEMORY: midsummer's eve

Midsummer's Eve, which occurs on June 23 in most places, is not much celebrated in the United States, but it's as important a holiday in Scandinavia as Christmas. It's widely celebrated in northern and eastern European countries and the British Isles. Bonfires, dress-ups, dances, and much fertility symbolism are incorporated in the rituals, most of which date from pre-Christian times. In Poland, for instance, people dress like pirates and maidens throw wreaths made of flowers into the sea, rivers, and lakes. When Europe became Christianized, the date was renamed "St. John's Day," though the pagan festivities continued unabated.

Modern-day wiccans—neopagans—call the holiday Litha, the Old English name for the time of year as set down by Venerable Bede (673–735 C.E.). Shakespeare, of course, wrote his brilliant comedy *A Midsummer Night's Dream* about this fecund time, and the play catches much of the mystery, eroticism, and sheer tomfoolery that characterize the festival to this day.

Some of the foods associated with this day include apple pancakes, black currants (called Johannisbeeren—St. John's berries—in Germany because of the association of Midsummer's Eve with St. John and the fact that the year's black currants ripen about this time), buttermilk scones, broccoli soup in bread bowls, cucumber soup with lemongrass and spinach, gooseberry fool, herbed roast chicken, herb and lemon cookies, mead, orange honey butter, strawberries, and zucchini bread.

In the eastern United States, summer is the season for bugs, especially if you grow your own food.

Lots of bugs.

We share our food with the bugs then, if we are growing crops of any type. At my property in Pennsylvania, I had Alden grapes, and aerial phylloxera made little orange pimples on the leaves in which the plant lice grew and hatched. Bugs punched holes in my filberts and took a share of them.

Cabbage loopers and green cabbage worms went after my crucifers: cabbage, collards, kale, kohlrabi, cauliflowers, broccoli, radishes, and others in that family. Striped and spotted cucumber beetles invaded my cucurbits—the melons, cucumbers, and squashes. They were joined by gray, shield-shaped squash bugs, stem borers, and others that liked my crops as much as I did.

Beautiful tomato hornworms ate the leaves of my tomato plants. The worms were fancy—green with yellow stripes and red "horns" that projected from their back ends. They and other caterpillars would be infected by ichneumon flies that laid their eggs right into the flesh of the caterpillars. The eggs grew into little white sacs, and when these hatched, the fly larvae had their food right there, carrying them around, ready to eat.

Leaf miners drew white lines in my spinach and beet leaves as they burrowed their way through the tissues of the leaves. Flea beetles ate shot holes in my radish leaves. Apple maggots and apple fruit flies burrowed into the apples in my orchard, becoming the notorious worms in the apples.

Butterflies of many types visited my gardens. The larvae of monarch butterflies lived on the juices in the milkweed in the meadow, and when they pupated, they made little gray-green hanging cases with projections tipped in gold that, if reproduced as jewelry, would have brought hundreds of dollars. Praying mantises moved deliberately in my garden, cocking their triangular heads, picking off whatever bugs were handy. Occasionally I would encounter a walking stick, looking exactly like a little stick, but suddenly getting up and walking away on Ent-like stems, à la *Lord of the Rings*.

Hoverflies would come to entertain me as I weeded the garden, hanging in the air just a foot or two from my face, wings beating so fast I couldn't see them, their eyes glittering green and red. Hummingbird moths came to show off their mimicry, looking for all the world like hummingbirds—but still, they were just moths.

In the evenings of early summer, the orchard and meadow were alive with lightning bugs, the females buried down in the grasses, flashing rhythmically to attract the males. But the males, with their thoughts elsewhere, floated upwards, blinking as they went, toward the starry sky until I couldn't tell where the fireflies ended and blinking stars began.

When I gardened, no-see-ums pinched at me and I slapped back. Flies from the nearby dairy farms came to make life unpleasant in my house, but I hung flypaper to defeat them—although their frantic buzzing as they tried to extricate themselves from the flypaper was disquieting. Slugs climbed the wet sides of the stone walls on the way to the springhouse. Wasps made paper houses in the barn. Hornets hung their big, round nests in the trees. Mosquitoes came to bite in the night.

Then in late August, the katydids started their nightly choruses. They grew in loudness until there were hundreds of thousands of them chanting all around my house in the woods: katydid, katydid, katydid. By the end of August they would be so loud I couldn't sleep if I thought of them as a botheration. So I thought of them as a chorale of Bach-like counterpoint, singing me to sleep. And to their thunderous chorus, exhausted from the day's labors, I would fall into their audible arms and sleep.

And now I live in California. "Isn't California great?" I hear people say. "The summer dryness means there are no bugs to contend with. We need no screens in the summertime. We're bug free!"

True. It's not that I miss the bugs I once shared the world with. It's just that I miss the challenge they presented and my ability to respond with careful kindness in dealing with it.

DIPS & SPREADS

Pinzimonio

Guacamole

Pico de Gallo

Hummus

Harissa

Baba Ghanoush

Raita

Tzatziki

Tomato Chutney

Roasted Red Pepper Tapenade

FINGER FOODS

Crudités

Sizzlin' Celery Sticks

Cheddar and Sardine Canapés

Bruschetta with Garlic, Tomatoes, and Basil

Prosciutto and Melon

Stuffed Grape Leaves

Stuffed Squash Blossoms

Southern-Style Fried Onion Rings

Deep-South Onion Rings

Corn Fritters

Maryland Crab Cakes

Argentine Empanadas

Hoisin Chicken Drumettes

Grilled Chicken Satay on Rosemary Skewers

Barbecued Pork Shish Kebabs

Shrimp on the Barbie

Fish Kebabs

DIPS, SPREADS, & FINGER FOODS

The warm weather is one of the greatest inspirations for gathering with family and friends. Always be prepared for last-minute guests by keeping these simple, crowd-pleasing recipes at hand. They are delicious in almost any scenario.

DIPS & SPREADS

pinzimonio
TUSCAN RAW VEGETABLE DIP

MAKES ½ CUP OR 2 SERVINGS

Italians are known for the simplicity of dishes that exalt the natural flavors of ingredients. And so they have *pinzimonio*, which is a dipping sauce for a tray of raw fresh vegetables. If you like, vary the dip with a bit of other seasonings such as spices or aromatics like garlic. (Don't overdo the extra flavoring, though; you don't want to overwhelm the vegetables.)

For a summer party, choose some or all of the following: small hearts of celery with leaves on, peeled and thinly sliced carrots, snap beans, thin asparagus spears, slices of sweet bell peppers, long sticks of peeled cucumber, trimmed radishes, scallions with roots and outer layer of skin removed, and fennel cut into strips. See Crudités (page 48) for more ideas. It's best if the vegetables are served cold.

½ cup best quality extra virgin olive oil
½ teaspoon coarse salt
½ teaspoon freshly ground black pepper, or to taste
Up to 6 cups raw fresh vegetables of your choice

Pour the oil into a shallow bowl. Stir in the salt and black pepper. (For easier reach at a large table or at a party, divide the ingredients into two shallow bowls.) Serve with the vegetables.

guacamole

MAKES ABOUT 1½ CUPS

Avocados are a summer staple at my house. They are so nutritious and their texture so buttery. Their mild flavor means they can be used with just about any other vegetable, especially the hot peppers that can give authentic Mexican guacamole its required kick. This recipe makes a particularly spicy guacamole. Kick up the heat by adding more peppers (or hotter ones), or take it down a notch by decreasing the amount.

2 ripe avocados, sliced in half, pits removed
1 lime cut in half
2 serrano chiles, minced
2 tablespoons minced onion
1 tablespoon finely chopped cilantro
¼ teaspoon salt
1 medium tomato, peeled, seeded, and chopped (optional)

1. Scoop the avocado flesh into a bowl and squeeze lime juice over it. Mash the flesh and juice together.

2. In a separate bowl, mash together the chiles, onion, cilantro, salt, and tomato, if desired. Add this mixture to the avocado and mix thoroughly. Serve immediately to avoid browning.

✳ Avocado

Technically, avocados are available year-round, but they find increased popularity in the warm-weather months when there are more outdoor parties, picnics, and get-togethers. Nothing says party food quite like a bowl of well-made guacamole.

There are two dominant varieties of avocados in the Americas: the Hass and the Fuerte. Hass avocados have greenish-black skin when ripe and a rich, buttery texture that makes them extra delicious.

Most avocados are still hard in the store; they will easily ripen on your kitchen counter. When shopping for ripe avocados, choose those that have a slight give when you gently press or squeeze down on the flesh.

Remove the flesh by cutting the avocado in half lengthwise, then twist the halves in opposite directions to pull them apart. Whack the pit lightly with the blade of a knife and twist to dislodge it, or scoop it out with a spoon. Scoop out the flesh by running a spoon just under the skin.

Properly storing any remaining avocado still in the shell will allow it to keep for an extra day or two. Sprinkle the flesh with the juice of a lemon or lime, then tightly wrap the avocado in cling wrap to avoid discoloration. Store it in the refrigerator.

1 ½ cups finely diced ripe tomatoes
1 cup mild chopped onion
1 ½ cups diced ripe avocado
3 serrano chiles, minced
3 tablespoons lime juice
¼ cup chopped cilantro
Salt and freshly ground black pepper to taste

In a bowl, mix together all the ingredients and refrigerate for 2 hours for the flavors to marinate. Serve with tortilla chips.

hummus

MAKES ABOUT 2 CUPS

The homemade version of this delicious (and healthy!) snack is quite simple to make. Some people swear by using dried chickpeas and reconstituting them, but I find that canned chickpeas are so much easier and give the more traditional flavor I'm looking for. They come packed in salted water, so it's necessary to rinse and drain them, but reserve the liquid in the can—you may need it to blend the ingredients to the proper consistency.

You can make a fine picnic out of just a container of hummus, a small bottle of olive oil, a container of Tabbouleh (page 117), several loaves of pita bread, and a chilled bottle of wine. What a great way to spend a summer afternoon!

WINE SUGGESTION: ROUSSANNE

One 16-ounce can chickpeas
Juice of 1 lemon
3 tablespoons tahini (ground
    sesame paste)

pico de gallo

MAKES 4 CUPS

This traditional Mexican salsa should be spicy enough to make you sit up and take notice, if you want it to be authentic. Reduce the amount of chiles if you must.

3 cloves garlic, chopped
Salt to taste
Extra virgin olive oil

1. Set a colander in a large bowl and pour in the can of chickpeas. Reserve the bowl of liquid. Rinse the chickpeas under cold water and drain.

2. Place the chickpeas, a little of the chickpea juice, the lemon juice, tahini, and garlic in a blender. Blend to a smooth paste, using only as much of the liquid from the chickpea can as necessary to get the ingredients to blend. You are looking for a smooth, creamy consistency, but not watery or thin. Taste and add salt, if necessary.

3. Transfer the hummus to a container, cover, and refrigerate for up to 2 weeks. To serve, place the hummus in a shallow bowl. Draw the back of a tablespoon down the middle of the hummus to form a shallow depression. Add a few tablespoons of oil to the depression and serve.

✱ VARIATIONS
- Add ½ teaspoon of ground cumin or 1 tablespoon Harissa (see below) for added flavoring.
- Garnish the hummus with a teaspoon of chopped, fresh parsley or with a quick shake or two of paprika for color.

harissa
MAKES ABOUT 1 CUP

Here's a sprightly, fiery sauce much favored in the hot countries of North Africa. Dried pasillas, chipotles, and habaneros represent increasingly hot levels of burn.

12 dried chiles
4 cloves garlic, coarsely chopped
½ cup extra virgin olive oil
1 teaspoon ground cumin
Salt to taste

1. Slice the chiles in half and remove the seeds. Rough chop the halves into coarse bits. Soak the bits in warm water for a half-hour, until they soften.

2. Drain and place the chiles in a blender with the garlic, olive oil, cumin, and salt. Blend until a smooth paste is formed.

3. Put the paste into a small jar with a lid and float a quarter-inch of olive oil on top. Refrigerate.

baba ghanoush
MAKES 2 CUPS

This favorite eggplant-based appetizer from the eastern Mediterranean is best served at room temperature or slightly chilled, along with pita bread. Any type of eggplant will do, but the younger the better—before hard seeds develop.

1 ½ pounds eggplant
3 tablespoons freshly squeezed lemon juice
1 teaspoon salt
2 cloves garlic, chopped
3 tablespoons tahini
¼ cup finely chopped flat-leafed parsley
2 tablespoons extra virgin olive oil
Warmed pita bread

1. Spread a piece of aluminum foil on an oven rack. Preheat the oven to 400°F. Prick the eggplants with a fork about 8 to 10 times around the surface and set on the aluminum foil to catch any juices.

2. Bake for 30 to 40 minutes for large purple eggplant, or 15 to 20 minutes for smaller Japanese eggplant. The eggplant is done when the flesh is soft throughout. Cut in half and scoop out the flesh into a measuring cup. You should have about 2 cups.

3. In a large bowl, add the cooked eggplant and lemon juice and mash together with a potato masher or beat with an electric mixer until smooth. In a separate small bowl, mash the salt, garlic, and tahini, and add mixture to the eggplant. When the mixture is cool, stir in the parsley and use a rubber spatula to scrape it into a serving bowl.

4. Draw the back of a tablespoon down the middle of the baba ghanoush to make a shallow depression and drizzle in the olive oil. Serve with warmed pita bread.

✳ VARIATIONS
Sprinkle the top with ½ cup lightly toasted pine nuts. Or add a cup of peeled, seeded, and chopped ripe tomato and 2 or 3 finely chopped scallions.

raita

MAKES ABOUT 2 CUPS

Raita is a cooling condiment that calms the fires of spicy Indian food. It's also a cooling and refreshing dish, not unlike Greek *tzatziki*, that belongs on the summer table.

Serve it as a dip for crudités or add it as a topping to burgers or any spicy foods.

6 ounces plain yogurt
1 medium cucumber, peeled and
   finely chopped
1 medium onion, finely chopped
¼ cup cilantro
¼ cup mint leaves
Pinch ground cumin
Pinch ground cinnamon
Pinch cayenne pepper
Salt to taste

Place all the ingredients in a blender and puree until smooth. Keep covered in the refrigerator for up to 2 weeks.

tzatziki

MAKES 1¼ CUPS

This cool and refreshing Greek dip is classically paired with pita bread, crackers, or toast, but it is equally delicious as a summery dip for crudités. Pair it with any dish with peppery heat that may benefit from a cool balance of flavors.

2 tablespoons extra virgin olive oil
1 teaspoon white wine vinegar
1 clove garlic, crushed
1 cup plain yogurt
Salt to taste (start with a pinch)
1 medium cucumber, peeled, deseeded, and
   finely diced or coarsely grated
½ tablespoon spearmint, freshly chopped,
   or ½ teaspoon dried

In a medium bowl, whisk together the oil, vinegar, and garlic. Add the yogurt and salt and beat lightly with a fork until the mixture is smooth and well combined. Mix in the cucumber and mint. Chill in a covered container until ready to serve. Keep covered in the refrigerator for up to 2 weeks.

2. Simmer, with a lid partially open, for 3 to 5 hours. Stir more frequently as the chutney thickens toward the end of the cooking period to prevent sticking and burning.

3. Can in pint jars according to the manufacturer's instructions, or store in the freezer. An opened jar will keep in the refrigerator for up to 3 weeks.

tomato chutney

MAKES ABOUT 8 PINTS

Let the tangy, delicious flavors of Mumbai inspire you on a hot summer evening. Serve some of this delicious chutney alongside your meat or fish main course. It's best made in high summer when the tomatoes are at their best, and needs a few weeks for the flavors to marry and ripen.

16 cups fresh, ripe tomatoes, peeled, seeded, and chopped
2 cups chopped onions
2 cups chopped tart green apples
8 ounces seedless dark raisins
8 ounces golden raisins
1 ½ pounds light brown sugar
3 cups cider vinegar
2 tablespoons whole mustard seeds
1 tablespoon ground cloves
2 teaspoons ground allspice
½ teaspoon ground cayenne
1 tablespoon kosher salt

1. Place a large stockpot (with a lid) over low heat and add all the ingredients. Stir to combine. Bring to a simmer, stirring occasionally.

MEASURING FRESH AND DRIED HERBS

Herbs that are packaged and dried may often contain strong flavors initially, but they quickly lose pungency as they age. Always use fresh herbs when possible to achieve the best flavor in your dish.

The general rule of thumb for most herbs is:

1 teaspoon dried = 1 tablespoon fresh

Fresh herbs will have the strong flavor of volatile oils that dried herbs lack, and some subtle flavors, too.

It's possible to substitute one herb for another in many recipes.

GOOD TO KNOW:
STAYING HEALTHY WITH SUMMER FOODS

Summertime is the season when the widest variety of plant foods is available to us, and that variety is key for our health. The wider the variety of food plants we eat, the more varied the phytochemicals we ingest. It's not the sheer volume of plant foods we eat, but rather the number of different foods that positively affects our health. These phytochemicals—naturally occurring plant compounds that include antioxidants and phenolics—surge through our bloodstreams, scavenging unhealthy free radicals, which bind with tissues in the arteries and veins, damaging them and leaving them open to vascular disease.

If you remember your high school chemistry, you'll remember that a radical is the negatively charged part of a chemical compound that dissociates from its positively charged partner when it's in a liquid solution. Some of these free radicals, as they are called, bind to cells in the arterial walls, causing lesions that the body tries to repair with sticky plaque. That in turn can cause clogged blood vessels, heart attacks, and strokes. Antioxidants bind to these free radicals before they attack the vascular system, rendering them harmless in our bodies.

Researchers at Colorado State University discovered that people who ate a wider variety of plant foods received more health benefits than those who ate as much volume, but less variety, of plant foods. "We saw more benefit from smaller amounts of many different phytochemicals than from larger amounts of a few," according to the study's lead author, Henry Thompson, Ph.D.

Americans are encouraged by the U.S. Department of Agriculture, through its Dietary Guidelines, to eat at least two portions of fruit and three of vegetables every day. A portion here is about two and a half ounces, which works out to slightly less than a combined weight of one pound. Notice that the guidelines use the term "at least" when recommending portions. And they don't mean "beans, beans with every meal." Beans count as one portion, no matter how many of them you eat a day. They mean five *different* fruit and vegetable portions daily. And potatoes, breads, and pasta don't count as vegetables, though they are plant-derived. They are classed as carbohydrates. Beans only count because they have such good stores of plant dietary fiber.

Of course, not all fruit and vegetable dishes are made from a single ingredient. Ratatouille (see recipe, page 215) is a mélange of eggplant, tomatoes, onions, bell peppers, summer squash, and garlic, along with herbs, oil, and condiments. That's six vegetables right there. A fruit salad (see recipe, page 105) can be made of as many seasonal fruits as you want. So a dinner that includes ratatouille and fruit salad might cover you for one day—and in the summer when the ingredients for many kinds of mixed dishes are at hand, it's not difficult to follow the government's guidelines.

roasted red pepper tapenade

MAKES 1½ CUPS

Here's a flavorful dip to serve with a tray of crudités or a basket of thinly sliced French bread. The only cooking is done on the outside grill—perfect for that backyard barbecue you've been planning!

3 red bell peppers
½ cup olives, pitted
3 cloves garlic, crushed through a
   garlic press
1 ounce feta cheese
2 anchovy fillets
1 teaspoon dried oregano or
   1 tablespoon fresh
2 tablespoons extra virgin olive oil

   1. Roast the bell peppers over a hot gas or charcoal grill until the skin is black and peeling. Place in a paper bag and tie with string so they cook some more in their own steam. After 10 to 15 minutes, open the bag and, using a paring knife, peel the peppers. Slice in half and take out the core and seeds. Place the prepared pepper flesh in the blender and add any accumulated juices, but no skin, stem, or seeds.
   2. Add the olives, garlic, cheese, anchovies, oregano, and oil and process until it forms a smooth paste. Serve as a dip.

FINGER FOODS

crudités

MAKES 4 SERVINGS

Think of all the advantages of cool, crunchy vegetables on a hot summer day: they're cold; they take no cooking (other than a minute's blanching for broccoli and cauliflower florets, which need that treatment to soften them); they refresh the palate and freshen the breath; and they are nutritionally superior because they are raw.

   This is one of the easiest items to pull together for a last-minute party or even just as a casual afternoon snack for the kids. No matter what combination of vegetables you choose to incorporate, the crudités tray is always a colorful and attractive addition to any meal.

WINE SUGGESTION: SPANISH ALBARIÑO

2 stalks celery
2 medium carrots
1 red, yellow, or green bell pepper
8 spears slender asparagus
12 yellow wax beans
3 red radishes
½ pint pear, cherry, or grape tomatoes
½ small head broccoli
½ small head cauliflower
1 cup high-quality extra virgin olive oil
Small bowl kosher salt

   1. Keep all the vegetables cool in the refrigerator until ready to use.
   2. Snap off the celery near the base and pull off as many strings that run up the

stalks as you can. Slice the stalks length-wise into ½-inch strips.

3. Wash the carrots and trim off the tops and the tips. Cut them in half and then into long strips. Cut the strips so none are more than ⅓ inch wide.

4. Trim off the top of the bell pepper and remove the seeds. Cut the pepper in half. Lay it skin side down and cut each half into ⅓-inch-wide strips.

5. Cut asparagus ends off, leaving 3 to 4 inches of the tips. Peel the remaining stem.

6. Trim tops and tips of wax beans and slice them in half lengthwise.

7. Trim tops and tips from the radishes and cut them crosswise into coins. Slice coins into ½-inch strips.

8. Wash and pick over the small tomatoes. Large cherry tomatoes can be cut in half.

9. Trim the broccoli and cauliflower heads to small florets. Blanch the broccoli and cauliflower for 1 minute. Plunge them into a bowl of ice water to stop the cooking. Drain and pat dry.

10. Arrange the vegetables artfully on a serving dish. Serve with a small bowl of the oil and a small bowl of the salt for dipping.

sizzlin' celery sticks

MAKES 18 PIECES

Cream cheese or peanut butter are considered the traditional filling for celery sticks. Why not spice things up and try this filling for your hot summer relish tray? In addition to the flavor boost, the filling is a healthful alternative to other fillings. The cashews aren't really raw, but rather unroasted as well as unsalted.

6 celery stalks
2 cups unsalted "raw" cashews

1 serrano chile, or to taste
2 cloves garlic, roughly chopped
½ teaspoon toasted sesame oil
½ tablespoon tamari

1. Trim tops and bottom of celery stalks. Snap one inch of celery at the bottom of the stalks backwards and pull toward the top, removing several strings. Wash the stalks and stand them upright in a pitcher of water and ice cubes.

2. Place the cashews, chile, garlic, sesame oil, and tamari in a food processor or blender. Process until a thick paste forms. If there's not enough liquid to process the ingredients, add water one teaspoon at a time, just until the ingredients blend.

3. Using a dinner knife, fill the celery hollows with the cashew mixture. Serve whole, or cut into 3-inch pieces (prior to filling them) and serve as part of a relish tray.

cheddar and sardine canapés

MAKES 4–5 CANAPÉS PER PERSON

These canapés may be simple, but they make a fine, quick snack or light lunch for a busy summer day. Assemble them and serve them on a tray at your cocktail party, or create a tray of the ingredients and let guests assemble their own.

Thin slices of cheddar, cut to fit the wafers
1 box reduced-fat baked woven wheat wafers
Sardines, packed in olive oil
Dijon mustard

Place a slice of cheese on a wafer, then top it with a sardine. Add a dab of mustard to the top of the sardine.

bruschetta with garlic, tomatoes, and basil

MAKES 4 SERVINGS

While the French may base their cuisine on butter, the Italians base theirs on olive oil—and they've undoubtedly drizzled their toast with olive oil since the founding of the republic and probably before. Over the years, they've tweaked the basic recipe by adding three more ingredients that make a match from heaven. The result is bruschetta—pronounced brew-sketta, not brew-shetta. It's best made with slices from a crusty loaf of Italian bread.

WINE SUGGESTION: ITALIAN REFOSCO

8 slices Italian bread, ¾ inch thick
6 ripe Italian plum tomatoes (Roma or San Marzano)
4 cloves garlic, crushed through a garlic press
Salt and freshly ground black pepper to taste
½ cup extra virgin olive oil, or more as needed
8 fresh basil leaves, minced

1. Slice the loaf of Italian bread on a diagonal, so the slices are long ovals rather than rounds. Toast the slices under the broiler or on the grill, until both sides are golden brown. Set aside to cool slightly.

2. Peel and seed the tomatoes and drain the remaining pulp, then cut it into ½-inch dice. Set aside.

3. Using your fingers or the back of a

small spoon, smear a little of the mashed garlic on one side of each piece of toast. Add 1 to 2 tablespoons of the diced tomatoes to each piece of toast. Sprinkle on a pinch of salt and 1 to 2 grinds of pepper. Drizzle the oil across all the pieces and top with a sprinkle of the fresh basil.

prosciutto and melon

MAKES 2 DOZEN PIECES

This simple combination showcases sweet summer melons at the pinnacle of subtle yet sumptuous flavor.

The prosciutto should be sliced very thinly. While you may be tempted to remove the fat, don't. It is an integral part of the ham's fragrance, texture, and flavor. The melon should be dead ripe and very sweet. Yellow-fleshed melons such as Crenshaw and cantaloupes pair better with prosciutto than green-fleshed kinds. This flavor combination needs no citrus juice, but may benefit from a simple grind of black pepper. Be careful not to overshadow the sweet, fragrant flavor of the melon or the salty, sweet taste of the prosciutto.

Planning to get an early start on your party prep? Cut the melon pieces and slices of prosciutto in advance, but don't wrap them until you're ready to serve.

WINE SUGGESTION: VERDICCHIO

1 yellow-fleshed melon, very ripe and chilled
¼ pound prosciutto, very thinly sliced

1. Cut the melon in half and remove the seeds. Cut each half in half so you have four melon slices in total.

2. Make 5 equally-spaced horizontal cuts along each slice and separate the flesh from the rind, resulting in 24 bite-size melon pieces.

3. Wrap each piece of melon with a thin layer of prosciutto. Place each wrapped piece on a toothpick to secure the ingredients.

stuffed grape leaves

MAKES ABOUT 4 DOZEN

These tidbits, also called dolmas, are quintessentially Greek, and are perfect when prepared in early summer when the grape leaves are tender. Greeks have used many leaves as wrappers for cooked foods, from fig leaves to cabbage leaves. The grape leaves add a nice tang of their own to the food that's wrapped inside. These can be served as an appetizer or main course.

WINE SUGGESTION: CALIFORNIA MERLOT

4 tablespoons olive oil
¼ cup minced onion
½ cup basmati or long grain rice
½ pound ground beef
1 clove garlic, minced
¼ cup finely chopped fresh dill
¼ cup chopped fresh Italian flat-leaf parsley
1 teaspoon ground cumin
1 teaspoon dried and crumbled mint
Salt and freshly ground black pepper to taste
1 egg, lightly beaten
4 dozen fresh grape leaves, young and
    unsprayed, or 1 jar store-bought
Juice of 2 freshly squeezed lemons

1. Place a large skillet over medium heat and add 2 tablespoons of the oil. Add the onions and sauté until they turn translucent.

Add the rice and stir for 3 to 4 minutes. Mix in the ground beef and cook until it is lightly browned all over.

2. Reduce the heat to low and add the garlic, dill, parsley, cumin, mint, salt, and black pepper. Add ½ cup water and stir to mix well. Cover the skillet and simmer for 20 minutes, stirring occasionally to prevent sticking. Add a little more water as necessary to prevent sticking, but at the end of the 20 minutes, the liquid should be entirely absorbed.

3. Remove the pan from the heat and uncover. When warm, not hot, stir in the egg. Trim any hard stems from the grape leaves, setting aside any leaves that are torn or broken. If using commercial leaves from a jar, rinse them well to remove excess salt.

4. In a Dutch oven, add the remaining 2 tablespoons oil and line the bottom of the pan with the reserved torn and broken grape leaves.

5. Lay a servable leaf on a flat surface, underside up. Place a generous teaspoon of the meat filling in the center of the leaf and fold up the bottom, then fold in the left and right sides, and finally roll the leaf upwards completely, toward the leaf tip. Place the dolma in the Dutch oven with the seam side down. Repeat until all the filling has been used.

6. Sprinkle lemon juice across the dolmas in the pan. Add 2 cups of water and place a plate on top of the stuffed grape leaves to hold them in place during cooking so they don't unfurl.

7. Place the Dutch oven over medium heat, covered. When the liquid is boiling, reduce the heat and simmer, covered, for at least 2 hours or until the rice is finished cooking through and the leaves are tender. Serve hot or cold.

✳ SUMMERY TAPAS

It is customary in Mediterranean countries to serve small bites or plates for everyone to share. In Spain, these little bites are called tapas. The tradition has spread, and tapas are as well-known in the United States now as they are in Spain.

Heavy, meaty, savory tapas are best reserved for the colder months and pairing with rich red wines. Here are some alternatives for the hot days, many of which pair well with chilled white or rosé wines or Agua Frescas (page 265).

✳ A small plate of apple slices, bites of cheese, and walnuts.

✳ A dish of sliced apricots sprinkled with lemon zest.

✳ Slices of avocado and grapefruit segments, sprinkled with lime juice. Or, avocado slices topped with chopped red onion and a splash of lemon juice.

✳ Fresh-picked green bean pieces lightly sautéed in butter, skewered on a toothpick with small pieces of bacon.

✳ Diced roasted beets lightly dusted with nutmeg.

✳ Custard-berry cubes: Place blackberries in the compartments of an ice cube tray, then fill with vanilla custard and refrigerate until set. The custard-berry cubes are gently pried out of the compartments with a butter knife and served with red raspberries.

✳ Peach-blueberry bites: Peel fresh peaches and slice them, then cut the slices into small squares. Add the peach bite and a fresh blueberry to a toothpick and splash the skewer with a mixture of freshly squeezed lemon and lime juices.

✳ Celery stalks cut into 1-inch pieces and the hollows filled with a pungent blue cheese.

✳ Cherry halves placed in shot glasses with brandy, then chilled before serving.

✳ Mini omelets: Place a gently beaten egg in a hot skillet, one tablespoon at a time. Add half teaspoonfuls of the following mixture: cooked chopped corn kernels, minced onion, and bits of bacon.

✳ Peeled cucumber rounds topped with dabs of crème fraiche and sprinkled with torn-up mint leaves.

✳ Eggplant coins: Long, slender eggplant cut into round slices, then sautéed in olive oil until soft. Add a spoonful of mashed garlic and a small piece of anchovy fillet to each round.

✳ Fresh figs quartered and marinated in Cointreau, then dusted with the merest pinch of cinnamon before serving.

✳ A true classic: Fresh fig quartered, then wrapped in prosciutto.

✳ Mini fruit kabobs made of alternating grapes, diced melon, and strawberries skewered on toothpicks.

✳ Fine-fleshed white fish cut into ½-inch cubes and soaked in lime juice overnight. The following day, alternate equal-sized cubes of fish and mango on toothpick skewers.

✳ Melon balls wrapped in prosciutto, held together with a toothpick, then topped with a slice of fresh strawberry.

✳ Peaches and crushed almonds served in small bowls, then drizzled with a splash of Grand Marnier.

✳ Mini brochettes of plum, apricot, and peach dice skewered on toothpicks and sprinkled with lemon zest.

✳ Slices of grilled pork tenderloin served atop slices of ripe apple.

✳ Melted chocolate drizzled over ripe red raspberries, then refrigerated so the chocolate hardens.

✳ Bits of grilled salmon topped with basil and bacon, served on thin-sliced bread.

✳ Baby summer squash halved, brushed with olive oil, and grilled. Cut the squash into 1-inch dice and sprinkle with grated Parmesan cheese.

✳ Hot chiles, salt, and tomato slices wrapped in pieces of red Swiss chard leaves, held together with toothpicks.

stuffed squash blossoms

MAKES 4 SERVINGS

Gardeners who grow zucchini will have more squash blossoms than they know what to do with, since the zucchini blossoms or fruits (as the squashes themselves are called) must be picked off daily if the plant is to continue making new blossoms and squashes.

For nongardeners, squash blossoms are sometimes available at specialty stores and farmers' markets, as are baby squash with the blossoms still attached. Male blossoms are slender, while female blossoms have a rudimentary squash at their base. Either will work for this recipe, but remove the stems, rudimentary squashes, and the stamens and pistils. Check carefully for the presence of striped or spotted cucumber beetles. They love zucchini even more than we do and may hide in the blossoms.

WINE SUGGESTION: FALANGHINA

Pinch salt
1 clove garlic, crushed through a garlic press
½ cup ricotta
½ cup grated Parmesan cheese
¼ cup shredded cheddar cheese
1 tablespoon minced parsley
1 tablespoon chopped fresh thyme
½ teaspoon freshly ground black pepper
12 squash blossoms
2 eggs, beaten
1 cup all-purpose flour
1 cup olive oil

1. In a large bowl, place the salt and garlic and mix well. Add the cheeses, parsley, thyme, and black pepper. Mix and mash the ingredients together to form a paste.
2. Gently open each squash blossom and add 1 tablespoon of the cheese mixture in each. Twist the ends of the blossoms shut and set them aside on a tray.
3. In a large bowl, beat the eggs. In a second large bowl, add the flour. Set the two bowls aside. Place a large skillet over medium heat, add the oil, and heat until fragrant but not smoking.
4. While the oil is heating, dip each blossom in the egg, then in the flour, shaking off any excess flour. Add the blossoms to the skillet 3 or 4 at a time, depending on space. Turn them gently several times until they are golden, about 3 minutes. Set the cooked blossoms on paper towels in a warm oven and continue until all the blossoms are cooked.

southern-style fried onion rings

MAKES 4 TO 6 SERVINGS

These deep-fried onions aren't hard to make, especially if you have a mandoline that can cut them to very thin ⅛-inch rings. For rings, sweet onions (Vidalia, Maui, Walla Walla, Granex, red onions) are best. Their sugar caramelizes in the hot oil, adding flavor to the finished product. Paprika adds a refreshing but mild kick, too.

The secret to perfect rings is to make sure the cooking oil is clean, fresh, and hot enough (370°F) to immediately seal the batter so it doesn't soak up oil and become greasy. Canola, grapeseed, refined peanut, and rice bran oils all have smoke points higher than 370°F, making them the best choices to prevent a burnt oil taste. Cook the rings in very small batches so they don't stick together.

3 large sweet onions
3 ½ cups pastry flour
2 cups buttermilk
1 ½ cups yellow cornmeal
2 teaspoons paprika
1 teaspoon salt
½ teaspoon ground cayenne
½ teaspoon freshly ground black pepper
Vegetable oil (canola or refined peanut oil
    are best) for frying
Kosher salt to taste

1. Slice the onions crosswise and separate into thin rings. Place them in a bowl, cover with cold water, and let stand 30 minutes. Drain well in a colander and pat dry.

2. Place 1 ½ cups of the flour into a plastic or paper bag and add the moist onion rings. Toss well to coat and, shaking off the excess flour, remove them to a baking sheet.

3. In a large bowl, add the buttermilk. Set aside. In a second large bowl, add the remaining 2 cups flour, the cornmeal, paprika, salt, cayenne, and black pepper, and mix well.

4. Dip the onion rings in the buttermilk, then into the flour-cornmeal mixture. Place the batter-covered onion rings on baking sheets lined with wax paper. Allow the rings to stand for 30 minutes to allow the dry ingredients to soak through and set the batter.

5. Place a large skillet over high (370°F) heat and add 2 inches of oil.* Add the rings, in small batches, and fry until they turn golden brown. Cooking time will vary depending on the thickness of the onions. Place cooked rings on a baking sheet lined with paper towels to drain. Wait 1 to 2 minutes between batches to allow the oil to return to the proper temperature.

6. Transfer the drained rings to a serving tray in a warm oven. Sprinkle very lightly with kosher salt just before serving.

*Be very careful with hot oil. If you have small children, keep them out of the kitchen during the cooking period.

deep-south onion rings
MAKES 4 TO 6 SERVINGS

Chopped pecans give these onion rings extra crispness. They are a welcome substitute for french fries and a fabulous accompaniment to burgers from the grill.

2 pounds yellow onions
2 eggs
1 cup buttermilk
2 cups pastry flour
1 cup cornmeal
½ cup pecans, finely chopped
1 teaspoon kosher salt
½ teaspoon freshly ground black pepper
Canola oil for frying

1. Slice the onions crosswise into ¼-inch-wide slices and separate into rings. Set aside.

2. In a large bowl, whisk together the eggs and buttermilk until well mixed. In a second large bowl, add the flour, cornmeal, pecans, salt, and black pepper, and mix well.

3. Place an 8-inch skillet over high (370°F) heat and add 2 inches of oil.* Dip the onion rings in the egg mixture, then coat with the flour-cornmeal mixture. Add the rings, 2 to 3 at a time, to the hot oil and cook, flipping once, until golden brown, just 1 or 2 minutes. Place cooked rings on a baking sheet lined with paper towels to drain. Wait 1 to 2 minutes between batches to allow the oil to return to the proper temperature.

4. Transfer the drained rings to a serving tray in a warm oven.

*Be very careful with hot oil. If you have small children, keep them out of the kitchen during the cooking period.

corn fritters

MAKES 4 TO 6 SERVINGS

Don't refrigerate leftover corn on the cob; it's too difficult to properly reheat it. Instead, cut the corn off the cob and refrigerate in an airtight container with a lid. Then use the leftover kernels to make these delicious fritters.

1 tablespoon unsalted butter
¼ cup chopped onion
¼ cup chopped sweet pepper, such as
    bell peppers
2 cups sweet corn kernels
¼ cup all-purpose flour
½ teaspoon baking powder
Salt and freshly ground black pepper to taste
2 eggs, lightly beaten
2 tablespoons milk
½ teaspoon Tabasco or other hot pepper sauce
2 tablespoons canola oil, plus more if
    necessary

1. Place a medium saucepan over medium-low heat and add the butter. When melted, add the onion and pepper and cook, stirring occasionally, for 6 minutes. Add the corn kernels and continue cooking for 2 minutes more, stirring periodically to heat the kernels through. Remove from heat and set aside.

2. In a large bowl, mix together the flour, baking powder, salt, and black pepper. Add the eggs, milk, and hot pepper sauce, and mix well. Add the corn mixture and stir to mix.

3. Place a large skillet over medium-low heat and add the canola oil. When the oil is hot, drop 4 or 5 heaping tablespoons of the fritter mixture into the pan. Using a spatula, flatten them slightly and cook about 5 minutes, or until lightly browned. Turn the fritters once and continue cooking for another 4 to 5 minutes.

4. Place cooked fritters on a baking sheet lined with paper towels to drain. Transfer the drained fritters to a serving tray in a warm oven. Re-oil the pan if needed, and continue with the remaining batches until the batter is finished.

Corn

Corn is one of the most popular summer staples, found at almost every barbecue or picnic. It's one of the most delicious and versatile vegetables.

When shopping for corn, don't strip the husks; instead, feel through the husks to determine whether the ear is full. Husk the corn when you're ready to cook. Peel the husks back, then grasp them all in one hand, gripping the ear in the other hand, and twist and pull the husks to remove them. Discard the corn silk as well.

When grilling corn on the cob, it's best to keep some of the husks on; just remove the tougher outer layers. Then soak the partially husked corn in cold water for about a half hour prior to cooking, to prevent burning on the grill.

SUMMER SPOTLIGHT

For several years, our friend Barry threw an annual blockbuster summer party at his house in Huffs Church, Pennsylvania. The party always centered around a huge pot of boiling water and an equally huge tub of fresh, live Maryland crabs that Barry would buy near Annapolis and haul up to his house. The water was seasoned with a spicy crab boil mix of peppers, herbs, and spices, and the crabs were all boiled and eaten on picnic tables with plenty of drawn butter and pitchers of beer from a tapped keg kept nearby. Well, *almost* all the crabs were boiled. One was allowed to live and roam at will through the partygoers, and each year carried the name Buster. People wearing flip-flops kept a sharp eye out for Buster.

If you've eaten fresh Maryland blue crab, then you know that their crabmeat is the choicest seafood in the world—better than lobster, better than any fish. It has a naturally buttery flavor and silky texture, and one person can easily eat a dozen of them because they're small compared to the Dungeness crabs of the West Coast. Shortly after moving to California, I was watching the news and the news anchor announced that an eastern blue crab had been pulled from San Francisco Bay. He wondered out loud, "I wonder if they're edible?" I was astounded. Having eaten more than my share of blue crabs and Dungeness crabs, I can vouch for the fact that there is no comparison. Dungeness crab is good, but it is second rate compared to blue crab. A small bowl of freshly picked lump backfin blue crabmeat is as good as seafood gets.

If you ever find yourself in the quaint Revolutionary-era town of St. Michael's on Maryland's Eastern Shore, wander out to The Crab Claw restaurant and they'll boil you up a mess of crabs and set you down at a picnic table with the crabs, french fries, and a pitcher of beer. Just watch out for Buster. He's around there somewhere.

maryland crab cakes

MAKES 6 SERVINGS

The best way to enjoy fresh crab (and the fresh summer air!) is to go down to the water and catch them yourself, then cook and pick them. However, you can also find delicious fresh crab at your local market.

My friends on the West Coast will be loath to hear it, but nothing—I repeat, nothing—compares to Maryland blue crabs for luscious flavor and texture. The local lump backfin crabmeat makes the most succulent, delicious crab cakes imaginable. They're light fare and perfect as an appetizer or main course on a hot night.

If you can't get Maryland crab where you live, substitute Dungeness, Stone, Peeky-Toe, or whatever crab you have locally. Dungeness crab may be frozen in the summer. This recipe is a classic down on Maryland's Eastern Shore.

WINE SUGGESTION: CHARDONNAY

2 large eggs
¼ cup mayonnaise
½ teaspoon celery salt
Pinch ground nutmeg
Pinch ground ginger
Pinch cayenne
Pinch paprika
½ teaspoon freshly ground black pepper
2 teaspoons Worcestershire sauce
1 teaspoon dry mustard
1 pound precooked lump backfin crabmeat
½ cup finely crushed crackers, such
    as Saltines
2 tablespoons peanut oil

1. In a large bowl, add the eggs, mayonnaise, celery salt, nutmeg, ginger, cayenne, paprika, black pepper, Worcestershire sauce, and dry mustard and mix well.

2. Add the crabmeat and crackers, and combine gently, so as not to break up any lumps of crabmeat, but thoroughly.

3. Using your hands, mold the mixture into 6 cake patties, about 3 to 4 inches in diameter and ¾-inch thick.

4. Place a large skillet over medium-low heat and add the peanut oil. When hot, add the patties in batches and cook for 5 to 7 minutes on each side, until golden brown. Place cooked patties on a plate lined with paper towels to drain. Serve hot.

argentine empanadas

MAKES ABOUT 10 EMPANADAS

These empanadas are a guaranteed crowd pleaser at any backyard party. An evening of Malbec and empanadas will have your guests dreaming about the tango and the pampas in short order. Visiting Argentina a few years ago, I was struck by the ubiquity of beehive ovens and fell in love with the luscious empanadas that emerged from them. My friend Alfredo said that the proper way to eat them is to stick out your rear end and lean forward before biting into them. This puzzled me until I took a bite and the wonderful, fragrant, savory juice spilled out. If I hadn't followed Alfredo's advice, the juice would have run down my shirt. You don't have to have a beehive oven to make these (but what a treat it would be).

WINE SUGGESTION: ARGENTINE MALBEC

The grape variety known as malbec is one of the five so-called Bordeaux varieties: cabernet sauvignon, merlot, cabernet franc, malbec, and petit verdot. In France, it adds a nice bass note to the vinous harmonies made at Bordeaux châteaux, but on its own, as a varietal wine, it is rather bland and not very interesting.

In the mid-1850s, the Argentine government began a program to improve its agriculture, and imported malbec vines as part of the program. The vines were taken to the western high desert around the town of Mendoza, and there a strange thing happened. Malbec started to yield wines of a richness and complexity unknown in France. The vine had found its promised land, much as the Croatian vine *Crljenak Kastelanski* did when it came to California and developed into Zinfandel.

In recent times, growers like Nicolas Catena planted malbec not only on the desert floor, but on the slopes of the snow-capped Andes to the west. Grown at altitude—up to 5,000 feet above sea level—Argentine malbec develops a superior aromatic profile, richer flavors, and even produces compounds in its skins that have been shown to reduce the body's ability to deposit plaque in the arteries.

Today Malbec from Argentina is being recognized as one of the world's great wines. It is the perfect wine for barbecues—not only for empanadas but for grilled meats and other rich, spicy foods.

CRUST

1 ½ cups all-purpose flour
Generous pinch salt
½ stick butter
About ⅓ cup milk

FILLING

1 pound ground beef, not too lean
2 tablespoons extra virgin olive oil
1 medium onion, finely chopped
1 red bell pepper, seeded and finely chopped
2 jalapeño chiles, seeded and minced
1 small red potato, peeled, boiled until just tender, and finely chopped
2 tablespoons golden raisins, chopped
1 teaspoon capers, drained
1 tablespoon paprika
1 tablespoon finely chopped fresh parsley.
Salt and freshly ground black pepper to taste

GLAZE

1 egg
1 tablespoon milk

1. Make the crust: In a large bowl, sift the flour and salt. Add the butter and, using 2 knives, cut it into the flour. Add just enough milk for the flour to come together into a ball that holds its shape. Wrap the dough in wax paper and refrigerate for at least 1 hour.

2. Make the filling: Meanwhile, place a large skillet over medium heat and sauté the beef until cooked through, mixing and dividing it into crumbles, but not letting it dry out.

3. Place another large skillet over medium heat, add the oil, the onion, bell pepper, and jalapeños, and cook, stirring frequently, until the onions are a translucent golden brown.

4. Add the vegetables to the meat and stir until well combined. Add the potato, raisins, capers, paprika, parsley, salt, and black pepper. Remove from heat and continue to mix thoroughly.

5. Make the glaze: In a small bowl, whisk together the egg and milk. Set aside.

6. Preheat the oven to 400°F. On a lightly floured cutting board or surface, roll out the dough to ⅛ inch thick and cut out 6-inch circles, using a cookie cutter or ring mold. Gather leftover dough, reroll, and cut more circles. Repeat until all the dough is used up.

7. Spoon a heaping tablespoon of filling onto one half of each circle. Fold the empty half over the filling and crimp the edges of the dough with the tines of a fork to seal. Cut a 1-inch slit at the top of each empanada to let steam escape.

8. Place the empanadas on an ungreased baking sheet, slit side up, and bake for 10 minutes. Reduce the heat to 350°F and continue baking until the top turns a light, golden brown. Remove the baking sheet from the oven. With a pastry brush, glaze the tops of the empanadas with the milk and egg mixture, then return to the oven and bake for 5 more minutes. Serve hot or at room temperature.

hoisin chicken drumettes

MAKES 6 SERVINGS

These are amazingly good chicken wings, and a crowd-pleaser at parties, cookouts, and summer pool parties. Hoisin is a Chinese bean-based barbecue sauce with a flavor intensity of 11 on a scale of 10. It really packs a flavor punch in these easy-to-make wings. Avoid small jars of hoisin at the supermarket and go for the large tins found at Asian markets.

WINE SUGGESTION: ZINFANDEL

5 pounds chicken drumettes
Nonstick cooking spray
2 cups hoisin sauce

1. Preheat the oven to 300°F. Place a large skillet over medium-high heat and spray with the nonstick cooking spray. Working in batches, brown the drumettes on all sides, then place in a large bowl.

2. When all the drumettes are added to the bowl, add the hoisin sauce and toss to coat.

3. Spray baking sheets with nonstick cooking spray and arrange the hoisin-coated drumettes in three rows, alternating the meaty ends with the smaller ends as you work. Place the drumettes on the middle rack of the oven to bake.

4. After 45 minutes, rotate the baking sheet, and continue baking for 45 minutes more. Bake until the sauce is baked onto the meat but stop before the sauce burns black. Remove the drumettes from the baking sheet and arrange them in a spiral or circular pattern on a serving platter.

grilled chicken satay on rosemary skewers

MAKES 4 SERVINGS

Fresh rosemary branches add that little something extra to your chicken satay. If you live in an area where rosemary can survive the winter, gather slender, woody rosemary branches and reduce them to foot-long skewers with pointed ends. Soak them by weighting them down under warm water with a plate for a half hour. If you don't have rosemary, use bamboo skewers from the supermarket, soaked for a half hour in a cup of warm water. When cooking, be sure to turn the skewers often; the plum sauce is sugary, and the sugar will burn black and bitter if left over the heat too long.

WINE SUGGESTION: PINOT NOIR

20 rosemary or bamboo skewers, soaked in
   warm water
4 boneless, skinless chicken breasts
Chinese plum sauce

1. Slice each breast lengthwise into at least 4 slices, each about 1 ½ inches wide and about 4 to 5 inches long.

2. Thread each piece of chicken onto a skewer. Lay the skewers in a tray or platter and pour Chinese plum sauce over them, turning to coat both sides.

3. Preheat the grill on high for about 15 minutes. Scrub the grates with a wire brush, and brush them with vegetable oil. Reduce the heat to low.

4. Place the skewers on the fire so that the bare ends of the skewers extend over the edge of the grill (so you don't burn your fingers turning them). Cook, turning the skewers frequently, about 5 to 6 minutes or

GOOD TO KNOW: GRILLING SHISH KEBABS

Traditional shish kebabs call for grilling different foods on the same skewer, which often mean the tomatoes turn to jelly before the potato chunks are even half-finished, while the chicken breast meat is dried out and overcooked before the pork chunks are much past medium-rare. What to do?

The answer is to grill all the same foods on their own skewers. The different meats go on their own skewers; the vegetable chunks each on their own skewer. Time your cooking by starting with the food that will take longest to cook. Then continue by adding the other skewers in descending order of cooking times, with the quickest-cooking food (such as shrimp) going on last.

By following the recommendations above, the skewers should then come off the grill at approximately the same time. You can then slide the food off the skewers into separate bowls, with a plate of clean skewers off to the side, and let guests choose their own combinations. Or serve everything in one big bowl, as a grilled medley.

until the meat is just cooked through. Remove from heat, place the skewers on a platter, and serve immediately.

✱ CHICKEN SATAY WITH PEANUT SAUCE
Instead of coating the raw meat with plum sauce, cook the satay skewers without sauce and serve them with traditional Thai-style peanut sauce for dipping.

barbecued pork shish kebabs

MAKES 8 SERVINGS

Shish kebabs can be broiled, but centuries of cooking meat on sticks means they are meant to be grilled. Prerequisite are eight long stainless skewers with edges. (Round skewers allow meat or vegetables to spin and flop around, making it hard to grill them evenly.) Serve these kebabs with a light salad of butterhead lettuce with oranges or strawberries, and dressed with a fruit vinaigrette. Note that the pork should be marinated for at least 1 hour before grilling.

WINE SUGGESTION: ZINFANDEL

8 stainless steel skewers
2 ½ pounds pork tenderloin (about 2), cut into 1-inch cubes
2 cups Homemade Barbecue Sauce (page 294) or store-bought
2 pints cherry tomatoes
4 young zucchinis (about 7 inches each) cut into 1-inch pieces
Extra virgin olive oil

1. In a large bowl, place the pork tenderloin pieces and add the barbecue sauce. Toss to coat. Cover the bowl with plastic wrap and allow it to marinate in the fridge for at least 1 hour, but preferably overnight.

2. Spear the pork pieces onto the skewers, allowing the excess sauce to drip off into the bowl. Alternate the meat with a cherry tomato and a piece of zucchini. Fill each skewer about 5 inches with meat and vegetables.

3. Preheat the grill to medium-high heat. Brush the skewers with oil and place them on the grill. Cook for about 5 to 6 minutes, then turn the skewers over and cook an ad-

ditional 5 to 6 minutes, or until the meat is well done. Serve immediately.

✳ TERIYAKI SHISH KEBABS
For a sweet Asian flavor, substitute teriyaki sauce for the barbecue sauce.

shrimp on the barbie

MAKES 4 SERVINGS

Some people grill shrimp as they come from the market—with shells and legs attached — letting guests deal with the shelling. But barbecuing shrimp usually welds the shells to the juicy flesh underneath, making them doubly hard to remove. Shrimp are much easier to shell and devein when they're raw. Any kitchen supply store should carry a shrimp shelling and deveining tool that magically shells and deveins a shrimp in just a few moments.

WINE SUGGESTION: AUSTRALIAN SEMILLON

8 bamboo skewers, soaked in warm water
1 pound (20 to 25) large shrimp
1 cup extra virgin olive oil
Juice of 1 lemon
1 teaspoon kosher salt

1. Shell and devein the shrimp.

2. In a bowl, whisk together the oil, lemon juice, and salt. Put the shrimp in the bowl and toss to coat. Cover the bowl with plastic wrap and allow it to marinate in the refrigerator for at least 1 hour.

3. Preheat the grill on high heat for 15 minutes. Scrub the grates with a wire brush, and wipe them down with oil. Reduce the heat to medium.

4. Spear the shrimp onto the skewers, using two skewers at a time (see sidebar).

Slide 5 or 6 shrimp onto four pairs of skewers.

5. Place the skewers on the grill and cook for about 3 minutes on each side, turning once, or until the shrimp are cooked through. Serve immediately.

✻ **SOY-GINGER-GARLIC SHRIMP ON THE BARBIE**
Marinate peeled, deveined raw shrimp in a soy-ginger-garlic sauce.

✻ **EXTRA-SPICY SHRIMP ON THE BARBIE**
Marinate the shrimp in a sauce made of white wine, toasted sesame oil, and Sriracha or other hot chili sauce such as Tabasco.

✻ **CITRUS-MARINATED SHRIMP ON THE BARBIE**
Make a marinade for shrimp of freshly squeezed lime juice whisked together with mashed garlic, a dash of soy sauce, a tea-spoon of ground coriander, and a few table-spoons of canola oil.

fish kebabs

MAKES 4 SERVINGS

Firm-fleshed fish such as cod, Chilean sea bass, escolar, ahi, and swordfish make the best kebabs, as they don't disintegrate into flakes when cooked. Chunks of nectarine cut to about 1-inch cubes, the same size as the fish, make a tasty match on the skewers and take about the same amount of time to cook. The recipe below calls for swordfish, but feel free to substitute any of the firm-fleshed options mentioned here.

WINE SUGGESTION: GERMAN RHEINGAU

8 bamboo skewers, soaked in warm water
Canola oil
1 pound swordfish steaks, cut into
    1-inch cubes
1 pound ripe nectarines, halved, pitted, and
    cut into 1-inch chunks

✻ GOOD TO KNOW: PREVENTING SKEWER TWIRL

Skewers are a fun and fast way to grill all kinds of food, but unless you spear each chunk of food exactly in the place where its weight is equal in all directions (unlikely), it can have a tendency to twirl on the skewer. This means uneven cooking—the heavy part may get all the heat and the top part little or none.

There are ways to prevent skewer twirl. The simplest is to use two skewers. If using bamboo skewers, soak them for ½ hour in warm water by weighting them down under the surface with a plate. Then they won't burn on the grill. Metal skewers simply need to be clean.

Push the first skewer through one side of the food, and the second through the other side. For instance, the first skewer might go through the head side of six shrimp, the second skewer through the tail side. Now they can't twirl. And having two skewer handles instead of one makes them easier to flip.

1. Preheat the grill to high for 15 minutes. Scrub the grates with a wire brush, and brush them down with some oil. Reduce the grill's heat to medium.

2. Use 2 skewers to spear 4 chunks of swordfish alternating with 3 chunks of nectarines. Brush the kebabs all around with oil.

3. Place the kebabs on the grill and cook uncovered for about 4 minutes. Turn them over—be careful when you lift not to pull off any fish that might be stuck to the grates; if you feel resistance, run a spatula blade gently under the kebabs along the grates to loosen. Cook for an additional 3 to 4 minutes, or until the fish is thoroughly cooked through. Serve immediately.

SANDWICHES & BREADS

Few foods are easier to make than sandwiches. They are a simple way to combine protein and carbohydrates, and if you add a smear of mayo and some lettuce, then you have your fats and greens, too.

Most two- or three-slice sandwiches have the summer virtue of being served cold. Roast turkey breast, sliced chicken, baked ham, slices of steak, and tuna salad all work beautifully when chilled.

Of course, we eat hot sandwiches in the summer, too—not hot, open-faced sandwiches with gravy maybe, but hot dogs and hamburgers, lobster rolls, sausage sandwiches, and oyster po'boys. The point is that all of them are easy to make.

When I was a boy, hot and sticky evenings when Mom was running late meant we had a build-your-own-sandwiches dinner of fresh cold cuts, condiments like mustard and mayo, lettuce, ripe tomatoes, and a stack of bread. It's still a good ploy when spending time in the kitchen just isn't all that appealing.

fish tacos

MAKES 3 TO 4 SERVINGS

These hearty tacos were inspired by the fish tacos I had at Soo Young Kim's Sooze Wine Bar Café in Petaluma, California. They're the best fish tacos I've ever had. They don't require much cooking heat, making them a perfect addition to your summer repertoire.

WINE SUGGESTION: PINOT BLANC

2 cups cornmeal
Salt and freshly ground black pepper
2 tablespoons Harissa (page 43)
2 tablespoons chopped jalapeño peppers
½ cup mayonnaise
3 eggs
¼ cup milk
1 pound orange roughy or other firm
    fish fillets
¼ cup olive oil
12 soft corn tortillas (6 inches across)
½ cup tomatillo salsa
1 head heart of romaine lettuce, thinly sliced
½ cup shredded carrots
1 red onion, thinly sliced
½ cup shredded tome or Jack cheese
9 lime wedges
¼ cup finely chopped cilantro

   1. In a small bowl, mix the cornmeal with salt and black pepper. Set aside.
   2. In a large bowl, combine the harissa, jalapeño, and mayonnaise. Set aside.
   3. In a large bowl, mix the eggs and milk together. Dip the fish into the egg mixture, then into the cornmeal mixture, and coat all sides well.
   4. Place a large skillet over medium-low heat and add the oil. When hot, add the fish in batches and cook for 3 to 4 minutes, then

flip and cook for 3 to 4 minutes more, or until the cornmeal coating is golden brown. Place the fish on a plate lined with paper towels to drain. Transfer the drained fish to a warm oven.
   5. Pour out the remaining oil and wipe the skillet clean with paper towels. Heat as many tortillas as will fit in the pan until hot, turning once. Place the tortillas on a plate and slide a piece of cooked fish onto each. Slather on the tomatillo salsa, lettuce, carrot, onion, cheese, and the mayonnaise mixture. Squeeze the juice of a lime wedge (¼ of a whole lime) onto each fish taco. Sprinkle on the cilantro. Fold and serve.

CLT on toast

MAKES 4 SANDWICHES

A twist on the classic BLT sandwich, but here, I substitute hearty chicken breast for the bacon. These quick-to-make sandwiches are healthy and hearty.

WINE SUGGESTION: SEMILLON

2 eggs, beaten
¼ cup plain yogurt
1 cup cornmeal
2 boneless, skinless chicken breasts, cut
    into ⅓-inch slices
½ cup extra virgin olive oil
8 slices whole wheat bread
4 teaspoons mayonnaise
2 medium tomatoes, sliced
1 head butterhead lettuce, torn

   1. In a large bowl, whisk together the eggs and yogurt. Set aside.
   2. In a large bowl, add the cornmeal. Dip

the chicken into the egg mixture, then dredge in the cornmeal. Set aside.

3. Place a large skillet over medium heat and add the oil. When hot, add the chicken in batches and cook, turning once, about 3 minutes on a side, or until they are cooked through. Place on a plate lined with paper towels to drain.

4. While the chicken is cooking, toast 2 slices of bread. Spread each piece with ½ teaspoon of the mayonnaise. Assemble the sandwich: add 1 or 2 slices of chicken breast over 1 slice bread, and top with 1 slice tomato and a handful of lettuce leaves. Top the sandwich with the second piece of toast. Repeat with the remaining ingredients.

multigrain club sandwich

MAKES 1 SANDWICH

Club sandwiches don't have to be reserved for lunch. They also make a delicious light dinner on a hot night when you don't want to be in a hot kitchen. Use whole wheat, seven-grain, or nine-grain bread to add complex carbohydrates to the meal. The following recipe makes one sandwich. Increase the recipe for the number of sandwiches you need.

WINE SUGGESTION: CHILLED ROSÉ

4 slices bacon
3 slices multigrain bread
¼ cup mayonnaise
2 romaine lettuce leaves
½ tomato, thinly sliced (about 4 slices)
Salt and freshly ground black pepper
4 thin slices roast turkey breast

1. Place a large skillet over medium-high heat and add the bacon. Fry the bacon until crisp. Blot away excess fat with a paper towel. Set aside.

2. While the bacon is cooking, toast the bread. Spread all three slices of toast with mayonnaise. Slice the romaine in half across the leaves and place 2 pieces on the first slice of bread. Top the lettuce with 2 tomato slices and a pinch of salt and black pepper.

3. Place 2 strips of bacon neatly on the tomato, folding if necessary, and top the bacon with 2 slices of turkey breast, folded to fit. Repeat this process on the second slice of bread, then carefully set the slice of bread on top of the first. Place the third slice of bread on top, mayonnaise side down.

4. Place 4 toothpicks in a diamond pattern in the sandwich—one at the top, two in the middle, and one at the bottom—to hold the pieces together. Using a serrated knife, make 2 diagonal cuts that cross in the middle of the sandwich. Serve immediately,

classic italian hoagie

MAKES 6 SANDWICHES

These easy-to-assemble sandwiches are what they eat in Philly when it's too hot for cheese steaks. They are a perfect addition to any picnic lunch in the park. Most delicatessens sell the requisite Italian lunch meats and cheeses. The rolls should be soft, about 10 inches long, and 3 inches thick in the middle. For added variety, substitute other Italian deli meats, such as coppa, sopressata, or various other kinds of salumi—but never pepperoni. Pepperoni is greasy and has a flavor that can overwhelm the other ingredients.

One of the best ways to celebrate the season is to enjoy the great outdoors, with great food and great company. Be it a picnic in the park, a snack on the beach, or dinner on the patio, eating outdoors is truly a pleasure in the warm summer months.

It's important to keep safety in mind when thinking about eating outdoors, or about transporting food from one location to another. Keep these tips in mind when preparing, cooking, and transporting your delicious dishes:

* Marinate food in the refrigerator, not out on the counter.

* Don't reuse marinade that was used on raw meat, poultry, or fish.

* Don't use the same platter or dish that previously held raw meat, poultry, or fish.

* Keep food cold when transporting from one location to another. Use a cooler with ice packs. Food should be kept at a temperature of 40ºF.

* Use separate containers or coolers for beverages and perishables.

* Pack food in the cooler in the reverse order you plan to eat it. This allows for easy access and minimizes the length of time the contents of the cooler are exposed to the elements.

* Wrap raw meat, poultry, and seafood securely so that the juices don't leak onto other raw foods.

* Pack dressings and vinaigrettes separately and toss just before eating.

* Always rinse raw fruits and vegetables before packing. Dry them with a paper towel.

* Keep coolers in the air-conditioned section of your car, rather than in the hot trunk.

* Keep cold foods cold, and hot foods hot.

* Always remember to wash your hands before beginning.

* Hot food should be kept at or above 140˚F, wrapped and insulated if necessary.

* Try not to keep perishables out for longer than 2 hours. Try to keep food in the shade as much as possible.

* Food should not be kept out for longer than 1 hour at temperatures at or above 90˚F.

For more information, visit www.foodsafety.gov.

To make the sandwiches as fresh as possible, do all the slicing and preparation first and then assemble the hoagies just before serving.

WINE SUGGESTION: CALIFORNIA SANGIOVESE

6 Italian or French bread loaves (or their equivalent)
¼ cup extra virgin olive oil
2 cups shredded iceberg lettuce
2 cups thinly sliced red onion
¼ pound provolone cheese, thinly sliced
¼ pound prosciutto, thinly sliced
¼ pound Genoa salami, thinly sliced
2 medium tomatoes, thinly sliced
2 tablespoons dried oregano
2 tablespoons dried basil or ¼ cup finely chopped fresh
3 hot pickled cherry peppers, thinly sliced
About ½ cup red wine vinegar
Salt and freshly ground black pepper to taste

1. Using a serrated knife, slice the rolls lengthwise, stopping right before breaking through to the other side. Lay them open on the work surface and sprinkle them lightly with oil.

2. Divide the lettuce and onions evenly among the rolls. Divide the provolone, prosciutto, and salami evenly among the rolls, lightly folding each slice so they fill the roll lengthwise.

3. Add 2 slices of tomato to each sandwich. Sprinkle pinches of oregano and basil into the sandwiches. Slice each of the cherry peppers into 4 slices and add 2 slices among the other fillings in each sandwich. Sprinkle 1 to 2 tablespoons vinegar over the filling. Add a pinch of salt and black pepper and close the roll.

4. Place each hoagie on a plate and slice in half across the middle. Secure the roll with a toothpick in each half if necessary.

✳ SPICY ITALIAN HOAGIES
Instead of the red wine vinegar, use the liquid in the hot cherry pepper jar. Substitute slices of pepperoncini for the cherry peppers.

steak and pepper sandwiches
MAKES 8 SANDWICHES

Philadelphia is famous for its Philly "cheese steaks," a delicious sandwich that's made up of steak and Cheez Whiz. These easy-to-prepare alternatives are not the authentic steak sandwiches of Pennsylvania. But they are oh-so-good anyway.

WINE SUGGESTION: SANGIOVESE OR CHIANTI

4 tablespoons olive oil
8 red bell peppers, seeded and cut into 8 pieces
1 medium onion, chopped
3 cloves garlic, minced
Salt and freshly ground black pepper to taste
¼ cup butter, melted
8 soft French rolls, halved
1 pound top sirloin steak, grilled medium rare

1. In a large skillet over medium heat, add 2 tablespoons of the oil. When hot, sauté the bell peppers, onion, garlic, salt, and black pepper for 3 to 5 minutes, or until the vegetables are tender.

2. In a large bowl, add the remaining 2 tablespoons oil and the butter and mix until well combined.

3. Brush the cut sides of the bread with the

oil and butter mixture and place under the broiler. Cook until the tops are lightly toasted.

4. Slice the steak against the grain into thin strips. Lay the strips on the bottom half of each roll and top with the pepper-onion-garlic mixture. Place top half on the sandwiches and serve.

tacos con carne asada
MAKES 4 TO 6 SERVINGS

There's nothing difficult about this classic Mexican dish. Serve it with rice, refried beans, Pico de Gallo (p. 42) and plenty of warm tortillas. For plenty of spicy heat, choose ground arbol chile powder. For less heat, choose chili powder (which is a mix of spices, some not so hot). Mix up the flavors by adding minced onions, salsa picante (hot pepper sauce), taco sauce, tomatillo sauce, or minced tomatoes.

WINE SUGGESTION: ZINFANDEL

2 tablespoons butter
2 pounds outside skirt steak, about
   1 inch thick
Salt and freshly ground black pepper to taste
1 cup loosely packed cilantro leaves,
   chopped
1 tablespoon finely grated lime zest
2 cloves garlic, crushed through a garlic press
1 teaspoon chili powder
12 corn tortillas

1. Preheat the grill to high, or set a larger skillet over high heat and preheat oven to 350°F. Add butter to the skillet and immediately put in the steak, partially covering the pan to direct smoke to an exhaust fan, if you have one. On the grill, cook the steak to medium-rare, 3 to 4 minutes on each side. If searing in the skillet, cook 3 to 4 minutes on one side, flip, and finish cooking the meat in a 350°F oven for an additional 10 minutes.

2. Slice the steak on the grain into ¼-inch-thick slices. Sprinkle with salt and black pepper on both sides and set aside to rest.

3. In a large bowl, combine the cilantro, lime zest, garlic, and chili powder. Set aside.

4. Add the steak to the bowl and toss to coat.

5. Place steak mixture on corn tortillas and serve.

GOOD TO KNOW: USING LEAVES TO WRAP FOODS

Soft and pliable edible leaves make fine wraps for finger foods. But not all greens are the same—butterhead lettuce will roll nicely, whereas iceberg or romaine are too stiff and will break. Grape leaves can be steamed to make them pliable. Spinach leaves are preferable to chard or beet greens, which are too coarse and earthy. Cabbage leaves also need steaming.

fried shrimp and mango wrap
MAKES 4 SERVINGS

This recipe is inspired by a Thai dish called *meang kam,* in which several ingredients such as dried shrimp, toasted coconut, crushed peanuts, and chutney are wrapped in leaves and eaten as finger foods. Here's a summer version of this Thai favorite.

WINE SUGGESTION: ITALIAN PROSECCO

1 head butterhead lettuce

1 Japanese cucumber, peeled and sliced
    into thin sticks

2 cups bean sprouts

½ bunch fresh mint

2 ripe mangoes

1 jalapeño pepper, minced

1 teaspoon sugar

Juice of 1 lime

Pinch salt

12 medium shrimp, peeled, deveined,
    and butterflied

½ cup all-purpose flour

2 eggs

¼ cup milk

1 ½ cups plain panko or breadcrumbs

Salt and freshly ground black pepper

Vegetable oil for deep frying

1. Separate the lettuce head into individual leaves and stack them. Wrap tightly in plastic wrap and keep cool in the fridge.

2. Peel and slice cucumber into long strips, then slice strips lengthwise into long sticks about ¼ inch wide. Cut the sticks into 2-inch pieces. Place in a bowl, cover, and refrigerate.

3. Wash, drain, and pat dry the bean sprouts. Wrap tightly in plastic wrap and keep cool in the fridge. Pick over the mint to remove stems and damaged leaves. Wash and pat dry. Wrap tightly in plastic wrap and keep cool in the fridge.

4. Peel and dice the mango flesh and place in a bowl with the jalapeño, sugar, lime juice, and salt. Mix well, cover, and refrigerate.

5. Place shrimp into a plastic bag with the flour and shake to coat. Remove shrimp to a plate, shaking off excess flour. In a large bowl, whisk together the eggs and milk. In a second bowl, add the panko, salt, and black pepper, and stir to mix. Dip the shrimp in the egg mixture, and coat with panko.

6. Place an uncovered Dutch oven or heavy pot over medium-high heat and add 2 inches of vegetable oil.* When the oil is hot but not smoking, shake off loose breadcrumbs from the shrimp and add a few at a time. Cook about 3 minutes, or until crispy and golden. Using a slotted spoon, remove the shrimp from the oil and let drain on paper towels. Cover with more paper towels. Repeat with remaining batches until all the shrimp are cooked.

7. Set the lettuce leaves, cucumber sticks, bean sprouts, mint leaves, shrimp, and mango salsa on individual dishes so guests can mix-and-match their own roll-ups.

*Be very careful with hot oil. If you have small children, keep them out of the kitchen during the cooking period.

✴ TWO SUPER-SPICY VARIATIONS

Increase the spiciness by substituting a minced serrano pepper for the jalapeño.

If you want over-the-top spiciness, substitute a minced habañero for the jalapeño. Warn people not to touch the habañero bits with their hands, but use the spoon provided. Remember to wear gloves while mincing the habañero, and wash your hands immediately.

lobster roll

MAKES 4 ROLLS

Nothing says summer quite like fresh lobster. You'll find these sandwiches offered all over coastal New England, from Connecticut to Maine. The authentic roll is a flat-bottomed, top-loading hot dog bun. If you can't find the top-loading roll, a regular hot dog bun will work as well. Be sure to use only lobster from a quality fishmonger—it's all about the lobster, after all.

1 small lobster, about 1 to 1 ½ pounds
½ cup minced celery stalk and leaves
¼ cup mayonnaise
1 tablespoon lemon juice
Salt and freshly ground black pepper to taste
2 tablespoons butter
4 hot dog buns

   1. Place a stockpot over medium-high heat and add water and some salt. Be sure to add enough water to cover the lobster completely.
   2. When the water is at a rolling boil, remove rubber bands from claws and hold the lobster by the rear of the carapace (spine), plunging its entire head into the water. When the lobster relaxes, drop it into the water and return the water to a full boil. Reduce the heat to a simmer and allow the lobster to cook for about 5 minutes.
   3. Place the lobster on a clean work surface. Crack the shell and pick the lobster so you have about 1 ½ to 2 cups of meat. Coarsely chop any large pieces.
   4. In a bowl, thoroughly mix the lobster meat with the celery, mayonnaise, lemon juice, salt, and black pepper. Set aside.
   5. Spread ½ tablespoon of butter on each hot dog bun. Toast the sides of top-loading buns under the broiler. If using regular hot dog buns, toast inside faces until lightly browned. Fill each bun with ¼ of the lobster salad and serve while still warm.

✳ CLAM ROLLS
For clam rolls, steam either soft-shell clams (preferred) or cherrystone clams. Dip the meats in a batter made of 2 eggs and ¼ cup of milk and roll in breadcrumbs. Fry in butter or canola oil over medium heat until lightly browned on all sides, about 3 to 4 minutes. Fill hot dog buns with fried clams and top with about as much tartar sauce as you'd use mustard on a hot dog.

olive bread
MAKES ONE 16-OUNCE LOAF

This is a simple bread to make, and just right for any Mediterranean-style meal.
WINE SUGGESTION: AGLIANICO

2 cups all-purpose flour
½ teaspoon salt
1 tablespoon dry yeast
½ cup lukewarm water
2 tablespoons olive oil
1 pint pitted purple oil-cured olives

   1. In a large bowl, mix the flour, salt, and yeast together, then add water, a little at a time, until the mixture forms a firm dough.
   2. Knead the dough on a floured board for 5 to 7 minutes, until smooth and elastic. Oil the bowl and place the dough in it, smooth side up. Set the bowl in a warm place, covered with a moist towel, and let rise for at least 1 hour.
   3. Preheat the oven to 425°F and place a baking stone or baking sheet in the upper rack. Return the dough to a floured board and knead again for 5 to 7 minutes, then roll out the dough into a rectangle about 8 x 12 inches. Press olives into the dough about 2 ½ inches apart in all directions, forming a pretty pattern.
   4. Cover the dough with a dry towel and let rise for 30 minutes. Using 2 spatulas, transfer the dough to the stone or baking sheet and bake for 15 minutes, or until golden brown. Remove from the oven, let cool for a few minutes, and serve.

FABULOUS HOMEMADE SANDWICH BREAD

MAKES 2 LOAVES

It's a lazy, sunny summer day and all you can think of is sandwiches made with fresh bread. And who can blame you? Nothing is more appetizing than the aroma and the reality of fresh-baked bread. There are easier and quicker ways to make bread, but the results of this method are astoundingly superior. I have used this recipe many times and find it to be superb. The recipe takes three days but only a few minutes, work are needed on the first two days. The third day requires some baking time, so keep this in mind when deciding when to begin this recipe.

You'll find your loaves will have a beautiful crust and an internal structure full of holes, with a slightly translucent, stretchy, deliciously chewy texture. The whole wheat, rye, and oats give real flavor to plain white bread. I enjoy inhaling the aroma of this bread almost as much as I do eating it. You'll also notice with pleasure that this bread will last for days and days without getting stale.

Tip: you'll be slashing your dough before baking and for this you'll need a very sharp knife or razor blade. Have it handy on baking day so you don't have to search for it.

FIRST DAY
2 cups all-purpose flour
2 cups lukewarm water
½ teaspoon dry yeast
1 heaping tablespoon kosher salt

1. In a large bowl, mix together the flour, water, yeast, and salt with a wooden spoon, until well combined.

2. Take a clean dish towel and soak it in hot tap water. Wring out the excess water, and cover the bowl, Place a dinner plate on top of the towel to hold it in place. Set the bowl in a cool area of the kitchen counter, away from drafts.

SECOND DAY
1 cup whole-wheat flour
½ cup rye flour
½ cup rolled oats
½ cup lukewarm water
Dough from Day 1

1. In a large bowl, mix together the flours, oats, and water, with a wooden spoon until well combined. Add this mixture to the one from Day 1 and stir it in well.

2. Re-wet the dish towel and cover the bowl with the towel and the plate again. Set the bowl back on the counter.

THIRD DAY
5 cups all-purpose flour
2 ½ cups lukewarm water
Dough from previous 2 days
All-purpose flour for flouring the board and kneading the dough
Olive oil
Yellow cornmeal

1. In a large bowl, mix the flour and water together. Transfer mixture to a floured surface and gently knead it for 2 to 3 minutes, then return it to the large bowl and let it rest for 30 or 40 minutes. The resting period is responsible for heightened flavor in the final bread.

2. After the resting period, uncover the bowl containing the poolish—the mixture that's been sitting for 2 days. It's now supercharged with active yeast ready to go. Using a spatula, scrape the poolish into the large bowl with the rested dough. Use your hands to squeeze and mix the poolish and the new dough together until they are fairly well incorporated. This mixed dough will be powerfully sticky.

3. Using both hands, transfer as much of the mixture as you can to a board or work surface heavily floured with all-purpose white flour.

4. Fold the dough in half, then gently pull it out to its former size. Give it a half turn, fold and pull. Use as much flour as you need to keep the surface from being too sticky to fold and pull. Spend 1 minute flouring, folding, and stretching the dough so it holds together and can be kneaded. Then knead it for 8 to 10 minutes to work up the gluten (gluten causes bread to be stretchy and chewy). Knead by pushing the dough with the heels of your palms, folding it toward you, giving it a quarter turn, and repeating the pushing, folding, and turning. If it begins to stick to the board, add more flour.

5. Thoroughly wash your large bowl with hot water. Dry it and wipe the inside of the bowl all over with a little olive oil. Being careful not to let your dough tear or pull apart, use both hands to transfer it from the board to the bowl. Cover the top with a dish towel soaked in hot water and then wrung out. Set the bowl aside in a warm (75°F to 80°F is ideal), draft-free spot and let the dough rise for 4 hours. It should nearly triple in size.

6. Gently pull the dough away from the sides of the bowl and deflate the dough into the bottom of the bowl. If any sticks, use a rubber spatula to free it. Cover it again and allow it to rise in your warm spot for 2 more hours. It should at least double in size.

7. To make two loaves, get two large bowls and wipe the inside all over with a little olive oil. Gently remove the dough from its bowl and place it on a lightly floured board. Divide the dough into equal halves with the slice of a sharp knife. Try not to deflate the dough any more than necessary. Once the dough is divided, gently pat the pieces into large rounds and place them with their smoothest side down in the bowls. Dust the top of the dough with a little yellow cornmeal. Cover each bowl by lightly floating a length of plastic wrap over the top. Don't tuck the wrap; just let it settle gently on top. Let the dough rise once more, for 1 hour.

8. Remove any oven racks from your stove except the middle one and the one below it. Place a cookie sheet on the middle rack and place a cast-iron cornbread mold (or cast-iron skillet) on the bottom rack. Preheat the oven to 500ºF while the bread finishes rising. Quickly open the oven door and sprinkle the cookie sheet with a dusting of cornmeal. Close the door quickly.

9. Dust 2 large plates with cornmeal. The cornmeal will allow you to slide the dough off the plates onto the cookie sheet in the oven, so use enough to completely cover the plates' top surfaces. Remove the plastic wrap from the bowls, and quickly invert one of the bowls onto a plate. Repeat with the second bowl. Using a sharp knife, make three quick, shallow slashes that cross in the center of the dough. Be sure the slashes don't tear and deflate the dough. Repeat with the second loaf.

10. Open the oven door and, giving the plate a sharp forward then backward shake, slide the dough onto one side of the cookie sheet. Slide the second loaf onto the other side of the cookie sheet. Toss 1 ice cube into each of the 8 segments of the iron cornbread mold, or all 8 into the iron skillet. Close the door immediately. The reason for the ice cubes is the same reason why professional ovens have steam injectors: the ice cubes turn to steam over the first 10 minutes or so of the bake and produce a beautiful, crispy crust.

11. Bake 15 minutes, then reduce the heat to 350°F for an additional ½ hour. Remove the cookie sheet from the oven. Turn a loaf upside down and thump the bottom. It should sound hollow. Set the breads right side up to cool on racks: round, wire-mesh pizza baking screens are ideal. Set the pizza screen atop a bowl so air can circulate freely around the loaf.

12. Cool slightly if using right away and cool completely if storing for later use. If storing, place the loaves in plastic bags to freeze. When you are ready to use them, allow the loaves to thaw out at room temperature in their plastic bags.

quicker homemade bread

MAKES ONE 24-OUNCE LOAF

Homemade bread is just the thing to accompany any summer meal. It's great for dipping into olive oil, for sandwiches, and for sopping up the remnants of your lunch or dinner.

In 2006, Mark Bittman of the *New York Times* described a method of making homemade bread that required no kneading, very little work, and makes a loaf as good as—if not better than—most commercial bakeries'. The method was developed by Jim Lahey at the Sullivan Street Bakery in New York City. And it's too good, too easy, and too simple not to share.

The result is delicious fresh bread, perfect when you don't have time for the longer three-day method described on pages 76–78. You'll need a heavy Dutch oven or enameled pot with a lid for this bread.

3 cups all-purpose flour
$\frac{1}{4}$ teaspoon active dry yeast
$1\frac{1}{4}$ teaspoons kosher salt
Cornmeal as needed

1. In a large bowl, mix together the flour, yeast, and salt. Add $1\frac{5}{8}$ cups of water and stir until blended into a shaggy, sticky dough. Cover the bowl with plastic wrap and set aside on a kitchen countertop (at about 70°F) for 18 hours.*

2. The dough will be ready when it's dotted with bubbles. Lightly flour a work surface and turn the dough out onto it. Sprinkle with just a little flour, then fold it over on itself once or twice, leaving it seam side down. Do not knead. Cover the dough loosely with plastic wrap and allow it to rest for 15 minutes.

3. Lay out a clean cotton or linen dish towel (not terrycloth) on a work surface and generously coat the center where the dough will rest with cornmeal. Using just enough flour on your hands to prevent sticking, quickly shape the dough into a ball.

4. Place the ball seam side down on the towel and dust the top with flour or more cornmeal. Cover it with a cotton towel and let it rise for 2 hours. It should about double in size.

5. Preheat the oven to 450°F and set the rack so the Dutch oven or enamel pot will fit. Place the empty, covered Dutch oven in the oven as it heats. When the dough is ready, pull out the rack and remove the pot lid. Slide your hand under the towel and turn the dough into the pot, seam side up. Cover with the lid, slide the rack back into the oven, and close the oven door. Bake for 30 minutes, then remove the lid and continue baking for an additional 15 to 30 minutes until the loaf is browned to your liking. Remove the bread from the pot with two spatulas and let it cool on a rack.

*If you're making this during the work week, make the dough before going to bed on one night and it should be ready when you get home from work the next day.

✳ QUICK RYE BREAD
Substitute $\frac{1}{2}$ cup rye flour for $\frac{1}{2}$ cup of the all-purpose flour to give a richer flavor to the loaf.

grilled garlic bread

MAKES APPROXIMATELY 12 GRILLED
BREAD SLICES

Robert Parker, the wine critic, often finds the aroma of grilled bread among the flavors and aromas of red wine. I think the toasted barrels and barrel heads impart some smokiness to the wine that reminds him of that scent. The following recipe captures that same smokiness in astonishingly good grilled garlic bread. Use these slices of garlic toast as the foundation for Bruschetta (page 50).

1 loaf artisanal Italian bread, cut into
   1-inch-thick slices
⅓ cup extra virgin olive oil
4 cloves garlic, crushed through a
   garlic press
Kosher salt

1. Preheat the grill on high for 15 minutes. Scrub the grates with a wire brush, and wipe them down with olive oil. Reduce the heat to low.

2. With a pastry brush, paint both sides of the bread with the oil. Place the bread on the grill and cover with the hood or lid. The lower the heat, the better the bread will toast. Turn once when the underside is golden brown. Cook an additional 1 to 2 minutes.

3. When the bread is toasted, use the pastry brush to brush each side with some of the crushed garlic—just enough to flavor. Sprinkle the bread with just a little salt and serve immediately.

SUMMER MEMORY: **ballpark food**

Time was, you went to the ballpark (Yankee Stadium mostly, in my case) and had maybe a hot dog and a soda (or a beer, if a so-called adult). Maybe some peanuts or Cracker Jack, but that was about it.

Now I live near San Francisco and Oakland, both of which have major league ballparks. I go to the Oakland Coliseum when the Yanks are in town and the Giants' new park when the Mets are in town—only because the Mets are from New York, even though they're disappointingly not the Yankees.

I am amazed by the foods you can now get at baseball stadiums. At the Giants' stadium, Acme Chophouse is built into the ground level of the park on Willie Mays Plaza. It's pricey: main entrées like New York steak and lamb chops start in the mid-$20s range and oysters are on the higher end as well.

Inside, you can still get a hot dog, Cracker Jack, and a beer, but plenty more besides. The California Wine Bar, for starters, offers Beringer, Fetzer, Buena Vista, Villa Mt. Eden, and Kendall-Jackson Cabernet Sauvignons. Use them to wash down your all-beef Vienna dog that's nicely browned on a griddle and comes loaded with tomatoes, pickles, relish, onions, peppers, mustard, ketchup, and chili powder. Or go downscale to the Doggie Diner for a Giant dog, which must refer to the team, not the paltry size of the wiener.

Gilroy garlic fries are superb and can be washed down with a brewpub-style Gordon Biersch beer, but that beer and fries will cost you more than $10. Yikes! It ain't cheap at the old ball game.

If a mere hot dog is too proletarian, Say Hey! Sausage Specialties will make you an Italian sausage sandwich with onions and green peppers. And—though we're not in Milwaukee—bratwurst is available, too. The California Sandwich Factory serves a teriyaki chicken roll, and deli sandwiches piled high with roast beef. Maybe as a nod to the many fine Japanese players in the big leagues these days, you can also get sushi.

Walking around the ramps, I've discovered stands selling pizza, buffalo wings, bacon cheeseburgers, crispy chicken, and Krispy Kreme doughnuts, and a stand named Orlando's (named after former Giant Orlando Cepeda) serving a Cha-Cha Bowl containing jerked chicken, black beans, white rice, bits of pineapple, and shreds of carrots and squash.

If you get seats on the park's View Level, you'll have admittance to the AAA Club—and to better food and full bars. There's a Carvery, where you can buy fresh fruit and a Carvery sandwich, brisket or turkey on a fresh-baked hoagie roll with dill pickle, orange or cranberry relish, dijon mustard, and barbecue or horseradish sauce. The Dip is about a half pound of brisket slices and a cup of meat juice for dipping. If none of this entices, you can find grilled corn on the cob, skewers of cherry tomatoes and mozzarella balls, and a berry combination fruit salad full of blackberries, raspberries, blueberries, and strawberries.

The Derby Grill serves its lemon garlic chicken breast sandwich: the white meat is marinated in lemon and garlic, grilled, and topped with aioli and sweet onions.

If you're lucky enough to have Field Club seats (those box seats around home plate and up toward the dugouts), you'll find another Carvery and Derby Grill, as well as Joe Garcia, a stand with Super Nachos con Queso, or beef or chicken soft tacos served with two red jalapeños, pickle, radish, lemon, and fries. You'll also see a quote from Tallulah Bankhead on the wall: "There have been only two geniuses in the world, Willie Mays and Willie Shakespeare."

Across the bay sits the Oakland Coliseum—home to the brawny, working-class A's. No nibbling daintily in this ballpark. Here's where ya get yer gooey, fatty, calorie-packed junk food, and plenty of it—except for the paltry hot dogs. The stadium dog will set you back three simoleons and is a skinny little puppy. But mostly, this fare feels like real baseball food.

Ultimate Nachos are vertical rows of round chips covered over with tasteless melted yellow cheese, but at least there are plenty of them. The All-Star Burrito is a bland wrap of shredded beef with beans and rice. A pork ribs dinner consists of seven pieces of very meaty ribs with a choice of either mild, medium, or spicy sauce, served with a clump of yellow potato salad and fluffy white bread. You can also get a whole slab of beef or pork ribs, or barbecued chicken and smoked beef links dinners.

The West Side Club is a members-only area with a long, full bar and a good wine list; an à la carte menu of barbecued chicken, Reuben sandwiches, pasta, burgers, and hot dogs; and a carver's buffet where you can get the cooks to slice off slabs of beef, or whatever else you want, to build your own sandwich. But you gotta be a member.

Saag's Specialty Sausages serves Italian sausage sandwiches, loaded with lots of grilled onions and red and green bell peppers. Saag's menu includes chicken Parmesan, bratwurst, hot links, linguiça, and Polish sausage—a sausage for every ethnicity, practically. The Heineken beer stand offers Popcorn Chicken and Fries. This is a plate full of bits of chicken coated with thick, crusty batter of no discernible flavor, accompanied by limp french fries. The stand also sells chicken strips with your choice of hot, barbecue, ranch, or honey-mustard sauces.

The big Budweiser stand on the main concourse, pretty close to a line drawn up from first base, sells an Italian sub—six slices of bologna, a slice of spicy salami, a slice of provolone, finely shredded lettuce, a slice of tomato, and some oil, vinegar, and herbs on a crusty, chewy roll. Also on the menu is shrimp cocktail, which is a large handful of tiny rock shrimp and a cup of "cocktail sauce" that tastes like ketchup. But my favorite is a hot pastrami sandwich on light rye, with the pastrami piled a couple of inches thick on the bread and covered with a slice of Swiss cheese. It comes with a half of a kosher dill pickle. It's not the Second Avenue Deli, but it's enough of an echo of New York for me to get the pastrami sandwich religiously whenever I go to see the Bombers play.

The food was a lot simpler when I was a kid, but watching my favorite team play while chowing down is still one of the highlights of summer, then and now.

GREENS

Baby Greens Salad
Lettuce Medley Salad
Mesclun Salad
Spinach and Bacon Salad
Mâche and Baby Arugula Salad
Chicory and Walnut Salad
Fresh Herbed Salad
Classic Caesar Salad
Greek Salad
Chef's Salad
Cobb Salad
Caprese Salad

VEGETABLE SALADS

Cucumber Salad
Cucumber, Tomato, and
  Olive Salad
Creamy Polish Cucumber Salad
Panzanella
Cold Roasted Beet Salad
Cold Green Bean Salad
Grilled Corn Salad
Summer Vegetable Salad
Summer Confetti Salad

FRUIT SALADS

Simple Fruit Salad
Minted Fruit Salad
Green Papaya Salad
Melon-Lime Salad
Watermelon Salad
Watermelon-Mango Salad
Watermelon, Fig, and Sweet
  Red Onion Salad
Grilled Peach and Fig Salad

POTATO SALADS

Classic American Potato Salad

SLAWS

Coleslaw
Midwestern Sweet-and-Sour
  Coleslaw
Ginger-Scallion Coleslaw
Summer Fruit Slaw

PASTA SALADS

Pasta Primavera Salad
Spicy Pasta Salad with Olives
  and Feta

Yogurt Pasta Salad
Couscous Salad with Pine
  Nuts and Summer Fruits
Tabbouleh
Citrusy Tofu and Rice Salad

POULTRY AND MEAT SALADS

Simple Chicken Salad
Chicken and Jasmine Rice
  Salad
Southwestern Chicken Salad
Steak Salad
Asian Steak Salad

FISH AND SEAFOOD SALADS

Salade Niçoise
Tuscan-Style Tuna Salad
Summery Shrimp Salad
Shrimp and Fennel Salad
Heirloom Tomatoes and
  Prawns
Lobster Salad
Crab and Cucumber Salad
Crab Louis
Ceviche

SALADS

Summer salads are sunlight and rainwater turned into luscious greens, succulent tomatoes, and crunchy peppers; they're the whole big, warm, summer season brought down into a friendly bowl on the kitchen counter, enriched with seeds and nuts, emboldened by tangy dressings, ready for lunch or dinner.

The variety and quality of salad ingredients explode in summer. Now greens have a delicate, tender crunch because they are dewy fresh. Sun-ripened local tomatoes and cinnamony basil are in season and at their most aromatic. Thin strips of spicy, rich salami add a savory note to the vegetables. A teaspoon of diced jalapeño adds some spicy heat. Dried fruits like raisins or chopped dried cherries add sweetness. Now summer herbs, such as chervil, summer savory, basil, and oregano are at their freshest and most intense. One of the best things about summer salads is the surprise of finding little bursts of varied flavors within each bite.

Most of those delightful summer salads require no cooking; you can throw them together quickly from easy-to-find ingredients. And most can be served chilled—an added pleasure on hot days. With the addition of vegetables, meats, cheeses, nuts, and seeds, a salad can be all that's needed for a whole, light meal.

To get the most pleasure from your salads, buy your ingredients as close to the time you'll use them as possible, keeping an eye out for the freshest, finest greens at your local markets.

If you haven't found one already, shop around for a generously sized wooden salad bowl—the one that will be your favorite for daily use. Rub its interior with a cut clove of garlic and wipe it down with a thin coat of olive oil between uses. It will become like an old friend and add a bit of flavor to every dish you put in it.

Most importantly, experiment with flavors you particularly favor. Many recipes in this chapter are classics, some are more experimental—but all are delicious. Chances are that any or all of them will win favor at your table. But don't hesitate to fine-tune a recipe to make it your own. I love the crunchy sweetness of red onions, and rare is the salad of mine that doesn't include some finely shaved ringlets.

GREENS

baby greens salad

MAKES 4 SERVINGS

Baby greens are just that—babies, not plants that are miniature when they're fully grown. They make the most tender and delicate salads. Their flavors only hint at the more aggressive flavors of mature plants. Their leaves tend to be soft, so they make a fine foil for crunchy ingredients like Candied Walnuts (page 288), seeds, or Croutons (page 289). A simple salad of baby greens makes a fine light summer lunch. It's never filling or heavy, and fresh, raw greens are always good for you.

Most baby greens have leaves that are 3 to 4 inches in length. You'll most likely find them as a blend of lettuces, chicories, arugula, endives, radicchio, Chinese greens, and spinach.

8 cups mixed baby greens
½ cup Classic Vinaigrette (page 282)

In a large bowl, add the greens. Add the vinaigrette, toss to coat, and serve immediately.

lettuce medley salad

MAKES 4 SERVINGS

A medley of lettuces can run the gamut of texture from firm and crunchy (romaine) to soft and tender (Bibb or butterhead types). Their colors can range from light to dark green, ruby-red, and even speckled, with flavors that are both buttery and icily sweet. You'll be able to find a wide variety of lettuces at most markets in the summertime. Lettuce medleys also come prepackaged. Add 1 cup of Croutons (page 289) for extra crunch. Make this salad in a large wooden bowl that's been rubbed with a cut clove of garlic.

1 head buttercrunch or other butterhead
   type lettuce
1 head romaine lettuce
4 cups loosely packed loose-leaf lettuces,
   red and green
1 small red onion, thinly sliced
½ cup Classic Vinaigrette (page 282)

1. Remove and reserve outer leaves from the buttercrunch lettuce. Trim the base from the head so the leaves separate and fall free. Check them for soil and rinse, if necessary, in cold water, then pat dry. Place these inner leaves in a large bowl.

2. Remove and reserve several layers of leaves from the romaine, until you are down to the inner leaves, about 7 or 8 inches long. Wrap the reserved buttercrunch and romaine leaves in a moist paper towel and place in a plastic bag in the vegetable crisper for other use. Trim the base of the romaine so the leaves separate and fall free. Check them for soil and wash, if necessary, in cold water, then pat dry. Cut them diagonally into 2-inch pieces. Place them in the bowl with the buttercrunch.

3. Add the loose-leaf lettuces to the bowl. Separate the red onion slices into rings and add to the bowl. Toss to mix and place the bowl in the fridge to keep the lettuces cool.

4. Add the vinaigrette to the salad, toss to coat, and serve immediately.

NO COOK ✳ MAKE AHEAD ◎ QUICK & EASY

✳ Lettuce—the Foundation of a Fine Salad

Here's a rundown on the common types of lettuce you'll find at stores. They are the foundation of most salads. Their delicate flavor can be enlivened with any of the salad greens in the box on page 92, with onions, olives, tomatoes, peas, cheese, or just about anything that strikes your fancy. Salad dressings (see pages 282–288) add the finishing touch.

* **BIBB LETTUCE**—Small, paddle-shaped leaves are delectable. This is usually sold as a loose-leaf kind of butterhead-type lettuce. If you find it fresh, use it as the main base for your salad. Also called limestone lettuce and sold as small, whole heads.

* **BUTTERHEAD LETTUCE**—You can find dozens of types of butterhead lettuces grown around the United States. Buttercrunch is a common cultivar, as are Merveille des Quatre Saisons, Cracoviensis, Boston lettuce, and the miniature heads of Tom Thumb, among others. All of them have a soft, buttery-textured quality that makes them a fine base for all kinds of salad.

* **CRISPHEAD LETTUCES**—Iceberg, good for crunchy texture but not a nutritional powerhouse, is one of the better-known crispheads. There is a variety called Summertime that is often grown for its durability in hot weather.

* **LOOSE-LEAF LETTUCES**—There are dozens of types of loose-leaf lettuces suited to summer cultivation, such as Green Oak Leaf, Lollo Rossa, Bibb, Slobolt, and Merveille des Quatre Saisons. You'll find them in mesclun mixes at the markets, usually as a medley. Lollo Rossa is a red-tinged type of frilled loose-leaf lettuce sold widely in whole-head form.

* **ROMAINE LETTUCES**—Besides green romaine—which, incidentally, is the nutritional champ among lettuces—there is a red type, plus many other cultivars such as Forellenschluss (Trout's Back), Bullet, Romulus, and Valmaine. All are crispy-crunchy and delicious.

mesclun salad

MAKES 2 TO 4 SERVINGS

Baby greens are delicate in taste and texture. A mixed lettuce salad is mildly flavored. But mesclun mixes mild and bold flavors to make a salad with real character. *Mesclun* is a French word that means mixed, and that's what it has come to mean in America—a mixture of just about any field greens.

Mesclun is sold all summer at farmers' markets because growers have learned to shade the mesclun patch and block out a percentage of the sun's rays, preventing the tender plants from wilting in the hot sun or bolting (goint to seed early).

Try for a balance of tender, delicate lettuces with stronger-flavored greens like arugula. The proportions can vary, but a ratio of 2 parts lettuce to 1 part stronger greens works fine. Looking for extra pizzazz? Include a few edible flowers for color, or add halved cherry tomatoes, fresh oregano leaves, and/or a pinch of freshly grated Parmesan cheese.

4 cups loosely packed loose-leaf lettuces, including red and green varieties
½ cup frisée endive
½ cup chervil, de-stemmed
½ cup escarole, cut into bite-size pieces
½ cup arugula
½ cup Classic Vinaigrette (page 282)

In a large bowl, add all the greens. Add the vinaigrette, toss to coat, and serve immediately.

EDIBLE FLOWERS FOR SUMMER SALADS

Edible flowers mostly dress up a salad, making it festive and pretty with their colors. Not many edible flowers add much in the way of taste, although the blossoms of nasturtiums, onion family members, dill, fennel, lavender, rosemary, and sage will certainly add flavor.

Don't overdo it with flowers. Sprinkle a small amount on top of finished salads, as the oils in a salad dressing penetrate delicate petals easily, turning them to unattractive mush.
Note: commercially grown flowers are usually treated with pesticides and fungicides. Make sure any flowers you add to a salad are from a clean place in the wild, from an unsprayed garden, or are organically grown. It's best to obtain them from a supplier who grows flowers specifically for consumption. Do not eat flowers from a florist.

Look for freshly opened flowers that are free of spots. Wash them thoroughly in a bath of salt water. Then drop them into a bowl of ice water for about 30 seconds to brighten and open the petals. Here are some recommended edible flowers:

✳ BASIL—Pull apart a flower spike and sprinkle the florets over the salad.

✳ BEEBALM—The florets of ornamental beebalm can be white, red, or pink. Wild beebalm's florets are light lavender.

✳ BORAGE—True blue flowers have a cucumber flavor.

✳ IMPATIENS—Yes, the Busy Lizzies are edible, although without much flavor. They do add pretty color.

✳ JOHNNY-JUMP-UP—These little violas look like miniature pansies. Their wild cousin, the white or violet violets, can be used in salads, too.

✳ NASTURTIUMS—The spicy, peppery taste and electric colors of nasturtium petals, torn up and sprinkled on, brighten a salad.

✳ ROSES—Tear a few petals into little pieces to toss with the salad.

✳ SAGE—The pure red florets of pineapple sage are a classic flower for salads.

✳ SCARLET RUNNER BEANS—These climbing beans produce pods after their scarlet flowers fade. Nab a few flowers first.

spinach and bacon salad

MAKES 2 SERVINGS

In the cool weather of spring and fall, spinach leaves grow large and meaty, but in the summer, the crop quickly wants to bolt, or go to seed, and quality is lost. So growers tend to pick their spinach young in the warm months, before the plants bolt. This is good for us lovers of fine spinach salads made from tender, young leaves.

Spinach doesn't need help in the salad bowl from other greens. It tastes complex enough all by itself. The dressing for this recipe calls for rice vinegar because of its lighter acidity, since spinach itself has some acid tang. I like it with a little minced onion for added zest. If you're concerned about bacon's fattiness, substitute turkey bacon.

WINE SUGGESTION: OFF-DRY CALIFORNIA CHENIN BLANC

2 slices bacon
4 tablespoons Japanese rice vinegar
1 tablespoon extra virgin olive oil
1 teaspoon minced Italian flat-leaf parsley
½ teaspoon dry mustard
½ teaspoon sugar
4 cups loosely packed baby spinach leaves

1. Place a large skillet over medium-high heat and add the bacon. Fry the bacon until crisp. Blot away excess fat with a paper towel. When the bacon is cool, crumble it, using your hands.

2. In a large bowl, whisk the bacon, vinegar, oil, parsley, mustard, and sugar thoroughly, until the sugar has dissolved.

3. In a serving bowl, add the spinach. Add the dressing, toss to coat, and serve immediately.

✳ **WARM SPINACH SALAD**
Heat the bacon dressing in the microwave until hot, but not boiling, about 1 minute. Pour over the spinach, toss, and serve immediately.

✳ **SPINACH AND SCALLOP SALAD**
Quickly sear one cup of bay scallops in a little oil over medium-high heat. Combine them with a finely crumbled strip of crisp bacon. Dress the spinach with ½ cup of Sherry Vinaigrette (page 283), then toss with the scallops and bacon mixture.

✳ **AVOCADO-ORANGE SPINACH SALAD**
Alternate slices of avocado and peeled orange segments on top of the dressed salad.

✳ **DRESSING VARIATION**
Add ½ teaspoon of minced onion or shallot to the dressing to give it added zest.

mâche and baby arugula salad

MAKES 2 SERVINGS

As summer arrives, both mâche (also known as corn salad), and arugula reach their peak flavors. In a salad, arugula sings soprano with its high-pitched herbaceousness, while mâche sing baritone with its nutty earthiness. Together the combination is delightful, especially when given a splash of this sweet and savory dressing.

4 small heads of young mâche
1 cup baby arugula, loosely packed
¼ cup grated carrot
¼ cup grated radish

¼ cup walnut oil
2 tablespoons balsamic vinegar
1 tablespoon summer savory
Salt and freshly ground black pepper to taste

1. Pick the leaves from the heads of mâche and place in a medium bowl. Add the arugula, carrot, and radish. Toss to mix.

2. Place the oil, vinegar, savory, salt, and black pepper in a jar with a lid. Screw on the lid and shake vigorously. Add the dressing to the salad, toss to coat, and serve immediately.

chicory and walnut salad

MAKES 2 SERVINGS

This recipe calls for Belgian endives (which are actually chicories; true endives include frisée and the Batavian "lettuce" known as escarole). The little endive heads are called chicons. This salad combines the slightly bitter but icily refreshing flavor of the endives with the nutty flavor of walnuts and the salty savor of blue cheese. It makes a fine centerpiece for a summer lunch or a side salad with grilled meat or vegetables for dinner.

WINE SUGGESTION: SPANISH ALBARIÑO

4 Belgian endive chicons
2 cups loose-leaf lettuce leaves,
    loosely packed
¼ cup chopped toasted walnuts
¼ cup Stilton, Maytag, Point Reyes, or other
    blue cheese
1 teaspoon red wine vinegar
1 teaspoon minced red onion
¼ teaspoon Coleman's dry mustard
2 tablespoons walnut or other vegetable oil

1. Preheat the oven to 350°F.

2. Rinse and pat dry the Belgian endive chicons. Cut them on the diagonal into ½ - inch pieces. In a large bowl, add the Belgian endive and lettuce leaves and toss until well mixed.

3. Spread the walnuts on a baking sheet. Toast for about 5 minutes, being careful not to let them burn or get too brown. Set aside for 5 minutes to cool. While the walnuts are toasting, crumble the blue cheese. Set aside. When the walnuts have cooled, add them and the blue cheese to the greens.

4. In a large bowl, whisk together the vinegar, onion, and mustard. Add the oil in a slow, steady stream until well incorporated. Add to the salad, toss to coat, and serve immediately.

fresh herbed salad

MAKES 3 TO 4 SERVINGS

Most herbs are strongly flavored and very aromatic, and they add an incomparable richness of flavors and aromas to a salad of bland lettuces or mixed greens. Some like parsley and cilantro carry lemony notes; peppermint and perilla are peppery, tingling the tongue. Some are resinous, like savory, thyme, and oregano. And some have a licorice flavor, like anise hyssop, chervil, and French tarragon. Coordinate these flavors— that is, use some of the resinous herbs together, or the anise-scented ones. Use them sparingly and take note of how they make an ordinary salad into a tapestry of tastes.

If you have the room, a small kitchen

garden can give you fresh culinary herbs—parsley, oregano, savory, sage, rosemary, mint, and thyme—all summer. If you can't grow herbs, they are plentiful in stores during the summer.

4 cups fresh lettuce or mixed greens
1 cup fresh herb leaves (See "Herbs for Summer Salads," page 95)
⅓ cup Classic Vinaigrette (page 282)

In a large bowl, add the greens and herbs. Toss to mix well. Add the vinaigrette, toss to coat, and serve immediately.

classic caesar salad

MAKES 2 SERVINGS

Here's a salad invented in a place that is *muy caliente*, so it's just right for a hot summer evening. This is the authentic recipe for the refreshing salad Caesar Cardini created at his Tijuana, Mexico, restaurant in the 1920s.

Start with the freshest, just-picked head of green romaine you can find, and refrigerate it so it's cold and delightfully crunchy when it hits the table. So many restaurants mislabel their salads of chopped romaine

FLAVOR PROFILE OF SALAD GREENS

Follow the French lead and mix mild greens with more intensely flavored varieties in a 2 to 1 ratio for a balanced salad or 1 to 2 for a salad with more pizzazz

MILD GREENS	MORE FLAVORFUL GREENS	MOST FLAVORFUL GREENS
Bok choy	Collards	Arugula
Butterhead lettuces	Kale	Belgian endive
Crisphead lettuces	Beet greens	Curly cress
Hearts of romaine	Spinach	Mustard greens
Loose-leaf lettuces	Mâche	Mizuna
	Chard	Dandelion greens
	Escarole	Radicchio
	Frisée	Watercress
	Romaine lettuce	
	Pea shoots	

tossed with a sticky, cheesy dressing as a Caesar, but don't be fooled. Make this authentic recipe and you'll know what a real Caesar salad is supposed to be.

Chef Cardini called for a coddled egg. We don't coddle eggs much anymore, but you can achieve the same effect by boiling an egg for 1 minute in rapidly boiling water. Place the egg on a tablespoon and slowly ease it into the boiling water to prevent the shell from breaking.

WINE SUGGESTION: ITALIAN FIANO DI AVELLINO

1 clove garlic, peeled, minced
1 teaspoon kosher salt
½ cup extra virgin olive oil
1 head romaine lettuce
1 egg, boiled for 1 minute
Juice of 1 lemon
Dash of Worcestershire sauce
½ cup grated Parmigiano-Reggiano cheese
Freshly ground black pepper to taste
½ cup Croutons (page 289)

1. In a small bowl, add the garlic and salt and mash together using a pestle or wooden spoon. Pour in the oil, mixing constantly with a fork until well combined.

2. Select only the finest inner leaves of the romaine.* They should be a light green and about 7 inches long. Trim the base of the romaine so the leaves separate and fall free. Check them for soil and wash, if necessary, in cold water, then pat dry.

3. In a large bowl, add the romaine leaves, drizzle with the garlic-oil mixture, and toss to coat. Break the egg into the salad and toss again until the egg is well incorporated.

4. Sprinkle the lemon juice over the salad and toss again. Add the Worcestershire

sauce, cheese, black pepper, and croutons. Toss again and serve immediately.

✳ CAESAR SALAD WITH ANCHOVIES

Chef Cardini didn't include anchovies in his original recipe. However, many people like a little anchovy flavor in their Caesar. There are two ways of achieving this.

- Heat a handful of flat anchovy fillets in their oil in a pan over medium-low heat until they soften and melt when squished with the back of a fork. Whisk the melted anchovies into the oil-garlic-salt mixture.
- The second option is to simply lay an anchovy fillet or two across the top of the finished salad.

*Save the remaining romaine leaves for making wraps or a salad another day. Wrap them in a sheet or two of damp paper toweling and place them in a plastic bag in the vegetable crisper of your fridge, for up to 5 days.

greek salad

MAKES 4 SERVINGS

The Greeks make this "peasant salad," as they call it, in the summer because that's when the heat is at its fiercest and tomatoes are at their best. Sun-ripened tomatoes are the heart of the salad. Note there's no lettuce in this recipe because traditional Greek salad does not contain any.

With this addictive salad, you do all the preparation of the ingredients and then assemble it just before serving. Make sure that the cucumber you use is a small one, because larger cucumbers have unpleasantly hard seeds.

The best salt for this salad is fleur de sel. It's gathered by hand from evaporation ponds in Brittany on the coast of France in high summer. Fleur de sel has the perfect crunchiness that releases bursts of intensely salty flavor to enhance the tomatoes and cucumbers.

If you grow or can find Greek oregano, all the better. It has a slightly resinous quality. The tomatoes, cucumber, and pepper should be refrigerator cold rather than room temperature.

WINE SUGGESTION: CHIANTI OR NERO D'AVOLA

3 vine-ripe tomatoes
1 cucumber
½ green bell pepper
1 small red onion
1 cup feta cheese
½ cup black kalamata olives
1 teaspoon fresh oregano
Salt to taste
3 tablespoons extra virgin olive oil
1 tablespoon red wine vinegar
½ teaspoon capers

1. Slice each tomato into 4 lengthwise slices, then cut each slice in half across the middle. Peel and cut the cucumber into ½ -inch chunks. Slice the bell pepper lengthwise into thin strips. Very thinly slice the red onion. Cut the feta into ⅓ -inch cubes. Pit the olives. Remove the oregano leaves from their stalks and petioles.

2. In a large bowl, mix all the ingredients together quickly and serve immediately.

chef's salad
MAKES 2 TO 3 SERVINGS

The 1940s certainly had style. Women wore hats with veils, and gloves, when they "went to town," even in the summertime. This stylish salad dates from that era. It was likely created at the Ritz-Carlton in New York, although no one knows with absolute certainty. Its chief virtue is that it can be made with items you have on hand, so feel free to substitute. It also makes a tasty no-cook dinner (except for the hard-boiled egg).

However, the better your ingredients, the better the salad will be. This recipe, for instance, calls for Gruyère cheese, although any firm cheese can be substituted. And it calls for prosciutto, the salt- and air-cured Italian ham sold widely in many markets these days. Make sure that the prosciutto is sliced almost transparently thin. Very thin slices of any firm domestic ham can be substituted. The chef's salad is a simple, delicious summer meal right from the fridge to the table.

WINE SUGGESTION: CALIFORNIA CHARDONNAY

4 cups very fresh salad greens
½ cup chicken breast, thinly sliced
2 ounces prosciutto, thinly sliced
2 ounces Gruyère cheese
1 vine-ripe tomato
1 hard-boiled egg
6 black olives
¼ cup Classic Vinaigrette (page 282)
¼ cup minced Italian flat-leaf parsley
Salt to taste (optional)
Freshly ground black pepper to taste

1. In a large bowl, place the greens. Cut the chicken and prosciutto slices into wedges. Cut the Gruyère into thin, rectangular slices, then cut those into wedges. Cut the tomato into 8 sections. Cut the hard-boiled egg into 8 slices. Pit the olives.

2. Add the vinaigrette to the greens.

3. Artfully arrange the chicken, prosciutto, cheese, tomato, egg, and olives around the top of the greens, and sprinkle on the parsley. Sprinkle on a pinch or two of salt, if using. Grind a little fresh black pepper on the salad and serve immediately.

HERBS FOR SUMMER SALADS

Herbs are at their flavorful best during the warm summer months. All that sun encourages the plants to make more of the volatile oils that give herbs their characteristic aroma and taste. So, what better way to add interest to a salad than to include a few leaves of fresh herbs?

Some herbs like full sun, some like partial sun, and some grow best in shade. Almost all grow well in pots, so keep a few pots full of easy-to-grow culinary herbs like thyme, oregano, and chives. Here are the champions for inclusion in salads:

✳ **Anise hyssop**—Pinch out the little growing tips of the shoots for a strong anise taste.

✳ **Basil**—One of the kings of summer herbs and a classic companion to tomatoes.

✳ **Borage**—A few true blue borage flowers (they taste like cucumbers) add color and flavor.

✳ **Chervil**—Before hot summer weather forces chervil to go to seed and lose its light anise flavor, its little leaves make a subtle addition to any salad.

✳ **Chives**—Either regular chives or garlic chives—and their flower heads pulled apart into florets—give an onion or garlic flavor, respectively, when snipped into little pieces for the salad.

✳ **Cilantro**—Some people love this herb—others can't stand it. If you like it, a few leaves make a noticeable difference. Best used by itself as it can drown out other herb flavors.

✳ **Dill**—Either a few leaves or bits of the umbrella-like flower heads go well with a vinaigrette dressing.

✳ **Lovage**—Lovage tastes like a very strong celery and so can be useful in salads. A little goes a long way.

✳ **Mint**—Cool, refreshing mint is most welcome in salads served during hot weather.

✳ **Oregano**—When a hard Italian grating cheese is part of a salad, oregano (or its close cousin marjoram) makes a fine partner.

✳ **Parsley**—Italian flat-leaf parsley is the best choice for inclusion in a salad, as it has more flavor and is easier to eat than curly parsley.

✳ **Perilla**—It's called *shiso* in Japan, where its red or green leaves are used to decorate plates of sushi or sashimi. A couple of torn-up perilla leaves add a fruity spiciness to a salad.

✳ **Sage**—Although we usually think of sage in its dried form, a few fresh leaves chopped and added to a salad add a delicious herby flavor.

✳ **Savory**—Summer savory, of course. Just strip the leaves from a stem and sprinkle them on your salad as a breath freshener.

✳ **Tarragon**—Make sure it's French tarragon with an anise flavor, not Russian or other tarragon with hardly any flavor. Taste a leaf before buying.

✳ **Thyme**—Thyme's strong herbal character is rich, and just the leaves from one short stem are all that is needed to add its resinous taste.

cobb salad

MAKES 2 TO 3 SERVINGS

It's hard to say why a particular combination of ingredients becomes a classic. But such is the case of the Cobb salad, created extemporaneously one night in 1937 by Chef Robert Cobb. He made it for theater owner Sid Grauman at the original Brown Derby restaurant in Hollywood, and it's still enjoyed worldwide to this day. Its popularity becomes understandable with the first taste. Think of a salad that combines the flavors of a BLT with blue cheese and moist chicken breast, and the lovely textures of buttery lettuce (although in the 1930s, Cobb undoubtedly used a crisphead lettuce like iceberg), avocado, and hard-boiled egg.

It can be an easy-to assemble and very nutritious main dish on hot summer nights when cooking is about as appetizing as paying the bills. It's also the perfect answer for dinner when you have cold chicken breast as a leftover in the fridge.

WINE SUGGESTION: WHITE CHATEAUNEUF-DU-PAPE

1 head butterhead lettuce, individual leaves torn into 2 to 3 pieces
5 slices cooked bacon (or turkey bacon), crumbled
2 hard-boiled eggs, sliced into ¼ -inch rounds
1½ cups cooked, skinned, boned, chopped chicken breast
1 tomato, seeded and chopped
2 ounces blue cheese, crumbled
½ avocado, pitted, peeled, and sliced into ¼ -inch slices
1½ cups chopped scallions
½ cup Cobb Salad Dressing (page 287) or Creamy Blue Cheese Dressing (page 285)

Arrange the lettuce in 2 or 3 individual-serving salad bowls and top evenly with the bacon, eggs, chicken, tomato, blue cheese, avocado, and scallions. Add the dressing evenly over the salads and serve immediately.

caprese salad

MAKES 3 SERVINGS

The justifiably famous caprese salad is named for the Isle of Capri off the coast of Naples, where the salad is said to have originated. It couldn't be simpler to make or more delicious to eat, taking just a few minutes to put together. Yet despite its simplicity, it has an exotic air about it. When the weather is warm, the caprese naturally comes to mind because its dominant flavors are those perfect partners, tomato and basil.

The tomatoes should be the most delicious, vine-ripe variety you can find. In the summer, you'll find fresh basil in the stores and markets. Look for the big, green leaves of the Genovese variety or the colored leaves of purple basil—but really, any basil will do. Domestic mozzarella is good, but if your market carries the Italian mozzarella made from water buffalo milk (in Italian, it's *mozzarella di bufala*), it will be super soft and silky with a rich, creamy flavor. Some people use balsamic vinegar along with extra virgin olive oil to dress the salad, but I think it's just as delectable without the vinegar.

To make a very special caprese, use burrata instead of plain mozzarella.

WINE SUGGESTION: ITALIAN AGLIANICO

2 medium vine-ripened tomatoes
One 7-ounce ball of mozzarella
3 to 4 leaves of fresh basil
2 tablespoons extra virgin olive oil

1. Slice the tomato into ⅓-inch-thick slices, discarding the stem and blossom ends, and arrange them on a plate.

2. Slice the mozzarella into as many rounds as you have tomato slices and top each tomato slice with mozzarella. Cut the basil into threads and sprinkle them onto the cheese. Drizzle the caprese with the oil.

✳ HOW TO HARD-BOIL AN EGG

Having a few hard-boiled eggs on hand gives summer-busy family members a quick, nutritious snack, or something good for the picnic basket.

But as anyone who has tried to hard-boil an egg by dropping it into a saucepan of boiling water knows, this can cause problems. The shell will often crack, and egg white will seep out to form a frilly skirt around the egg. When the egg is peeled and sliced, the white will be rubbery and discolored and the yolk have a sickly greenish hue and chalky texture.

Here's a method of hard-boiling an egg that prevents all those problems: Place the egg in a saucepan with enough cold water to cover it by an inch. Place the saucepan on medium heat and bring the water to a boil. As soon as it boils, immediately remove the pan from the heat, cover, and set a timer for 12 minutes. The egg will be perfect at sea level, but might take a minute or two longer at high altitudes.

✳ CAPRESE SKEWERS

For a different presentation, slide cherry tomatoes, cubes of mozzarella, and folded basil leaves onto bamboo skewers. No need to cook them, but do drizzle them with olive oil and balsamic vinegar.

VEGETABLE SALADS

cucumber salad

MAKES 2 TO 3 SERVINGS

It is thought that cucumbers are indigenous to southern India, a region of ferocious summer heat, where they have been culti-vated for the last 4,000 years. Their cooling properties are a welcome relief from hot weather anywhere in the world. This refreshing cucumber salad is very easy to make. The cucumbers add a cold crunch and the vinegar adds a tangy note.

1 cucumber, peeled and thinly sliced
1 tablespoon extra virgin olive oil
2 tablespoons red wine vinegar
1 tablespoon minced parsley
Salt and freshly ground black pepper
  to taste

1. Arrange the cucumber slices in a serving dish and place in the fridge until cold.

2. In a cup, mix the oil, vinegar, and parsley. When ready to serve, lightly sprinkle the cucumber slices with salt and black pepper, add the dressing, and serve immediately.

GOOD TO KNOW: HOW TO START A CONTAINER GARDEN

Anyone with a sunny balcony, porch, or deck can grow wonderfully flavorful cherry tomatoes easily. All you need is a five-gallon container with drainage holes in the bottom, a plastic tray to catch drainage water so it doesn't stain the porch or deck, a sack of potting soil, and a cherry tomato seedling. All these items are available at any garden center.

Look for Sweet 100 or Sungold varieties. Sweet 100 is very prolific, producing hundreds of sweet, red, 1-inch-diameter fruits over the growing season. Sungold has superior flavor but is less productive. Both are indeterminate plants, meaning they keep growing from sideshoots that arise in the leaf axils—the place where leaves attach to the vine. And they are vining, so grow them by a drainpipe and tie them loosely to it. When planting the cherry tomato, remove all leaves except those at the top 6 inches of the plant and bury the root and stem up to just below the top 6 inches. A buried tomato stem will sprout roots, and the resulting larger root system will make the plant healthier and more vigorous. Keep the soil moist but not sopping wet.

Salad greens can be grown in containers, too. Again, they need drainage holes in the bottom. Three or four 18-inch-diameter plastic buckets with seven holes drilled in the bottom will work. Plant five loose-leaf lettuce plants in each container in a sunny spot. Keep the soil moist but not sopping wet. If you have room in your yard, cut and lift the sod from a 4 x 4-foot space square that's in a sunny area. Empty a sack of compost and smooth it out over the bare soil surface. Then, using a shovel or a spade, turn the soil 6 to 8 inches deep to incorporate the compost. Plant loose-leaf lettuce plants 6 inches apart in all directions. You'll be able to plant about 50 plants this way. Set a lawn sprinkler to cover the area and run it for at least 20 minutes or until the lettuce patch soil is thoroughly and deeply moistened. Keep the soil moist but not sopping wet. Save your grass clippings and use them as mulch to cover the bare soil around the lettuce plants. This keeps in moisture and keeps down weeds. If you have rabbits in your area, drive 5-foot stakes at the four corners and attach 3-foot chicken wire to them with brads or staples to fence out the bunnies. Make sure the wire touches the ground, as rabbits will scoot through seemingly small gaps to get at the tender lettuces.

When the lettuces have overcome their transplant shock and are growing again—about two weeks—take two or three leaves from the outside of each plant. The lettuces will keep sending up new leaves that will develop into more outer leaves as long as you don't damage the crown (the growing point in the center) or the roots.

This kind of loose-leaf lettuce is called a "cut-and-come-again" crop. Some good varieties to look for, or to get seed for, include Black Seeded Simpson, Deer Tongue, Royal Oak Leaf, Salad Bowl, and Slobolt among green lettuces, and Lollo Rosso, Red Deer Tongue, Red Oak Leaf, and Ruby among red types.

By late July or early August, you may see some plants starting to send up a leafy stalk from their centers. They are getting ready to flower and set seed. Quality drops off drastically at this stage and they turn bitter, with milky sap. Pull them and replant their spots with seedlings from the garden center or seeds you've started yourself. By replanting two or three times over the summer, you'll have homegrown salad greens until the frosts arrive.

Making a salad will be as simple as gathering leaves and cherry tomatoes, adding thin-sliced red onion, and tossing with your favorite dressing.

cucumber, tomato, and olive salad

MAKES 3 TO 4 SERVINGS

If you've ever traveled in Greece in the summer, where the heat is intense and the need for simple, cooling dishes just as intense, you'll have seen this easy-to-make salad in tavernas and homes across the land and on the Greek islands. All the ingredients contribute to its succulence, and the cucumbers add a cooling effect.

2 cucumbers, about 8 inches long, peeled
2 medium vine-ripe tomatoes
12 kalamata olives, pitted and halved
2 tablespoons crumbled feta cheese
3 tablespoons extra virgin olive oil
2 tablespoons red wine vinegar
1 tablespoon chopped fresh oregano

1. Cut the cucumbers in half lengthwise. Remove the seeds. Cut them into thin strips about 1½ inches wide. Cut these strips in half across their width. Cut the stem and blossom ends from the tomatoes and cut the tomato in half, then remove seeds. Slice into half-rounds.

2. Place alternating rows of the cucumbers and tomatoes on a platter. Arrange pitted kalamata halves on the tomatoes and cucumbers. Sprinkle crumbled feta over the tomatoes and cucumbers. Whisk together the oil, vinegar, and oregano. Drizzle over the salad and serve immediately.

creamy polish cucumber salad

MAKES 2 TO 3 SERVINGS

This is a traditional summer recipe in American cities with large Polish populations, like Milwaukee and Chicago. Although it takes just a few minutes to prep, there is an hour's wait for the salt to work its deliquescent effect.

Instead of sour cream, you can substitute yogurt or crème fraiche. If using yogurt, place it in a bag made of two thicknesses of cheesecloth and hang it on the kitchen sink's faucet to drain for an hour, or it will make the salad too watery.

1 firm cucumber, peeled and thinly sliced
  into rounds
Salt to taste
1 cup sour cream
Juice of 1 lemon
Freshly ground black pepper

1. Arrange the cucumber in a single layer on a plate. Sprinkle the slices with salt. Set the plate aside for an hour so most of the liquid runs out of the cucumber slices.

2. Rinse the slices under cold water and press them between sheets of paper toweling.

3. Mix the sour cream with the lemon juice. Fold the mixture into the drained cucumber slices. Add the black pepper.

panzanella

MAKES 4 TO 6 SERVINGS

Panzanella is one of those inspired Italian creations your nonna (grandmother) would have made if you had a nonna. The secret to a great panzanella is to use a big crusty loaf of Italian bread, or another of the Italian bread types like focaccia or ciabatta. Use the finest tomatoes and cucumbers you can find. Heirloom tomato varieties show up in most markets in summer and they are packed with flavor—just right for panzanella.

Italian bread
3 ripe red tomatoes
Pinch, plus ½ teaspoon fleur de sel or
    kosher salt
1 clove garlic, peeled
1 tablespoon capers, drained
2 anchovy fillets, drained
¼ ripe red bell pepper
¼ cup extra virgin olive oil
1 tablespoon red wine vinegar
1 cup cucumber, peeled and minced
½ onion, peeled and sliced thinly
Freshly ground black pepper to taste

1. Cut enough ½-inch-thick rounds of Italian bread to make 2 cups of diced bread with the crusts trimmed off and the bread diced. Trim the crusts and gently toast both sides of the bread to a light brown either in the toaster or under the broiler. Cut the bread into ½-inch dice and place in a bowl.

2. Puree 1 of the tomatoes in a blender or food processor and mix the puree with the bread and the pinch of salt. Set aside to allow the bread to soak up the tomato's juices.

3. Squeeze the garlic through a garlic press into a serving bowl. Add the capers and anchovies, then mash together until a smooth paste forms. Remove the seeds and ribs of the bell pepper and cut into ¼-inch dice. Add the bell pepper, the ½ teaspoon salt, the oil, and vinegar to the garlic-anchovy paste and toss to mix well.

4. Peel the remaining 2 tomatoes by blanching in boiling water or peeling them with a paring knife. (Peel over a bowl to catch the juices.) Roughly chop the tomatoes into ½-inch pieces. In the serving bowl, add the bread, chopped tomatoes, cucumber, onion, and black pepper and toss to mix well. Serve immediately.

 Beets

Beets are a love 'em or hate 'em vegetable. Many people find the flavor too strong for their tastes, but they are missing out on one of the most delicious flavors of summer.

Red beets, perhaps the most commonly known, have an earthy sweetness, while golden beets have brighter color and flavor. White beets have the least flavor, but they do add a nice decorative element to many dishes.

Look for beets with smooth skin and no visible rough spots. When shopping for the beet root only, be sure they are firm and the stem stub is still attached (old beets have the stems trimmed off).

Before cooking, cut off the green tops, leaving about 1 inch of the stem attached. Reserve the green tops for another use. As with all tough vegetables, wash the beet carefully using a vegetable brush so no loose soil remains.

SUMMER SPOTLIGHT

cold roasted beet salad

MAKES 4 SERVINGS

WINE SUGGESTION: PINOT NOIR

Give your friends a real treat by arriving at their backyard barbecue party with a big bowl of this salad. They'll want the recipe. Be sure to tell them that the reason it's so delicious is that the beets are roasted. Try adding destemmed arugula or a small bunch of destemmed watercress to the lettuce to further enliven the salad. You may consider doubling the recipe, because it will disappear quickly!

½ pound medium-sized yellow beets
½ pound medium-sized red beets
3 tablespoons extra virgin olive oil
1 tablespoon sherry vinegar or rice vinegar
1 teaspoon Dijon mustard
Pinch of sugar
Salt and freshly ground black pepper to taste
1 small head butterhead lettuce, torn into
    bite-size shreds

1. Preheat the oven to 350°F. Trim off the long root and all but ½ inch of leaf stalks from the beets. Place them on aluminum foil in the oven. Bake for 90 minutes and check for doneness. They're done when the beet has pulled away from the skin. (See sidebar.) Allow to cool. Peel and cut the beets into ½-inch dice.

2. In a medium bowl, whisk together the oil, vinegar, mustard, sugar, salt, and black pepper.

3. Add the beets and toss to coat. Using a slotted spoon, remove the beets to a separate plate and add the lettuce. Toss and serve immediately.

cold green bean salad

MAKES 4 SERVINGS

In summer, the new crop of fresh local snap beans comes in, and with it, the season for a cold green bean salad. The beans take center stage here, and it's their crunchy texture and herby-beany flavor that make the salad a stand-out. Look for fine, young, slender, tender beans, such as French filet beans. If you are growing them in your garden, pick them when they're no more than 4 inches long. Trim the stem and blossom ends, but don't french them.

Serve them as I've noted in the recipe, or top the salad with finely minced shallots, thin slices of red onion, julienned and blanched carrots or tomato wedges. One serving is about ¼ pound—or 1 cup—of beans before trimming. You can cook the beans the night before and refrigerate them in a covered container until you're ready to make the salad the next day.

Try adding winter savory (it grows well in summer and can be found in spice racks in dry form) or dried thyme— the flavors will enhance any bean salad.

1 pound fresh young green beans
⅔ cup Classic Vinaigrette (page 282)

1. Trim the beans. Blanch in boiling salted water for 1 minute if they're 3 to 4 inches long, 2 to 3 minutes if they're 5 to 7 inches long. Place in a colander and run cold water over to stop the cooking. Drain and pat dry. Place in a serving bowl.
2. Toss with the vinaigrette. Cover and place in the fridge for at least 1 hour or until ready to serve.

grilled corn salad

MAKES 4 TO 6 SERVINGS

The barbecue is hot, the summer corn is milky sweet and fresh—now's the time to make a Southwest favorite, grilled corn salad. With today's supersweet varieties, corn can taste like it was just picked, even if it's a day or two old. Grilling gives the corn, and hence the salad, an irresistible light smokiness. Besides tasting delicious, it's a pretty salad.

WINE SUGGESTION: FRENCH CÔTES DU RHÔNE

6 ears of fresh corn, shucked
⅓ cup extra virgin olive oil
1 large ripe tomato, roughly chopped into ½-inch pieces
½ cup pitted and sliced black olives
¼ cup sliced scallions, white part and some green parts
Juice of 1 lime
Juice of 1 orange
Juice of ½ lemon
1 tablespoon chopped fresh basil

1. Preheat the grill, then turn the heat down to medium. Brush the corn with some of the oil. Place on the grill and cook, turning frequently, 5 to 7 minutes or until the kernels are golden brown.
2. Into a serving bowl, cut the kernels from the cob. Add the tomato, olives, and scallions.
3. Place the citrus juices, basil, and remaining oil in a blender. Pulse until smooth and add to the salad. Toss to coat and serve immediately.

✳ VARIATIONS
Serve this salad over freshly picked field greens or lettuces. You may also add ⅓ cup

finely crumbled blue cheese when you toss. Add ¼ cup finely diced red sweet pepper for color. If you like the spiciness of Southwest cooking, mince a serrano pepper and add it in step 2.

summer vegetable salad

MAKES 3 TO 4 SERVINGS

In early summer, local farmers will be bringing in their first summer squash, fresh garden peas, and sweet onions, all beginning to swell to full size. Consider this exciting and refreshing salad that makes use of all three ingredients.

WINE SUGGESTION: PINOT GRIS

1 small sweet onion (Walla Walla, Vidalia, Maui, or red), thinly sliced
Juice of ½ lemon, strained
1 pound fresh peas in pods
2 young zucchini, 6 to 7 inches long
Generous pinch fleur de sel
3 tablespoons extra virgin olive oil
1½ ounces goat cheese, crumbled
2 basil leaves, chopped
Freshly ground black pepper to taste

1. In a small bowl, place the onion and lemon juice.
2. Shell the peas and blanch in them in boiling water for 2 minutes. Place in a colander and run cold water over to stop the cooking. Drain and pat dry. Place in a medium bowl.
3. Trim off the blossom and stem ends of the zucchini, then slice very thinly. Place in the bowl with the peas. Using two forks, scoop up the onions and add them to the zucchini and peas, allowing lemon juice to drip back into the small bowl.
4. Add the salt and oil to the bowl with the lemon juice. Whisk together. Drizzle over salad.
5. Sprinkle the salad with the cheese and basil. Add the black pepper and serve.

summer confetti salad

MAKES 3 TO 4 SERVINGS

What a great way to tempt your family to dig into a nutritious salad—give it a dash of visual fun and an inviting name like "confetti salad." A fresh-from-the-market head of romaine or butterhead lettuce is the basis of the salad. The rest can be made from whatever you have on hand, but think about getting as many colors into the salad as possible.

I was inspired by the contents of my fridge to make this combination of ingredients. Feel free to do the same. Your ingredients may differ. The point is to make something new out of those veggies in your crisper. Not only was this salad delicious, but it was a nutritious meal using eight different vegetables, plus nuts, in a colorful way.

WINE SUGGESTION: MUSCADET

1 head butterhead lettuce, torn up
½ carrot, grated
1 medium tomato, thinly sliced
2 tablespoons grated raw beets
½ red onion, thinly sliced
¼ cup crushed walnuts
½ cup julienned raw zucchini

¼ cup julienned raw yellow
    crookneck squash
½ cup finely diced red bell pepper
Salt and freshly ground black pepper
    to taste
½ cup Russian Dressing (page 285)

1. Wash the lettuce, tear it, and pat dry. Place in a salad bowl.

2. In a separate bowl, mix together the carrot, tomato, beet, onion, walnuts, zucchini, crookneck squash, bell pepper, salt, and pepper.

3. Add to the lettuce. Toss to mix.

4. Serve with the Russian dressing on the side.

FRUIT SALADS

simple fruit salad

MAKES 6 TO 8 SERVINGS

Fruit salads in the summertime can be heavenly affairs, rich and sweet and juicy with the opulent flavors of summer's superstars: strawberries, raspberries, blackberries, blueberries, black or red currants, elderberries, cherries, apricots, plumcots, nectarines, peaches, sweet melon balls, and seedless grapes. The more the merrier as they join the staples of apples, pears, oranges, and bananas.

WINE SUGGESTION: CALIFORNIA SPARKLING WINE

1½ cups freshly squeezed orange juice
Zest of 1 lemon

2 tablespoons freshly squeezed lemon juice
⅓ cup honey or ½ cup sugar
2 green apples
1 pear
1 orange, peeled and seeded
1 banana, without brown speckles
1½ pounds assorted fresh summer fruits

1. In a large serving bowl, add the orange juice, lemon zest, lemon juice, and honey. Stir to mix thoroughly and dissolve the honey.

2. Add the fruits to the bowl as you work. The citrus juice and sugar will prevent them from browning. Peel and core the apples and pear, cut into ½-inch dice, and add them to the bowl. Remove the orange segments from their membrane, and cut into 1-inch pieces.

3. Thinly slice the banana. Prepare the fresh summer fruit. Destem elderberries and add to the bowl whole. Halve apricots, plumcots, peaches, and nectarines. Pit them, slice into ⅓-inch wedges, and add to the bowl. Pit cherries and add the halves to the bowl. Slice seedless grapes in half and add to the bowl. (Strawberries and raspberries will be added later.)

4. Cover the bowl with cling wrap and refrigerate for about 3 hours, but not longer as the fruits will start to fall apart. If using strawberries and raspberries, wash them, but don't prepare them until about 20 minutes before serving, as they tend to disintegrate if macerated for any length of time. The strawberries should be cut in half and the raspberries added whole.

5. Remove the fruit from the fridge and spoon into individual bowls, making sure each bowl gets some of the juice. Leftovers will keep for a day in the fridge, though some quality of texture will be lost.

✳ MACÉDOINE

To make the fruit salad the Europeans call a macédoine, add two ounces of Maraschino, the Italian liqueur, to the recipe. This delicious liqueur is made from marasca cherries, a small, sour cherry variety from Croatia and Italy. It gets its inimitable flavor from the almond-flavored oil in the pits, which are ground with the cherries when they're mashed to make the liqueur.

minted fruit salad

MAKES 4 TO 6 SERVINGS

Mint adds a refreshing flavor to a fruit salad, giving it a cooling effect on a hot summer day. This is an excellent salad to bring to summer potlucks and parties, as most folks won't have had the added pleasure of mint in a mixed fruit salad before. It's surprising, but pleasantly so. Spearmint is the ideal mint to use. This recipe is party-sized, but you can halve the amounts in the ingredients list for everyday use.

¼ cup fresh mint, destemmed
3 tablespoons sugar
Juice of 1 lime
½ pound blackberries
½ pound sweet cherries, halved and pitted
3 medium peaches, halved, pitted, and cut into ⅓-inch-thick wedges
1½ cups halved seedless grapes
2 cups destemmed and halved strawberries
1 cup blueberries

1. Place the mint and sugar in a food processor or blender and blend until reduced to fine particles. Or mince the mint

and add it to the sugar in a small bowl, crushing it into the sugar with the back of a spoon until well incorporated.

2. In a serving bowl, place the mixture. Add the lime juice and stir to mix. Add the rest of the fruit and toss well to coat.

green papaya salad

MAKES 2 SERVINGS

This salad is almost always available in good Thai restaurants. The lively flavors of garlic, tomatoes, hot chiles, sweet sugar, fish or soy sauce, tangy lime juice, and crushed toasted peanuts intrigue the palate. Although green papaya gets top billing in this classic Thai salad, its mild taste is not the chief contributor to the flavor. It absorbs flavors from the rest of the ingredients, but remains the textural foundation of the dish.

You can find already shredded green papaya and dried shrimp in many good Asian markets. If all you can find is a whole green papaya, peel it with a vegetable peeler and use a cheese grater to make long shreds. When you get close to the core, discard any white seeds you may find. By eliminating the shrimp and substituting soy sauce for the fish sauce, this is a good vegetarian or vegan salad.

Follow the salad up with homemade satay sticks cooked on the grill and served with a peanut sauce. If you're having guests over, just double or triple this recipe. They will be delighted to get away from the summer staples of burgers and hot dogs.

WINE SUGGESTION: RIESLING FROM MOSEL, GERMANY

1 clove garlic, peeled
6 green beans
5 cherry tomatoes
2 Thai bird peppers or serrano chiles
2 cups shredded green papaya
1½ tablespoons sugar
½ teaspoon fish or soy sauce
Juice of 1 lime
1 tablespoon dried shrimp
2 tablespoons toasted crushed peanuts

1. Squeeze the garlic through a garlic press into a salad bowl. Blanch the green beans in boiling water for 1 minute. Place in a colander and run cold water over to stop the cooking. Drain and pat dry. Cut the beans lengthwise. Halve the cherry tomatoes.

2. Add the beans and tomatoes to the bowl with the garlic and pound them with the back of a spoon a few times to get their juices flowing. Crush the chiles just a little until a small amount of juice runs and add them to the bowl. A little of their fiery juice will suffuse the salad. For more heat, crush them more. Add the green papaya and the remaining ingredients to the bowl. Toss well to coat and serve immediately.

melon-lime salad

MAKES 4 SERVINGS

When the first really sweet summer melons arrive at the markets, by all means, eat them plain and let the tastes you've loved since childhood wash over you. And then, try some variations, in-cluding this one that adds a touch of citrus sweetness to the melons' own sweet juices.

WINE SUGGESTION: GERMAN RIESLING

4 cups bite-size ripe melon, cantaloupe
    and/or honeydew
Juice of 1 lime
1 tablespoon Seville orange marmalade
1 tablespoon sugar
1 teaspoon spearmint, minced

1. In a large serving bowl, place the melon.

2. In a small bowl, whisk together the lime juice, marmalade, sugar, and mint until the sugar has dissolved.

3. Add the dressing to the melon, toss to coat, and serve immediately.

watermelon salad

MAKES 4 SERVINGS

Cold, juicy watermelons practically define summer eating. No other fruit beats the heat like watermelon. Once upon a time they were bothersome—full of seeds, although watermelon seed-spitting con-tests provided fun at outdoor picnics and barbecues. Nowadays we have seedless watermelons with red, pink, or yellow flesh that are especially user friendly because their small size allows them to chill in the fridge until needed. Choose a cold, seedless watermelon—preferably red—to make this delicious summery salad.

WINE SUGGESTION: SAUVIGNON BLANC

1 watermelon, about 4 to 5 pounds.
1 sweet onion
¼ cup red wine vinegar
Salt and freshly ground black pepper
    to taste
½ cup extra virgin olive oil
2 tablespoons fresh mint, chopped
4 ounces feta cheese, crumbled

1. Cut the watermelon into bite-size pieces, or use a melon baller. Slice the onion into rings.

2. In a small bowl, whisk together the vinegar, salt, and black pepper, until the salt has dissolved. Slowly drizzle in the oil, whisking, until all the oil is mixed in. Taste and adjust the seasoning, if necessary. Add the chopped mint. Stir to mix in.

3. In a serving bowl, place the watermelon, onion, and cheese. Add the dressing, toss gently to coat, and serve immediately.

watermelon-mango salad

MAKES 4 TO 6 SERVINGS

The secret of this refreshing summer salad is to serve it well chilled. It will be much appreciated either before the meal or afterwards as a dessert.

WINE SUGGESTION: GRECO DI TUFO

4 cups bite-size cubes seedless
    watermelon
2 cups cubed ripe mango
2 tablespoons freshly squeezed lime juice
1 tablespoon honey
1 teaspoon lime zest

1 teaspoon balsamic vinegar
Pinch salt

1. In a serving bowl, combine the watermelon and mango.

2. In a small bowl, whisk together the lime juice, honey, lime zest, vinegar, and salt.

3. Pour over the fruit, cover the bowl, and refrigerate until quite cold, stirring occasionally.

watermelon, fig, and sweet red onion salad

MAKES 6 SERVINGS

While this dish sounds like an unlikely combination, it's actually a fabulous mix of flavors. For added taste and texture, crumble a little feta cheese over the greens before adding the watermelon. Note the 30-minute marinating time, which softens the raw onion flavor.

WINE SUGGESTION: ITALIAN ARNEIS

1 tablespoon finely minced scallions
¼ cup raspberry, red wine, or other fruit
    vinegar
¼ cup raspberry puree from fresh red
    raspberries, strained to remove seeds
¼ cup freshly squeezed orange juice
2 teaspoons honey, or to taste
¼ cup extra virgin olive oil
Salt and freshly ground black pepper to
    taste
1 medium sweet red onion, cut into rings
    and soaked briefly in ice water
2 small bunches watercress or arugula,
    destemmed

8 cups cubed (1-inch) seedless watermelon
6 large ripe fresh figs, quartered
3 mint leaves, julienned

1. In a small bowl, whisk together the scallions, vinegar, raspberry puree, orange juice, honey, and oil. Season with salt and black pepper.

2. Drain the onions, pat dry, and separate into rings. Pour the vinaigrette over. Refrigerate for 30 minutes. Chill 6 salad plates.

3. To serve, divide the watercress equally among the chilled plates. Top with cubed watermelon. Arrange onions and figs around the outside and drizzle with vinaigrette. Sprinkle a few threads of mint leaves over the top and serve immediately.

grilled peach and fig salad

MAKES 4 SERVINGS

While the grill is hot, you might as well grill the main stars of this fine salad, which is only possible to prepare in late summer when the best peaches and fresh figs are in. This recipe is the invention of Chef John Ash, my friend and occasional dinner partner when I review restaurants in California wine country. John's insights and trenchant analyses of the dishes we're served are invaluable.

WINE SUGGESTION: PROSECCO

2 tablespoons minced shallot
6 tablespoons rice vinegar
2 tablespoons honey
4 tablespoons freshly squeezed
    lemon juice

5 tablespoons olive oil
2 large firm-ripe peaches, halved and
    pitted
4 large ripe figs, halved
3 cups lightly packed spicy mixed greens,
    such as arugula, endive, and watercress
6 very thin slices of salumi
5 to 6 shavings (about 2 ounces) of hard
    cheese, flaked with a vegetable peeler

1. In a small bowl, whisk together the shallot, vinegar, honey, lemon juice, and oil.

2. Preheat the grill, then lower the heat to medium-high. Brush the peaches and figs with the vinaigrette and place them cut side down. Grill just until the peaches are lightly browned, about 2 to 3 minutes. Thickly slice the grilled peaches.

3. In a medium bowl, toss the greens with a half cup of the vinaigrette. Store the rest of the vinaigrette, covered, in the fridge, for up to 1 week. Divide the greens among 4 plates. Place equal amounts of the peach slices and figs artfully on each plate and top with the salumi and cheese.

NO COOK　　MAKE AHEAD　　QUICK & EASY

POTATO SALADS

classic american potato salad

MAKES ABOUT 1½ QUARTS OR 6 TO 7 CUPS

WINE SUGGESTION: GRÜNER VELTLINER

At picnics, outdoor barbecues, softball games, potlucks, and other rituals of summer get-togethers, people will always be looking for the potato salad. Fluffy, tangy, and luscious, this version is an American classic. Keep it cold until ready to serve, as mayonnaise can spoil quickly in the heat. Take it to outdoor functions in an insulated cooler with a bag or two of ice.

I call for "new potatoes," which most people think of as the red-skinned potatoes at the markets. They're fine, but if you can find young, thin-skinned, waxy potatoes freshly dug from the soil, you'll find their taste superior and their texture velvety. If they're young enough, their tissue-paper skins won't even need peeling.

3 pounds new potatoes
¼ cup Classic Vinaigrette (page 282) or red wine vinegar
½ cup finely chopped red onion
¼ teaspoon salt
Freshly ground black pepper
1 tablespoon chopped parsley
½ cup mayonnaise
⅔ cup chopped celery
½ cup chopped dill pickle

1. Scrub the potatoes under cold water. Boil them in plenty of water until just barely tender. Cooking time will vary with the size of the potatoes, but 3-inch new potatoes will take about 15 minutes at a full boil. Overcooking turns them mealy, and undercooking leaves them hard.

2. When done, remove from the heat and drain. Peel by holding each potato up on the point of a knife or tines of a fork and pulling off the skins using a paring knife. Cut into 1-inch dice. While still warm, gently (so the potatoes retain their shape) toss with the vinaigrette and the onions, and season them with the salt and black pepper.

3. Let stand for 30 minutes, so the potatoes can absorb the dressing. Add the parsley, mayonnaise, celery, and pickle, and gently fold in until mixed.

Variations in potato salads are usually cultural, brought to America with immigrants from Europe, enriching the American experience with each new culinary twist. You can easily find German potato salad in Cincinnati and Milwaukee, for instance. Here are the most common variations.

FRENCH POTATO SALAD

MAKES 6 TO 8 SERVINGS

3 pounds waxy-fleshed new potatoes
½ cup herbed vinaigrette (page 283).
¼ cup Classic Vinaigrette (page 282) or red wine vinegar

Boil the potatoes until just tender as directed in American potato salad. Peel, slice, or dice them, and while the potatoes are still warm, pour the dressings over and gently toss to coat. Serve still warm.

GERMAN POTATO SALAD
MAKES 6 TO 8 SERVINGS

3 pounds new potatoes
4 strips bacon
1 stalk celery, with leaves, finely diced
1 small onion, finely diced
1 slice kosher dill pickle, finely chopped
½ cup vegtetable stock
¼ cup apple cider vinegar
1 teaspoon sugar
1 teaspoon ground paprika
½ teaspoon dry mustard
Salt and pepper to taste
2 sprigs parsley, finely chopped

1. Cook, peel, and slice or dice the potatoes as directed in American potato salad. Place the potatoes into a serving bowl in a warm oven. In a skillet, fry the bacon until crisp. Blot away excess fat with a paper towel. When the bacon is cool, crumble it, using your hands. Add the bacon to the potatoes in the warm oven. Pour off the excess bacon fat from the skillet, but retain 1 to 2 tablespoons.

2. Add the celery and onion to the skillet with the bacon fat over medium heat, stirring occasionally until the vegetables are golden. This will take 3 to 5 minutes.

3. Add the dill pickle, vegetable stock, apple cider vinegar, sugar, paprika, dry mustard, and salt and pepper to taste. Bring to a boil, and as soon as the mixture boils, pour it over the potatoes and gently stir to mix.

4. Garnish the salad with chopped parsley or little snips of chives and serve while hot, the traditional way to serve it, but you can also serve it at room temperature, or even cold.

SLAWS

coleslaw
MAKES 4 TO 6 SERVINGS

Great coleslaw is a matter of balance between sweet sugar and sour vinegar. When these tastes balance, the result is neither sweet nor sour, but a heavenly synthesis of the two that exalts the crunchy cabbage. The term coleslaw comes from the Dutch *kool sla*, which means cabbage salad. A small dish of cold coleslaw and a sandwich of cold cuts is a simple but delicious evening meal on a hot night when cooking seems out of the question. There are many recipes for coleslaw—probably a variation for everyone who makes it. This recipe makes a wonderful—and balanced—slaw. Substitute crème fraiche, light sour cream, plain yogurt, or any combination of these, for the mayonnaise.

½ head green cabbage, cored and outer
    leaves removed
¾ cup mayonnaise
⅓ cup red wine vinegar
1 teaspoon Dijon mustard
2 teaspoons sugar
½ teaspoon celery seed
Salt and freshly ground black pepper to
    taste
½ cup grated carrot
1 ½ tablespoons sweet paprika

1. Fill a large bowl half full of cold water and add a couple of trays of ice cubes. Set

aside. If you have a mandoline, now's the time to use it, for you want to slice the cabbage as finely as possible. If you're using a knife, try for the thinnest slices you can manage. When the half head of cabbage is entirely sliced, place the cabbage shreds in the ice water and set aside. They should soak for 1 hour.

2. Place a colander in the sink and drain the cabbage, discarding any remnants of the ice cubes.

3. While the cabbage is draining, combine the mayonnaise, vinegar, mustard, sugar, and celery seed, and season with a little salt and black pepper.

4. Place the thoroughly drained cabbage in a bowl, add the carrots, and toss. Add the dressing and toss. Sprinkle with a shake or two of sweet paprika. If you are serving in individual small bowls, shake ¼ teaspoon paprika on top of each dish.

midwestern sweet-and-sour coleslaw

MAKES 4 SERVINGS

Hazel Hardebeck's coleslaw was always the best. My mom hailed from Covington, Kentucky, and showed her German heritage in this dish. I looked for years until I found the exact same slaw she made, this version from Carlos at Nicola's Delicatessen in Calistoga, California. This recipe makes one quart of coleslaw dressing, which is enough for two batches of slaw. The extra pint of dressing can be kept refrigerated for up to a week and used for a second batch.

½ head of savoy cabbage, cored and outer leaves removed
½ grated carrot
¼ red bell pepper, minced, about ½ cup
3 cups egg mayonnaise
1 teaspoon celery seed
1 cup white vinegar
1 cup sugar

1. Fill a large bowl half full of cold water and add a couple of trays of ice cubes. Set aside. If you have a mandoline, now's the time to use it, for you want to slice the cabbage as finely as possible. If you're using a knife, try for the thinnest slices you can manage. When the half head of cabbage is entirely sliced, place the cabbage shreds in the ice water and set aside. They should soak for 1 hour.

2. Place a colander in the sink and drain the cabbage, discarding any remnants of the ice cubes. Pat dry between dish towels.

3. Place the cabbage in a bowl and add the carrot and bell pepper.

4. In a separate bowl, combine the mayonnaise, celery seed, vinegar, and some of the sugar, and mix until the sugar has dissolved. Taste the mixture; it's right when you can't taste only vinegar or sugar, but the whole becomes an integrated flavor. If you can still make them out, add more sugar or vinegar, a bit at a time, and taste, until the dressing is balanced.

5. Add half of the dressing to the cabbage mixture, reserving the rest for the your next batch of slaw. It will last in the fridge for a week.

6. Toss to mix well and serve immediately.

ginger-scallion coleslaw

MAKES 4 TO 6 SERVINGS

Every Korean home refrigerator contains a jar of kimchi, its crunchy cabbage pickled and spicy-hot. The flavor of this Asian slaw has resonance with kimchi, and makes a fine partnership with typical Korean dishes like cold buckwheat noodles, barbecued pork ribs, or beef and vegetable casserole. As opposed to the ice water bath that renders cabbage crunchy, this method uses the Korean technique of salting the cabbage to draw out water, giving it a nice crunchy texture. Use a fresh-as-possible head of cabbage. A mandoline does the best job of reducing the cabbage to fine shreds, but careful work with a sharp knife will suffice.

Note that this slaw is made well ahead—even 1 day ahead—of the time it will be served, so it can marinate in the fridge.

WINE SUGGESTION: DRY SAKE

½ head green cabbage, cored and
    outer leaves removed
1 tablespoon salt
1 cup plain rice vinegar
½ cup sugar
2 tablespoons peeled and grated
    fresh ginger
2 tablespoons finely chopped scallions,
    white part only
½ teaspoon red pepper flakes
1 cup grated carrot

1. While this recipe calls for green cabbage, you can use savory cabbage, napa, or Chinese cabbage, all of which work well. Slice the cabbage as finely as possible. If you're using a knife, try for the thinnest slices you can manage. When the cabbage is entirely sliced, place the cabbage shreds in a bowl. Sprinkle with the salt and toss to incorporate thoroughly.

2. Place the salted cabbage into a colander in the sink or in a large skillet and set a plate over the top to add pressure to the cabbage. Set heavy weights on the plate. (Cans of food, a canister of flour, etc.—the heavier the better.) Drain the cabbage for 3 hours. Rinse it with cold water and drain. Pat dry between paper towels.

3. In a serving bowl, whisk together the vinegar, sugar, ginger, scallions, and pepper flakes until the sugar has dissolved. Add the carrots to the cabbage and toss. Add the cabbage-carrot mixture to the dressing and toss well. Cover the bowl and set it in the fridge overnight. Toss once more before serving.

summer fruit slaw

MAKES 8 SERVINGS

With so many summer fruits to enjoy, we sometimes find extra peaches and plums on our windowsills. Better use them before they pass the point of perfection. Here's a fruit slaw that combines these sweet fruits of summer and the richness of dark brown sugar with the tangy sourness of apple cider vinegar in a magic marriage of flavors. They all disappear into something uniquely different from any of them. The use of napa cabbage gives the soft fruits a fine, firm texture. Chill the slaw well before serving. If a mango isn't available, substitute ripe nectarine or apricot.

WINE SUGGESTION: PINOT GRIGIO

6 cups finely shredded napa cabbage (or
   bok choy if napa cabbage is unavailable)
2 cups coarsely chopped fresh plums
2 cups coarsely chopped peeled fresh
   peaches
1 cup diced (½-inch) mango
½ cup raisins
1 cup finely chopped or crushed walnuts
1 cup walnut oil
½ cup apple cider vinegar
2 teaspoons dark brown sugar

1. In a serving bowl, place the cabbage,
plums, peaches, mango, and raisins.

2. In a jar with a tight-fitting lid, place the
chopped walnuts, walnut oil, vinegar, and
sugar and shake well to dissolve the sugar
and mix the dressing. Add the dressing to
the salad and toss to coat.

3. Cover and refrigerate until chilled.

PASTA SALADS

pasta primavera salad
MAKES 6 TO 8 SERVINGS

Primavera is Italian for "spring," but there's
no better time to make a pasta primavera
salad than the summertime. This dish is a
luscious way to get your vegetable servings
for the day—even the kids will love it.
Look for young, tender vegetable and
quickly blanch them in boiling water or
lightly steam them, rather than cook them

heavily, so they retain a pleasant crunch.
The salad is versatile: it can be served hot
or cold, as an appetizer, side dish, or main
dish. It is a staple of potlucks everywhere—
and always welcome. While it's easy to
make, its quality rests solely on the quality
of the vegetables you select.

WINE SUGGESTION: ITALIAN FRIULI

2 cups shelled fresh garden peas
1½ cups broccoli florets, stems trimmed
2 cups diced (⅓-inch) summer squash
1 cup diced (¼-inch) carrots
3 tablespoons extra virgin olive oil
1 cup cherry tomatoes, halved
1½ cups half-and-half
1 cup grated Parmesan cheese
1 tablespoon butter
Salt to taste
2 bay leaves
1 pound whole wheat spaghetti, fettucini,
   or linguini
Freshly ground black pepper to taste

1. Blanch the peas, broccoli, squash, and
carrots separately until tender but still
crunchy in a perforated colander set into a
pot of boiling water. Blanch the peas about
1 minute, the broccoli and squash about 2
minutes each, and the carrots 3 to 4
minutes. Plunge blanched vegetables into
cold water to stop the cooking, then place
them together in the same bowl to drain.
When all the vegetables are in the bowl, tilt
it to drain off any water that has accumulated in the bottom.

2. Place a skillet over medium heat and
heat 2 tablespoons of the oil. Add the
cherry tomatoes and sauté for 1 to 2
minutes. Remove from the heat and
reserve. Place a shallow saucepan on low

heat and gently heat the half-and-half, ½ cup of the cheese, and the butter, mixing to melt the butter and the cheese. Keep warm.

3. Place a large stock pot over medium-high heat and add the remaining 1 table-spoon of oil and a pinch of salt. Add the bay leaves. Add the pasta and cook until al dente. Drain in a colander, removing the bay leaves.

4. Place the pasta in a large sauté pan and add two-thirds of the vegetables (except the cherry tomatoes) and the cheese mixture. Place over medium heat and stir to mix and heat through. Season with salt and black pepper. Pour the primavera onto a serving platter, top with the remaining veg-etables and the cherry tomatoes, and serve with the remaining ½ cup cheese on the side.

✱ **CHILLED PASTA PRIMAVERA**
If the primavera is to be served as a cold salad, omit the cream and cheese mixture and toss with a vinaigrette (page 282). You can flavor the cold salad with basil shreds and toasted pine nuts.

spicy pasta salad with olives and feta

MAKES 4 SERVINGS

Here's a flavorful and spicy salad guaran-teed to prep the taste buds for grilled meats and fire-roasted veggies. Something of the hot, smoky taste of meat and vegetables from the grill just begs for a spicy accompa-niment. Mediterranean dishes are not only good for you, they are quintessential summer fare because they demand fresh produce in season to taste their best. This salad can be served hot, but it's better if cooled to room temperature. It stores well in the fridge for a week, but let it warm to room temperature before serving.

Flat-leaf parsley has a more intense parsley flavor than the curly sort. If you think an entire serrano may make the salad too hot, use a quarter of the pepper and taste the result. Add more minced serrano if needed. *Penne rigate* are little fluted tubes. *Fusilli* are little spiral pastas, and *conchiglie* are shell-shaped and hold the other ingredients well.

WINE SUGGESTION: SPANISH TEMPRANILLO OR ITALIAN BARBARESCO

1 serrano pepper, minced
½ cup chopped Italian flat-leaf parsley
2 cloves garlic, minced
1 tablespoon fresh oregano
1 tablespoon capers
¼ cup extra virgin olive oil
4 ounces feta cheese, crumbled
12 black oil-cured olives, pitted and chopped
½ cup diced ripe red bell pepper
Freshly ground black pepper to taste
Pinch of salt
2 bay leaves
10 ounces pasta (*penne rigate, fusilli,* or *conchiglie*)
1 small red onion, thinly sliced into rings

1. In a serving bowl, place the serrano pepper, parsley, garlic, oregano, capers, oil, feta, olives, bell pepper, and black pepper.

2. Place a large stock pot over medium-high heat and add a pinch of salt. Add the bay leaves. Add the pasta and cook until al dente. Add the onion rings during the last minute of cooking. Drain the pasta and onion in a colander, removing the bay leaves. Pour the pasta-onion mix into the serving bowl and toss to mix.

yogurt pasta salad

MAKES 3 TO 4 SERVINGS

This creamy salad is full of little crunchy veggie bits that burst their garden-fresh flavors onto your taste buds. It looks sinfully fatty, but is almost fat free. Back in the day, Grandmom made a creamy pasta salad with full-fat dairy products. With the advent of products like nonfat yogurt, we can be more calorie and fat conscious without giving up one ounce of flavor.

WINE SUGGESTION: CALIFORNIA GEWURZTRAMINER

⅔ cup nonfat plain yogurt
Pinch of salt
4 ounces pasta (elbow macaroni or
    penne rigate)
1 tablespoon red wine vinegar
1 clove garlic, minced
½ teaspoon sugar
½ cup very thinly sliced fennel
½ cup diced (¼-inch) ripe red bell pepper
3 tablespoons minced red onion
2 tablespoons minced fresh basil
Salt and freshly ground black pepper to taste

1. This salad will be too watery if the yogurt is used straight from the container. Set a fine-mesh sieve over a deep bowl and add the yogurt. Let gravity drain the excess liquid from the yogurt into the bowl over a 2-hour period on the kitchen counter. When the yogurt is nearly finished draining, cook

the pasta. Place a large stock pot over medium-high heat and add a pinch of salt. Add the pasta and cook until al dente. Drain the pasta in a colander and run cold water over to stop the cooking. Drain.

2. Place the drained yogurt in a serving bowl. In a separate bowl, whisk together the vinegar, garlic, and sugar until the sugar has dissolved. Add to the yogurt, stirring to mix it in.

3. Pour the pasta into the serving bowl and toss to coat. Add the fennel, bell pepper, onion, and basil and stir to mix well. Add the salt and black pepper and give the salad a final stir. This salad is good at room temperature, but chilling it slightly is preferred.

couscous salad with pine nuts and summer fruits

MAKES 4 TO 6 SERVINGS

Most recipes for a couscous salad call for dried fruit, but now it's summertime when the fruit is fresh, and using fresh fruit only adds to the pleasure of this wonderful salad. The resinous pine nuts and richly flavored apricots have an affinity for each other that brings this salad to life. Make sure the pine nuts taste fresh and piney. They so easily (and so often) turn rancid and acquire a fusty taste. Use North African instant couscous, not the larger Israeli type.

WINE SUGGESTION: VALPOLICELLA

3 tablespoons golden raisins
2 ¼ cups chicken broth
1 tablespoon butter
2 cups uncooked instant couscous
¼ cup lightly toasted pine nuts

½ ripe red or yellow bell pepper, cut into
  ¼-inch dice
2 tablespoons finely chopped green onion
4 fresh apricots, pitted and chopped
¼ cup vinaigrette made with lime juice
  (See "Vary Your Vinaigrette," page 283)
Salt to taste

  1. Plump the raisins in warm water.
  2. Add the chicken broth to a stockpot
and set over high heat. Bring to a boil and
reserve ¼ cup. Add the butter and couscous
to the broth in the pot and stir to melt and
mix in the butter. Cover and set aside, off
the heat, for 5 minutes. Pour the couscous
into a serving bowl, add the reserved ¼ cup
broth, and fluff the couscous.
  3. Drain and add the raisins to the couscous, then add the pine nuts, bell pepper,
green onions, and apricots. Add the vinaigrette and salt and toss well. Taste and
adjust the seasoning, if necessary.

✱ NORTH AFRICAN COUSCOUS SALAD
  • Add ¼ teaspoon ground cumin for true
    North African flavor.
  • Add two tablespoons fresh red and/or
    black currants when you add the fresh
    apricots. If cherries are in season, pit
    and halve them and add them in lieu of
    the currants.

tabbouleh

MAKES 4 SERVINGS

Tabbouleh is a Middle Eastern dish from a
region where the temperatures can really
soar. And it's at its best when the tomatoes
are sun-ripened and the herbs are full of

flavor. Fresh-picked tomatoes, parsley, scallions, and mint—what a refreshing and delicious harmony of ingredients.
  Serve this salad with grilled lamb
kabobs, pita bread, and a dish of garlicky
hummus with a shallow lake of really good
extra virgin olive oil in its center.

1 cup bulgur wheat
2 medium vine-ripe tomatoes
5 tablespoons freshly squeezed lemon
  juice
¼ teaspoon kosher salt
⅔ cup finely chopped scallions
1 cup finely chopped fresh parsley
½ cup chopped fresh mint
⅓ cup extra virgin olive oil
Freshly ground black pepper to taste

  1. Place the bulgur in a bowl and cover
with cold water. Set aside for 1 hour. Halve
the tomatoes and gently squeeze out the
juice and seeds. Finely chop the pulp. Place
the tomatoes in a small bowl, add 1 tablespoon of the lemon juice and the salt, and
set aside.
  2. Drain and squeeze the bulgur
between paper towels to remove any
excess water.
  3. Transfer the bulgur to a serving bowl.
Fluff it with a fork and add the tomatoes,
scallions, parsley, and mint. Mix the remaining 4 tablespoons lemon juice with the
oil and fold it into the bulgur mixture. Add
the black pepper and mix everything well.
Cover the serving bowl and place it in the
fridge for 1 hour, until it's cold, and serve.

✱ VARIATION
Add ½ teaspoon ground allspice along with
the black pepper in step 3 of the instructions.

A 10-by-10-foot herb garden will have you smothered in fresh, aromatic herbs for your summery dishes from the first day of the season to the last—and beyond.

Lay out the garden as a square with three-foot paths running down the middle from top to bottom and side to side. This will give you four 3½-foot-sided squares for planting. That's 12¼ square feet each, or 49 total square feet of space for your kitchen herbs—plenty of room in a very small space.

First, with a shovel or a tiller, turn the soil, burying any grass or weeds as you turn over each shovelful. At your garden store you'll find three-foot-wide weed barrier cloth. Lay it down in the pathways, then cover the weed barrier cloth with cocoa bean hulls, wood chips, or thick layers of lawn grass clippings. All will look nice and keep the mud off your feet.

Improve the soil in three of the squares with bags of ready-made compost from the garden store. Use one 20-pound bag per square. Dig the compost into the soil to a depth of 8 to 10 inches, using a spading fork or a shovel.

Many herbs don't like too much nutrition, and respond to it by cutting back on their aromatic qualities. Don't add compost to the soil in the fourth square. Instead, dump in a bag of builder's sand and turn it in to a depth of 8 to 10 inches. This is where you'll plant your Mediterranean herbs. They like poor, dry soil and are called the herbs of Provence—rosemary, sage, thyme, and oregano, and its cousin, marjoram. Mediterranean herbs become more aromatic in poor soil. They like to struggle for nutrients and water. Let them have their way.

Now water the garden thoroughly and deeply. Cover the three composted squares with thick mulch. Chopped leaves, lawn grass clippings, old newspapers—anything that was once living and will decay into the soil will work. The mulch smothers weeds, holds in soil moisture, and feeds the soil as it decays. When you go to plant, punch holes through the mulch or move it aside and plant in the moist soil underneath, then tuck the mulch back around the stems of the plants.

Plant your Provençal herbs in bare soil with no mulch. In the other three squares, plant summer and winter savory, parsley (both Italian and curly-leaf), any of the basils but especially Genovese and Thai basil, caraway, catnip (if you want to give your cats a treat), chervil, chives, cilantro, dill, lavender, lemon balm, sweet marjoram, mint (both spearmint and peppermint) oregano, and French tarragon. That's about six or seven herbs per square, with each getting a couple of square feet in which to grow. Some are larger than others—thyme is small, Genovese basil is large. Some will want to take over the whole square (like lemon balm), while others like winter savory are well behaved.

The Provençal herbs probably won't need water unless you're having a real drought. They thrive, after all, in the Mediterranean climate where it seldom rains from late spring to early fall. Water the other squares as needed.

Now when you need herbs bursting with garden-fresh potency, you've got them—and all from a 10-by-10-foot piece of soil.

citrusy tofu and rice salad

MAKES 4 SERVINGS

Tofu has nutritional advantages, but when it comes to flavor, it's a mirror, absorbing any flavors it's paired with. The sweet-and-sour sesame citrus dressing coats the tofu with a mixture of Asian flavors: soy sauce, ginger, toasted sesame oil, green onions. Prepare this summery salad with whichever greens are freshest at the market. It puts an intriguing Asian twist on any main course it accompanies.

WINE SUGGESTION: CALIFORNIA RIESLING

½ cup dry white wine
Pinch salt
½ cup jasmine rice
One 14-ounce package firm tofu, rinsed
    and cut into ¾-inch cubes
10 tablespoons Sesame-Citrus Dressing
    (page 284)
8 cups mixed field greens
1 medium carrot, grated
1 young cucumber, peeled and chopped
2 scallions, white part only, minced

1. Place the wine in a rice-cooking pot with a lid. Add ½ cup water and a pinch of salt. Turn the heat to high, and when the water and wine mixture comes to a boil, add the rice. Boil rapidly, uncovered, for 3 minutes, then turn the heat to low and cover. Let it cook for 45 to 60 minutes, until the rice has absorbed all the liquid and is tender.

2. Spray a large skillet with nonstick spray and place over medium-high heat. Add the tofu and 2 tablespoons of the dressing. Turn every 2 minutes or so, until the tofu is golden brown, about 15 minutes. Remove the skillet from the heat and add 1 tablespoon of the dressing. Turn the tofu to coat. Add the rice to the skillet and mix well with the tofu.

3. In a serving bowl, toss the greens, carrot, cucumber, and scallions with the remaining 7 tablespoons dressing. Scatter the tofu and rice over the top of the salad and serve immediately.

POULTRY AND MEAT SALADS

simple chicken salad

MAKES 4 SERVINGS

Chicken salad spooned onto lettuce leaves could be the quick and easy—and delectable!—answer to a hurry-up summer lunch or dinner. It has a warm, meaty flavor and a low-fat profile. Or slide the lettuce and chicken salad between two pieces of whole wheat toast and delight the kids.

A *poussin*—a small and tender young chicken you can order from your butcher—would be perfect for this salad. Roast it for 45 minutes at 350°F, or until done, and then skin it and dice all the meat—you should have about 2 cups. If you're in a hurry, nab a rotisserie chicken at the store and dice equal parts white and dark meat, then follow the rest of the recipe.

WINE SUGGESTION: CALIFORNIA CHARDONNAY

3 stalks celery
2 cups diced roasted chicken meat, dark
and white
¾ cup light mayonnaise
Salt and freshly ground black pepper
to taste
12 buttercrunch lettuce leaves
2 tablespoons chopped French tarragon

1. Wash the celery. Grab the stalks at the base and snap off a piece from the concave toward the convex part of the stalks, then pull the snapped piece up the convex side toward the top of the stalk to remove as many strings as possible. Cut into ¼ -inch dice. In a bowl, place the celery and the chicken. Add the mayonnaise, salt, and black pepper and mix well.

2. Spoon ¾ cup chicken salad onto three lettuce leaves on each of four plates, then sprinkle the tops with a bit of the chopped tarragon.

✳ TUNA SALAD
If you're really in a hurry, open a 6-ounce can of tuna and substitute it for the chicken, adding a half teaspoon of dry mustard, a few capers, and the juice of ½ lemon to the recipe when mixing the mayonnaise, salt, and pepper to make a tuna salad that you can serve on lettuce leaves or on toast as a tuna salad sandwich. Add one tablespoon of finely chopped tarragon to the salad. If you don't have tarragon, use parsley.

chicken and jasmine rice salad
MAKES 4 SERVINGS

What to do with those wonderful summer-ripe red or yellow bell peppers that usually cost an arm and a leg but now, at the peak of their season, are sweet, crunchy, and inexpensive? One idea is to use them in a whole grain and chicken salad that's chock full of protein and brimming with flavor. It makes a tasty side dish with ratatouille. The brown jasmine rice is fragrant and delicate. Use regular brown rice, bulgur, quinoa, or amaranth as a substitute for the brown jasmine rice. Substitute Jack or a mild cheddar for the Comte.
WINE SUGGESTION: PINOT GRIS (OR PINOT GRIGIO)

2 pinches salt
1 cup brown jasmine rice
1 bone-in, skin-on chicken breast
2 teaspoons red wine vinegar
1 teaspoon Dijon-style mustard
¼ cup extra virgin olive oil
½ cup diced (¼-inch) Comte cheese
1 red or yellow bell pepper, cut into
¼-inch dice
½ cup black oil-cured olives, pitted
and chopped
4 brined green olives, pitted and chopped
3 tablespoons chopped cornichons

1. Preheat the oven to 425°F. Place a pot over medium-high heat, add 2 cups water, and cover. Bring to a rolling boil. Add one pinch salt and the rice. Cook uncovered for 3 minutes at a full boil, then turn heat down to low and cover. Cook for 45 to 60 minutes, until the water is absorbed and the rice is cooked.

2. While the rice is cooking, bake the

chicken breast, skin side up, for 20 minutes. Turn the breast over and continue baking for 5 to 10 minutes more, until the meat is cooked through. Set aside to cool.

3. In a small bowl, whisk together the vinegar, the second pinch of salt, and the mustard until smooth. Add the oil and whisk until well mixed.

4. Spoon the rice into a large serving bowl to cool. Remove the skin from the chicken breast and carefully cut the meat away from the bone with a sharp boning knife. Cut the meat into ½-inch dice.

5. When both the rice and chicken are room temperature, add the chicken to the rice. Whisk the dressing once more and toss it with the rice and chicken mixture. Add the cheese, bell pepper, olives, and cornichons, and toss again to mix.

southwestern chicken salad

MAKES 4 SERVINGS

The prominent flavors of this salad are lime and cumin, but there's so much more going on: tomato, cilantro, and chili powder wrapped around luscious textures of juicy chicken and buttery avocado, plus crunchy toasted pumpkin seeds.

Though this salad is a little more elaborate than a simple chicken salad, it has more layers of flavor and it isn't difficult to assemble at all. Note that the salad needs a couple of hours in the fridge for the flavors to marry before serving.

You may substitute whole butterhead lettuce leaves for the shredded cabbage, if you wish.

WINE SUGGESTION: LIGHT PINOT NOIR

2 bone-in, skin-on chicken breasts
1 large ripe tomato, seeded and diced
1 ripe avocado, pitted, peeled, and diced
½ medium red onion, finely diced
½ cup fresh cilantro, chopped
¼ cup extra virgin olive oil
¼ cup fresh lime juice
½ teaspoon lime zest

GOOD TO KNOW: TAKING THE BITE OUT OF ONIONS

Raw yellow storage onions—as opposed to sweet onions like Walla Walla, Vidalia, or Maui—can bite the tongue. Here's how to defang onions destined to be included raw in salads.

Peel and slice the onion very thinly crosswise so it separates into rings. Place the rings in a large bowl and cover with cold water. Let stand about 5 minutes, then lift them out with your hands and squeeze out as much juice and water as you can. Set the onions aside on a clean counter or paper towel. Pour out the water in the bowl and put the onions back in. Cover them again with fresh cold water. Let stand another 5 minutes, and wring them out as before. Repeat this procedure a third time, then cover them with fresh cold water and set aside until you're ready to assemble the salad. Before adding them, wring them out one final time and pat them dry with paper towels. You'll have all the sweetness the onions have to give without any bite.

1 teaspoon ground cumin
½ teaspoon chili powder
Salt and freshly ground black pepper
   to taste
½ cup pumpkin seeds (*pepitas*)
4 cups red and green cabbage, shredded

1. Preheat the broiler. Broil the chicken breasts, bone side up, for 10 minutes. Turn them over and broil 7 to 10 minutes more, until they are done through. You can grill the chicken as well: Preheat the grill to high. Grill the breasts bone side down for 10 to 12 minutes. Turn them over and grill 8 to 10 minutes more, or until just done.

2. Let the chicken cool down to warm. Remove the skin and carefully cut the meat away from the bone with a sharp boning knife. Cut the meat into ⅓-inch dice.

3. In a bowl, toss the chicken with the tomato, avocado, onion, cilantro, oil, lime juice and zest, cumin, chili powder, salt, and black pepper. Cover and chill in the fridge for 1 to 2 hours. While the salad is chilling, lightly toast the pumpkin seeds in the oven until just beginning to color and crush them in a mortar with a pestle or in a blender.

4. Place a cup of the shredded cabbage on each of four salad plates. Divide the salad evenly among the plates. Top with the crushed pumpkin seeds and serve while cold.

steak salad

MAKES 4 SERVINGS

The earthy, peppery flavor of arugula complements steak, tomatoes, and onion, and you'll love the way a simple vinaigrette gives the slices of steak a tangy enhancement. For this salad, think ahead a couple of days to a summer meal that's quick and easy: if you're going to grill a steak this evening, grill more than you need so that you'll have cold steak in the fridge tomorrow or the day after.

Cold steak salad is a fine way to use that leftover steak—it's filling and nutritious and you don't have to cook. Flatiron steak is a tender cut that goes well in this dish when you're making it from scratch the night you're going to serve it. These thin cuts of beef cook quickly—just a few minutes on each side on the grill to medium rare.

We've learned these days that 4 to 5 ounces of red meat per person is a healthy amount. Therefore a pound and a half of steak will serve four or five people, especially in the form of steak salad.

WINE SUGGESTION: CALIFORNIA PINOT NOIR

2 bunches arugula
3 large ripe tomatoes, cut into ½-inch dice
1 small red onion, thinly sliced
Salt and freshly ground black pepper to
   taste
1½ pounds flatiron steak (or New York or
   top sirloin—see sidebar below)
1½ cups Classic Vinaigrette (page 282)
4 tablespoons shaved Parmigiano-
   Reggiano cheese

1. Wash and dry the arugula to remove any soil, and place it in a large bowl. Add the tomatoes and onion, and toss.

2. Lightly salt and pepper both sides of the steak. Grill the steak, or cook by stovetop method (see sidebar below) and place in the fridge to cool. Slice into ¼-inch-thick strips.

3. Add the vinaigrette to the salad, toss, and divide evenly among 4 plates. Top each plate with 1 tablespoon of cheese shavings. Top the salad plates with equal amounts of the steak and serve immediately.

asian steak salad
MAKES 4 SERVINGS

Mint, arugula, and watercress bring this zesty salad to cool, refreshing life. The added pleasure of Southeast Asian flavors and the sweet, hearty taste of grilled steak make it a stand-out at any table. Cilantro is optional, depending on your fondness for this controversial herb. If you're taking this to a picnic, barbecue, or friend's house for dinner, keep the greens cold and covered, and keep the dressing and steak separate. Combine just before serving.

WINE SUGGESTION: RHONE ROSÉ, SUCH AS TAVEL

2 bunches watercress, destemmed
1 bunch arugula, washed and patted dry
1 ¼ cups fresh mint leaves
½ cup fresh cilantro leaves (optional)
8 red radishes, thinly sliced
1 small red onion, thinly sliced
2 tablespoons lemon zest
½ cup canola or peanut oil
½ cup fresh lime juice
2 tablespoons fish sauce
1 tablespoon soy sauce
1 teaspoon sugar
¼ teaspoon red pepper flakes
Salt and freshly ground black pepper to taste
2 pounds flatiron, New York, or top sirloin, grilled and sliced to ½-inch strips (see sidebar)

1. In a serving bowl, place the watercress, arugula, mint, cilantro, radishes, onions, and lemon zest and toss to combine.

2. In a small bowl, whisk together the oil, lime juice, fish and soy sauces, sugar, red pepper, salt, and black pepper.

3. Add the steak and dressing to the greens and toss well. Serve immediately.

GOOD TO KNOW: COOKING STEAK THE RIGHT WAY

There are two great ways to prepare a delicious, juicy steak: grilling and searing. Both methods have their benefits, though nothing beats grilling outdoors on a warm summer evening.

GRILLING: Grill New York or top sirloin as usual, 5 to 8 minutes on a side, over hot coals or on the gas grill.

SEARING: You can cook the steak inside if you have a stovetop with an exhaust fan to remove the smoke. Preheat the oven to 350°F. In a large skillet over highest heat on the stovetop, add 2 tablespoons of butter. When the butter has melted and is beginning to smoke, add a 1½-inch- to 2-inch-thick New York or top sirloin steak to the melted butter. Partially cover the skillet with a lid so the smoke goes into the exhaust fan. Sear for 3 to 4 minutes, or until dark brown to almost black, then flip the steak, remove from the heat, and place on the top shelf in the oven for 12 minutes. Transfer the steak to a plate and allow to cool, then slice into thin strips against the grain.

FISH AND SEAFOOD SALADS

salade niçoise

MAKES 6 SERVINGS

Palm trees, blue skies, casinos, and the Cannes Film Festival—you're in Nice on the French Riviera. And what to eat on a balmy, sunny Mediterranean day? The famed, eponymous niçoise salad, of course. It's typically made with canned tuna in this country, but you can also make it with an ahi tuna steak that you grill until just done through. The grilled tuna adds that extra deliciousness to the salad. The niçoise is good anytime, but it's especially good when the tomatoes are vine-ripened and bursting with flavor at the height of the summer season. Although it is simply prepared, allow yourself enough time to prepare each of the ingredients. You can serve this simply, as presented here, with all the ingredients in a bowl, or compose a decorative platter, with each component placed separately.

WINE SUGGESTION: WHITE BURGUNDY SUCH AS MEURSAULT

1 clove garlic, peeled and halved
2 cups cooked, peeled, diced, cold red
   potatoes
2 cups cooked, sliced, cold snap beans
⅓ cup Classic Vinaigrette (page 282)
Salt and freshly ground black pepper
   to taste
3 medium, ripe tomatoes, quartered
3 hard-boiled eggs, peeled and quartered

12 pitted niçoise olives
One 6-ounce can of chunk light tuna
   packed in water (or 6 ounces of grilled
   ahi steak)
6 anchovy fillets (or more to taste)
1 tablespoon capers
2 tablespoons finely chopped chervil

   1. Rub a wooden salad bowl with the cut side of the garlic. Add the potatoes, beans, vinaigrette, salt, and black pepper to the bowl, and toss to coat.
   2. Arrange the tomatoes, eggs, olives, tuna, anchovies, and capers on top in a decorative way. Sprinkle the chervil over the salad, and serve immediately.

tuscan-style tuna salad

MAKES 6 SERVINGS

Here's a light, summery salad just bursting with crunch and flavor.

WINE SUGGESTION: VERNACCIA DI SAN GIMIGNANO

Two 6-ounce cans tuna packed in olive oil
½ cup good-quality extra virgin olive oil
½ cup freshly squeezed lemon juice
Salt and freshly ground black pepper
   to taste
2 tablespoons French tarragon, chopped
¼ cup Italian parsley, chopped
1 small head fennel, diced
2 stalks celery, diced
1 cup diced red onion
1 pound mixed summer greens (loose-leaf
   lettuce, radicchio, arugula, etc.)
1 red bell pepper, julienned
½ cup pitted and sliced kalamata olives

1. Chill six salad plates.

2. Drain the oil from the cans of tuna into a large measuring cup. You should have about ¼ cup. Add the olive oil, lemon juice, salt, black pepper, tarragon, and parsley and mix well.

3. Into a bowl, lightly crumble the tuna. Add the fennel, celery, onion, and about ½ cup of the dressing, and toss to coat.

4. In a second bowl, toss the greens with the remaining salad dressing.

5. Divide the greens equally among the chilled plates. Top with the tuna mixture. Garnish the plates with the red pepper and the olives.

summery shrimp salad
MAKES 4 SERVINGS

This dish goes together in no time but tastes wonderful. It's just the dish after you've been doing all that plein air painting, trying to capture that elusive color of the phlox. How did Monet do it?

WINE SUGGESTION: ITALIAN VERMENTINO

1 pound wild-caught shrimp
7 cloves garlic, minced
1 cup pitted, oil-cured black olives,
    coarsely chopped
½ cup extra virgin olive oil
5 ultra-thin slices peeled lemon
1 tablespoon capers, rinsed
Freshly ground black pepper
1 heart of romaine lettuce

1. Peel, devein, and de-tail the shrimp. Steam them until just done, about 2 minutes. Run the shrimp under cold water, then chop coarsely. Place in a medium bowl.

2. Add the garlic, olives, and oil to the shrimp, and toss to coat. Remove the seeds from the lemon slices. Cut each slice in half and then in half again. Add the lemon, the capers, and a few grinds of black pepper to the shrimp mixture and toss well. Refrigerate for at least ½ hour.

3. Cut the root end from the romaine heart and thinly slice the heart crosswise. Divide the sliced lettuce among 4 plates and top each with a quarter of the shrimp mixture, making sure to drizzle some of the liquid from the bottom of the bowl over each salad.

shrimp and fennel salad
MAKES 4 SERVINGS

This feast for a hot night or a social lunch-eon takes no cooking, very little time to prepare, and is nutritious and flavorful without a lot of calories. Have all the ingredients except the salt and pepper refrigerator cold.

WINE SUGGESTION: WELL-CHILLED GRECO DI TUFO

4 large heirloom tomatoes
¾ pound coldwater (aka bay) cooked and
    peeled shrimp
1 cup chopped fennel
Freshly squeezed juice of ½ lemon
⅓ cup low-fat mayonnaise
Salt and freshly ground black pepper to
    taste
1 head butterhead (Bibb) lettuce

1. Slice the top ½ inch off the stem ends of the tomatoes and hollow them out over a bowl to catch the juice, seeds, and the

segment flesh. Set hollowed tomatoes and tops aside. In a bowl, place the shrimp, fennel, lemon juice, mayonnaise, salt, black pepper, and 2 tablespoons of the reserved tomato juice. Mix well.

2. Fill the tomatoes to overflowing with the shrimp and fennel salad. Garnish the stuffed tomatoes with the cut-off top. Place 1 or 2 leaves of the butterhead lettuce on each of four plates and place the tomatoes on the leaves.

✳ VARIATION

Instead of tomatoes, hollow avocado halves, mixing the avocado flesh with the other ingredients, and adding 1 or 2 dashes of hot pepper sauce. Fill the hollow shells with the salad.

heirloom tomatoes and prawns

MAKES 6 SERVINGS

This was in the cold case at my local market one day and everyone at my house loved it. The layers of flavor keep giving and giving, but it's a simple recipe to put together. It's an appetizer, or on a day when eating light is called for, a main course. The summer-fresh heirloom tomatoes bring this dish, created by Mike Talavera, to life. You may substitute raspberry vinegar for the Japanese rice vinegar, if you wish.

WINE SUGGESTION: CALIFORNIA SAUVIGNON BLANC OR EAST COAST SEYVAL BLANC

8 ounces cooked bacon (6 to 8 strips)
2 organic (or well-washed) lemons, zest removed and finely chopped, and juiced
½ cup dry white wine
1 teaspoon salt
2 cups prawns, peeled, deveined, and de-tailed
6 medium to large heirloom tomatoes
1 cup fresh raspberries
1 cup baby arugula, destemmed
⅔ cup Classic Vinaigrette (page 282)

1. Place a large skillet over medium-high heat. Cut the bacon into ¼-inch dice and place it in the pan with ½ cup water. When the water evaporates, turn the heat down to low and stir until the bacon is evenly browned. Place the bacon bits on a paper towel to drain and cool.

2. Place a 2-quart pot over high heat and add the lemon juice, 2 cups water, the wine, and salt. Bring to a boil. Have a strainer and a medium-size bowl of ice water nearby. Place the prawns into the pot and poach for 2 minutes. Remove using a strainer and slotted spoon and quickly immerse them in ice water to stop the cooking. Drain and give them a few minutes to cool further, then chop them into small pieces and set aside.

3. Wash the tomatoes, raspberries, and arugula. Core and cut the tomatoes into ¾-inch dice.

4. In a serving bowl, add the bacon, lemon zest, tomatoes, raspberries, arugula, and prawns. Add the vinaigrette, toss to mix, and serve cold in a bowl or platter.

✳ VEGETARIAN HEIRLOOM TOMATO SALAD

By omitting the prawns and bacon, you can make this dish is suitable for vegetarians and vegans.

lobster salad

MAKES 4 SERVINGS

This is a grand salad for those special summer evenings and special guests you'd like to be sure to please. The salad can be made well ahead of time and served cold. You may substitute lump crabmeat or slices of shrimp, but nothing quite compares to the lobster. The flavor of this salad marries the salty taste of the ocean with the earthiness of the mushrooms, the herbaceous quality of the asparagus with the meatiness of the lobster, and the fruitiness of the wine with the condiments of brandy and chili sauce. There's a lot going on, but it all comes together quite beautifully.

WINE SUGGESTION: POUILLY FUMÉ

One 1 ½-pound live lobster
1 bunch asparagus
1 cup very thinly sliced button mushrooms
⅓ cup mayonnaise
2 tablespoons chili sauce
1 tablespoon brandy
Salt and freshly ground black pepper
    to taste
4 teaspoons unflavored gelatin
⅓ cup dry white wine, such as
    Sauvignon Blanc
2 cups fish stock (or any light stock)
Sweet paprika, for garnish

1. Bring a large pot of salted water to a full boil. Hold lobster head down from just behind the carapace, remove the rubber bands from its claws, and plunge its head into the boiling water. As soon as it relaxes, drop it fully into the boiling water and let it cook for 15 to 20 minutes, depending on whether the lobster weighs a little less or a little more than 1 ½ pounds. Alternatively, after killing the lobster in the boiling water bath, you may discard the water and steam the lobster for 18 to 20 minutes, depending on its size.

2. When the lobster is cooked, free the tail meat in one piece and slice it into 8 rounds. Set aside the rounds and the shell. Crack the claws and joints to get as much meat as you can, and dice it into little pieces, about ⅓-inch. Reserve the meat and the shells.

3. Steam the asparagus spears, then cut 1-inch-long pieces of the tips, and other 1-inch-long pieces from right behind the tips. Set aside the rest of the spears for another use. In a mixing bowl, add the asparagus pieces, the lobster, mushrooms, mayonnaise, chili sauce, brandy, salt, and black pepper. Add the tomalley* and any coral-red roe if you had a female. Toss to mix well. Spoon the mixture into 4 salad bowls. Top each bowl with 2 slices of the tail meat and place the bowls in the fridge to chill.

4. Place the gelatin in the wine until it softens, about 5 minutes. Place a stockpot over medium heat and add all the leftover lobster shells and the light stock. Bring to a boil and cook for 5 minutes more, then remove from the heat. Pass the liquid through a strainer to remove the shells, and stir in the gelatin-wine mixture. Set this aspic aside to cool.

5. When the aspic has cooled, but not set, remove the salad bowls from the fridge, drizzle a scant ½ cup of the aspic over each bowl, enough to glaze the salad, and put the bowls back in the fridge to chill,

allowing the aspic to set. When it's set, sprinkle just a small pinch of sweet paprika over each bowl for color. Cover each bowl with plastic cling wrap and keep refrigerated until ready to serve.

*Tomalley is the greenish liver of the lobster. It intensifies the lobster flavor of the salad here.

crab and cucumber salad

MAKES 6 SERVINGS

If you spend some summer days at the Eastern seashore, send that 13-year-old who does nothing but play video games all day down to the docks with a net and some bait, and have him or her bring home a couple of fat blue crabs. What a fantastic way to begin this scrumptious salad.

Of course, if you aren't near the ocean, you can simply purchase some blue crabs at the local fish market. On the West Coast, you can buy Dungeness crab at the market in the summer, but it will have been frozen. You may substitute king crab legs or lobster meat, if you wish. Chill 6 salad plates along with the cucumbers and crabmeat.

WINE SUGGESTION: CHILLED SANCERRE

1 ½ cups crabmeat (1 Dungeness or 2 blue crabs)
½ cup freshly squeezed lemon juice
1 tablespoon red wine vinegar
1 teaspoon minced scallions
¼ cup extra virgin olive oil
Pinch of salt
Freshly ground black pepper to taste
1 tablespoon chopped chives

1 tablespoon chopped chervil
3 medium cucumbers, well chilled and peeled
Lemon wedges

1. Place the crabmeat in a bowl. Cover and refrigerate until cold.

2. In a small bowl, mix together 2 tablespoons of the lemon juice, the vinegar, scallions, oil, salt, and black pepper. Add the chives and chervil. Add the mixture to the chilled crabmeat and toss well with a fork to coat.

3. Peel the cucumbers. If you have a mandoline, now's the time to use it, for you want to slice the cucumbers as finely as possible. If you're using a knife, try for the thinnest slices you can manage. Take off strips from one side until you reach the seeds. Turn the cucumber over and cut more wide strips, again until you reach the seeded core. Discard the core. Each of the 6 salads will have 6 strips, so you need to 36 strips—12 from each cucumber. Pour the remaining lemon juice into a shallow bowl and dip in each cucumber strip, then lay them out on wax paper.

4. Measure out 6 portions of the crab salad—about ⅓ cup for each serving. Place a cucumber strip on a chilled plate and some crab salad on it. Place another strip on top and fold and push and twist the strips so the folds contain crab salad. Continue until you've used up 6 strips and the ⅓ cup of crab salad. Continue with the remaining ingredients. Serve immediately or return the salads to the fridge to chill further until lunch or dinner is to be served.

 NO COOK   MAKE AHEAD  QUICK & EASY

crab louis

MAKES 4 SERVINGS

Crab Louis is old-fashioned fun and a great summer salad, with the flavor of cold and salty crabmeat, thousand island style dressing, and the rich, buttery texture of avocado.

It's spelled Louis but pronounced "looie." This classic American dish dates from the turn of the 20th century, but precisely when and where it was created, no one can say for sure. Some say Seattle, some say San Francisco. Victor Hirtzler, the chef at the St. Francis Hotel in San Francisco from 1904 to 1926, has a recipe in his 1910 cookbook for "Crab à la Louise" that sounds rather like our modern crab Louis.

On the West Coast, where the dish inarguably originated, the native Dungeness crab is available fresh in northern California only in late fall and winter, although some fresh and frozen crab is shipped down from the Pacific Northwest and British Columbia in the summer. In the summertime, the dish often morphs into what's called either shrimp Louis or seafood Louis, made with little bay shrimp. Bay shrimp are coldwater shrimp, sold cooked to a fine pink color, the heads, shells, and tails removed. They're caught in the Pacific, from Alaska to northern California. Sometimes bay shrimp are mixed with Dungeness crabmeat to make seafood Louis.

On the East Coast, fresh eastern blue crab is available all summer. If you live within driving range of the mid-Atlantic coast's inland bays and estuaries, you can get them live and kicking. Their meat is harder to pick than Dungeness, but with a more elegant, buttery texture and a better flavor. Crab Louis made with blue crab backfin lump crabmeat—sometimes sold ready picked and in containers—is out of this world. Just remember—local is best.

WINE SUGGESTION: CALIFORNIA VIOGNIER

1 small head iceberg lettuce, chopped
12 ounces fresh crabmeat
1 avocado, peeled, pitted, and sliced into long, thin strips
3 small ripe tomatoes, quartered
½ pound asparagus spears, steamed and trimmed to the top 3 inches
1 cup mayonnaise
½ cup ketchup
½ cup sweet pickle relish
½ cup chopped black olives
2 hard-boiled eggs, chopped

1. Spread the chopped lettuce on a large serving platter. Artfully arrange the crabmeat, avocado, tomatoes, and asparagus on the lettuce.

2. In a medium bowl, mix together the mayonnaise, ketchup, relish, olives, and eggs. Add the dressing to the salad in generous dabs and serve immediately.

ceviche

MAKES 4 SERVINGS

Ceviche is a simple dish to prepare, as this recipe attests. Any firm, white fish will work as long as you choose fillets so there are no bones. Among the best are halibut, tilapia, and Chilean sea bass. The ceviche needs at least 3 hours marinating time before serving, so make it at noon for the evening meal or in the morning for later in the day. You may omit the spicy chiles if you wish.

WINE SUGGESTION: SAUVIGNON BLANC

1 pound firm, white fish fillet, cut into
    ½-inch cubes
5 cloves garlic, peeled and chopped
1 teaspoon chopped fresh cilantro
1 hot chile (jalapeño, serrano, or habañero),
    seeded and chopped
Juice of 6 limes, or enough to cover the fish

½ teaspoon salt
¼ teaspoon freshly ground black pepper
1 red onion, thinly sliced, rinsed, and
    drained

1. In a large bowl, combine all the ingredients except the red onion. Toss until well combined.

2. Scatter the red onion rings over the top, cover with plastic wrap, and refrigerate for at least 3 hours. To serve, mix again, incorporating the onion rings, and distribute the ceviche in individual bowls.

COLD SOUPS

Chilled Fresh Tomato Soup

Sweet-and-Tart Gazpacho

Cold Avocado-Tomato Soup

Cold Cucumber Soup

Cold Avocado-Cucumber Soup

Cold Summer Squash Soup

Cold Corn Soup

Vichyssoise

HOT SOUPS

Beef Consommé

Zuppa Toscana

New England Clam Chowder

Steamed Mussels in Broth

Leek and Celery Soup Avgolemono

Minestra di Verdura

Chili con Carne

SOUPS

Yes, it seems incongruous to make soup in summer, but truthfully, there is no "wrong" time to make a delicious bowl of comforting soup. Whether it be hot or chilled, a bowl of soup can calm and comfort in a way that no other food can. Summer is a great time to experiment with flavors, as there are so many vegetables and herbs in season; it's an excellent way to experience summer's wonderful bounty.

The base of many soups is a good, hearty stock or a consommé. While you can easily find store-bought versions, they pale in comparison to a homemade base. Prepare a large batch early in the season—as the cool brisk spring weather still looms and your warm kitchen still feels cozy. Freeze the stock consommé in small batches so you have it handy at a moment's notice all season long.

COLD SOUPS

chilled fresh tomato soup

MAKES 4 TO 6 SERVINGS

The best time to make this soup is when those wonderfully flavorful heirloom tomatoes are at the peak of their season. Tasteless tomatoes yield an ordinary, tasteless soup. This is so simple, yet so good. For creamier texture, add a dollop of crème fraiche in the center to be stirred in. Or top the soup with finely minced cucumber marinated in vinegar. Japanese rice vinegar works best; use red wine vinegar if you prefer.

4 pounds ripe heirloom tomatoes,
    coarsely chopped
¼ cup unflavored (Japanese) rice vinegar
Salt and freshly ground black pepper
    to taste
Extra virgin olive oil

1. Place the tomatoes in a blender or food processor and puree. Pour the puree into a medium mesh strainer and press the pulp through using a flexible spatula to separate it from the seeds and pieces of skin. Season to taste with the vinegar, salt, and black pepper. Refrigerate until very cold. Place 4 to 6 soup bowls in the fridge as well.

2. When ready to serve, ladle it into the cooled bowls and drizzle each with a little extra virgin olive oil. You can halve the recipe to make fewer servings.

sweet-and-tart gazpacho

MAKES 4 TO 6 SERVINGS

The sweetness in this soup comes from watermelon, the sourness from acidic tomatoes and vinegar. It's served cold and is refreshing in so many ways as a summer soup.

3 pounds ripe tomatoes
1 pound seedless watermelon flesh,
    coarsely chopped
1 cup cucumber, diced, peeled, and seeded
2 tablespoons red wine vinegar
1 tablespoon extra virgin olive oil
Salt and freshly ground black pepper
    to taste

1. Place a large stockpot over medium-high heat and bring water to a boil. Add the tomatoes and cook for 1 minute, or until the skins begin to crack. Immediately remove the tomatoes and plunge them into a bowl of ice cold water.

2. Set a strainer over a large bowl. Working over the strainer, peel the tomatoes and halve them across their middles. Allow the juice, skins, and seeds to fall into the strainer. Place the peeled, seeded tomatoes on a cutting board and chop them coarsely. Squeeze the skins and seeds so all the juice is caught in the bowl Add the chopped tomatoes to the juice in the bowl.

3. Place the tomatoes, watermelon, and cucumber in a blender and pulse until coarsely pureed—the result should be a little lumpy rather than homogenously smooth. Pour the soup into a serving bowl and add the vinegar, oil, salt, and black

pepper and stir to mix well. Cover the bowl and refrigerate until cold.

✳ **GAZPACHO WITH A SPICY KICK**
Mince 1 shallot and 1 serrano or jalapeño pepper and mix with chopped cilantro and 1 squeeze of lime juice. Place 1 to 2 spoonfuls of this mixture into the center of the soup after it's placed in individual serving bowls.

cold avocado-tomato soup

MAKES 4 SERVINGS

This thick and flavorful soup benefits from a generous portion of lime juice and coconut water. Chill it for several hours before serving, as the vegetables are at their best here when cold.

3 ripe avocados, sliced in half, pits removed
2 cups fat-free milk
¼ teaspoon kosher salt
Pinch ground cayenne
2 tablespoons freshly squeezed lime juice
1 cup coconut water (not coconut cream)
1 tablespoon freshly squeezed lemon juice (optional)
12 small cherry tomatoes, halved (optional)
1 teaspoon parsley, chopped (optional)

1. Scoop the flesh from 2 avocados and place in a blender with the milk, salt, and cayenne. Puree until mixture is smooth and homogenous. Add the flesh of the third avocado, the lime juice, and the coconut water and puree again.

2. Pour the soup into a serving bowl. Sprinkle the surface with the lemon juice to prevent browning, or press a piece of plastic wrap to the surface. Refrigerate for at least 3 hours and serve cold.

3. For added refreshment, place 4 soup bowls in the freezer about ½ hour before serving. Then mix in the tomatoes, sprinkle with parsley as a garnish, and serve in the chilled bowls.

cold cucumber soup

MAKES 4 TO 6 SERVINGS

On hot, humid days, you want something to cool you down quickly. This soup refreshes and cools the palate, especially if you're eating spicy-hot food. The cucumbers are

Cucumbers are such a light, refreshing summer vegetable, and so incredibly versatile. You can use them in just about anything, from soups to salads, desserts, and of course, pickles.

There are a number of cucumber varieties available, not just the smooth, dark green vegetables often found in America. In addition to those slicers, you will likely come across pickling, hothouse, cornichons, Middle Eastern, and Asian cucumbers, all with their own unique flavor profiles and textures.

Always look for firm cucumbers that have a uniform green color all around. You can store them for up to 1 week in the refrigerator.

not peeled, which gives this soup its pleasant green color. Make it a day ahead so it has plenty of time to get icy cold in the fridge.

2 unpeeled hothouse cucumbers, coarsely
　　chopped
2 cups plain, whole-milk yogurt
1 clove garlic, minced
1 teaspoon white vinegar
¼ teaspoon salt
¼ teaspoon freshly ground black pepper
½ red radish, cut into very thin rounds, then
　　into slivers
4 basil tips, sliced into strips

　1. Place the cucumber and yogurt in a blender and puree until mixture is smooth and homogenous. You may need to do this in several batches.

　2. Pour the soup into a large serving bowl. Add the garlic, vinegar, salt, and black pepper, then cover the bowl and refrigerate overnight.

　3. When ready to serve, ladle the soup into bowls and top each bowl with a pinch of radish slivers and a pinch of basil strips.

cold avocado-cucumber soup

MAKES 4 SERVINGS

As nutritious as it is tasty, this cold soup is the right starter for a meal including a seafood salad, Cobb Salad (page 96), or Asian Steak Salad (page 124).

WINE SUGGESTION: PINOT GRIGIO

2 unpeeled young cucumbers, coarsely
　　chopped
2 ripe avocados, peeled, pitted, and flesh
　　scooped out
1 small shallot, chopped
⅔ cup plain yogurt
⅔ cup milk
1 cup vegetable broth
1 tablespoon lemon juice
1 teaspoon (Japanese) rice vinegar
1 tablespoon mint, chopped
Pinch ground cayenne
Pinch salt

　1. Place all the ingredients a blender and puree for 3 to 4 minutes, or until smooth.

　2. Set a strainer over a bowl and strain the puree through the strainer, working the soup gently through with a spoon so that any hard bits remain in the strainer. Add a few drops of water to thin the soup if it's too thick.

　3. Cover and refrigerate the bowl for 4 hours or overnight. Adjust the seasoning before serving.

cold summer squash soup

MAKES 2 TO 4 SERVINGS

Here's a spicy and easy-to-make soup to help you use some of those delicious yellow crookneck, patty pan, or zucchini squashes found in such abundance now at the markets or in your garden. Served chilled, it's a delightful way to start a summer dinner. Make this on a weekend morning, stash it in the fridge, and it's ready to eat at dinnertime.

1 pound yellow summer squashes, trimmed
    and coarsely chopped
¼ cup extra virgin olive oil
Pinch crushed red pepper
¼ teaspoon cumin seeds, toasted and
    crushed
¼ teaspoon coriander seeds, toasted
    and crushed

Pinch ground turmeric
Salt and freshly ground black pepper
    to taste
2 teaspoons freshly squeezed lime juice

1. Place a large stockpot (with a lid) over high heat. Add the squash, oil, red pepper, cumin, coriander, turmeric, salt, and ¾ cup water. Bring to a boil, uncovered. Reduce the heat to low, cover the pot and simmer about 15 minutes, or until the squash is very tender.

2. Slowly pour the contents of the pot into a blender and puree until smooth.

3. Set a strainer over a bowl and strain the puree through the strainer, working the soup gently through with a spoon so that any hard bits remain in the strainer. Allow the soup to cool, then add the black pepper, lime juice, and more salt, if needed. Refrigerate until cold and serve in individual bowls.

✳ THE SCENT OF A TOMATO

Does anything say "summer" more than the heady, volatile scent of fresh, sun-warmed tomato stems and foliage crushed between the fingers? It's a scent we all know from early childhood, for just about everyone grows tomatoes, even if they don't grow anything else.

And the taste and aroma of a ripe tomato, just pulled off the vine, is a rare treat, for even locally grown tomatoes lose something on their way from farm or truck patch to the market and then home.

Tomatoes do quite well in ordinary potting soil—not too rich or it will force the plants to grow nothing but stems and leaves—in a large pot with good drainage. So that makes tomato culture possible even on a sunny porch. Tie the elongating stems to a drainpipe, or insert a tall stick into the pot and tie the stems to it as they grow.

There are hundreds of varieties of tomatoes available to us. You can peruse them at www.tomatogrowers.com, where you can order seeds online. My favorites: Brandywine, beefsteak, Early Girl, and Giant Paste.

---

cold corn soup

MAKES 4 SERVINGS

When sweet white corn is fresh and the hot days are soggy, think about a bowl of cold corn soup. It's not only refreshing, it is the distilled flavor of high summer.

WINE SUGGESTION: CHARDONNAY

2 tablespoons sweet butter
3 to 4 shallots, thinly sliced
Pinch of curry powder
4 cups fresh, raw white corn kernels
4 cups chicken stock
1 cheesecloth bag containing 4 whole black

peppercorns, 6 whole coriander seeds, and 3 stems of parsley, tied up at the top
1 cup unsweetened coconut milk (or whole milk)
Salt to taste

1. Place an uncovered Dutch oven over medium heat and melt the butter. Add the shallots and cook for 3 to 4 minutes or until soft, but don't let them brown. Add the curry powder and stir, cooking 1 minute more.
2. Add the corn and chicken stock.
3. Add the cheesecloth bag of spices. Reduce the heat to low and simmer, stirring occasionally, for about 20 minutes. Take the pot off the flame, add the coconut milk, cover, and let it rest for 20 minutes.
4. Remove the cheesecloth bag and discard it. Slowly pour the soup into a blender, reserving 1 cup. Puree the soup until smooth.
5. Set a strainer over a bowl and strain the puree through the strainer, working the soup gently through with a spoon so that any hard bits remain in the strainer. Add the reserved 1 cup soup to the bowl for added texture. Mix well and add salt, if needed. Cover the bowl with plastic wrap and refrigerate until cold.

vichyssoise
MAKES 4 TO 6 SERVINGS

Vichyssoise is a potato-and-leek soup that has been enriched with half-and-half. It can be served warm, but it is also delightful served cold on warm days. Like tomatoes and basil, and chocolate and raspberries, potatoes and leeks are a classic combination of flavors whose whole is better than the sum of its parts. Commercial chicken stock generally has plenty of salt, so taste the soup before adding more.
WINE SUGGESTION: CHARDONNAY

3 leeks, white part only
3 tablespoons butter
5 cups chicken stock
4 medium potatoes, peeled and thinly sliced
1 small ham bone (ask your butcher for one)
2/3 cup half-and-half
1/4 teaspoon freshly ground black pepper

1. Remove the outer layer from the leeks and wash them thoroughly. Coarsely chop the white part. Set aside.
2. Place a large stock pot over medium-low heat and add the butter. When it's melted, add the chopped leeks, and cook, stirring occasionally, for 15 to 20 minutes, or until the leeks are tender, but not browned.
3. Add the chicken stock. Then add the sliced potatoes and the ham bone. Increase the heat to high until the soup comes to a boil, then reduce to a simmer and cook for 1 hour.
4. Remove the ham bone. Slowly pour the soup in a blender or food processor, and puree until smooth. Set a strainer over a bowl and strain the puree through the strainer, working the soup gently through with a spoon so that any hard bits remain in the strainer. Add the half-and-half and black pepper and stir to mix. Allow to cool, then refrigerate until cold.

HOT SOUPS

beef consommé

MAKES ABOUT ½ GALLON

Whereas most meat-based broth is murky, consommé is sparkly clear. Served cold, it provides delicious flavors as it refreshes you.

Consommé takes some time to make, but once made it can be frozen or stored in the fridge for up to one week. It serves as the base for all kinds of soups, hot and cold, so make a batch early in the season (before it gets too hot!) and keep it on hand for quick soups anytime.

The secret to making this sophisticated version of bouillon is to make sure all your equipment is squeaky clean and the meat you use is very lean with as little fat as possible.

5 egg whites
1 pound leanest ground beef
2 medium onions, 1 chopped, 1 whole
1 carrot, chopped
1 stalk celery, chopped
1 medium tomato, diced
2½ quarts beef broth
Extra virgin olive oil, for cooking
1 bay leaf
¼ teaspoon dried thyme
¼ teaspoon freshly ground black pepper
4 stems parsley
4 stems chervil
1 whole clove
Salt to taste

1. In a small bowl, lightly whisk the egg whites, just until frothy. In a large stockpot or iron pot, place the egg whites, beef, chopped onion, carrot, celery, and tomato. Add the cold or room temperature beef broth, making sure you remove any fat from the broth, and mix.

2. Cut the whole onion in half. Place a large skillet over medium-high heat and add some oil. Add the onion cut side down and cook until the surface browns, about 5 minutes.

3. Place the onion halves, bay leaf, thyme, black pepper, parsley, chervil, and clove in cheesecloth and tie with string to form a pouch. Put the pouch in the broth. Add salt to taste.

4. Slowly bring the mixture to a simmer, stirring all the while so the egg whites don't congeal and stick to the hot metal at the bottom of the pot. Heat to just barely simmering—that is, steam will rise from the liquid, but it will not boil. Stir until the egg whites and other ingredients rise to the top in a mass. Immediately stop stirring when this happens or you'll be stirring particles that cause haziness back into the broth. Gently break a hole in the center of the mass to allow the broth to come through.

5. Simmer for 1½ hours. Carefully ladle the clear consommé through the hole and pour the consommé through a cheesecloth-lined colander set into a container to catch the liquid.

6. Cool the consommé in the fridge until cold. Degrease if any fat congeals on the top. Store the consommé in a covered container until ready to use.

zuppa toscana

MAKES 4 TO 6 SERVINGS

This white bean soup is traditional in Tuscany and one bite transports you right to the villas and fields there. This recipe makes enough for leftovers that can be easily heated up for a rapid addition to a summer lunch or dinner. Note that the beans must be started the day before you make the soup.

1 pound dried white beans
¼ cup extra virgin olive oil, plus a dash
   for serving
2 medium yellow onions, diced
5 stalks celery, diced
1 clove garlic, minced
3 medium carrots, scrubbed and diced
5 cups chicken or vegetable broth
1 teaspoon dried sage
Salt and freshly ground black pepper
   to taste
Juice of ½ lemon
¼ cup grated Parmesan cheese

1. Place beans in a large bowl with enough water to cover. Soak overnight. The next day, rinse the beans well and drain them in a colander.

2. Place a large stock pot over medium-high heat and add the oil. Add the onions and cook for 5 to 7 minutes, or until the onions are clear. Add the celery, garlic, and carrots and cook for 10 minutes more, stirring frequently.

3. Add the broth, white beans, sage, salt, and black pepper. Bring the soup to a boil. Cover, reduce the heat to low, and simmer for 1 hour.

4. Slowly transfer 3 cups of the soup to a blender or food processor, and puree until smooth and creamy. Add the lemon juice and seasoning to taste. Set aside and repeat with the remaining batch of soup. When ready to serve, add a dash of oil and sprinkle with Parmesan.

THREE SUPER-SIMPLE CONSOMMÉS

CHICKEN CONSOMMÉ
Replace the beef with ground chicken thigh meat.

FISH CONSOMMÉ
Replace the beef with any ground white fish, such as cod.

DUCK CONSOMMÉ
Replace the beef with ground duck leg meat.

new england clam chowder

MAKES 4 TO 6 SERVINGS

"Chowdah" is an essential part of the New England clambake and is best made with tender soft-shelled clams (also called steamers or Ipswich clams). Large cherry-stone clams, called *quahogs* (pronounced co-hog) in New England, are tough fellows best put through a meat grinder to be rendered edible and not suitable for making a chowder. If you live on the West Coast and have access to razor clams, those choice beauties will be an excellent substitute for the steamers.

Note that the chowder is made a day

ahead. Ask your fishmonger to give you enough clams so you can shuck out a pound of clam meat. Clams vary greatly in the shell-to-meat weight ratio by the type and size of the clams, so it's hard to say exactly how many pounds of clams you'll need.

BÉCHAMEL SAUCE

2 tablespoons butter
2 tablespoons all-purpose flour
¾ cup chicken stock
¼ cup heavy cream
Pinch salt
Two grinds of black pepper

BRINE

⅓ cup noniodized salt
1 gallon water

CHOWDER

2 strips bacon
3 tablespoons butter
1 medium onion, chopped
About 1 pound steamer clam meat
2 pounds waxy-flesh potatoes (red skinned), peeled and cut into ½-inch dice
3 cups whole milk
2 cups half-and-half
Salt and freshly ground black pepper to taste

1. Make the béchamel sauce: In a saucepan over medium heat, melt the butter. Remove from the stove and mix in the flour. Put the pan back over medium heat and cook about 1 minute, stirring constantly.

2. Add the stock and stir as you bring it to a boil. Add the cream, salt, and black pepper. Cook, stirring continuously, for 1 to 2 minutes, or until the sauce thickens. Remove from heat and set aside.

3. Make the chowder: In a Dutch oven, fry the bacon over medium heat until crisp. Remove the bacon strips and place them on a dish lined with paper towels to drain. Leave the bacon grease in the pot to add a delicious and necessary smoky pork fat flavor to the chowder.

4. Add the butter to the pot and stir until melted. Add the onion and cook, stirring occasionally, 5 to 6 minutes, or until transparent. Remove from the heat and set the pot aside.

5. Inspect the clams. Make sure all the clams are closed, or, if any are open, they quickly close when tapped. Discard any that won't close.

6. Make the brine: In a large bowl or pot, combine the salt and water and stir until the salt dissolves. Soak the clams in the brine for about 15 minutes to remove any residual dirt or grit. Pour the clams into a colander or strainer and place under a stream of cool water to rinse. Scrub each clam thoroughly with a metal brush.

7. Place a large stockpot with a steamer insert over medium-high heat. Add about 1 to 2 cups water, add the clams, cover, and steam for several minutes, until they open. Discard any that have not opened. Pour the clam broth (the water at the bottom of the steamer) into a bowl, leaving any sand or sediment behind. Reserve.

8. Scoop out the clam meat and divide. Measure 1 cup of whole clam meat and set aside. Place the remaining meat on a flat work surface with sides, such as a baking sheet (to collect residual clam juice) and mince. Pour the clam juice into the bowl of clam broth.

One day, my wife, Susanna, had a yearning for steamed clams. "I know a place where you can get a whole bucket of clams for a dollar," I said, remembering a fish house in Atlantic Highlands, New Jersey, where my brother and sister-in-law would take me on summer evenings when I was in my early teens. The place smelled of salt water and hot fat from the deep fryer, and you could see Sandy Hook from the north windows of the room, built on pilings out over the water. A sign on the wall read, "Bucket of Clams $1."

"When exactly did you get this bucket of clams for a dollar?" she asked, giving me the squint-eye.

I thought. Geez, it must have been. . .decades ago, realizing that the price would be much higher nowadays.

"Uh-huh," she said, and shook her head.

Those were the days. My brother lived in an old Victorian in Rumson, New Jersey, and when I visited, my days were spent enjoying the sand, sun, and surf at nearby Sea Bright. In the early evenings, lightning flickered inside dark gray thunderheads as they rolled southeast across the ocean. Jersey corn and tomatoes were always on hand for dinner. At night, the kids gathered at the park near Hunt Street; the girls were perfumed, and I always wondered if they knew just how great they looked. Reflections of lights in Locust, a small town across the Navesink River from Rumson, danced on the water. Boats, tied up or at anchor, bobbed slowly in the small waves.

Summer: heady, rich with promise, sensuous and sensual—that's how it was before summer jobs stole time and college stole time and work stole time. Though we may never get back those long, empty stretches of summertime, we mustn't forget them. We can still find a few hours or a few days to sit quietly on the beach and watch the lightning flash far out over the sea. But we'll never return to the dollar bucket of clams. That's history.

9. Add the potatoes to the onions in the Dutch oven. Pour the contents of the broth bowl onto the potatoes, again being careful to leave any sand or sediment behind. The liquid should just cover the potatoes. If it's scant, add water. Turn the heat to medium and cook the potatoes for 15 to 20 minutes, or until just tender.

10. Add the clams—whole and minced— milk, half-and-half, béchamel, salt, and black pepper and bring to a boil, stirring so the bottom doesn't scorch. Boil for 1 minute, then turn off the heat and put the lid on the Dutch oven. Allow to cool and refrigerate overnight. The next morning, skim any congealed fat from the surface. Reheat before serving.

steamed mussels in broth

MAKES 2 TO 4 SERVINGS

A big bowl of these mussels is quick to prepare and the results are very delicious. Look for mussels with their "beards" (byssal threads) still attached, which ensures that they'll be alive. (When these byssal threads are removed, the mussels start to die.)

The shellfish need a little preparation. Soak them in fresh water for 20 minutes and they will disgorge sand and salt. Next, using a towel, grasp the fibrous "beard" and pull it out and back toward the pointed, hinge end of the mussel. Don't pull toward the front opening or you'll tear the mussel meat. Then, using a brush, scrub the mussels under running cold water. Provide a bowl for the empty shells and make sure everyone gets some of the broth. Serve Italian bread to sop up the broth.

WINE SUGGESTION: PINOT GRIGIO

3 pounds fresh mussels, soaked, debearded, and scrubbed
½ cup white wine
3 cloves garlic, minced
3 basil leaves, chopped
2 medium tomatoes, chopped

1. Inspect the mussels. Discard any mussels that won't close when tapped.

2. Place a large stock pot (with a lid) over high heat. Add the wine, garlic, basil, and tomatoes and boil uncovered for 2 to 3 minutes, or until the tomatoes soften and begin to disintegrate.

3. Add the mussels and put the lid on the pot. Steam the mussels until they open, about 3 minutes. Discard any that fail to open. Transfer the mussels to a serving bowl. Pour the liquid in the pot over the mussels. Serve immediately.

leek and celery soup avgolemono

MAKES 6 TO 8 SERVINGS

Avgolemono refers to a group of Mediterranean sauces made with eggs and lemon juice, then combined with a warm broth, such as chicken or seafood. It adds a smooth, creamy texture to this laid-back soup.

AVGOLEMONO SAUCE
3 egg yolks
⅓ cup lemon juice, strained
1 cup chicken broth

SOUP
3 pounds fresh leeks
1 pound celery, leaves included

4 tablespoons extra virgin olive oil
8 cups water
Salt and freshly ground black pepper to
   taste
¼ teaspoon ground cumin
2 tablespoons parsley, finely chopped

1. Make the avgolemono: In a small bowl, whisk the egg yolks until frothy. Slowly add the lemon juice, continuing to whisk. Add ⅓ cup of the broth to the bowl, stirring constantly, then add the remaining ⅔ cup broth until all is well incorporated.

2. Place a small saucepan over medium-low heat. Add the egg mixture, and cook (without boiling), stirring constantly, for 3 to 5 minutes, or until the mixture is thick enough to coat the back of a spoon. Set aside.

3. Make the soup: Remove tough green part of the leeks and cut the white part into very thin rounds. Wash and finely chop the celery.

4. Place a large stockpot over medium-high heat and add 2 tablespoons of the oil. Add the leeks and celery and sauté until the leeks are translucent. Add the water, salt, black pepper, and cumin. Cover, bring to a boil, reduce the heat to low, and simmer for 1 hour, or until the vegetables are tender.

5. Using a slotted spoon, transfer the solids from the stockpot to a blender. Add the remaining 2 tablespoons oil to the blender. Puree until smooth, then return to the stockpot and continue cooking over low heat for another 10 minutes.

6. Remove the pot from the heat and let cool for 3 minutes, then slowly beat in the avgolemono. Serve warm with a sprinkle of parsley.

minestra di verdura
MAKES ABOUT 2½ QUARTS

In Italian, this literally means "vegetable soup." Note that this is not a vegetarian soup. The hearty broth base is chicken broth here; you can use vegetable broth or water if you need to, but if you don't, go for the chicken broth for best flavor.

Why not call it minestrone? Because *minestrone* technically means "mix-up" or "confusion" in Italian, but there's nothing confused about this wonderful soup, made in the summertime from the freshest possible vegetables. Some of the finished soup can be frozen for eating later in the year, bringing the flavor of summertime to the winter table.

WINE SUGGESTION: SICILIAN NERO D'AVOLA

2 quarts chicken broth
1 small fennel bulb, coarsely chopped
3 roma or fresh Italian paste tomatoes,
   sliced
2 stalks celery, cut into 1-inch pieces
1 medium onion, coarsely chopped
2 medium carrots, cut into coins
⅓ bunch Italian flat-leaf parsley,
   destemmed and chopped
1 red bell pepper, seeded and chopped
3 small red potatoes, cut into quarters
1 teaspoon dried marjoram
¼ teaspoon ground cayenne
Salt to taste (less is more)

1. Place a large stockpot over medium-high heat and add the chicken broth. Add the prepared vegetables, marjoram, cayenne, and salt and bring to a boil, then reduce heat to low, cover, and simmer for 5 to 7 minutes, or until the harder vegetables—carrot and potato—are tender.

2. Working in batches, slowly transfer the vegetables and broth to a blender and pulse until the vegetables are reduced to small pieces, just a few seconds. Do not puree until smooth.

3. Return the processed soup to the stock pot and bring to a boil. Adjust the seasoning as needed and serve while hot.

*Note: Allow any unused soup to cool, then refrigerate or freeze. Refrigerated soup will last for 3 days, frozen soup for 6 months.

GOOD TO KNOW: HOMEMADE CHICKEN BROTH

The use of your homemade chicken broth makes these soups even more wonderful. When I'm finished with a rotisserie or roasted whole chicken, I throw all the leavings—bones, skin, any leftover meat—into a stockpot with 3 quarts of spring water and add 7 peppercorns, ½ teaspoon salt, a handful of bay leaves, 1 onion cut in half, and 1 or 2 stalks of celery, and simmer it covered on the lowest heat until the liquid level reduces by a third. Then I strain the broth and store it in the refrigerator to cool.

The following day, I skim the congealed fat off the top, then distribute the broth among small freezer-safe containers. I recommend placing a strip of masking tape on top of each container to mark the contents and the date. The resulting stock will thaw into a slightly jelly-like consistency, but it tastes infinitely better than any store-bought version. Make some early in the season and you'll have it at the ready through the summer.

chili con carne
MAKES 4 TO 6 SERVINGS

There are as many recipes for chili con carne as there are folks who cook it—witness the ubiquitous chili cook-offs that pop up around America like thunderheads on a hot summer afternoon. Here's a straight-ahead recipe that you can tweak toward more spice, less spice, more meat, fewer beans, or a shot of Jack Daniels—whatever is your pleasure. It's always a hit as a covered dish at a potluck and as a main course at casual gatherings.

WINE SUGGESTION: SYRAH

Two 15-ounce cans of red kidney beans
1 tablespoon canola oil
1 large onion, chopped
1 red bell pepper, seeded and chopped
1½ pounds ground beef
One 14.5-ounce can crushed Italian plum tomatoes
One 8-ounce can green chile peppers, drained
1 fresh jalapeño pepper, halved, seeded, and minced
One 8-ounce can tomato sauce
1 tablespoon chili powder
1 teaspoon salt
½ teaspoon ground cayenne
Pinch ground cloves
1 bay leaf

1. Pour the beans into a colander or strainer and drain the liquid. Rinse them under cold water and drain again. Set aside.

2. Place a large skillet over medium-high heat and add the oil. Cook the onion, bell pepper, and ground beef, breaking up any clumps of meat, about 5 minutes.

3. Add the remaining ingredients, stirring to mix well. Reduce heat to a simmer, cover, and cook for 90 minutes, adding a few table-spoons of water if the liquid level reduces. Stir occasionally to prevent sticking.

4. Add the beans and continue stirring. Continue cooking until the beans are hot. Remove from heat, adjust the seasoning and serve immediately.

PASTA

Farfalle with Heirloom
  Tomatoes
Summer Squash with Pasta
Pasta Primavera with Sausage
Easy Cheesy Dinner
Homemade Pasta

CHICKEN & POULTRY

Chicken Meatballs
Grilled Chicken Burgers
Grilled Lime Chicken Breasts
Grilled Chicken Thighs
Grilled Chicken Halves
Southern Fried Chicken
Pan-Roasted Garlic Chicken
Cold Roast Whole Chicken
Rotisseried Chicken on
  the Grill
Easy Indian Chicken and
  Rice Dinner
Grilled Turkey Legs

MEAT

Classic Meatballs
Hamburger from Scratch
The Jerk Burger
The Down-Home Burger
California Burger
The Spicy-Spicy
  Cheeseburger
Blue Cheese and Bacon Burger
Grilled Beefsteak
Simplest Grilled Steak
Grilled Pork Tenderloin
Grilled Pork Chops
Pork and Fennel Roast
Pork and Veal Terrine
Bourbon-Hoisin Baby
  Back Ribs
Grilled Butterflied Leg
  of Lamb
Grilled Veal Chops
Greek Lamb Chops

FISH & SEAFOOD

Grilled Fish
Plank-Grilled Fish
Mango Shrimp
Shrimp with Garlic and
  White Wine
Lemon-Garlic-Butter Scallops
Scallops in a Saffron
  Cream Sauce
Crab Delights
Grilled Oysters
Grilled Oysters and Clams
Baked Salmon with Chiles
Saturday Night Fish Fry

VEGETARIAN

Mushroom Burgers
Summer Vegetable Casserole

SURF & TURF: MAIN DISHES

Summer means easy-to-make dishes that are fun to eat. Think sticky fingers. Think straight from the refrigerator to the table. Think about which light foods are meant to be consumed late, when the sky still glows slightly in the west but the stars are beginning to glitter above.

Many of these dishes will inspire you to plan ahead and keep extras on hand for those hot nights when you don't want to cook. Not every summer night is hot and humid, although it sometimes seems that way in the dog days of August. So some cooked dishes are included here, but they are not elaborate ones that take a lot of preparation. It's summertime, and the livin' is supposed to be easy.

PASTA

farfalle with heirloom tomatoes

MAKES 6 TO 8 SERVINGS

If you can't find or don't want to use heir-looms, use the freshest, ripest tomatoes available.

WINE SUGGESTION: ZINFANDEL

3 large heirloom tomatoes
3 cloves garlic, minced
¼ cup destemmed and chopped fresh Italian parsley
¼ cup destemmed and chopped fresh basil
1 tablespoon destemmed and chopped fresh oregano
1 tablespoon destemmed and chopped fresh thyme
Fleur de sel or kosher salt and freshly ground black pepper to taste
½ teaspoon crushed red pepper
1 pound *farfalle* (bowtie) pasta
½ cup extra virgin olive oil

   1. Core and chop the tomatoes to about ½-inch dice and place in a medium bowl. Add the garlic, parsley, basil, oregano, thyme, salt, black pepper, and crushed red pepper to the bowl.
   2. Place a stockpot over high heat and add water and a little salt. Bring to a boil. Add the pasta and cook according to the instructions on the package.
   3. Drain the pasta in a colander and transfer to a large bowl or back into the pot. Add the oil and stir to mix. Add the tomato mixture and stir to mix well.

summer squash with pasta

MAKES 2 TO 4 SERVINGS

This dish is quick, easy, and packed with energy-replenishing fuel—just the thing after a day of swimming (and lying out by the pool).

WINE SUGGESTION: CALIFORNIA MERLOT

1 pound summer squash, washed, cut into ⅓-inch dice, and steamed
½ cup olive oil, plus a dash for cooking the pasta
8 cloves garlic, minced
Salt
12 ounces linguini
1 cup grated Parmesan cheese
Crushed red pepper flakes

   1. Run a bowl under hot water to heat. Transfer the steamed squash to the warm bowl. Cover with a plate, and set it aside.
   2. Set a small skillet over medium-low heat and add the oil. When it's hot (not smoking), add the garlic. Sauté until golden brown, 5 to 7 minutes.
   3. Meanwhile, place a stockpot over high heat and add water, some salt, and a dash of oil. Bring to a boil.
   4. Add the pasta and cook according to the instructions on the package. Fill a serving bowl with hot water. When the pasta is cooked, pour out the water from the serving bowl. Drain the pasta in a colander and transfer to the heated serving bowl. Add the squash and the heated garlic oil to the serving bowl. Toss to mix and serve immediately with the Parmesan and red pepper flakes on the side.

SUMMER MEMORY: giant zucchini

One of the first garden vegetable crops I ever grew was a zucchini plant I bought at a garden center. I didn't have a garden, but I did have a five-gallon bucket with drainage holes in the bottom that I filled with store-bought compost, in which I planted the little squash seedling.

I kept the bucket watered and the zucchini plant quickly grew until one day I noticed that it was flowering. The rich yellow flowers were soon followed by little zucchini which also quickly grew into giant zucchini. Had I known what I was doing, I would have harvested the zucchini when they were about five to six inches long. I didn't know two very important things about summer squash in those days. First, in order for it to keep producing squash, the zucchini must be harvested almost daily, before they grow large enough to ripen their seeds. And second, that the fruits—as the squashes are called in garden-speak—would keep enlarging, seemingly forever.

What I ended up with was six huge zucchini about two feet long and 10 inches in diameter—and an exhausted plant that quit producing squashes. Of course, I proudly brought these giants into the office to give away, but nobody knew what to do with them and nobody wanted them. They eventually went into the garbage.

We learn more from our failures than our successes, and now I plant one green zucchini, one yellow crookneck, and one golden patty pan squash in the garden each year. By visiting the plants daily and harvesting the fruits when they are small and tender, I have more than enough summer squash for our table all summer long.

pasta primavera with sausage

MAKES 3 TO 4 SERVINGS

When you don't have much time, try this quick dinner.

WINE SUGGESTION: ZINFANDEL

4 tablespoons extra virgin olive oil, plus a dash for cooking the pasta
4 Italian sausages
2 medium tomatoes, chopped
6 cloves garlic, chopped
6 basil leaves, chopped
¼ cup red wine
1 pound angel hair pasta
½ pound grated Parmesan
Crushed red pepper flakes

1. Place a stockpot over high heat and add water, some salt, and a dash of oil. Bring to a boil.

2. While the water is heating, place a skillet over medium heat and add the oil. Remove the sausage casings, add the contents to the skillet, and stir for 5 to 7 minutes or until browned. Transfer to a small bowl and set aside.

3. Return the skillet to the heat and add the tomatoes, garlic, basil, and wine. Cook for 5 to 7 minutes, or until the tomatoes break down and most of the liquid has evaporated. Return the sausage to the skillet and mix to heat through. Reduce the heat to a simmer.

4. Add the pasta to the boiling water in the stockpot and cook according to the instructions on the package. Fill a serving bowl with hot water. When the pasta is cooked, pour out the water from the serving bowl. Drain the pasta in a colander and transfer to the heated serving bowl. Add the sausage-tomato mixture to the pasta and toss to mix. Serve with Parmesan and crushed red pepper flakes on the side.

✳ VARIATIONS
Use 1 pound hamburger instead of sausage. Add 1 diced onion to the skillet and cook until clear before adding the tomatoes, garlic, basil, and wine.

easy cheesy dinner

MAKES 6 TO 8 SERVINGS

Okay, this isn't haute cuisine, but it's quick, easy, and guaranteed to please the kids. It's just the dinner for a hot summer night when you're running late.

One 8-ounce package egg noodles
1½ pounds ground beef
1 medium onion, chopped
One 8-ounce can tomato sauce
2 tablespoons tomato paste
One 11-ounce can corn kernels, drained
½ teaspoon kosher salt
¼ teaspoon freshly ground black pepper
1 cup shredded Parmesan cheese

1. Place a stockpot over high heat and add water and some salt. Bring to a boil. Add the pasta and cook according to the instructions on the package.

2. While the water is heating, place a skillet over medium heat, add the beef and onions, and cook for 5 to 7 minutes, or until the beef is no longer pink. Add the tomato sauce, tomato paste, and ½ cup water.

Bring to a boil, reduce the heat, cover, and cook for 10 minutes on low heat.

3. Drain the noodles and add them to the skillet. Stir in the corn, salt, black pepper, and cheese. Continue stirring until the cheese is completely melted.

homemade pasta
MAKES ABOUT 1½ POUNDS OF PASTA

We often have more free time in the summer, so it's a great time to learn or get back to doing culinary tasks that reap rich rewards. You don't need a pasta machine to make lovely homemade pasta. A rolling pin and a sharp knife will do. You'll be surprised how easily the noodles come together, and what a difference using your own ingredients will make. The best topping for the pasta? My favorite is Raw Tomato Sauce (page 292).

3 cups all-purpose flour
1 teaspoon kosher salt, plus more for cooking
3 large eggs
4 tablespoons heavy cream
1 tablespoon extra virgin olive oil

1. In a large bowl, add the flour and salt and mix well. Make a well in the center of the flour mixture and break the eggs into it. Sprinkle the flour and eggs with the cream. Break the yolks and begin working the flour into the eggs, turning the bowl as you work, until a ball of dough forms.

2. Transfer the dough to a floured board and knead it for 15 minutes to work up the gluten by pushing the dough with the heels of your hands, folding it over on itself, turning it 90 degrees and repeating. The dough will become smooth, firm, and elastic.

3. Coat a small bowl with the oil and add the dough. Cover with a plate and refrigerate it for 30 minutes.

4. Cut the dough into 2 pieces and set one back into the bowl. Roll out the first piece of dough on a floured surface. Beginning in the middle, roll outwards in all directions. Flip the dough, add more flour and continue to roll, until very thin.

5. To cut the strips, roll up the well-floured dough into a tube and cut thin rounds, then shake them out. You should have long strands. Put 2 chairs back to back and stretch out a fine dish towel over the tops of the backs. Lay the strips over the towel to air dry. Cut into wide strips for lasagna or pappardelle, into fettucini or linguini-sized strips about ¼ inch wide, or into thin, long noodles. Repeat process with the second piece of dough. Let the second batch air dry for at least 15 minutes.

6. Place a stockpot over medium heat and add water and some salt. Bring to a boil. Add the pasta and cook for 3 to 5 minutes. Don't overcook, as homemade pasta has a tendency to get flabby when overcooked. Drain the pasta in a colander and transfer to a large bowl or back into the pot. Serve immediately with your favorite pasta sauce or some fresh Pesto (page 293).

CHICKEN & POULTRY

chicken meatballs

MAKES 4 SERVINGS

These meatballs are light and delicious—
just right for a summer pasta supper or
stuffed inside toasted ciabatta bread for a
tasty meatball sandwich.

WINE SUGGESTION: RIOJA

MEATBALLS
1 pound ground chicken thighs
½ cup plain breadcrumbs, plus 2 cups
   for rolling
¼ cup finely chopped parsley
6 ounces mushrooms, finely chopped
1 egg
7 cloves garlic, finely chopped
1 teaspoon thyme
½ teaspoon cayenne
½ cup shredded Parmesan cheese
Salt and freshly ground black pepper to taste
¼ cup olive oil

SAUCE
4 tablespoons olive oil
1 medium onion, finely diced
1½ quarts Heirloom Tomato Sauce
   (page 293)

1. Make the meatballs: In a large bowl,
add all the meatball ingredients except the
2 cups breadcrumbs. Using wet hands,
knead together until well mixed, then mold
the meatballs. Place the 2 cups breadcrumbs in a bowl. Roll the meatballs in the
breadcrumbs to coat.

2. Place a skillet over medium heat and

add 4 tablespoons of the oil. Working in
batches, fry the meatballs, about 3 minutes
on each side, until evenly browned. Remove
the meatballs from the skillet and let drain
on paper towels. Repeat with remaining
batches.

3. Make the sauce: Preheat the oven to
350°F. Place a Dutch oven over medium
heat and heat 2 tablespoons of the oil.
Add the onions and sauté until translucent, about 5 minutes. Remove from heat
and spoon the onions into a bowl. Set
aside.

4. Add the meatballs to the Dutch oven
and cover with the tomato sauce. Cover the
Dutch oven and bake 1 hour. Add the
onions back into the pot and mix well.
Serve immediately.

grilled chicken burgers

MAKES 2 SERVINGS

Markets sell ground chicken breast meat
these days, but avoid it. It makes a dry and
tasteless burger. Ground chicken thigh
meat makes superior burgers with less fat
than beef. The secret with ground chicken
thigh meat is to handle it as little as possible, and to cook it slowly. Adding a little
olive oil to the meat helps it cook evenly
and retain juiciness.

WINE SUGGESTION: AUSTRALIAN SHIRAZ

Olive oil for the grill
1 pound ground chicken thighs
3 teaspoons extra virgin olive oil
Salt and freshly ground black pepper
   to taste
2 hamburger buns

1. Preheat the grill on high for 15 minutes. Scrub the grates with a wire brush, and wipe them down with oil. Reduce the heat to medium. Lay a sheet of wax paper on the cutting board. Cut the ground meat in half and gently form patties. Swirl 1 teaspoon oil over each patty. With a fork, stab each patty 4 or 5 times over its surface to help the oil seep into the meat, then pat the sides to firm up the patties.

2. Salt and pepper both sides of the patties and place them on the grill, oiled side up. Cover with the grill lid and cook for 5 to 7 minutes, then flip and cook for 5 to 7 minutes more. Depending on the exact heat of your grill, they may need a little more time. When done they will be firm and springy. Don't undercook them.

3. Transfer to a plate and set aside. Lightly toast the hamburger buns face down on the grill. The burgers will be juicier if you wait for 5 minutes before placing them on the buns and serving them.

✱ VARIATION

Substitute ground turkey for ground chicken. The flavor is stronger and the texture a little firmer, but the resulting burger, like chicken, is a low-fat, high-protein replacement for beef.

GOOD TO KNOW: MAKING CHICKEN BURGERS

To reduce your consumption of red meat, use ground chicken thigh meat for your burgers. It's wonderfully tasty. Thigh meat is dark meat, and like the leg, aids the chicken in walking and moving itself around in a relaxed manner. White meat—the breast meat—on the other hand, is for explosive movement, such as when the chicken is startled and suddenly bursts into flight.

Dark meat gets its energy from fat stored in the tissues, while white meat gets its energy from glycogen, which is why leg and thigh meat is juicier than white meat. The fat in the dark meat bastes the muscle tissue as it's being cooked, while the glycogen in white meat is soon depleted by cooking, allowing white meat to overcook easily and become dry and chewy.

Because of the type of muscle tissue in dark meat and its content of fat and amino acids, it has more flavor than white meat, and so makes superior burgers. When forming it into patties for the grill, you'll notice that it's very sticky and hard to work with. Wash your hands thoroughly before handling the thigh meat, but don't dry them. There'll be very little sticking with wet hands. Be sure to wash your hands after handling the raw chicken, too. To avoid placing raw chicken meat on the cutting board, I lay down a length of wax paper and work on that. The chicken meat also won't stick to the wax paper, or if it sticks slightly, you can always lift one end of the wax paper and flip the patty into the palm of your other hand.

If cooking in a stove-top skillet, cook the burger slowly on low heat, 8 to 10 minutes on a side. It's done when it has lost its red color all the way through.

grilled lime chicken breasts

MAKES 4 SERVINGS

Quick, easy, and oh-so-tasty—that's this artful combination of chicken and lime juice. On the way home from work, buy the chicken breasts and a few limes, and whip up some freshly made Guacamole (page 41) or Pico de Gallo (page 42) to go with it.

WINE SUGGESTION: CHARDONNAY

1 tablespoon extra virgin olive oil, plus more
    for the grill
4 boneless, skinless chicken breasts
Juice of 3 limes
½ teaspoon salt

1. Preheat the grill on high for 15 minutes. Scrub the grates with a wire brush, and wipe them down with oil. Reduce the heat to medium. Place the chicken breasts in a shallow pan. Pour the lime juice over them. Add the salt and 1 tablespoon oil. Flip the breasts to coat well.

2. Place the chicken breasts on the grill and cook for 8 to 10 minutes, then flip and cook for 8 minutes more. Check for doneness (no pink in the thickest part of the breast).

3. Remove from heat, slice into strips and serve with guacamole on the side.

grilled chicken thighs

MAKES 4 SERVINGS

Chicken connoisseurs know that the thigh meat has a better texture and better flavor than breast meat. Many markets sell boneless, skinless thighs, or thigh and leg meat together as one piece. Thighs tend to have pockets of fat that are easily trimmed off, but you don't have to be obsessive about it, as some fat helps the thighs retain their juiciness. The finished thighs make great sandwiches for lunch or main meat course for dinner.

WINE SUGGESTION: RIOJA

¼ cup olive oil, plus more for the grill
2 to 3 pounds boneless, skinless thighs
    (about 8 large, 10 medium, or 12 small
    thighs)

1. Preheat the grill on high for 15 minutes. Scrub the grates with a wire brush, and wipe them down with oil. Reduce the heat to medium high.

2. Place the thighs in a shallow bowl with ¼ cup oil and toss to coat.

3. If using a charcoal kettle, maintain a hot fire and remove the cover. Place the thighs on the grill and cook for 5 to 6 minutes on each side for large thighs, or for 3 to 4 minutes for smaller ones. If using a gas grill, cook the chicken with the hood closed and the heat set at medium high.

✱ VARIATIONS
Rub the thighs with rubs, such as Jamaican jerk, Asian five-spice, Indian spices, or other rubs. Or cook the thighs, interior side down, and brush the tops with barbecue sauce. Turn once, but reduce heat so the sauce, which contains sugar, doesn't burn, and cook until done through. Or mix spices such as coriander, ginger, garlic, cayenne, and cumin with olive oil and marinate the chicken, covered in the fridge, for 2 to 12 hours before cooking.

Summer cooking is all about the wonderful flavors that we can't get any other time of year. And the major tool we use to achieve those flavors is the backyard grill. Successful grilling is a craft to be learned, and in the hands of those who have mastered the craft, can be an art. That comes from within the person preparing the food. The emergence of creativity from a solid foundation in the craft is one of the true joys of cooking. And one of the main benefits of summer grilling is that you keep all that heat out of the house.

It's important to understand how food interacts with the fire and the heat (two different, though related, things) and with the grilling unit itself. These joys easily cross gender lines. Guys who don't go near the stove in the house suddenly become master chefs when the grilling season starts. Once, when visiting friends, I was standing by the barbecue grill and thought I'd be helpful by turning the hamburgers. I'd just turned the first one when the owner of the property came running up, snatched the spatula out of my hand, and growled, "You never touch a man's grill!"

Whether gas grill or charcoal kettle, there are two chief processes that cook the food—the direct heat that food gets when it's placed above the fire, and indirect heat that bakes or roasts food that's not directly over the fire. For indirect cooking on a gas grill, you simply turn on the burner or burners on one side of the unit, place the food to be cooked on the other side, and close the hood. On a charcoal kettle, you build or rake the fire to one side, place the food over the empty side, and put on the top. There is a third way that food cooks on a grill, and that is from the heat of the hot metal grillwork, but the hot metal is there whether you are cooking over direct heat or indirect heat, whether the grill is gas or charcoal, and whether the hood or lid is up or down. Its main function is to make those satisfying grill marks on the food. To get good-looking grill marks, turn the meat or vegetables just once.

When you're cooking over direct heat, be aware that gas and charcoal grills are quite different in how they work. Gas grills provide an even, steady heat and temperature that only changes if you raise or lower the flame. A graph of the charcoal grill's temperature over time would show a curve that starts cool, rises as the charcoal ignites, reaches a peak, and slowly descends as the charcoal burns to ash. With some practice, it's not difficult to keep the charcoal at a fairly even temperature by adding a few chunks or briquettes now and then.

Then, there's the question of whether to grill with the lid off or on. For obvious reasons, you can't cook with indirect heat while the lid is off (or up) because the heat simply escapes into the air. With indirect cooking, the heat under the lid does the cooking, which requires the top to be on and the air holes set wide open for maximum heat, or partially open for slower heat. Closing the air holes completely on a charcoal grill results in the fire going out. Gas grills usually have openings in the bottom or back so plenty of air can mix with the propane gas. With all the burners on and set to high, the temperature under the hood can reach 500°F or more.

When I want to cook something slow and easy on my gas grill, I place the food directly over the burners set to low and leave the top up. Slow and easy cooking on a charcoal kettle means cooking with the lid on because you have better control over air flow to the charcoal—and thus the heat level—and over the rate at which the charcoal burns itself out. Keeping the lid on the charcoal grill also reduces flare-ups from burning fat because there is only so much air allowed in the unit. Indirect cooking also minimizes fat flare-ups. (Having a spray bottle filled with water can come in handy, too.)

Much of the wonderful smoky flavor of grilled food comes not from the charcoal and certainly not from burning propane, but from the smoke generated by the fat that drips onto hot metal bars or fake stone in the gas grill or onto burning charcoal in the kettle and turns into puffs of smoke. To enhance the smoky flavor, you can use wet hickory wood chips tossed onto the charcoal during the cooking process. Of all woods, hickory makes the most deliciously aromatic smoke. Most gas grills come with a metal basket to hold hickory chips, or you can place chips in an iron skillet over an otherwise unused burner set to high.

Direct heat can be applied to food on either a gas or charcoal grill with the hood or lid up or down. Indirect cooking requires the hood or lid to be down so the hot air and smoke recirculate. Think of direct heat as broiling from the bottom up and indirect cooking as similar to a convection oven.

Most people chiefly cook meat on their grills, and there are some rules of thumb that will ensure success. When using a charcoal kettle, use direct heat on meat that will cook in 20 minutes or less—thin steaks and chops, hamburgers, sausages and hot dogs, vegetables, and so on. Use indirect heat when cooking roasts, chicken halves, and large cuts of meat. If you want to sear the meat quickly and finish it by roasting, start it over direct heat and finish it by indirect heat. This works well with steaks 2 inches or thicker, which take about 3 to 5 minutes on a side over the coals, and then 15 minutes in indirect heat for medium rare.

If using a gas grill, the same rules apply except that long, slow cooking can be achieved by setting the burners to low and cooking the meat with the hood up. If your gas grill has a rotisserie feature, here's what I do. I position a whole chicken on the skewer so that it will be in the middle of the grill. I place a drip pan under the chicken. My grill has four burners, so I turn on two of them, one on the far left and one on the far right, close the hood, and turn on the motor. The chicken cooks with indirect heat and comes off the grill juicy and succulent. If using a gas grill with two burners, turn them both on to low or medium. The presence of the drip pan will prevent direct heat from roasting the chicken.

I find that the secret to grilling success is patience. Haste makes for burnt poultry or meat. Wait for the charcoal to be completely covered with ash and for the heat to subside somewhat, then maintain a gentle, even heat by occasionally adding more fuel. On the gas grill, the food tastes better and is cooked better at lower temperatures and gentler heat. The exception to this rule is when cooking a thick steak and you want a very hot fire to sear the meat before finishing it with indirect heat at a lower temperature.

Regarding the tendency of food to stick to the grill: placing food on a cold, greasy grate and turning on the heat guarantees the food will weld itself to the metal. To prevent sticking on a charcoal kettle, get the fire very hot and scrub the hot grates with a wire brush, then use olive oil on both sides of the food. With a gas grill, turn all burners to high and close the hood. Wait 15 to 20 minutes, then scrub the hot grates with a wire brush. Oil the food, place it on the grill, and reduce the heat to whatever level you want.

grilled chicken halves

MAKES 4 SERVINGS

Grilling time depends on the size of the chicken, but birds called broilers or fryers generally weigh from 2 ½ to 3 ½ pounds. Have your butcher split whole fresh chickens in half and remove the backbones. A serving once was a half chicken per person, but nowadays a quarter chicken is more appropriate. Cutting a barbecued chicken between the breast and thigh yields a dark meat quarter of thigh and leg and a white meat quarter of breast and wing. Poultry shears make short work of this task, but it's also easily done with a sharp, heavy knife.

For safety's sake, never let a cooked chicken touch surfaces where raw chicken has been. For instance, when transporting raw chicken halves on a platter to the grill, thoroughly wash the platter in soap and hot water and dry before using it to transport the cooked chicken to the table.

WINE SUGGESTION: CHARDONNAY

1 young chicken, split in half
Olive oil
Kosher salt

1. Rinse and pat the chicken dry with paper towels.

2. Preheat the gas grill on high for 15 minutes. Scrub the grates with a wire brush and wipe them down with oil. Reduce the heat to medium. If using a charcoal grill, wait until the briquettes have turned white with ash, then scrub the grates with a wire brush and wipe them down with oil before adding meat or vegetables. Get a strong fire going in the charcoal kettle and wait until heat is medium before putting chicken on the grill.

3. Brush the chicken on both sides with oil. Sprinkle both sides with a little salt. Place the chicken bone side down on the gas grill, over the fire. Cover with the grill lid and cook for 15 minutes, then flip and cook for 15 minutes more. Flip again and cook for 15 more minutes. Flip once more and cook 10 to 15 minutes more, depending on doneness. Check to see if the leg joint moves freely. If it does, the chicken is done. Prick the thigh and notice the color of any juice that runs out. If it's clear or yellowish, that's a sign of doneness. If it's at all pink, the chicken needs more time on the fire. On the charcoal grill, grill uncovered with bone side down for 20 minutes. Then turn three or four times over the next 40 minutes, checking for doneness after the last turn.

❋ VARIATION
Brush the chicken with barbecue sauce (to make your own, see Homemade Barbecue Sauce, page 294) at every turn and cook on medium-low heat for 1 ½ hours, turning every 15 to 20 minutes, as the sugar in the sauce will burn if cooked at too high a heat.

southern fried chicken

MAKES 4 SERVINGS

Real Southern fried chicken has to be at the top of anyone's list for summer picnics, lunches, and dinners. When the chicken is done right, it has a salty, toothsome mixture of crunch and succulent meat that's making me hungry just writing about it. There are, of course, hundreds of variations of "real" Southern fried chicken. My mom, a Kentucky lady, gave me this one and it does just fine by me.

You can leave the skin on, but it is rich in cholesterol, and so I remove it. The bacon drippings were her secret ingredient—the one she'd leave out when giving people her recipe. But I saw her cook this recipe enough times to know better. It was the secret ingredient in her hash browns, too.

WINE SUGGESTION: GERMAN MOSEL

12 pieces of broiler or fryer chickens (4 each of breasts, thighs, and legs, bone-in and skinless)
6 cups all-purpose flour
3 tablespoons baking powder
3 teaspoons freshly ground black pepper
1 teaspoon kosher salt
3 eggs
½ cup water
Peanut oil for frying
2 tablespoons bacon drippings

1. Allow the chicken pieces to reach room temperature.

2. Place 2 cups of the flour in an airtight plastic bag and add the chicken pieces in two 6-piece batches, twisting the bag shut and shaking the pieces in the flour bag. Shake off any excess flour as you remove them from the bag. The pieces should have just a fine coating of flour all over them.

3. In a bowl, combine the remaining 4 cups flour, the baking powder, black pepper, and salt, and mix well. In a second bowl, beat the eggs and water until well combined.

4. Place a deep-sided skillet over medium heat and add the peanut oil and bacon drippings so that together, the oils are 1 inch deep. Gently heat the oil to about 325°F. The oil will be ready when a tiny drop of water sizzles and evaporates from its surface within a few seconds. Don't let the oil smoke.

5. Dip the chicken in the egg mixture, then dredge in the flour mixture, patting them gently so the dry mix adheres to the chicken. Alternatively, place the dry ingredients in an airtight plastic bag and shake a few pieces of egg-coated chicken at a time until they are all coated.

6. Transfer the chicken to the skillet and fry for 8 to 10 minutes on one side. turning once and cooking for another 6 to 8 minutes on the other side, or until the coating is golden brown and juices run clear when a thigh is pricked with a knife tip. Serve immediately or refrigerate for picnic baskets, lunch pails, and cold chicken dinners.

✳ VARIATIONS

There are many, but the most popular probably include substituting buttermilk for the water, or adding 2 tablespoons garlic salt and/or 2 teaspoons Bell's poultry seasoning and/or 1 tablespoon paprika to the dry coating ingredients.

*Be very careful with hot oil. If you have small children, keep them out of the kitchen during the cooking period.

The Internet really has changed everything.

Once upon a time, if you wanted real Milwaukee bratwurst and Polish sausage, you had to go to Milwaukee with a cooler and some bags of ice and bring them home with you.

But today, you can order those brats and sausages online and they'll be overnighted to your home, still frozen in a cold pack. Your friends and family will discover why frankfurters, as good and summery as they are, just aren't in the same league with Thuringer-style grilled brats or real Polish sausage. Check out the Bavarian Sausage website at the end of this text.

And it's not just Milwaukee's regional specialties that are available. Want something out of the ordinary and wholly delicious for the barbecue? How about elk steaks, raised in downstate Illinois? See the website for Pea Ridge Elk products below.

The best red meats I've ever tasted were reindeer from Alaska and antelope from west Texas and New Mexico. Both are farm raised, but that doesn't mean confined to a pen, unless you understand that the pens enclose thousands of acres where the animals run free and browse on their natural foods until they're slaughtered, so you are getting the true taste of the wild. Both meats are low fat, high protein, and full of nutrients. Best of all, they are wonderfully delicious. Both are available through Exotic Meat Sales, see below. Note: they are not cheap, but for a special occasion for a summer barbecue, they will be unsurpassed.

Spice up your summer evening with real Cajun andouille sausage on the grill. You can be guaranteed you're getting true Louisiana andouille—woo-EE! that's très épicé!—when you order Jacob's World Famous Andouille from the Cajun Sausage Co. in LaPlace, Louisiana. See the website below.

Down East along the New England coast, summer means lobsters and steamer clams (see page 193). You can have a clambake right in your own backyard by ordering both live lobsters and steamers from Simply Lobsters, below.

Get creative with Google and you'll find that the entire world of regional American (and other countries, too) summer foods is now at hand.

Real Milwaukee bratwurst: www.bavariansausage.com

Elk meat: www.pearidgeelk.com

Reindeer and antelope meat: www.exoticmeatsales.com

Cajun andouille: www.cajunsausage.com

Live lobsters and steamer clams: www.simplylobsters.com

pan-roasted garlic chicken

MAKES 4 SERVINGS

Here's an easy way to make a wonderfully delicious chicken main course without using the oven.

WINE SUGGESTION: SOAVE

2 tablespoons extra virgin olive oil
1 tablespoon butter
One 2 ½ pound chicken, cut into 2 legs,
    2 thighs, and 2 breasts
Two 7-inch sprigs fresh rosemary (or 4
    sprigs fresh thyme)
3 cloves garlic, peeled
Salt and freshly ground black pepper
    to taste
½ cup dry white wine

1. In a large skillet over medium heat, add the olive oil and butter. When the butter stops foaming, place the 6 pieces of chicken skin side down and brown on both sides, about 3 to 4 minutes on a side, turning them skin side down at the end.

2. Arrange the rosemary among the pieces and add the garlic cloves. Add salt, black pepper, and wine. Let the wine sizzle in the skillet for 15 to 20 seconds to cook off the alcohol, then reduce the heat to a simmer and cover the skillet, leaving the lid slightly ajar.

3. Cook for 1 hour, checking close to the end of cook time that there is still liquid in the skillet. Add a little water, if necessary. The chicken is done when the thigh meat is tender and the meat comes easily away from the bone when prodded with a fork. Transfer to a serving dish.

4. Discard the herb sprigs. Tilt the skillet and spoon off any excess oil, leaving a little

in the skillet. Mash the garlic cloves into the liquid and increase the heat to medium. Scrape up the browned bits and let the liquid boil until there's just a small amount left. Pour the contents of the skillet over the chicken and serve at once. You can garnish the serving dish with a sprig or two of fresh herbs if you wish.

MARCY'S GARLIC CHICKEN

Here's a recipe from Marcy Smothers that impressed Susanna and me when she quietly whipped these together one roister-ous summer night. You can make these chicken thighs in the oven, in a Dutch oven, or on a hot outdoor covered grill.

8 cloves garlic, minced
½ cup olive oil
Salt and freshly ground black pepper
    to taste
6 small chicken thighs, bone in and skin on
6 rosemary sprigs
2 lemons, sliced ⅓-inch thick

1. Preheat the oven to 400°F. In a small bowl, pound together the garlic, oil, salt, and black pepper to create a paste-like mixture. Slip the mixture under the skin of the thighs and rub what's left on your hands over the skin.

2. Lay the lemon slices in the bottom of a cooking dish or Dutch oven. Top each with a bit of rosemary sprig. Set a thigh, skin up, on top of each lemon slice. Roast for 35 to 40 minutes, until thighs are tender. If using a Dutch oven, roast covered.

cold roast whole chicken

MAKES 1 WHOLE CHICKEN

Many markets sell rotisserie chickens these days, and they are convenient and quite good. In the summertime, when kids are running in and out of the house and meals are made on the fly, it's always nice to have a cold roast chicken in the fridge. But store-bought rotisseried chickens don't compare to plump organic chickens turned on the spit at home. Many gas grills have rotisserie features, but don't fret if you don't have one—roasting a chicken in the oven is simple. And the leftovers are great to use the next day in a salad or sandwich.

WINE SUGGESTION: ROSÉ

5 feet butcher's string
One 3- to 4-pound whole chicken
4 sprigs rosemary
1 lemon, cut in half
2 tablespoons olive oil
Salt and freshly ground black pepper
   to taste

  1. Preheat the oven to 450°F. Remove the giblets and neck from the bird's body cavity. Rinse the cavity, pouring out the water completely. Pat dry. Lightly salt the cavity, then add the rosemary and lemon halves.
  2. Truss the bird by girdling it with string and tie down the wings. Cross the legs and tie them securely together at the "ankles." Place the bird on a roasting pan and rub it all over with the oil. Sprinkle with salt and black pepper.
  3. Place in the oven on the center rack and reduce the heat to 350°F. Roast for 20 minutes per pound, or until a meat thermometer registers 180°F in the thickest part

of the thigh. Let cool on a platter, cover with plastic wrap when cool, and refrigerate.

Note: The breast will be juicier if you roast it breast down, turning it breast up for the last 20 minutes of roasting to brown the skin.

rotisseried chicken on the grill

MAKES 4 SERVINGS

Many gas grills—and even some charcoal grills—have a motor attachment that turns a spit. Rotisseried chickens from the market are okay, but you can seek out whole organic chickens or extra flavorful breeds like Rhode Island Reds to achieve truly spectacular results, with both white and dark meat emerging succulent and juicy.

WINE SUGGESTION: WHITE BURGUNDY

5 feet butcher's string
One 3- to 4-pound whole chicken
Kosher salt
½ lemon (optional)
Fresh rosemary sprigs (optional)
Olive oil

  1. Preheat the grill on high for 15 minutes.
  2. Remove the giblets and neck from the bird's body cavity. Remove any metal tags from the wings. Rinse the cavity, pouring out the water completely. Pat dry. Lightly salt the cavity, then add the lemon and or rosemary, if desired.
  3. Slide a pronged holder onto the spit with the prongs facing the tip of the spit. Slide the spit through the bird's cavity, distributing its weight as evenly as possible around the spit. Add the second holder, prongs facing the spit's handle. Insert the pronged holders into

the bird to hold it securely in the center of the spit. Truss the bird to tie down the wings and legs. Coat the chicken's entire surface with oil and sprinkle with a little salt.

4. Place a drip pan in the center of the grill to catch drippings. Insert the spit tip into the motor and close the hood. Adjust heat to maintain a steady 350°F in the grill. Cook for 70 to 90 minutes, depending on the bird's weight. When done, remove the spit from the grill and, with the bird still on it, place it on a serving platter and let it rest

for 5 to 10 minutes. Remove the outer prong. Slide the bird off the spit onto the platter and remove the other prong and the butcher's string.

easy indian chicken and rice dinner

MAKES 2 TO 4 SERVINGS

Sometimes you don't want to do all the prep work yourself, and so you shop the markets for a few ingredients to bring home for a quick and easy summer dinner. Here's a simple one that tastes fantastic. *Tikka* means bits of chicken and *masala* means any mixture of Indian spices.

WINE SUGGESTION: NEW ZEALAND SAUVIGNON BLANC

1 cup brown jasmine rice
¼ teaspoon salt
1 small rotisserie chicken
One 15-ounce container of tikka masala sauce
¼ cup white wine
2 tablespoons olive oil
1 eggplant, cubed

1. Place a saucepan over high heat and add 2 cups of water. Bring to a boil. Add the rice and salt and allow it to boil vigorously for 5 minutes, then reduce heat to low, cover, and simmer for 45 minutes or until the rice is tender.

2. Remove the skin and bones from the chicken and pull off the meat into a skillet with your fingers. Turn heat to medium and add the tikka masala sauce. Add the white wine and stir until the chicken is coated. Reduce the heat to low.

3. Place a skillet over medium heat and heat the oil. Add the eggplant and sauté, turning frequently, until soft and lightly browned, about 10 minutes. Add the eggplant into the chicken tikka masala and stir to mix. Serve hot over rice.

grilled turkey legs
MAKES 4 SERVINGS

Turkey legs are delicious, especially when grilled. And they pair beautifully with Dr. Brown's Cream Soda. Kids love playing caveman and cavewoman as they gnaw their way into the complexities of the leg. And truth be told, adults will appreciate the combo, too. Leg sizes can vary from less than 1 pound to almost 2 pounds, so grilling time will have to be adjusted accordingly.

WINE SUGGESTION: GEWURZTRAMINER OR PINOT NOIR

¼ cup olive oil, plus more for the grill
4 turkey legs
Salt and freshly ground black pepper
    to taste

1. Preheat the grill on high for 15 minutes. Scrub the grates with a wire brush and wipe them with oil. Reduce the heat to medium-low.

2. Rub the turkey legs all over with the ¼ cup oil. Sprinkle with salt and pepper.

3. Place the turkey legs on the grill, uncovered, and flip every 10 minutes until the interior of the leg reaches at least 170°F or the meat is very soft and easily separates from the bone, 70 to 90 minutes for a medium-size leg.

MEAT

classic meatballs
MAKES 4 SERVINGS

What's a dinner of pasta without fresh meatballs? These are a true classic. Make extras and use them in a meatball sandwich the next day. (Some people like cold next-day meatballs better than fresh cooked.)

WINE SUGGESTION: MONTEPULCIANO D'ABRUZZO

1 pound ground beef
1 egg
Pinch of salt
¼ teaspoon freshly ground black pepper
½ cup breadcrumbs
½ cup finely chopped parsley leaves
1 cup panko (or additional breadcrumbs)
    or more as needed
½ cup olive oil
1 ½ quarts Heirloom Tomato Sauce
    (page 293)
½ cup red wine

1. Preheat the oven to 350°F. In a mixing bowl, place the ground meat, egg, salt, black pepper, breadcrumbs, and chopped parsley. Start mixing by cutting the mixture with two knives. When fairly well mixed, wet your hands and finish incorporating the ingredients with your fingers.

2. Make meatballs about the size of golf balls and set them on a sheet of wax paper (approximately 20 total). Place the panko in a shallow bowl and roll each meatball in the panko to cover. Place the finished meatballs back on the wax paper.

3. Place a large skillet over medium-low heat and add the oil. When the oil is hot

(not smoking), place the meatballs in the pan and brown, about 3 minutes. Turn all the meatballs over and cook an additional 3 minutes. Repeat until all sides of the meatballs are browned. Remove from heat and let drain on paper towels.

4. Place the meatballs in an oiled Dutch oven. Pour the tomato sauce and red wine over, cover, and bake for about 1 hour.

hamburger from scratch

MAKES 4 BURGERS

To achieve the most delicious hamburgers, grind the meat yourself. So bring your food processor with you when you travel to your summer home (or simply imagine you're in a glamorous summer home, even if you've never left your kitchen). Prepackaged, store-bought hamburger can't compare. You can use an old fashioned meat grinder* if you wish, but a food processor gives quicker, if not better, results.

This recipe yields basic hamburger meat and calls for meat with some fat in it. Fat gives the burgers their juicy, tender quality.

WINE SUGGESTION: SPANISH MONASTRELL

1 ½ pounds Choice grade beef chuck roast
½ pound pork shoulder
Salt and freshly ground black pepper to taste
Olive oil for the grill

1. Cut the beef and pork into 2-inch cubes and put them in the food processor. Pulse until the meat is chopped, not too fine. Use a spatula to gently remove the meat from the processor.

2. Handling the meat as little as possible, divide into fourths and mold into patties. Season with salt and black pepper as desired.

3. Preheat the gas grill on high for 15 to 20 minutes. Scrub the grates with a wire brush, and wipe them down with oil. Reduce the heat to medium high. Or, make a medium-hot fire in the charcoal kettle.

4. Place the patties on the grill and cook for about 4 minutes, then flip and cook for 4 minutes more. Keep a spray bottle of water nearby to control any flare-ups. Serve on your favorite hamburger buns with your favorite condiments.

* If using a hand-cranked meat grinder, note the meat's coarseness after the first grind in Step 1. It should be fine with one pass through, but if it seems too chunky and coarse, put it through again, but not more than twice in total.

GOOD TO KNOW: FLAVORING BURGERS

One of the best things about making your own burgers from scratch is having the flexibility to customize the flavors to your liking. Try one of the combinations below, or create your own unique flavors. Add:

* Chopped onion or minced garlic
* A splash of bourbon and some fennel seeds
* Minced hot chile pepper
* A handful of grated Parmesan
* Minced parsley, basil, or thyme (add to the processor before pulsing.)

the jerk burger

MAKES 4 TO 6 BURGERS

Amaze your friends! Surprise your enemies! Make your enemies your friends by adding Jamaican jerk seasoning to your grilled hamburgers! This burger definitely has zip and even some zing. You'll find the jerk seasoning in the international section of most supermarkets, but my homemade version (page 291) is much more flavorful than anything you'll find in the store.

Try using bison meat instead of ground beef. It's leaner and contains far fewer calories and cholesterol than beef or even chicken.

Note there's a 30-minute (or overnight in the fridge) rest period, so plan ahead.

WINE SUGGESTION: ZINFANDEL

2 tablespoons unsalted butter
1 medium onion, finely chopped
3 cloves garlic, finely chopped
4 ounces mushrooms, chopped into
    ⅓ -inch pieces
½ tablespoon dark rum
2 pounds ground beef or bison
1 tablespoon Jamaican Jerk Spice Rub
    (page 291)
2 tablespoons finely chopped Italian flat-
    leaf parsley
Salt and freshly ground black pepper
    to taste
Olive oil for the grill
6 hamburger rolls
1 bunch arugula
Spicy mustard
6 thin slices of ripe tomato
3 red onion slices, pulled apart into rings

1. Place a large saucepan over medium heat and add the butter. When melted, add the onion, garlic, and mushrooms and sauté for 3 minutes until the vegetables are soft but not browned. Add the rum and stir, cooking for 2 minutes more.

2. Transfer the contents of the saucepan to a large mixing bowl and add the ground meat, jerk seasoning, parsley, salt, and black pepper. Gently mix using 2 forks; too much handling will make the burgers tough.

3. When well mixed, form into 6 fat patties. Place the patties on a baking sheet, cover with plastic wrap, and place in the fridge for at least 30 minutes.

4. Preheat the grill on high for 15 minutes. Scrub the grates with a wire brush, and wipe them down with oil. Reduce the heat to medium high. Place the burgers on the grill and cook for 5 minutes on each side for medium rare or 7 to 8 minutes on each side for medium.

5. Cut the rolls in half and grill cut side down for 1 to 2 minutes until lightly toasted. Place 3 sprigs of arugula on the bottom of each roll, top them with a burger, then top the meat with mustard, a slice of tomato, and several onion rings. Place the roll top over and serve.

✱ **VARIATION**

Instead of mustard, use a mix of the juice of 1 lime, 3 to 4 tablespoons of mayonnaise, 1 clove of garlic crushed through a garlic press, and 1 tablespoon of jerk seasoning.

MARINADES: The marinade penetrates the ground meat, adding flavor throughout rather than just on the surfaces, especially if you poke through the ground meat here and there with a thin skewer.

FLAVOR WITH ALCOHOL: Mix your favorite marinade with vodka or with an acidic liquid like wine. The alcohol in vodka will help tenderize the meat and carry the marinade's flavor components deep into the interior of the ground meat. Besides adding flavor and alcohol, the acid in the red wine will tenderize the meat.

SOME USEFUL TIPS ON MARINATING: Use a food-safe storage bag to marinate. Place the ground beef or other meat in the bag, pour in the marinade (at least ½ cup per 2 pounds of ground meat) and close tightly. Set the bag in a baking dish and place it in the fridge—never at room temperature on the counter for fear of the development of microorganisms in summer heat. Turn the bag from time to time while marinating.

OTHER SAFETY TIPS: Discard marinade that's been in contact with uncooked meat. If you want to use the marinade as a baste or sauce, reserve a portion for this use before you add the rest to the ground meat. Never save and reuse a marinade that's been in contact with raw meat. When seeking a flavor burst, marinate for 30 minutes to 2 hours. Drain the meat before making it into patties for grilling.

the down-home burger

MAKES 10 BURGERS

Grind your own chuck or round for true meaty flavor. The bread soaks up the acidic vegetable juice and feeds it back to the meat as it cooks. The result is marvelously juicy and appetizing.

WINE SUGGESTION: CABERNET SAUVIGNON

3 slices of good-quality Italian bread, like ciabatta
One 11.5-ounce can vegetable juice, such as V8
3 pounds ground chuck or ground round
1 large egg
1 teaspoon salt
1 teaspoon freshly ground black pepper
Olive oil for the grill
10 hamburger buns

1. Chop the bread into ¼-inch dice. In a large bowl, add the vegetable juice and bread. Using your hands, mix until the bread has soaked up all the juice it can. Discard the leftover juice.

2. Add the ground meat, egg, salt, and black pepper. Gently mix using 2 forks until all is well combined; too much handling will make the burgers tough.

3. Divide the mixture into 10 equal parts and gently shape into patties. Preheat the grill on high for 15 minutes. Scrub the grates with a wire brush, and wipe them down with oil. Reduce the heat to medium high. Place the burgers on the grill and cook with the hood or lid on for 5 minutes on each side for medium rare and 7 to 8 minutes for medium well.

4. Slice the buns in half and grill cut sides down for 1 to 2 minutes, until lightly toasted. Serve the buns and patties separately, along with seasonings, condiments, vegetables, or relishes of your choice, and allow guests to build their own burgers.

california burger

MAKES 4 BURGERS

When I lived back East, I'd occasionally see a "California burger" on a menu. This usually meant a hamburger with a salad of lettuce, tomato, onion, and possibly avocado, on top of the meat patty.

Here in California, hamburgers just come with salad on them and they are known simply as "hamburgers." The quintessential and iconic California hamburger, or cheeseburger, is served at a chain of fast-food places called In-N-Out Burger. Burgers at In-N-Out are amazingly good and put other fast food burgers to shame. Create a healthier version (that's equally comforting and delicious) using this recipe.

WINE SUGGESTION: ANY GOOD, INEXPENSIVE RED WINE

4 hamburger buns
1 pound ground beef
Dash salt
4 slices American cheese
4 tablespoons Thousand Island dressing (See headnote for Russian Dressing, page 285)
4 large tomato slices (or 8 small slices)
4 large lettuce leaves
1 whole red onion, sliced into thin rings

1. Preheat a frying pan over medium heat. Lightly toast the hamburger buns face down in the pan. Set the buns aside.

2. Gently form the ground beef into thin patties slightly larger than the bun. Lightly salt, and cook for 2 to 3 minutes on one side. Flip, and immediately place the cheese on top. Cook for 2 to 3 minutes.

3. Assemble the burger in the following order from the bottom up: bottom bun, Thousand Island dressing, tomato, lettuce, beef patty with cheese, onion slice, and top bun.

the spicy-spicy cheeseburger

MAKES 4 BURGERS

There's a reason that people who live in hot climates eat a lot of hot peppers. Yes, the capsaicin acts as pest repellent, but even more, it triggers perspiration, and when breezes blow across glistening skin, the body is cooled. The same is true for us in the hot days of summer.

Evaporative cooling can't happen if there's nothing to evaporate. So get your sweat on with the spicy-spicy burger. The degree of spiciness depends on your tolerance for the burn. An Anaheim pepper is just mildly spicy, a jalapeño is medium spicy, a serrano is very spicy, and a habañero is a masochist's delight. In all cases, you can reduce the flames by halving, coring, and seeding the peppers before mincing them. If you like every bite to be spicy, you'll mix the minced chiles into the meat before forming the patties. But you can control the heat much better and get the same perspiration-inducing effect by mincing the chiles and topping your burger with them.

WINE SUGGESTION: *ZINFANDEL*

¼ cup olive oil, plus more for
  the grill
2 pounds ground beef
Salt and freshly ground black pepper
  to taste
4 slices of pepper Jack cheese
4 hamburger buns
4 thin slices of sweet onion
4 tablespoons smoky chipotle
  barbecue sauce
2 chiles, destemmed, cored, seeded,
  and minced

1. Preheat the grill on high for 15 minutes. Scrub the grates with a wire brush, and wipe them down with oil. Reduce the heat to medium.

2. Divide the meat into 4 equal parts and gently form them into patties. Brush both sides with the ¼ cup oil. Season the top with salt and black pepper. Place on the grill and close the top. Cook for 5 to 6 minutes, then flip, add the cheese, and cook for 5 to 6 minutes more. (If using charcoal, make half the kettle high heat and reduce the coals on the other half so heat is medium—high heat, you can only hold your hand just above the cooking grates for 1 or 2 seconds; medium heat, you can hold your hand just above the grates for only 4 to 5 seconds. Place the patties over the high heat side and grill uncovered for 1 minute, then flip for 1 more minute. Then move patties to the medium heat side. Grill for 5 minutes on medium heat, then flip them and place a slice of cheese on top and cook until it melts.)

3. Place the patties on a platter and let rest for 5 minutes. This allows the juices, which had been driven into the center of the burger, to seep back out to the periphery and render the burger juicy throughout.

4. While the burgers are off the heat, slice the buns in half and grill cut sides down for 1 to 2 minutes, until lightly toasted.

5. Assemble the burgers in this order: bottom bun, cheeseburger patty, onion slice, chipotle barbecue sauce, and minced chiles.

* VARIATION

Load your burger as you wish with the usual toppings: tomato slice, lettuce, mustard, and so on. You can't really go wrong. But for the real spicy-spicy burger, follow this recipe at least once before trying to improve it.

blue cheese and bacon burger

MAKES 4 BURGERS

Although this sandwich isn't heart healthy at all, it is absolutely delicious. And so, following the rule, "moderation in all things, including moderation," we all may indulge at least once in a while.

WINE SUGGESTION: FRENCH BANDOL

4 tablespoons olive oil, plus more for
   the grill
2 pounds ground chuck
Salt and freshly ground black pepper
4 strips smoky platter bacon
4 ounces good quality blue cheese, at
   room temperature
4 hamburger buns

1. Preheat the grill on high for 15 minutes. Scrub the grates with a wire brush, and wipe them down with oil. Reduce the heat to medium high.

2. Divide the ground chuck into 4 equal

---

* GOOD TO KNOW: CHILE PEPPERS—THEY HURT SO GOOD

How hot are your peppers? Their heat level is measured in Scoville units, named after Wilbur Scoville, a scientist who over 100 years ago devised a way to measure the heat in peppers. Here's a rundown of some common (and some not so common) peppers and their capsaicin content as measured in Scoville units. Capsaicin is the compound in peppers that makes them hot.

1,001,304	Naga-Bih Jolokia pepper
923,000	Dorset Naga pepper
577,000	Red Savina Habañero pepper
350,000	Habañero pepper
325,000	Scotch Bonnet
225,000	Bird's Eye pepper
150,000	Jamaican pepper
125,000	Carolina Cayenne pepper
110,000	Bahamian pepper
100,000	Tabiche pepper
80,000	Red Amazon pepper
75,000	Thai pepper
75,000	Chiltepin pepper
50,000	Pequin pepper
50,000	Super Chili pepper
50,000	Cayenne pepper
50,000	Tabasco pepper
30,000	de Arbol pepper
23,000	Serrano pepper
10,000	Hungarian Hot Wax pepper
10,000	Chipotle pepper
4,000	Jalapeño pepper
4,000	Guajillo pepper
2,000	Pasilla pepper
2,000	Ancho pepper
2,000	Poblano pepper
2,000	Anaheim pepper
1,000	New Mexico pepper
500	Pepperoncini
0	Sweet bell pepper

parts, then gently shape into patties. Sprinkle them with salt and black pepper and brush with the 4 tablespoons oil on both sides.

3. Fry the bacon to crisp and let drain on paper towels.

4. Place the burgers on the grill and cook

for 5 minutes. Flip, and place a folded strip of the bacon over, then top each burger with a 1-ounce slice of the cheese. Cover the grill with hood or lid and cook for 5 minutes. Remove the burgers to a platter to rest for 5 minutes. While the burgers are resting, slice the buns in half and grill cut sides down for 1 to 2 minutes, until lightly toasted.

5. Place burgers on the bottom bun and serve next to the top bun with condiments and flavorings of your choice.

GOOD TO KNOW: CLEANING THE GRILL AND GRATES

Both kettle and gas grills accumulate grease over time, so to keep things clean and sanitary, you need to degrease them. The best way to do this, I've found, is with EZ Off (sodium hydroxide spray that turns grease into soap over 24 hours) and a pressure washer. It's a 2-day process. On Day 1, spray the greasy insides of the grill with the EZ Off. The next day, pressure wash the insides. This leaves the grill clean and ready for more unavoidable greasy buildup.

Grates can be cleaned with a wire brush, but there is a product that will do a better job. It's called the Grill Daddy. You fill its reservoir with water and heat the grill. As you work its scrubbing brush on the hot grates, water is released, turning into steam and loosening grease and stuck-on food particles. When the fine work is finished, you flip the tool over and use the main brush to clean the grates back to their original metal surface. It's a definite advance over a plain wire brush. See more at www.buygrilldaddy.com.

---

grilled beefsteak

MAKES 4 SERVINGS

All those whose childhood memories include sultry summer evenings with Dad out back grilling steaks, raise your hands. Hmmm—just about everyone. Now it's our turn to impart memories.

Make them even more memorable by following a few simple rules for achieving perfection: 1) Choose organically raised meat; it's grown without hormones or antibiotics and it's been raised and slaughtered humanely. 2) Choose tender cuts of beef such as New York strips, rib-eyes, filets mignons, or T bones. 3) Allow the steaks to warm to room temperature before grilling them. This allows them to cook more evenly. (Figure 1 hour for them to warm up.) Serve them with Southern-Style Fried Onion Rings (page 54). Top with Sautéed Mushrooms (page 214)

WINE SUGGESTION: CABERNET SAUVIGNON OR BORDEAUX

Extra virgin olive oil
Four 10-ounce steaks, 1 inch thick
Salt and freshly ground black pepper to taste

1. Preheat the grill on high for 15 minutes. Scrub the grates with a wire brush, and wipe them down with oil. Rub the steaks with salt and black pepper and brush with extra virgin olive oil on both sides.

2. One-inch-thick steaks will cook to medium rare with 4 minutes on a side over the hottest part of the fire. (If you're using the frequent flipping technique described in "Grilling Steak," figure about 12 minutes total time for medium rare to medium.) For thicker steaks, grill over the hottest part of the fire for 3 minutes on a side, and then move them to a part of the grill that receives indirect or lower heat until they're medium rare. Determining that moment is the art of grilling and depends on what degree of doneness you want, the temperature of the fire, and the cut of meat. Check doneness by opening a small slit in the thickest part of the steaks or use a grilling thermometer and take them off the fire when they're 140°F. in the center.

3. Let them rest on a serving platter for 10 minutes before slicing or serving.

GOOD TO KNOW: GRILLING STEAK

Steaks come in all shapes, sizes, thicknesses, and degrees of fattiness. Preferences for doneness come from raw (steak tartare) to ruinously overdone. Markets sell sirloin steak, rib-eyes, T-bones, porterhouse, New York steak, flatiron steak, filets mignons, whole tenderloins, bavettes, and tri-tips, among other names and cuts. So, there's no hard-and-fast rule that applies to all, except to grill them over a very hot fire as quickly as you can, flipping them from side to side as often as you can until they reach the stage of doneness you prefer. That frequent flipping is important, because it gives the surfaces of the steaks lots of quick flashes of heat that seal in the juices, rather than a long searing heat that can draw out the juices and evaporate them. The thicker the cut, the more total time they can spend on the very hot grill. Most need only a little oil, salt, and pepper to ready them for the grill, but marinating them overnight can add flavor.

simplest grilled steak

MAKES 4 SERVINGS

Imagine rummaging around the fridge to find a chunk of grilled steak, medium rare, ready to be sliced thin for sandwiches or just for a snack by itself. Follow this easy recipe and you'll have plenty of richly flavored leftovers to use for sandwiches, salads, and more.

WINE SUGGESTION: CABERNET SAUVIGNON

3 pounds châteaubriand, about
   2 inches thick
Freshly ground black pepper

1. Turn a gas grill to high and close the lid for 15 to 20 minutes, then scrub the grill with a steel brush. Or prepare a hot charcoal fire in a kettle grill (ready when white ash completely covers the coals and you

can't hold your hand over the coals for more than 3 seconds).

2. Grind black pepper on both sides of the steak, then place the meat over the coals without the lid or above the burners on the gas grill with the hood up. Cook on high heat for 8 minutes on a side.

3. Brush the coals to one side of the charcoal grill and place the meat over the other side so it's off the direct heat, put on the lid, and crack the air holes a bit to allow some draft. On the gas grill, move the meat away from the burners and close the hood. Roasting time will vary with your preferences.

4. When done, move the meat to a platter and cover loosely with aluminum foil for 20 minutes, then carve against the grain.

grilled pork tenderloin
MAKES 4 SERVINGS

Pork tenderloins are at their sweet best when grilled. The smoke from the fire mingles with the rich flavor of the pork to make a special treat. Most weigh from 1 to 1½ pounds, just the right amount for a small get-together of four people. This recipe calls for simple flavoring, but pork tenderloins also take beautifully to dry rubs, North African spices, and marinades.
WINE SUGGESTION: ZINFANDEL

Olive oil
1 pork tenderloin
Salt and freshly ground black pepper to taste

1. Heat the grill on high for 15 minutes. Scrub the grates with a wire brush, and

wipe them down with oil. Reduce the heat to medium high.

2. Coat the pork tenderloin with oil and sprinkle with salt and black pepper.

3. Place the tenderloin on the grill and cook for 8 to 10 minutes, then flip and cook 8 to 10 minutes more.

4. Remove the tenderloin to a platter and cover lightly with aluminum foil for 5 to 7 minutes. Slice into 1-inch-thick medallions and serve.

✱ STUFFED PORK TENDERLOIN
Using a cylindrical rod such as a knife sharpening steel, skewer the tenderloin lengthwise through its center. Make a chopped ripe fruit mixture (use figs, plums, peaches, nectarines, or berries, or any mixture of these) and push the fruit mixture into the center hole until the loin is stuffed. Add an extra minute per side to the cooking time.

grilled pork chops
MAKES 2 SERVINGS

Pork is the sweetest of meats and irresistible when grilled to a rich smokiness.
WINE SUGGESTION: ZINFANDEL

2 tablespoons extra virgin olive oil, plus more for the grill
2 center-cut pork loin chops, boneless or bone-in, 1½ inches thick
Salt and freshly ground black pepper to taste

1. Preheat the grill to medium high. Scrub the grates with a wire brush, and wipe them down with oil. Rub each chop on both sides with 1 tablespoon oil and sprinkle with salt and black pepper.

2. Place the chops on the grill and cook for 6 minutes per side for boneless and 8 minutes for bone-in chops. Serve immediately.

pork and fennel roast

MAKES 4 TO 6 SERVINGS

Big, juicy bulbs of fennel are a summer treat and there are so many ways to use its light anise flavor to good effect. One way is to pair it with sweet pork.

WINE SUGGESTION: SYRAH

½ cup fennel leaves (packed) or ¼ cup finely chopped fennel root
2 cloves garlic, minced
¼ teaspoon freshly ground black pepper
1 cup dry white wine
1 ¼ cups *verjus*
One 3- to 4-pound boneless pork roast
½ cup chicken stock

1. Mix the fennel leaves, garlic, black pepper, wine, and 1 cup of the *verjus* in a large glass bowl or baking dish.
2. Pierce the pork so the marinade can penetrate through. Add the pork to the bowl and marinate at room temperature 2

✳ GOOD TO KNOW: TESTING MEAT FOR DONENESS

When I was a young man, I occasionally saw professional chefs poking oven-roasted and grilled meats, sometimes using a long-handled fork or spoon, but most often using their index finger. I assumed this let them know how the cooking was going. When I learned to cook, I discovered the reason to poke is to see the degree to which the meat is done.

Whether beef, pork, or lamb, a quick poke or two gives you the following information.

✳ If the meat feels soft and squishy, it's either not done or is rare.

✳ If the meat yields to pressure but has lost the squishiness, it's medium rare.

✳ If the meat yields slightly to your finger pressure, and springs back readily when pressed, it's medium.

✳ If the meat feels firm and doesn't yield to pressure, it's well done.

Visual cues are not always helpful in determining when a steak is done to your liking. Use a meat thermometer to ensure that the meat has cooked evenly and is ready to be taken off the grill.

Rare	140°F
Medium rare	145°F
Medium well	160°F

Chicken should be cooked through (to 180°F) and so the meat should feel firm. Chicken is a more tender meat than beef, pork, or lamb, however, and so will not be as firm as well-done beef.

hours or for a few hours in the fridge, turning the meat several times. If marinated in the fridge, remove 2 hours before cooking so the roast reaches room temperature.

3. Preheat the oven to 425°F. Roast the pork in a roasting pan for 20 minutes. Reduce the heat to 350°F and cook for 1 hour, basting with a little bit of the marinade every 20 minutes.

4. Remove the pork to a carving plate and place in a warm—not hot—oven. Pour and scrape drippings into a pan. Add the remaining ¼ cup *verjus* and chicken stock and reduce over medium heat until thick and syrupy. Slice the pork and serve with the sauce.

pork and veal terrine

MAKES ABOUT 20 SERVINGS

A well-made terrine is the definition of a make-ahead dish. It's not difficult and the result is worth it, which is why it has long been a great party food. Since the terrine is served cold, it makes a marvelous summertime appetizer and shows off the cook's prowess in the kitchen. Ask the butcher for some butcher's string when you buy the meat.

WINE SUGGESTION: RUSSIAN RIVER PINOT NOIR

5 feet of butcher's string
1 ¼ pounds boneless lean veal
¼ pound boneless lean ham
¼ cup brandy
¼ teaspoon salt
¼ teaspoon freshly ground black pepper
¼ teaspoon dried thyme
¼ teaspoon ground nutmeg
1 tablespoon minced shallot
¾ pound lean fresh pork shoulder
1 pound bacon
2 large eggs, beaten
¼ teaspoon ground ginger
½ teaspoon poultry seasoning
1 clove garlic, crushed through a
   garlic press
1 bay leaf

1. Cut ½ pound of the veal and all of the ham into ¼-inch-thick strips, then cut the strips to 4-inch lengths. In a shallow dish, place the brandy, salt, black pepper, thyme, nutmeg, and shallot, then add the sliced meat. Marinate for 2 to 3 hours.

2. Place the pork shoulder, ½ pound of the bacon, and the remaining ¾ pound of the veal through a meat grinder or food processor until well ground and smooth. Add the eggs, ginger, poultry seasoning, and garlic. Strain the marinade from the veal and ham strips and set the strips aside. Add the liquid to the processed meat mixture. Mix everything together thoroughly.

3. Preheat the oven to 350°F. Use some of the remaining ½ pound bacon strips to line the bottom and sides of a 2-quart round, straight-sided, ovenproof casserole or baking dish that has a tight-fitting lid. Put one-third of the processed meat mixture on the bottom, smooth it out, and cover with half the reserved ham and veal strips. Add the second third of the meat mixture, smooth it out, and cover with the remaining half of the veal and ham strips. Add the remaining third of the meat mixture and smooth it out.

4. Cover the top completely with bacon strips. Place the bay leaf on top. Cover the lid with a double thickness of aluminum foil and tie it down tight with butcher's string, then trim off the loose ends. Place the casserole in a pan of hot water so that the water reaches about halfway up the sides of the casserole. Place the pan and casserole in the oven on the center rack and bake for 1 ½ hours. Add more water to retain the level of the water bath as it evaporates.

5. Remove from the oven and unseal. The terrine should have shrunk away from the sides of the casserole and the juices should be clear yellow with no trace of pink. If the terrine isn't quite done, reseal and cook for another 20 minutes. Remove from the oven and take out of the water bath. Remove the aluminum foil, take off the bay leaf and bacon strips from the top, and set a plate over the terrine to press on the cooked mixture. Weight the plate with a closed jar from the pantry and allow the terrine to cool on the counter for a few hours, then refrigerate, still weighted, overnight.

6. The next day, remove the weight, loosen the edges of the terrine from the casserole with a knife, lower the casserole halfway into a pan of very hot water for 3 minutes to heat the bottom, then invert the casserole onto a platter. Remove the remaining bacon from both the casserole and the meat and remove any excess fat. Return the terrine to the casserole or another serving dish, or keep it on the platter. Slice to serve.

✳ VARIATION
Make an aspic flavored with sherry and pour it over the cleaned-up terrine when it's back in its casserole, then refrigerate until the aspic sets. It can then be served as is, or turned out onto a platter.

bourbon-hoisin baby back ribs
MAKES 2 TO 4 SERVINGS

You will be the star of the party when you lay these ribs out before the crowd. Double or triple the recipe, depending on how many people you're feeding. One whole slab will feed 2 or 4, so figure accordingly.
WINE SUGGESTION: RICH, SPICY-FRUITY ZINFANDEL

1 cup hickory wood chips
1 slab pork baby back ribs
1 teaspoon garlic crushed through a
   garlic press
2 tablespoons bourbon
½ cup hoisin sauce
2 tablespoons rice vinegar
2 tablespoons real maple syrup
1 ½ teaspoons peeled, grated ginger
1 ½ teaspoons freshly squeezed lime juice
Salt and freshly ground black pepper to taste

1. Soak the wood chips in a bowl of water, placing a small plate on them and submerging them for 30 minutes. Drain well before using.

2. The ribs will be cooked over indirect heat (see page 158): for a gas grill, light burners on one side only; for a charcoal kettle, get the briquettes burning all across the bottom, then rake them to one side when you're ready to cook.

3. Place a stockpot over high heat on the kitchen stove and add water and some salt. Bring to a boil. Add the ribs, making sure they are completely covered with boiling water. Parboil for 3 to 4 minutes. Drain and pat dry.

4. In a bowl, whisk together the garlic, bourbon, hoisin, vinegar, maple syrup, ginger, and lime juice. Sprinkle a little salt

Before I was born, my family came east to New York from Kentucky, where Mom and Dad both were reared. When my parents said they were "going home," I knew that meant a long car ride from Long Island to Kentucky. As a kid, I never paid much attention to the liquors they were drinking, but I now know that when they were "home," they drank bourbon, just like everyone else. My dad told me stories about his grandfather—a Civil War vet—who "liked his cigars, his pinochle, and his bourbon."

One of my uncles lived in Louisville, near Bardstown, the center of the bourbon-making area of Kentucky. As fate would have it, I did my active duty service in the Army at nearby Fort Knox, and I spent a lot of time in Louisville, sampling the demimonde's delights, which included some cheap bourbons. On visits to Churchill Downs to wager a few bucks on the ponies, I encountered the middle-aged women sitting up in the stands, drinking from pints of Heaven Hill bourbon that they called "Old Heaven and Hell" and yelling themselves hoarse—or should I say "horse"?

Heaven Hill was rough stuff, but today the bourbon picture is much brighter. Fine artisanal bourbons are easy to find and identify—they are the expensive ones. One of the most expensive is Pappy Van Winkle's 20-Year-Old Reserve. It's worth every penny, having received 99 out of 100 points in a blind tasting by the Beverage Tasting Institute in Chicago—the highest mark ever given to any whiskey. If you'd like to discover how great tasting and silky smooth fine bourbon can really be, find a bar that stocks it and try a shot neat. Just don't use it in marinades, barbecue sauces, or mixed drinks. It deserves to be savored on its own.

and black pepper over the meaty top of the ribs, then slather the top with the hoisin-bourbon mixture.

5. Put the wood chips in the gas grill's smoker attachment or toss them onto the gray briquettes of the charcoal kettle. Place the ribs where they'll get indirect heat, bone-side down, sauce-slathered side up. On the gas grill, turn heat to medium low and lower the hood. On the charcoal grill, adjust the air vents for a medium-slow burn and place the lid on. Cook for 35 to 45 minutes, until done and the sauce has cooked onto the meat.

grilled butterflied leg of lamb
MAKES 8 TO 10 SERVINGS

To butterfly a leg of lamb is to debone it. It's best to have a butcher do this for you. You can then spread the meat easily so it lies out flat on your work surface, about 2 to 2½ inches thick. This is the way I prefer to grill the cut. Its greater surface area gives it more flavor, and a whole butterflied leg will serve 10 people after it's grilled and sliced. It's one of the most elegant grilled meats you can serve at a barbecue and will surely impress your guests.

You may find butterflied leg of lamb at your local market stuffed into flexible mesh bags that can be roasted in the oven. For grilling, simply remove it from its mesh bag and open it up flat.

Note that this recipe requires letting the meat marinate in its seasonings for at least 1 hour before it goes on the grill. More time is better. Ideal would be to season the meat in the morning and grill it for dinner.

WINE SUGGESTION: PINOT NOIR

6 cloves of peeled garlic, mashed
¼ cup finely chopped fresh rosemary (or 2 tablespoons dried)
¼ cup olive oil, plus more for the grill
Kosher salt and freshly ground black pepper
1 butterflied leg of lamb (about 4 to 5 pounds)

1. In a small bowl, mash together the garlic, rosemary, the ¼ cup oil, salt, and black pepper. Spread the lamb out on a working surface and generously rub both sides of the meat with the garlic-rosemary mixture. Place the seasoned lamb on a platter, cover with plastic wrap, and refrigerate for at least 1 hour so the garlic and rosemary can penetrate the meat.

2. Preheat the grill on high for 15 minutes. Scrub the grates with a wire brush, and wipe them down with oil. Turn the heat down to medium.

3. Add the meat, boned side up, and cook for 12 minutes, then flip and cook for 12 minutes more, for medium-rare. Add 1 more minute of cooking time to each side for medium-well.

4. Remove the meat from the grill to a serving platter and let rest for 5 to 7 minutes. Slice on the bias into 1-inch-thick slices.

grilled veal chops
MAKES 4 SERVINGS

We've all had steaks served with herbed butter and I always grimace at the thought of all that hard fat on top of red meat. But Italians use heart-healthy olive oil to

The time it takes to grill chops depends entirely on their thickness and the type of meat. Here are some quick rules of thumb:

LAMB CHOPS: Rib chops, cut from the rack, are usually thinner than loin chops and so take just 3 to 4 minutes a side over medium-hot heat. Loin chops take 5 to 6 minutes a side. Both of these times yield medium-rare chops. Add 1 to 2 minutes more for medium. Lamb is most tender when still pink inside.

PORK CHOPS: Center-cut pork chops are the most tender, but also the most expensive. Pork chops are sold in a variety of thicknesses from 1/2 inch thick to 2 or more inches thick. Figure 8 to 10 minutes per side over medium-low heat per inch of thickness, until cooked through. Let pork chops rest after grilling for 5 minutes so internal juices return to the whole chop.

VEAL CHOPS: These are usually sold as 1- to 1 1/2-inch-thick chops, but sometimes can be found thicker. Grill them over medium-high heat for 5 to 6 minutes per side, per inch of thickness. For medium to medium well, add 1 to 2 minutes more per side. Veal chops take beautifully to dry rubs.

increase the juiciness, flavor, and aroma of their grilled meats.

WINE SUGGESTION: BARBERA D'ALBA OR SANGIOVESE

Extra virgin olive oil
2 cloves garlic, mashed through a garlic
    press
1 tablespoon dried rosemary leaves or
    2 tablespoons fresh
3 tablespoons dried sage
Four 1-inch-thick veal chops (about 12
    ounces each)
Kosher salt and freshly ground black
    pepper to taste

1. Preheat the grill on high for 15 minutes. Scrub the grates with a wire brush, and wipe them down with oil. Reduce the heat to medium high.

2. In a large, shallow dish, mix 2 tablespoons of the oil with the garlic, rosemary, and sage and set the dish aside.

3. Generously season the chops on both sides with salt and black pepper and drizzle them with oil. Place the chops on the grill and cook for 6 minutes per side, turning only once to achieve good grill marks. Test for doneness (see page 179).

4. Transfer the chops to the dish with the oil and herbs, drizzling more oil over the meat. Turn to coat them.

5. Place the chops on a warm serving platter and spoon some of the oil, herbs, and meat juices over them. Serve immediately.

greek lamb chops

Yes, lamb is tasty enough to be served by itself. But try something different that requires only an outdoor grill and no other cooking. The flavor of lamb has natural partners that show up in this dish.

WINE SUGGESTION: ARGENTINE MALBEC

2 tablespoons extra virgin olive oil, plus more for the grill
8 lamb loin chops
20 very small cherry tomatoes, halved
¼ cup minced red onion
2 tablespoons chopped mint
2 ounces feta cheese, crumbled
½ teaspoon kosher salt

1. Preheat the grill on high for 15 minutes. Scrub the grates with a wire brush, and wipe them down with oil.

2. Place the chops on the grill and cook for 3 to 4 minutes, then flip and cook for 3 to 4 minutes more. Remove from heat and allow to cool. Carve meat from bones and slice across the grain into ¼-inch-thick slices. Place the meat in a bowl and set aside.

3. Add the tomatoes, onion, mint, and cheese to the bowl. Add the salt, drizzle the oil, and toss all together. Spoon onto 4 plates and serve.

FISH & SEAFOOD

grilled fish

MAKES 2 TO 4 SERVINGS

Whether ocean-going fatty fish like Atlantic bluefish and Pacific salmon, or light, low-fat fish like halibut and flounder, or freshwater fish like trout, walleye, catfish, or tilapia, all fish should be cooked gently over a medium-low fire until just done. Some recipes call for searing fish on high heat, then finishing on medium heat. That's too much heat, in my book. Overcooked fish is tough and dry. Fish also has a habit of sticking to hot grills and, because it has such a delicate texture, can be hard to pry loose without tearing it.

When firing up the grill, get it very hot, then reduce heat to medium low just before putting the fish on to cook. Coat the fish on both sides with olive oil and coat the grates with olive oil. (Never use non-stick cooking spray directly on hot grates; it could catch fire, travel back up the spray to the can, and explode.) Or, invest in a long-handled fish cooking basket and make sure the basket and fish are well oiled. Grilling adds a delightful smoky flavor to delicate fish.

WINE SUGGESTION: POUILLY FUMÉ

Olive oil
1 wild king salmon fillet, skin on (about 16 to 20 ounces)
2 sprigs dill weed
4 lemon wedges

1. Preheat the grill on high. Scrub the grates with a wire brush, and wipe them down with oil. Turn heat down to medium low.

2. Brush both sides of the fillet with oil. Place in oiled cooking basket or on oiled grates and cook 4 to 5 minutes starting with the skin side up, then flip and cook 4 to 5 minutes more, or until the skin is crisp. Place skin-side down on the serving platter and garnish with the dill weed and lemon wedges.

✱ VARIATION
Before grilling, rub the fillet's flesh side with crushed fennel seeds, lemon zest, kosher salt, crushed dill seeds, or a combination of these.

plank-grilled fish
MAKES 4 SERVINGS

Here's another way to serve those fish fillets you worked so hard to bring home— all those hours bent over a hot fishing pole. Well, here's your reward.

1 wooden fish plank (14 x 7 x 1, alder, pecan, cedar)
¼ cup extra virgin olive oil
4 fish fillets
2 tablespoons Cajun seasoning*
2 summer squashes, sliced
1 yellow onion, sliced
1 red bell pepper, sliced
2 lemons, cut into rounds ¼-inch thick

1. Submerge the plank under water for at least 4 hours, preferably overnight. Preheat the grill on high. Remove the plank from the water and smear the top with the oil.

2. Lay the fillets on the plank, overlapping them just slightly. Layer the fillets with 1 tablespoon of the seasoning, the squash, onion, bell pepper, and lemon slices. Top with the remaining 1 tablespoon of the seasoning.

3. Position the plank directly over the hottest part of the heat and close the lid. Cook for 20 to 30 minutes, depending on the thickness of the fillets. Slide the cooked fillets and vegetables from the plank onto a warmed serving platter and serve

4. Save the plank. It can be used again and will provide more flavor the second time.

* Either purchase prepared Cajun seasoning or make your own using the recipe on page 292.

mango shrimp
MAKES 4 SERVINGS

Check with your fishmonger to see if you can find fresh (never frozen) wild-caught shrimp from the Gulf of Mexico. Most shrimp sold in the United States are grown in Thailand or Vietnam, frozen, and thawed out here. They can't compare to Gulf shrimp. When you do find these choice crustaceans, try this spectacular recipe. The shrimp are good spooned over a plateful of hot jasmine rice, so time the rice to finish when the shrimp are ready to serve.

Kosher salt
1½ cups jasmine rice
1½ pounds raw Gulf shrimp, peeled and deveined
2 tablespoons freshly squeezed lemon juice

Freshly ground black pepper to taste
1 tablespoon olive oil
1 tablespoon unsalted butter
2 tablespoons minced shallots
¼ cup rum
½ cup half-and-half
½ tablespoon crushed red pepper flakes
1 ripe mango, peeled and flesh diced

1. Place a pot with a cover over high heat and add 3 cups water and some salt. Bring to a boil. Add the rice. Allow to boil, uncovered, for 3 minutes, then reduce heat to low and cover. Place a serving bowl in a warm oven.

2. In a bowl, place the shrimp, lemon juice, salt, and black pepper. Set aside for 15 minutes. Place a skillet on high heat and add the oil and butter. Immediately add the shrimp, and cook, stirring constantly for about 3 minutes, turning the shrimp as you stir.

3. Add the shallots, rum, half-and-half, and red pepper flakes and cook on high for 1 minute.

4. Add the mango and cook until heated through, about 1 minute.

5. Spoon the rice into the warmed serving bowl. Using a slotted spoon, top the rice with the shrimp and mango. Bring the sauce in the skillet to a full boil for about 30 seconds, then pour over the shrimp and mango. Serve immediately.

shrimp with garlic and white wine
MAKES 2 TO 4 SERVINGS

If you have 15 minutes, you can make this dish that tastes like you've been working on it for hours. The secret is in having enough flour clinging to the shrimp to make a thick, soupy sauce when the wine is added. Serve over linguini or rice with a side salad for a quick, complete meal.

WINE SUGGESTION: CHARDONNAY

1 tablespoon salt, plus more for the pasta
1 teaspoon freshly ground black pepper
1 cup all-purpose flour
1 pound shrimp, peeled, deveined, and
    butterflied
¾ pound linguini
¼ cup extra virgin olive oil
6 cloves garlic, finely chopped
1 cup dry white wine, plus more if
    necessary
Juice of ½ lemon
2 tablespoons butter
1 cup grated Parmesan cheese

1. Place the 1 teaspoon salt, black pepper, and flour in an airtight bag and shake to mix well. Add the shrimp to the bag and shake to coat the shrimp.

2. Place a stockpot over high heat and add water and some salt. Bring to a boil. Add the pasta and cook according to the instructions on the package.

3. Place a large skillet over medium high heat. When hot, add the oil, then the shrimp, shaking off some of the excess flour coating, but not all. Stir the shrimp for 4 to 5 minutes, or until they turn pink and are done. Add the garlic and stir for 1 to 2 minutes, or until it turns golden. Don't let the garlic brown or scorch or it turns bitter. Add the wine, using more, if necessary, so the flour makes a smooth sauce. Add the lemon juice and butter and stir to incorporate.

4. Drain the linguini and place in a

serving bowl. Serve pasta and shrimp topping separately. Place the cheese in a serving bowl on the dinner table. Top pasta with the shrimp mixture and the grated cheese.

lemon-garlic-butter scallops

MAKES 2 TO 4 SERVINGS

By summertime, the season's fresh garlic has replaced the winter and spring heads that have turned slightly bitter as they push out their little yellow-green shoots trying to grow again. A fine use for the new garlic is a plate of sweet, light scallops—a natural for a summer dinner overlooking the harbor or the lake. Use large, deep-sea scallops rather than the small bay scallops. The finished scallops can be turned out of the pan onto a bed of pasta or couscous, or onto grains like rice or quinoa.

WINE SUGGESTION: FRENCH CHABLIS

12 deep-sea scallops (about 1 ¼ pounds)
Salt and freshly ground black pepper to taste
2 tablespoons unsalted butter
½ cup white wine
2 lemons, zested and juiced
5 cloves garlic, minced

1. Pat the scallops dry with paper towels and sprinkle with salt and black pepper.

2. Place a large frying pan over medium-high heat and add the butter. When the butter stops foaming, add the scallops and cook until browned on both sides, 3 to 4 minutes total. Remove the scallops from the pan and set aside.

3. Deglaze the pan immediately with the wine and lemon juice. Add the garlic and cook for 2 minutes, or until the liquid is slightly reduced. Add the scallops back to the pan and cook until they warm through again. Sprinkle the zest over the top and serve.

scallops in a saffron cream sauce

MAKES 2 TO 4 SERVINGS

It's the summer-fresh basil that gives these scallops a unique and refreshing flavor. It's an easy, quick meal for any summer evening. Use half-and-half if you want a lighter sauce.

WINE SUGGESTION: CHARDONNAY

1 tablespoon extra virgin olive oil
1 tablespoon unsalted butter
1 pound bay scallops
1 cup heavy cream
1 teaspoon saffron threads
½ teaspoon salt
3 fresh basil leaves, cut into thin shreds

1. Place a large skillet over medium-high heat and add the oil and butter. When hot, add the scallops and cook, stirring frequently, until the scallops are cooked through, 3 to 4 minutes total.

2. Add the heavy cream, saffron, and salt. Reduce heat to medium, and heat the mixture until simmering. Simmer until it has reduced slightly and thickened, 2 to 3 minutes.

3. Garnish the scallops with basil shreds. Serve immediately.

crab delights

MAKES 8 SERVINGS

This excellent dish, so perfect for a summer evening is easy to assemble. Its success depends on the quality of the crabmeat. Fresh lump crabmeat from Maryland's Eastern Shore is best, or, if your fish store has precooked crab, pick the meat yourself. Beware of crabmeat produced overseas. It tends to be tasteless.

1 pound fresh lump backfin crabmeat, cold from the fridge
¼ teaspoon Coleman's dry mustard
Juice of 1 chilled lime
1 tablespoon minced chives
¼ teaspoon fleur de sel or kosher salt
¼ teaspoon freshly ground black pepper
4 ripe avocados
2 lemons, chilled and halved

1. In a medium bowl, place the crabmeat, mustard, lime juice, chives, salt, and black pepper. Toss to combine well. Place in fridge until ready to fill avocados.

2. Cut avocados from stem end to blossom end, all the way around, down to the pit. Separate the halves. (See Summer Spotlight: Avocado, page 42). Take a large spoon and loosen the avocado flesh from the skin, but let the flesh remain in the skin. Drench each half with juice squeezed from a lemon half. Do this before moving on to the next avocado. It prevents browning.

3. Fill each half with the crab mixture, piling it high. Serve immediately.

Cuts of red meat, poultry, fish, and shellfish like scallops and shrimp can benefit mightily from a swim in a good marinade before grilling or cooking. Remember a few rules, though.

* Because raw meat has been sitting in the marinade, either discard it after use or boil it well if you intend to use it for braising or basting meat on the grill or cook with it in other ways.

* Pat the surface of marinated meats dry before grilling or browning, or the meat won't brown well.

* Always marinate meats in the fridge.

* Small pieces of meat and fish can be marinated for 3 to 5 hours, whole or half chickens and roasts for no more than 6 hours, and large meats like leg of lamb overnight.

* A leakproof, food-grade plastic freezer bag makes a fine marinade container. Never marinate food in aluminum, iron, copper, or other reactive metal, as the acid in the marinade may eat away at the metal.

The best marinades have generous amounts of acidic ingredients like citrus juice, dry white wine, *verjus*, and vinegar—but keep the marinades containing vinegar away from lemon juice, wine, or *verjus*, as vinegar clashes with these flavors. Vinegar marinades have a marvelous effect on hunter's meats like wild rabbit, squirrel, white-tailed deer, and pheasant, which lose some of their gaminess when marinated for 4 hours in a liquid containing ½ cup vinegar in 4 cups of water flavored with bay leaves, peppercorns, salt, and chopped onion.

 NO COOK MAKE AHEAD QUICK & EASY

A few years ago I worked for a man who is a great fly fisherman. Wet fly, that is, where you have heavy line that lies on the water, and with a back-and-forth motion of your arm, you snake dozens of yards of line far out onto the surface of the lake. At the end of the line is a wet fly, and line and fly sink under the water. You slowly reel it toward you in such a way that lake trout find it irresistible, hit the lure, and you have breakfast, lunch, or dinner, depending on what time of day you're fishing.

This is opposed to dry fly fishing, where you loop out enough line and leader to make the dry fly dance realistically at the surface of the water, so when the trout rise for breakfast, they get a hook along with a fake fly.

I was going for a two-week summer vacation on Long Pond in northern Maine, in an area so remote there was no electricity and the roads were simply dirt tracks through the piney woods. My boss, who was also my friend, gave me a short lesson on using the wet fly technique, lent me his equipment, and I was off for the summer woodlands of Maine.

My accommodations were spartan—just a cabin with a small woodstove, for it could get cold at night in Maine, even in the summer. The main house had a generator, and every night when dinner was served, the owner would turn on the generator and a light bulb in the dining room, and a record player on which he played the same scratchy old vinyl recording of Chopin piano études.

My first morning I was up at dawn and out on the vast lake with the fishing equipment and a warm cup of coffee in a Thermos bottle. I had a small rowboat at my disposal, and soon, out on the water, I hauled in the oars and let the boat drift and simply listened. It was the first time in my life I heard complete silence—to the point where the loudest sound was my own blood pulsing through the vessels closest to my ears. The silence was broken occasionally by the far-off chittering of a red squirrel floating across a mile of water from the other side of the lake. And then I heard the slight sound of fish rising and moving the water.

Hurriedly I assembled the equipment and—inexpertly—managed to get the wet fly about 80 feet out from the boat. After about five or six casts, a trout hit the lure. I'd grown up fishing the trout streams of eastern Pennsylvania, so I knew how to set a hook and reel in a scrappy trout, and soon I had the fish in my net and into the creel. It was a beautiful trout, about 12 inches, and somehow I knew it was a female. As it gasped out the last of its life, I had a grateful feeling for this fish; it would be my breakfast and it gave its life for me.

I rowed back to shore, pulled the rowboat up on the bank, took my equipment and walked back to the main house, where the owner took the fish and cooked it for me. To him it was no big deal. This wilderness lake was teeming with trout. But I felt a strange mixture of happiness that I would get to eat a fish that not an hour before was swimming in its lake, gratefulness to the fish for its life that mine could be sustained, and a kind of melancholy that I had somehow intruded on a wild, pristine world that was not my world, and diminished it.

But when the fish, pan-fried and sparkling fresh, came to the table, and I saw its salmon-colored flesh indicating that it had eaten nothing but its natural food of summer bugs, I dropped my moping thoughts and dug in. It was sweet and very delicious, and its flesh came off its bones in lovely, tender flakes. With a second cup of coffee, it was the best breakfast I've ever had and undoubtedly the best fish I've ever eaten. The meal somehow filled me with delight. I had come to Maine to fish and eat fish and my work was done. I stowed the fishing gear in my cabin and left it there.

For the next two weeks I wandered the woods—saw a big dark spruce grouse hopping along a fallen log, found spongy lichens and moss so thick on the forest floor that I could almost bounce on them, saw places where the red squirrels made huge mounds of husks of pine seeds and empty cones, saw where the moose walked, and where the deer bedded down, and mostly, listened to that summer silence. It was thick and heavy, and I needed no more fish to infuse my time away from work with the energy that only the wilderness can give.

grilled oysters

MAKES 2 SERVINGS

The best way to eat an oyster is still to slurp it cold and raw from its shell, but grilling them and dressing them with a spicy sauce may be the next best way. And don't worry that June, July, and August don't have an R in their names—oysters these days are perfectly safe to eat in the summer, although Pacific oysters can get "creamy" (a bit muddy tasting) when they spawn in summer. Eastern oysters, on the other hand, don't have that habit. Look for Malpeques, Wellfleets, or Blue Points for top quality, or ask your fish monger to tell you what's fresh.

WINE SUGGESTION: FIANO DI AVELLINO

SAUCE
²⁄₃ cup extra virgin olive oil
2 tablespoons butter, melted
8 cloves garlic, minced
4 tablespoons minced shallots
2 tablespoons minced parsley
2 tablespoons minced basil
2 teaspoons hot sauce (your choice, but Tabasco is always good)
1 teaspoon Worcestershire sauce
1 teaspoon freshly squeezed lemon juice

OYSTERS
2 dozen fresh oysters in their shells
1 box rock salt
4 strips bacon, fried and finely diced

1. Prepare the sauce: Place all the ingredients in a bowl and whisk to combine well. Set the bowl aside while you prepare and cook the oysters. This will give the sauce time for the flavors to marry.

2. Prepare the oysters: Spread a layer of rock salt on a platter large enough to hold all the oysters. The salt is simply to give the oysters a steady bed, so they don't tip and spill.

3. Preheat the grill to high. Inspect the oysters. Discard any oysters that are open. Set the oysters directly over the flame with the flat side down. In about 8 minutes, they'll pop open. Discard any that haven't opened after 10 minutes. Use an oven mitt or tongs to handle the hot oysters and snuggle them down into the bed of rock salt, trying not to spill the "liquor," or natural juices of the oysters.

4. Spoon a tablespoon or two of the spicy sauce over each oyster, then sprinkle on a pinch or two of bacon bits.

grilled oysters and clams

MAKES 2 TO 4 SERVINGS

Some people like their oysters and clams cooked. They gain flavor when cooked on the grill. Pick through your oysters and clams and tap any that are even slightly open. If they don't immediately snap shut, discard them. After being cooked them on the grill, they will open of their own accord. Discard any that aren't open after cooking.

WINE SUGGESTION: SAUVIGNON BLANC

1 box kosher salt
24 oysters and clams
Lemon wedges

Heat the grill to medium. Spread a layer of kosher salt on a platter large enough to hold all the oysters and clams. The salt is simply to give them a steady bed, so they don't tip and spill. Discard any oysters and clams that are open. Set the oysters and/or clams on the grates over the fire. After a 6 to 8 minutes on the fire, they will open. Let them cook for a couple of minutes more after they open to cook through. Discard any that haven't opened. Use an oven mitt or tongs to handle the hot oysters and clams and snuggle them down into the bed of kosher salt, so they sit upright as if in sand. Serve with lemon wedges for squeezing.

✳ VARIATION

Serve with a mignonette sauce made by reducing a ½ cup of dry white wine and 1 tablespoon of rice vinegar by half, then adding a finely chopped shallot and freshly ground pepper to taste. Chill before serving with the oysters.

baked salmon with chiles

MAKES 4 SERVINGS

When the king salmon comes in from Alaska in mid-July, buy a fillet. If you don't feel like firing up the barbecue, cooking it at low heat in the oven will yield the tenderest salmon you've ever had. This spicy chili sauce keeps the top from turning tough and crusty. How spicy do you like your food? At the mild end of the scale, use Anaheim peppers. Jalapeños give a little more heat. Serranos are nice and hot, and habañeros are for those who can withstand a blow-torch of heat. Use whichever you prefer in this recipe.

WINE SUGGESTION: PINOT NOIR

✳ GOOD TO KNOW: MAKING STEAMED CLAMS

The three types of clams you'll most likely find in markets are—in descending order of frequency found—cherrystones, manila, and steamers, also known as soft-shelled clams, long-necked clams, or even piss clams (their siphon shoots out an arc of saltwater when a clamming fork is inserted in their bed and the handle is lowered to pry them up from the muck.) Steamers are wicked good, but are a regional specialty of New England. If you have steamers, remove the blackish skin from their necks. They are usually served with a cup of clam broth from the vessel in which they were steamed. Dip them to remove any sand. They are also served with a small cup of melted butter.

Cherrystones, or hard-shell clams, are sold around the United States, and high-quality, little manilas are usually farmed on the West Coast. Mussels make an excellent substitute for clams and they are farmed on both coasts, but are not typical of clambake fare. The blue mussel is typically farmed on the East Coast, while the Mediterranean mussel is farmed on the West Coast.

Figure at least a dozen clams per person at a minimum, and two dozen if your guests are hungry. With steamers, the count can go up considerably.

Pick over your clams for any that won't close tightly and immediately when tapped. Discard them. Steam the clams for 5 to 8 minutes until they open. Pick them over again and discard any that haven't opened. Pour the clam broth into cups for dipping, and also serve small cups of melted butter if you wish.

GOOD TO KNOW:
STARTING WITH A LIVE LOBSTER

Lobsters can be steamed, boiled, broiled, or grilled. In a real Maine clambake, a pit is dug in the sand and driftwood burned in the pit all day until there's a deep bed of glowing coals. Then rockweed, also called bladderwrack, which is a common seaweed with many small vesicles that keep its fronds afloat, is dumped by the basketful on the coals. Mesh bags of steamers, corn on the cob, and lobsters are placed on the steaming rockweed and more of the seaweed is laid on top. Then wet burlap bags are used to cover the pit. It doesn't take long for the clams, corn, and lobsters to be steamed to perfection. I've done this at home away from the seashore, using wet burlap bags under and over the food, but the burning burlap is rather acrid and the results aren't worth the trouble. Better to choose one of the following methods of cooking your lobsters. Most lobsters are between 1 and 2 ½ pounds. The clams? They're called steamers for a reason.

STEAMED LOBSTER—Place a rack above 2 inches of water in the pot. Bring the water to a rapid boil, remove the rubber bands from the lobsters' claws, and put the lobster in. Put the lid on snugly and hold it down until the lobsters stop thrashing. Steam for 10 minutes for a 1 pound lobster and add 2 minutes for each additional ½ pound, until they are bright red.

BOILED LOBSTER—Have a pot large enough so the lobsters will be covered by the boiling water. Salt the water well. Bring the water to a rolling boil. Holding the lobster by the tail, plunge it head first into the water, but only up to the carapace behind the head. The lobster will soon lose consciousness and stop wiggling. When that happens let the lobster slide entirely under the water. This prevents the lobster from tightening up its tail meat. When all the lobsters are in the pot, return it to a boil, then reduce the heat to a simmer and cook for 4 minutes for a 1-pound lobster, 5 minutes for a 1 ½-pounder, and add 2 minutes for each additional pound. The lobsters will have their characteristic red color when done.

GRILLED LOBSTER—Lobsters need to be split in half, from head to tail, to be grilled. Since we're not barbarians, you will need to kill the lobsters before splitting them. There are two ways to do this. Hold the lobsters by the barrel of the tail and plunge their heads into boiling water until they stop wiggling. Or, with a very sturdy chef's knife, insert the point just behind its head and plunge the knife straight down, then quickly cut through the head without decapitating it. Split the lobster forward through the head then backward toward the tail, cutting straight down the center of its back. Place the lobster halves, shell side down, on a medium grill and grill for about 10 minutes. Brush the meat with melted butter so it doesn't dry out.

BROILED LOBSTER—Follow the directions for killing and splitting lobsters for grilled lobster. Preheat the broiler to 375°F. Place the halves shell side up on a baking sheet given a little butter where the lobster will lay and broil for about 10 minutes, until the tail meat is white and feels firm when you press it.

If you don't have lobsters close at hand, there are businesses in Maine that will be happy to ship you live lobsters, steamers, and clam chowder. Just Google your desire and you'll find them online.

1 large king salmon fillet, about 1 ½ pounds, skin removed
3 tablespoons extra virgin olive oil
1 tablespoon chopped fresh chervil
1 chile of your choice, destemmed, seeded, and minced
1 clove garlic, crushed through a garlic press
Salt and freshly ground black pepper to taste

1. Preheat the oven to 300°F. Set an ovenproof pot of water on the stove to boil. Coat one side of the fillet with 1 tablespoon of the oil. Place it oiled side down on a baking sheet covered with aluminum foil with the edges turned up all around.

2. In a bowl, mix the remaining 2 tablespoons oil, the chervil, chile, garlic, salt, and black pepper. Mash the contents of the bowl together into a lumpy paste and smear this over the top of the fish.

3. Place the boiling water on a lower rack in the oven and the baking sheet with the fish on the middle rack. Cook for exactly 30 minutes, then gently scrape the paste off the top of the fish, transfer the fish using two spatulas to a warmed serving platter and serve.

GOOD TO KNOW: WHAT TO DO WITH LOBSTER TOMALLEY

Tomalley is the green goo found behind the head of a lobster. It functions as both liver and pancreas in the crustacean and many people who are unaware of what it is, throw it away with the shells. Those in the know, however, consider it a delicacy. It has a mild yet rich lobster flavor and silky texture. Some spread it on toast. Others add it to soups or sauces as a flavoring. I've seen people at a Maine-style clambake use bits of lobster meat to scoop it out of the shell and down it with relish. If your lobster is a female with eggs, you will find the roe next to the tomalley. This turns a coral color when cooked. You may want to mix it with the tomalley and spread it on toast.

A word of caution: the Canadian Health Service says that lobsters may ingest the toxin called Paralytic Shellfish Poisoning, which is filtered by the tomalley. It can cause tingling and numbness or even paralysis in humans if tomalley is eaten in quantity. It recommends that adults eat no more than the tomalley from two lobsters a day, and children, one. Boiling a lobster dissolves the toxin, however.

saturday night fish fry

MAKES 6 SERVINGS

So you've spent the day at the lake and come home with a mess of bass, lake trout, or maybe even pike (if you're lucky). Fillet those beauties and follow this recipe for a special treat.

6 fish fillets (about 2 to 3 pounds)
2 cups all-purpose flour
3 large eggs
1 cup whole milk
2 cups cornmeal
½ cup cornstarch
1 teaspoon kosher salt
1 clove garlic, very finely minced
1 teaspoon freshly ground black pepper
½ teaspoon ground cayenne
½ teaspoon fresh oregano
½ teaspoon fresh thyme
Peanut oil for frying
6 lemon wedges

1. Place the fillets in a plastic bag with 1 cup of the flour and shake.

2. In a bowl, whisk together the eggs and milk.

3. Place the cornmeal, remaining 1 cup flour, the cornstarch, salt, garlic, black pepper, cayenne, oregano, and thyme in a one-gallon resealable bag.

4. Place a skillet over medium (350°F) heat and add about ¼ to ½ inch peanut oil. The oil is hot enough when a bit of bread bubbles when placed in the oil.

5. Remove one fillet from the flour bag, shaking off excess flour, and dip it all over in the egg mixture. Place it in the resealable bag. Shake the bag and place the thoroughly dredged fillet in the skillet. Repeat

until skillet is nearly full. Fry for 2 to 3 minutes on each side, depending on the thickness of the fillets, until golden brown. Drain on paper towels and then transfer to a plate in a warm oven to keep them warm while the rest of the fillets are cooking.

6. Serve one fillet per person with a lemon wedge.

VEGETARIAN

mushroom burgers

MAKES 4 SERVINGS

Having some vegetarian friends over for a backyard barbecue? Serve them these portobello mushroom burgers. These are absolutely delicious alternatives to traditional beef burgers.

WINE SUGGESTION: CALIFORNIA SYRAH

1 large or 2 small red bell peppers
4 portobello mushroom caps, each about 5 inches in diameter
2 tablespoons olive oil
¼ pound thinly sliced Alpine lace cheese
4 round burger buns
Salt and freshly ground black pepper to taste
1 cup destemmed watercress leaves, rinsed and patted dry

1. Roast the bell pepper over a hot gas or charcoal grill until the skin is black and peeling. Place in a paper bag and tie with string so it cooks some more in its own steam. After 10 to 15 minutes, open the bag

and, using a paring knife, peel the bell pepper. Slice in half and take out the core and seeds. Chop into ½-inch dice.

2. Brush off the mushroom caps, trim off the stems, and rub them with the oil on top and on the gills. Place the mushrooms gill side down on a hot gas or charcoal grill. Close the hood on the gas grill. Cook for 4 to 5 minutes, or until the juices start to run. Turn the mushrooms over and cook 5 to 6 minutes more, or until the caps are no longer firm and are flexible.

3. Spoon equal portions of the diced peppers into each cap and place a slice of cheese on the peppers. Turn heat to medium and cook until the cheese melts, 2 to 3 minutes.

4. While the cheese is melting, cut the rolls in half and grill cut side down for 1 to 2 minutes until lightly toasted, then remove them to a platter. Place a mushroom with peppers-and-cheese side up on each bun bottom, season with salt and pepper, and top with the watercress. Place the bun top on and serve.

summer vegetable casserole

MAKES 4 SERVINGS

This casserole comes together quickly and makes a fine complete meal containing a starch, vegetables, and protein from cheese. Serve it with a salad for a healthful and light dinner, or as a side dish.

WINE SUGGESTION: CHARDONNAY

Butter for the casserole
1 tablespoon extra virgin olive oil
1 medium onion, chopped
1 red bell pepper, destemmed, seeded, and chopped
1 large red potato, peeled and cut into ½-inch dice
2 cloves garlic, minced
2 small yellow crookneck squash, cut into ½-inch dice
2 small zucchini, cut into ½-inch dice
½ cup yellow cornmeal
¼ cup all-purpose flour
½ cup grated Parmesan cheese
1 tablespoon fresh thyme
Salt and freshly ground black pepper to taste
1 cup whole milk
2 large eggs

1. Preheat the oven to 350°F. Butter the inside of a 9-inch round, ovenproof casserole dish.

2. Place a large skillet over medium heat and add the oil, onions, bell pepper, and potato, and cook, stirring frequently, for 5 minutes. Add the garlic and cook 2 minutes more, stirring so the garlic softens. Add the squash and zucchini and cook for another 5 minutes, stirring often, until vegetables are almost tender. Take the skillet off the heat.

3. In a large bowl, mix the cornmeal, flour, ¼ cup of the Parmesan, thyme, salt, and black pepper. In a separate bowl, whisk together the milk and eggs. Pour the egg mixture into cornmeal-flour mixture. Mix well, add the vegetables to the batter, and mix again. Pour into the prepared casserole dish.

4. Bake for 30 minutes, sprinkle the remaining ¼ cup Parmesan over and bake for 5 minutes more. Serve warm.

ON THE SIDE

While entrees may be the stars of the lunch or evening meal, it's the bit players—the side dishes—that bring the production to life. In fact, when we're eating light in the hot summertime, just a few side dishes may be all the food we need. And looking over these recipes, you'll find them every bit as enticing as entrees.

One of the secrets to putting together easy summer meals is to have side dishes already prepared and ready to join an entree for the dinner party. Spending a couple of hours making side dishes that can be refrigerated or frozen can free up scads of time for summer fun later on.

homemade applesauce

MAKES ABOUT 4 CUPS

This recipe is so simple and yields such great results, you'll want to make it often. Use the first apples of the season—such as Lady apples or Gravensteins. The advantage of homemade applesauce is that you know exactly what's in it, with no added sugar or preservatives. If you use organic apples, it can be safely fed to babies.

3 to 4 pounds fresh apples, peeled and cored
½ teaspoon ground cinnamon

1. Slice the apples. Cut the slices in half crosswise and place them in a saucepan. Add ½ cup water.
2. Place the saucepan over medium heat and cover. Cook, stirring occasionally, about 20 minutes, or until the apples are soft. Mash with a potato masher.
3. Add the cinnamon, stir to mix, and remove from the heat. Serve immediately or store in a closed container in the fridge for up to 2 weeks, or freeze.

stir-fried asparagus with beef

MAKES 4 TO 6 SERVINGS

Some people think asparagus is just a spring crop—but why then is it fresh in the markets all summer? The answer is that it's not *just* a spring crop—asparagus shoots can be harvested from the plant any time during the growing season, using a harvest-ing technique developed at the University of California–Riverside.

Since the tough, stringy part of the asparagus is in the peel, it's worth peeling the stalks before cooking the spears, although not necessary. If you marinate the beef in this recipe the night before or early in the morning, it will take only a few minutes at dinnertime to put together this Asian-style stir fry. A wok isn't necessary; a skillet will work just as well. Serve over jasmine rice, if desired.

WINE SUGGESTION: CALIFORNIA GEWURZTRAMINER

MARINADE
2 tablespoons tamari
2 tablespoons oyster sauce
2 tablespoons ponzu sauce
2 tablespoons white wine
1 teaspoon cornstarch
1 teaspoon brown sugar
½ teaspoon Worcestershire sauce
½ teaspoon freshly ground black pepper

BEEF
1 pound top sirloin steak

STIR-FRY
3 tablespoons white wine
4 tablespoons canola or peanut oil
1½ pounds asparagus, trimmed, peeled, and cut into 1-inch pieces
1 piece fresh ginger, about 1½ inches long, peeled and chopped
2 cloves garlic, minced

1. Make the marinade: In a large bowl, combine all the marinade ingredients and mix well.
2. Prepare the beef: Trim fat from the steak and slice it against the grain into 1-inch-wide strips, about 2 to 3 inches long.

Add the meat to the bowl of marinade and swirl it around until all sides of the meat are well coated. Cover and refrigerate at least 1 hour, but preferably overnight.

3. Prepare the stir-fry: Place a sieve over a large bowl and pour in the contents of the beef marinade so the beef drains and you catch the liquid in the bowl. Measure 3 tablespoons of the marinade liquid into a separate cup and add the white wine. Mix well.

4. Place a wok or skillet over high heat. When hot, add 2 tablespoons of the oil and the beef, stirring and turning the pieces for about 2 minutes, or until browned. Remove the meat from the wok, add the remaining 2 tablespoons of oil, then add the asparagus and ginger. Cook for 2 to 3 minutes, stirring.

5. Add the garlic and continue stirring for about 15 seconds. Then mix in the marinade–white wine mixture and reduce the heat to low. Cover and cook slowly for about 4 minutes, or until the asparagus is tender. Add the beef back to the wok and cook for about 1 minute, or until the meat is cooked through. Serve immediately.

Asparagus

Asparagus season runs from early spring through September. Its appearance at local farmers' markets sends out the call that the warm weather is on the way. You'll find green, purple, and white asparagus, all of which are delicious, though white asparagus has a bit less flavor.

Look for stalks that are firm and have tightly closed heads and a well-hydrated (not dry) base. You can store asparagus in the refrigerator for up to 3 days. Wrap the stalks tightly in plastic, or stand the bunch upright in a small amount of water with a plastic bag to cover them.

To remove the tough ends of the asparagus, grasp the cut end of the spear in one hand, and a spot a few inches from the tip in the other hand. Bend each side until the spear breaks.

Planning to add asparagus to a grilled vegetable medley? Use a grill basket with wire mesh, to keep the spears from slipping through the grill grates. Add any seasoning you wish, though olive oil and salt add simple, clean flavor.

pickled beets with red onions

MAKES ABOUT 2 QUARTS

Summertime for me has always meant a jar of cold, sweet-and-sour pickled beets and red onions in the fridge. It's a healthy, low-calorie snack, a fine side dish at dinner, or even a guilty pleasure at bedtime. Beets used to be boiled for making pickled beets, but roasted beets make a richer version. For dinner al fresco, that jar of beets in the fridge provides a quick, cold, and delicious accompaniment to grilled meats and salads.

Two 1-quart canning jars, with lids
8 medium beets
1 large red onion
2 tablespoons pickling spices
1 cup red wine vinegar
1 teaspoon salt or to taste
½ cup sugar

1. Wash and dry the jars. Set aside. Preheat the oven to 350°F. Lay a sheet of aluminum foil on the oven rack, to catch juices from the vegetables as they roast.

2. Cut off the slender roots of the beets and remove all but 1 inch of the tops. Arrange the beets on the aluminum foil, leaving enough space between them so they don't touch. Roast for 90 minutes, or until the skin of the beet collapses when squeezed before touching the beet inside. Remove from the oven and set aside to cool.

3. When the beets have cooled, peel them and cut into ¼-inch slices. Peel the onion and slice it into thin, ¼-inch strips lengthwise. Alternate layers of beet slices, onion slices, and sprinkles of pickling spices in the jars, pressing them in tightly.

4. Place a small saucepan over medium-high heat. Add the vinegar, salt, sugar, and I cup water and bring to a boil. Pour the boiling mixture over the beets, leaving about 1 inch of headspace. If you need a little more liquid, repeat step 4 to make more as needed.

5. Put on the lids and allow the jars to cool on the counter. When cool, place the jars in the fridge for at least 1 week before using. They will keep in the fridge for 3 or 4 weeks.

north african–style carrots

MAKES 4 SERVINGS

Carrots are nutritious—all that beta-carotene turns into vitamin A in our bodies. But a bowl of bland, steamed carrots doesn't make an exciting side dish at dinnertime. One way to bring them to life is to match them with spices. The flavor of

carrots goes particularly well with North African spices. Carrots are one of those vegetables that have the most interesting flavor the fresher they are, so if you have a garden, use them in this dish right after you pull them and wash them. If you don't have a garden, look for young carrots with their green tops still attached at your market.

WINE SUGGESTION: RUSSIAN RIVER PINOT NOIR

1 pound carrots
1 teaspoon sugar
½ teaspoon ground cumin
¼ teaspoon ground cinnamon
Pinch cayenne
Pinch salt
Freshly ground black pepper to taste
3 tablespoons extra virgin olive oil
2 garlic cloves, minced
1 tablespoon freshly squeezed lemon juice

1. Wash but don't peel the carrots, to retain the flavor in the skins. Using a knife or a mandoline, cut the carrots into ¼-inch slices.

2. Place one or two inches of water in a large stockpot with a steaming basket in the bottom over high heat and bring water to a boil. Add the carrots and steam for 10 minutes, or until tender. Be careful the water doesn't all boil away. Add more if necessary. Turn the carrots once or twice to ensure that all parts are thoroughly cooked.

3. While the carrots are steaming, in a small bowl, mix together the sugar, cumin, cinnamon, cayenne, salt, and black pepper. Set the bowl aside.

4. Place a large skillet over medium-low heat and add the oil. When hot, add the garlic and cook, stirring, for 1 minute or until golden brown. Add the carrots and the

spice mixture to the pan and stir to coat the carrots completely. Cook for 1 minute, or until the sugar dissolves. Add the lemon juice and stir to mix. Transfer into a serving bowl and allow it to cool before serving.

savory simmered corn
MAKES 4 TO 6 SERVINGS

When summer corn is at its freshest and sweetest best, thrill people with this tasty corn dish to serve on the side. The flavors in this dish have a synergy that will surprise you—it's greater than the sum of its parts. The medley of colors makes for a pretty presentation, too, served at the table.

WINE SUGGESTION: CALIFORNIA CHARDONNAY

5 ears very fresh corn, husked and desilked
2 medium leeks, white and light green
    parts only
3 slices bacon, cut into ½-inch squares
1 tablespoon unsalted butter
½ jalapeño pepper, seeded and minced
Freshly ground black pepper to taste
4 cups chicken broth
1 large potato, peeled and cut into
    ½-inch dice
1½ teaspoons chopped fresh thyme
4 tablespoons heavy cream
Salt to taste
3 spears chives, finely chopped

1. Cut the kernels from the corn and transfer to a large bowl. Slice the leeks into very thin rounds.

2. Place a Dutch oven or large saucepan over medium heat and add the bacon. Fry until crisp, then transfer to paper towels to drain. Pour off all but 1 tablespoon of the bacon fat from the pan.

3. Place the pan back over medium heat and add the butter. When melted, add the leeks, jalapeño, and several grinds of black pepper. Cook, stirring often, for about 5 minutes, or until leeks are soft.

4. Add the chicken broth, corn, potato, and thyme and increase the heat to high. When the mixture reaches a boil, reduce to a simmer and stir, simmering about 15 minutes, or until potatoes are soft,.

5. Transfer 1 cup of the stew to a blender and puree until smooth. Return the puree to the pan. Add the cream and stir to mix well. Add salt. Sprinkle the chives and bacon over the surface of the stew. Remove from heat and serve while hot.

cool corn and tomato mix
MAKES 4 SERVINGS

The air may be heavy and humid ("close" as they say in the Midwest), but that kind of summer weather just brings the corn and tomatoes to perfection. It is the best time to make this simple, wonderfully tasty, cool side dish.

WINE SUGGESTION: PINOT GRIGIO

8 leaves from butterhead lettuce
4 small, ripe tomatoes
Salt to taste
⅓ cup Creamy Buttermilk Dressing (page 285)
1 tablespoon parsley, minced
Generous pinch freshly ground black
    pepper

Generous pinch cayenne
1½ cups cooked fresh corn kernels
⅓ cup shredded havarti or Jack cheese
2 tablespoons chopped red-ripe sweet
    pepper, such as bell pepper
2 tablespoons peeled and chopped
    cucumber
2 tablespoons chopped onion or shallot

1. Chill 4 plates in the refrigerator or freezer. Remove when ready to assemble.

2. Place 2 lettuce leaves on each plate. Place each tomato, stem end down, on a cutting board and cut into—but not through—the tomato to make 6 wedges that are held together by the stem end. Set each tomato on one of the plates, spreading the wedges open. Sprinkle the wedges with a little salt.

3. In a small bowl, whisk together the dressing, parsley, black pepper, and cayenne.

4. In a large bowl, place the corn, cheese, sweet pepper, cucumber, and onion. Add the dressing mixture and toss lightly to coat. Fill the tomatoes with the corn mixture and serve immediately.

corn and baby lima bean succotash

MAKES 8 SERVINGS

The Narragansett Indians were making succotash before the Pilgrims arrived. The Pilgrims must have liked it, since we still enjoy this traditional dish today. Corn and lima beans reach their peak in summer. Make this dish using the freshest vegetables possible, then freeze the leftovers. You'll appreciate the fresh taste when summer has flown away. For a healthier alternative, replace the butter with ¼ cup extra virgin olive oil.

WINE SUGGESTION: WHITE BURGUNDY

About 3 ears corn
About 2 pounds baby lima beans, still in
    their pods
2 tablespoons butter
½ teaspoon salt
½ teaspoon thyme

1. Place a large stockpot over medium high heat and add water. Add the corn, bring to a boil, and cook for about 5 minutes, or until corn is cooked through. Drain the corn in a colander. Cut the kernels from the cobs into a bowl and cover with a plate so the corn stays hot.

2. Return the stockpot to medium-high heat and add more water. Add the lima beans, bring to a boil, and cook for 7 to 8 minutes, or until soft and cooked through. Test a lima to see if the bean is soft and done through. If it needs more time, continue boiling the pods for 3 to 5 minutes more and test again. When done, drain and let the pods cool enough so they can be handled. Shell the limas into the corn.

3. Add the butter, salt, and thyme and toss until the butter is melted. If the succotash is too cool, return it to a saucepan and stir constantly over medium heat just until it's hot. Serve immediately.

grill-roasted corn on the cob

MAKES 4 SERVINGS

Summer brings us fresh corn on the cob. It used to be that corn would lose its sweetness shortly after it was picked, but breeders have developed new sugar-enhanced and super-sweet varieties that remain sweet for days after picking. You'll see them advertised as such at the store. It is still a good idea to eat your corn as soon as possible; flavor compounds (other than sweetness) can be lost by waiting.

Corn reaches its best flavor when roasted on the grill, where it acquires some smokiness as the husks dry and brown and the kernels turn a deep golden yellow as some of that prized sugar caramelizes. Instead of twirling the hot, cooked ear on a stick of butter and salting it, simply drizzle the ear with extra virgin olive oil as a healthy—and tasty—alternative. You can also try mixing a bit of spice like chili powder or smoked paprika into the olive oil.

12 ears of corn in the husks
½ cup extra virgin olive oil for brushing, plus more for the grill
Bowl of water to quench husks that catch fire on the grill

1. Prepare the corn: Remove the tough outer husks from each ear. Pull the remaining husks away from the ears but don't detach them. Remove as much of the silk as you can and discard. Brush the kernels with a light coating of olive oil, then smooth the attached husks back over the ears. Place ears in a large pan or in the sink with enough water to cover them. Soak for 30 minutes.

2. Preheat the grill to medium-high. Scrub the grates with a wire brush, and brush them with oil. Place the ears on the grill and cook until underside of husks has turned blackish-brownish-gray. If husks catch fire, sprinkle the ears with a few finger flicks of water from a bowl. Rotate the corn by a quarter turn and continue cooking. Keep turning until the ears have made one complete rotation. Check an ear to see if the kernels have turned golden brown in spots. If they have, the corn is done. If not, replace the ear and keep turning until kernels are golden-brown.

3. Place the ears on a serving platter and provide guests with a large, empty bowl in which to place their husks and finished cobs. Serve with butter and salt or extra virgin olive oil, or both.

✳ **GRILL-ROASTED CORN WITH LIME**
Heat butter just until it melts in a small saucepan and add the juice of a lime and a pinch of salt if the butter is unsalted. Don't allow the lime juice to cook. Stir to mix thoroughly and serve with the grilled corn.

piccalilli

MAKES 15 ½-PINT JARS

Piccalilli is a vegetable pickle, best made in high summer when the ingredients are cheapest but of the highest quality—especially if they are from your own garden. You can use any combination of vegetables you wish, but this recipe shows you my favorite way. Piccalilli finds its true home used as a relish on hot dogs, bratwurst, and hamburgers

GOOD TO KNOW:
GRILLING VEGETABLES AND FRUITS

Although there's nothing quite like fresh, ripe fruits and vegetables, their flavors can be enhanced, changed, or intensified by grilling.

Grilling quickly over high heat caramelizes natural sugars, making the flavors richer, yet keeps the integrity of the fruit or vegetable. In addition to the caramelization, the grill can add a light smokiness that's an added pleasure. And quick cooking softens hard vegetables. However, not all fruits and vegetables respond well to high-heat cooking. Ears of corn, pineapple slices, and delicate oyster mushrooms do best over moderate or low heat, especially when it's indirect heat. If you're making shish kebabs, cut veggies into long strips and skewer them, rather than making large dice that cook slowly.

I have two grilling baskets that I use for a variety of foods, but especially slices of fruit or vegetables that might otherwise slip through the grill grates. I always heat the grates on high heat for at least 10 minutes, though preferably 15 or 20 minutes. Then I brush the grates with a steel brush. Some grill chefs will wipe down the grates with olive oil, but it's often easier and has the same effect to oil the vegetables. Fruits are full of sugar, which will weld itself to the grates, so wiping the grates with a little vegetable oil before laying on the fruit can help prevent sticking.

Very watery fruits like watermelon and other melons don't adapt to grilling very well. And neither do the watery vegetables like cucumbers and celery. The best fruits for grilling are the stone fruits, pineapples, figs, mangos, and kiwis. Mix a little rum with fresh lime juice as a marinade or dip for these fruits before grilling. When grilling the stone fruits of summer, such as peaches and apricots, keep a little dish of salt handy. Just a tiny pinch over grilled fruit enhances its flavor.

The best veggies for grilling include asparagus, corn, eggplant, fennel, leeks, mushrooms, onions, Italian paste tomatoes, and summer squashes like zucchini. I always oil my veggies—even corn—before grilling. It helps with the color and prevents sticking on the grates. Most times, vegetables can also use a pinch of salt and a grind of black pepper before going on the grill.

Reduce the bitterness of certain salad greens with a little time on the grill. Wrap radicchio with prosciutto and hold it together with a wet toothpick, then give it a light grilling. Or wrap a *chicon* of Belgian endive with pancetta and grill it.

cooked on the grill. It can also be used as a topping for red meats. Increase or decrease its spiciness to suit your taste. Note that the piccalilli is made over 2 days.

Fifteen ½-pint jars

BRINE
⅔ cup kosher salt
5 cups cold water

VEGETABLES
2 pounds mixed vegetables, including:
½ pound pearl onions
⅔ pound cauliflower florets
1 small cucumber, peeled
¼ pound celery root, peeled
¼ pound bell peppers
3 radishes
1 serrano chile

SPICED VINEGAR
2 cups malt vinegar
1 teaspoon pickling spices

SAUCE
2 tablespoons all-purpose flour
1 tablespoon dry mustard powder
2 teaspoons turmeric
2 teaspoons ground ginger
3 tablespoons malt vinegar

1. Make the brine: In a large bowl, dissolve the salt in the water, leaving plenty of room for the vegetables. Set aside.

2. Prepare the vegetables: Place a large stockpot over medium heat and bring water to a boil. Add the onions and cook for 2 minutes. Remove from the water and peel.

3. Trim the cauliflower to small florets. Chop the cucumber, celery root, bell

peppers, radishes, and chile into ½-inch pieces.

4. Put the vegetables in the brine and weight them down with a plate to hold them under the surface of the water. Cover the bowl with a dish towel, and allow to sit for 24 hours.

5. The next day, place the jars, lids, and bands in a large pot of water and boil for 10 minutes, then remove from heat and cover until ready to use.

6. Make the spiced vinegar: In a small saucepan over high heat, add the vinegar and the pickling spices and bring to a boil. As soon as the mixture boils, reduce the heat to simmer and cover, simmering for 15 minutes. Remove from the heat and set it aside.

7. Make the sauce: In a large saucepan, mix the flour, mustard, turmeric, and ginger. Add the vinegar and mix to make a smooth paste. Pouring through a strainer, stir the 2 cups of spiced vinegar, a bit at a time, into the paste. Discard any pickling spices caught by the strainer.

8. Place the saucepan over low heat and stir until the mixture becomes thick enough to adhere to a wooden spoon without running off, about 15 minutes. Remove the sauce from the heat.

9. Drain but don't rinse the vegetables, as the salt that clings to the vegetables is needed in the piccalilli. Add the vegetables to the thickened sauce, stir well, then return the pan to low heat. When the mixture reaches a simmer, let it cook for about 2 minutes, then remove it from the heat and stir well.

10. Spoon the piccalilli into the sterilized jars, leaving about ½ inch of headspace. Put on the lids and the bands, and tighten the bands finger tight. Place the jars into

the canner so they are at least 2 inches under rapidly boiling water and boil for 10 minutes. Remove the jars with tongs and allow them to seal themselves.

11. When they're cool, remove the bands, label them with the date, and store in a cool, dark place.

chow-chow

MAKES 6 QUARTS

Chow-chow is an old-fashioned way to use up some of summer's bounty. It's actually a pickle to be served as a side dish with sweet meats like roasted pork, or with sausages or grilled burgers. Pick through a farmers' market for fresh, organic vegetables and give them the following treatment. You'll be enjoying their sunshiny goodness now and when the snow is flying. You can double this recipe.

3 green tomatoes
5 medium onions
3 medium green bell peppers
3 medium red bell peppers
1 head cauliflower
¼ cup kosher salt
8 cups white vinegar
2½ cups sugar
1½ tablespoons dry mustard
2 teaspoons turmeric
1 teaspoon powdered ginger
2 tablespoons whole mustard seeds
1½ tablespoons celery seed
1 tablespoon pickling spices

1. Chop the tomatoes, onions, and bell peppers and place them in a large bowl.

Trim the cauliflower to small ½-inch florets and add to the bowl. Stir in the salt. Cover and let stand on the kitchen counter overnight. Drain off the liquid from the vegetables.

2. In a large pot, mix the vinegar, sugar, mustard, turmeric, and ginger. Cut two 10-inch squares from a roll of cheesecloth and place them together to form a double-thickness 10-inch square. Place the mustard seeds, celery seed, and pickling spices in the center and tie up the ends with butcher's string to form a bag. Add the bag to the liquid in the pot and bring it to a boil over high heat. Reduce the heat and simmer gently for 30 minutes. Add the vegetables and return to a simmer, then cook for 30 more minutes.

3. Remove the spice bag and pack hot, sterilized canning jars with vegetables and pot liquid and seal. Process according to jar manufacturer's instructions (usually 10 to 15 minutes at a full boil in a canner). Store jars in a cool, dark place.

✱ VARIATIONS
You can use other vegetables in the mix, especially snap beans, carrots, celery root dice, and the stems of chard cut to ½-inch pieces, but keep the proportion of vegetables to other ingredients the same.

caponata

MAKES ABOUT 3 CUPS

Caponata is Italian for "first born," but why this enticing relish is called that in its native Sicily is beyond me. Here's a quick way to prepare it, although a Sicilian might devote hours to it.

Freeze it in a plastic freezer container with a lid. There are many ways to enjoy it when the weather is hot and you don't want to spend much time cooking. Here's one: cook some pasta, thaw a few spoonfuls of caponata in the microwave (or simmer for a few minutes on the stovetop), then dress the pasta with it.

1 tablespoon extra virgin olive oil
½ cup oil-cured black olives, pitted and chopped
1 medium eggplant, peeled and cut into ½-inch dice
½ onion, chopped
2 cloves garlic, minced
¼ cup chopped flat-leaf parsley
¼ cup red wine vinegar
2 large ripe tomatoes, diced
Salt and freshly ground black pepper to taste

1. Place a large skillet over medium-high heat and add the oil. When hot (not smoking), add the eggplant, and sauté until the eggplant is golden brown. Cover the skillet, reduce the heat to low, and cook for 10 minutes, or until the eggplant is soft.

2. Add the onion and garlic and cook for 2 minutes. Add the parsley, vinegar, tomatoes, salt, and black pepper. Cook covered for 3 minutes. Uncover and simmer, stirring occasionally, for 5 to 8 minutes, or until the mixture thickens.

✱ VARIATIONS
Sicilians often flavor caponata with anchovies, pine nuts, almonds, and/or capers. My advice is always go easy on the capers—if I were to add them here, I'd use about ½ teaspoon.

grilled eggplant and tomato caponata
MAKES 4 TO 6 SERVINGS

The downside of August is a spate of oppressively hot and humid dog days. But the upside is that the best eggplants and heirloom tomatoes arrive in our stores about the same time. Take advantage of them with this wonderfully flavorful Mediterranean dish. You can use any eggplants, but look especially for the slender purple and white varieties. They have the most exquisite taste. Use as a side dish or relish with grilled meats or as a topping for pasta.
WINE SUGGESTION: REGALIALI RED

3 pounds eggplant, sliced into rounds and grilled (see page 207)
½ cup extra virgin olive oil plus 3 tablespoons
Salt and freshly ground black pepper to taste
4 cloves garlic, slivered
2 large heirloom tomatoes, cored and chopped
1 ¼ cups basil leaves, coarsely chopped

1. Cut grilled eggplant rounds into ½-inch-wide strips. Place a large skillet over medium heat and add ½ cup of oil. When hot, add the eggplant. Sauté, stirring occasionally every few minutes, for about 10 minutes. Add salt and black pepper.

2. While the eggplant is cooking, place a saucepan over medium-low heat and add the remaining oil. Add the garlic and cook for about 2 minutes, or until slightly golden. Add the tomatoes and 1 cup of the basil. Increase the heat to medium and cook, stirring every few minutes, for 15 minutes.

Taste and add salt and/or black pepper, if needed.

3. Place the eggplant and tomato-basil sauce in a serving bowl and mix well. Garnish with the remaining basil. Serve warm.

grilled fennel and tomatoes
MAKES 4 SERVINGS

This grilled, smoky dish is the soul of Mediterranean cooking and an excellent accompaniment to grilled meats.

2 fennel bulbs
4 fresh paste tomatoes (Roma or San Marzano)
½ cup extra virgin olive oil, plus more for the grill
Salt and freshly ground black pepper to taste
½ cup oil-cured black olives, pitted and chopped
¼ cup fresh basil leaves, destemmed and coarsely chopped
Juice of 1 lemon

1. Trim the fennel bulbs, being careful not to remove the soft white tissue at the base. Slice the bulbs lengthwise into ½-inch-thick slices. Cut the tomatoes in half. Brush all sides of fennel and tomatoes with ¼ cup of the oil, and season with salt and black pepper.

2. Preheat the grill on high for 15 minutes. Scrub the grates with a wire brush, and wipe them down with oil. Reduce the heat to medium. Place the fennel and tomato on the grill, and cook for 4 to 5 minutes on each side, or until soft and smoky.

3. Transfer the vegetables to a serving bowl with the olives, basil, lemon juice, and the remaining ¼ cup of the oil. Toss to coat and serve while hot.

green bean and tomato medley
MAKES 4 SERVINGS

When fresh green beans are in season, we often steam them and drizzle them with olive oil—a process that yields a good, but prosaic, result. Here's another way to use them: pair them with tomatoes and herbs. Have trouble getting the kids (or even other adults in your household) to eat their veggies? This dish will tempt them.
WINE SUGGESTION: CALIFORNIA ROSÉ

2 tablespoons extra virgin olive oil
2 shallots, finely diced
1 clove garlic, minced
2 large tomatoes, peeled and chopped
1 pound green beans, ends trimmed
1 tablespoon chopped fresh thyme leaves
1 tablespoon chopped fresh parsley leaves
Salt to taste
¼ cup vegetable stock

1. Place a Dutch oven or skillet (with a lid) over medium-low heat and add the oil. When the oil is fragrant and hot, add the shallots and garlic and cook, stirring occasionally, for 5 minutes.

2. Add the tomatoes, beans, thyme, parsley, salt, and stock, and cover. Reduce the heat to low and simmer for 30 minutes. Serve hot in shallow bowls.

✳ VARIATION
Substitute a tablespoon of dill weed for the thyme to give a more intense flavor.

✳ Tomatoes

More than 30 percent of Americans have some kind of garden in the summer, even if it's just a few tomato plants. And in fact, tomatoes are the most planted home garden crop in America.

It's easy to see why. There's nothing quite as delicious as a vine-ripened tomato, still warm from the sun, pulled right off the vine and eaten out of hand, with all its runny, meaty, juicy-sweet goodness tempered by a fine acidic edge.

Flavor-wise, tomatoes are the most vivid vegetable, compared to the delicate flavors of most other garden veggies. It takes herbs of equal intensity such as basil, oregano, and thyme to stand up to tomato's rich flavor.

It doesn't take much space to grow tomatoes. Cherry tomatoes, especially, will grow just fine in a big tub of potting soil, as long as there are drain holes in the bottom.

If you do grow some tomatoes at home, there's one fact you should know if you want tomatoes all season long. Tomatoes are either determinate or indeterminate. Determinate types set a big crop of fruit, ripen it pretty much all at once, and then stop producing. Indeterminate types keep producing new shoots that will continue to bear fruit right through the season until cold fall weather sets in. You'll want to make sure the plants or seeds you buy are of indeterminate types.

Or at least, plant one determinate and one indeterminate tomato. That way you'll have a big crop for canning and a few tomatoes coming ripe throughout the whole season.

When frost threatens to bring down your tomato vines at the end of the season, pick the green tomatoes and wrap each separately in newspaper, then set them in a dry, well-lighted place in the house. They'll slowly ripen over the next few weeks, extending your tomato season well into the fall.

green beans with mushrooms

MAKES 4 SERVINGS

Green beans are now referred to as snap beans instead of string beans because plant breeders have long since bred the strings out of them. They are a heat-loving annual crop, so high summer is the best time to enjoy them.

The herbaceous flavor of fresh green beans is complemented by the earthy, savory flavor of mushrooms. This makes a wonderful dish for parties. Reheat it gently if it has cooled before serving.

1 pound green beans, trimmed at top and
    tail, and cut in half diagonally
1 tablespoon extra virgin olive oil
½ pound mushrooms, sliced
2 tablespoons minced shallots
Salt and freshly ground black pepper
    to taste

1. Add an inch or two of water to a large stockpot with a steaming basket in the bottom. Set over high heat and bring water to a boil. Add the beans and steam for about 12 minutes, or until tender. Set aside and keep warm.

2. Place a large skillet over medium heat and add the oil. When hot, add the mushrooms and shallots and cook, stirring frequently, about 5 minutes. The mushrooms will absorb the oil at first, but then yield it back to the pan while turning brown.

3. Add the beans, salt, and black pepper to the skillet. Stir to incorporate all the ingredients thoroughly and heat up the beans. Remove from heat and serve warm.

✱ GREEN BEANS, MUSHROOMS AND ALMONDS
Add ¼ cup slivered almonds when adding
the beans in Step 3.

simple steamed greens

MAKES 2 TO 4 SERVINGS

The freshest greens are available in our
markets during the summer. The best ones
for steaming are also the most nutritious:
curly-leaved kale, collards, dinosaur kale,
chard, spinach, and beet greens. And
steaming is a nonfat way to preserve more
of their nutritional elements than any other
cooking method. Some cooks remove the
tough center ribs of kale and chard, but they
can add a pleasant crunchiness to the otherwise soft steamed leaves.

Collapsible metal steaming baskets are
available at most supermarkets and cook-
ware shops. Place one in a pot with a lid,
with an inch of water in the bottom, add the
greens, cover, and bring the water to a boil.
When the greens are done, transfer them
into a serving bowl and toss them with a
light dressing.

1 bunch chard, kale, collards, beet greens,
   or spinach
2 tablespoons soy sauce

1. Wash the greens and shake them dry.
Use them whole, destemmed or with stems
in, or cut across the bunch into ½-inch-
wide strips, as you prefer.

2. Place a large stockpot with a steamer
inside over medium-high heat and add
water. Bring to a boil, then add the greens to
the steamer. Steam the greens until tender,
about 3 to 5 minutes, depending on the
level of tenderness you prefer.

3. Drain the greens in a colander and
transfer them to a serving bowl. Drizzle the
soy sauce and toss lightly to coat. Serve hot.

✱ GOOD TO KNOW: PRESERVING THE COLOR OF VEGETABLES

Ever notice how green vegetables quickly
turn an appealing rich green when dropped
into boiling water? That's because there's
air trapped around the cells of the vegetables' tissues and it diffuses the color of the
chlorophyll when the vegetables are raw.
The hot water drives off these tiny pockets
of air, allowing all the green color to show
through.

Continued cooking, you'll have noticed,
eventually renders the vegetables an un-
appealing muddy, grayish-green color (or
other muted color if orange, red, purple, or
another color). That's because the boiling
water or steam has begun to break
down the cell walls of the plant tissue, re-
leasing their naturally occurring acids.
When these acids hit chlorophyll, the color
gets diluted. The disintegration of the cell
walls begins shortly after 5 minutes of
boiling or steaming.

To preserve the bright green color, cook the
vegetables for less than 5 minutes, and then
plunge them into ice water or the coldest
water you have. This stops the cooking
process and preserves the color.

grilled leeks

Summer leeks are the most tender, and they acquire a nice smokiness from grilling that augments savory meat or fish. Grilled leeks are a great side dish with any barbecued meat.

¼ cup extra virgin olive oil
2 tablespoons lemon juice
2 tablespoons chopped fresh marjoram or
    2 tablespoons chopped fresh oregano
1 teaspoon salt
Freshly ground black pepper to taste
8 medium leeks

1. In a large bowl, add all the ingredients except the leeks. Mix together to create a marinade and set aside.

2. Trim the coarse tops and roots from the leeks and wash thoroughly, but don't cut off the sole plate. Cut the leeks in half without cutting through the sole plate, so that the two halves are connected at the root end.

3. Preheat the grill to medium. If using a gas grill, light only one burner; if using a charcoal grill, move the coals to one side. Place the leeks on the grill so that they are not above the flame and receive strong but indirect heat. Brush them with the marinade. Cook, rotating the leeks every 3 to 4 minutes so all sides are cooked evenly, brushing them with marinade each time.

4. Continue cooking for 25 to 30 minutes, or until soft. Transfer directly over the hottest part of the fire for 2 minutes on each side. Serve hot.

sautéed mushrooms

Traditionally grilled steaks were "smothered with onions," but this accompaniment is even better.

2 cups beef broth
4 tablespoons unsalted butter
1 pound mushrooms, cleaned and cut into
    ¼-inch slices
Salt and freshly ground black pepper to taste
⅓ cup brandy

1. Place a large pot over medium-low heat and add the broth. Simmer about 10 minutes, or until reduced by half. Set aside.

2. Place a skillet over medium-high heat and add 2 tablespoons butter. When the butter stops bubbling, add the mushrooms and cook, stirring frequently, for about 5 minutes, or until they begin to brown and soften. Add a pinch or two each of salt and black pepper and stir. Reduce heat to low. Transfer the mushrooms from the pan to a bowl.

3. Return the pan to the heat and pour in the brandy. The liquid may immediately burst into flame.* When the flame disappears, turn the heat up to high and use a wooden spoon to incorporate the pan bits into the brandy. Reduce the liquid to a few tablespoons. Add the reserved beef broth. Continue cooking and stirring for 3 minutes more, until the liquid thickens slightly.

4. Add the mushrooms and any accumulated juices and the remaining butter to the skillet, and stir until hot and well mixed. Serve warm.

* Be extremely careful when heating liquids with high alcohol content such as brandy. The liquid will immediately burst into flames, so take extra caution to lean back from the stove and wear a heat-resistant oven mitt if necessary. Keep the kids away from the kitchen.

polenta with mushrooms and cheese

MAKES 4 SERVINGS

Polenta is a staple in Italian cuisine. It is cornmeal, making it a good starchy base for all kinds of dishes with savory sauces. I learned to make polenta this way from Marcella Hazan's wonderful book *Essentials of Classic Italian Cooking*, and it has since become one of my staples.

Polenta can be served warm immediately after cooking, or refrigerated and reheated in the microwave. It also freezes beautifully as slices placed in resealable freezer bags. You can also slice cooled polenta and pan-fry it quickly in some olive oil, making the perfect side dish when you don't have a lot of time or it's too hot to spend all evening in the hot kitchen. This recipe lists the slow method of cooking polenta, but the results are incomparable.

WINE SUGGESTION: MERLOT

7 cups water
1 teaspoon salt
1 ²/₃ cups dry polenta
1 ½ cups mushrooms, coarsely chopped
1 cup freshly grated Parmesan cheese

1. Fill a large deep bowl with cold water and reserve.

2. Place a large heavy pot (iron or enameled) over medium-high heat and add the water and salt. Bring the water to a rapid boil. Add the polenta in a thin stream, not all at once, stirring frequently so no lumps form.*

3. Reduce heat to medium and stir constantly and slowly, bringing cornmeal up from the bottom and scraping it off the sides.

Cook for about 30 minutes, stirring constantly. The polenta will become more difficult to stir as it thickens. Continue stirring until the polenta easily slides away from the sides of the pan. Add the mushrooms and cheese, and stir thoroughly.

4. Empty the cold water from the reserved bowl but don't dry it. Immediately scrape the polenta from the pot into the bowl. Fill the cooking pot with cold water before setting it aside, for easier cleanup later.

5. Let the polenta rest in the bowl for 10 to 15 minutes, then cover the bowl with an upside-down serving plate. Quickly invert the bowl and plate, then gently lift the bowl to remove. The polenta will make a nice cake that can be cut into slices to serve right away, or can be cooled and covered with plastic wrap before storing in the refrigerator.

*Cooking polenta is like deep-frying with hot oil—it gets hot very quickly and has a tendency to spatter initially, until the polenta thickens later in the cooking process. Protect yourself from getting burned by wearing gloves and a long-sleeved shirt. Keep children away from the hot stove while the polenta is cooking.

ratatouille

MAKES 4 TO 6 SERVINGS

Similar to, although more complex than, the Italian caponata, ratatouille is one of those summer dishes that uses tomatoes and eggplants when they're at their flavorful best. The dish doesn't look like much—sort of a soupy vegetable stew—but it bursts with complex flavors. While it's certainly good right from the pan to the table, it actually gains charm in the fridge overnight. This means that on hot days, it can be served cold with smoky-good meats from the grill. With ratatouille, you get all your vegetables at once.

½ pound eggplant
½ pound young zucchini
2 large tomatoes, peeled, seeded, cut into
    quarters
Extra virgin olive oil as needed
1½ cups onion, thinly sliced
1 cup red, yellow, or green bell peppers,
    sliced lengthwise
2 cloves garlic, minced
Salt and freshly ground black pepper to taste
3 tablespoons parsley, finely chopped

1. Peel the eggplant by cutting ½-inch thick rounds, then zipping off the skin. Slice the rounds lengthwise into inch-wide strips and cut these to about 3 inches. If the eggplant is watery, salt it thoroughly, set aside for 30 minutes, press, rinse, drain, and pat dry. Cut the zucchini to similarly sized strips. Cut the tomato quarters into ½-inch-wide strips.

2. Sauté the eggplant in a few tablespoons of olive oil at medium heat for one minute on each side, and do the same with the zucchini. Set them aside. In the same pan, cook the onions and peppers, adding a little more oil if necessary, for about 10 minutes, until they're softened but not browned. Stir in the garlic and add salt and black pepper to taste. Place the tomato strips on top of the onions and peppers. Cover the pan and cook on low heat for about 5 minutes, until the tomato juice starts to run. Remove the lid and spoon

some of the pan juices over the tomatoes, then turn up the heat to medium and let the juice reduce until it's almost all gone. Remove from the fire.

3. In a casserole dish with a lid or a Dutch oven with lid, spoon about a third of the tomato mixture into the bottom, and shake a tablespoon of the parsley over it. Cover this with half the zucchini and eggplant strips. Spoon half the remaining tomato mixture over the strips and shake another tablespoon of parsley on it. Top with the remaining eggplant and zucchini strips. Finish by spooning the rest of the tomato mixture and the last tablespoon of parsley over the top.

4. Cover the casserole and cook on low heat for 10 minutes. Remove the lid and spoon the juices over the vegetables, then cook uncovered on medium-low heat for another 15 minutes. Correct the seasoning. Spoon the juice over the vegetables several more times until it is almost entirely gone. Be careful not to let it all evaporate and scorch the vegetables.

corn risotto with lime
MAKES 4 SERVINGS

Risottos can be made to reflect any season—think of porcini and pancetta in fall—and summer's bounty brings them alive with wonderful fresh ingredients. They make a great side dish, or serve as a base for simple grilled chicken.

I've learned over the years to precook everything but the rice when making risotto. Trying to cook ingredients in the rice while the risotto is being made interferes with the rice's natural progression to doneness and can result in ingredients that aren't cooked properly; they can be underdone or over-done. For added flavor, try grilling the corn instead of boiling it. This will lend a nice smoky flavor to the dish.

WINE SUGGESTION: FRENCH VIOGNIER

2 cups freshly cooked corn kernels, cut off the cob (page 204)
6 cups chicken broth
¼ cup olive oil
⅔ cup arborio rice
½ cup white wine
Juice of 2 limes
½ cup freshly grated Parmesan cheese

1. Cut the kernels off the cobs and set aside in a small bowl.

2. Place a large stockpot over medium-low heat and add the chicken broth. Heat it to just below a simmer—so it's hot but not boiling. Keep it at a low simmer.

3. Place a large skillet over medium-high heat and add the oil. When hot (but not smoking), add the rice. Stir the rice con-stantly, moving all of it around the hot pan, for 2 minutes. Add the wine. It will sizzle and get absorbed almost immediately. Stir in the chicken broth 1 cup at a time, waiting to add the next until each is ab-sorbed. Continue stirring for 20 to 25 minutes, or until rice has a faintly chalky center.

4. Add the corn kernels and the lime juice and stir to incorporate and heat everything through. Add the cheese and stir until the cheese melts into the risotto. Serve imme-diately.

shrimp and summer vegetable risotto

MAKES 4 TO 6 SERVINGS

Here's one of my favorite summer risottos—fresh-tasting and colorful. It allows many other summery vegetables to be added to it, such as tomatoes, fresh herbs, and diced summer squash. Try adding shellfish like clams and scallops instead of the shrimp.

I generally make my own chicken broth (see sidebar on page 146), but store-bought broth will work just as well when you're short on time or have used up all your frozen homemade stock.

WINE SUGGESTION: VERNACCIA DI SAN GIMIGNANO

1 yellow summer squash, finely diced
1 small zucchini, finely diced
½ red bell pepper, seeded and finely diced
6 cups chicken broth
2 tablespoons extra virgin olive oil
2 cups Arborio rice
1 cup dry white wine
1 pound shrimp, steamed, peeled, and chopped
1 cup boiled fresh corn kernels (from 2 small ears or 1 large)
Juice of 2 limes
½ cup grated Parmigiano-Reggiano cheese
2 tablespoons chopped Italian flat-leaf parsley
Salt and freshly ground black pepper to taste

1. Steam the squash, zucchini, and bell pepper until just tender (see page 213). Set aside.

2. Place a large stockpot over medium-low heat and add the chicken broth. Heat it to just below a simmer—so it's hot but not boiling. Keep it at a low simmer.

3. Place a large skillet over medium-high heat and add the oil. When hot (but not smoking), add the rice. Stir the rice constantly, moving all of it around the hot pan, for 2 minutes. Add the wine. It will sizzle and get absorbed almost immediately. Stir in the chicken broth 1 cup at a time, waiting to add the next until each is absorbed. Continue stirring for 20 to 25 minutes, or until rice has a faintly chalky center.

4. Add the shrimp, squash, zucchini, bell pepper, corn kernels, lime juice, Parmigiano, parsley, salt, and black pepper. Stir all together well, allowing the added ingredients to heat through. Serve immediately.

✳ VARIATIONS

There are as many variations as your imagination can conceive. The rice is mild and accepts the flavors of your favorite savory summer foods: okra, green beans, peas, spinach, and more. Just about any meat can be used, especially smoky bacon. Shellfish works well, as does salmon. Delicate white fish, like sole and halibut, tend to get lost among the flavors.

sautéed okra with caramelized onion
MAKES 4 SERVINGS

The freshest okra arrives in mid to late summer. It's a snap to prepare and very tasty. It can be used to thicken stews like the traditional jambalaya and gumbo, but shines when prepared simply. It makes a nice side dish with grilled foods.

Pay close attention when cooking the okra. The sizzling oil will sear the cut ends of the okra pieces, turning them chewy-crispy. Too little cooking leaves them unpleasantly mucilaginous. Too much will cause blackened ends that are bitter.

1 pound young okra pods, about 4 to
    5 inches long
½ cup extra virgin olive oil
1 small onion, diced
Salt to taste

1. Wash, destem, and slice the okra into ⅓-inch rounds, placing them in a bowl. Don't discard the white seeds.

2. Place a large skillet over medium-low heat and add the oil. When hot (but not smoking), add the okra and onion. Using a spatula, stir and turn the pieces frequently. Add salt to taste.

3. Remove them from the heat when the okra is browned on both sides and tender and the onions are caramelized, about 12 to 15 minutes. Serve immediately.

✳ CRISPY FRIED OKRA
Coat the okra pieces in an egg wash (2 eggs and ¼ cup milk whisked together). Then coat pieces in cracker meal mixed with salt and freshly ground black pepper to taste. Fry the pieces in 1-inch of vegetable oil (peanut or canola oil are good) for 4 to 5 minutes, turning occasionally.

✳ SAUTÉED OKRA WITH TOMATOES AND GARLIC
Prepare okra as directed in main recipe above. Peel and chop 2 medium tomatoes and crush 2 cloves garlic through a garlic press, then add them to the okra when it's nearly finished in Step 2. Keep cooking until the tomatoes release their juice and boil. Serve in small serving dishes.

quick skillet squash

MAKES 4 TO 6 SERVINGS

This stir-fry works best with squash that's been salted and pressed (see sidebar on page 226). It's a simple, yet hearty side to any meat dish.

WINE SUGGESTION: LONG ISLAND CHARDONNAY

2 pounds summer squash, diced into
   ½-inch pieces
¼ cup olive oil
1 small onion, diced
2 cloves garlic, minced
1 teaspoon thyme
Salt and freshly ground black pepper
   to taste

1. Salt, drain, rinse, and press the squash as directed on page 226. Set aside.

2. Place a large skillet over medium-high heat and add the oil. When the oil is fragrant, add the onions and cook, stirring frequently, for about 1 minute. Add the squash and cook, stirring occasionally, for about 4 minutes. Add the garlic and thyme and cook, stirring occasionally, for about 4 minutes, or until the squash is tender. Add salt and black pepper and serve hot.

✽ SUMMER SQUASH FRITTATA

Beat 4 eggs together with ½ cup grated Parmesan cheese and add the mixture to the skillet in Step 2, when the squash is just tender. Reduce heat to medium-low and cook for 4 to 5 minutes, or until egg mixture is almost set through. Gently flip the frittata over and cook for an additional 1 to 2 minutes.

hoppin' john

MAKES 6 TO 8 SERVINGS

Food historians believe Hoppin' John was a dish invented by slaves on the plantations of the Old South. This traditional Southern dish can be made ahead of time and frozen in meal-size portions. It tastes better thawed and reheated than when first made, since the smoky, mildly spicy flavors will be more infused and pronounced.

WINE SUGGESTION: ZINFANDEL

1 pound dried black-eyed peas
2 small smoked ham hocks
2 medium onions, 1 cut in half, 1 minced
3 cloves garlic, peeled and cut in half
1 bay leaf
1 cup long-grain rice
2 large tomatoes, diced, with juice
   reserved
1 medium red bell pepper, seeded
   and chopped
½ green bell pepper, seeded and chopped
3 ribs celery, chopped
2 jalapeño or other spicy chiles, minced
2 teaspoons Creole seasoning
½ teaspoon dried thyme leaves
¾ teaspoon ground cumin
¾ teaspoon kosher salt
4 scallions, sliced into ½-inch pieces

1. In a heavy pot or Dutch oven, combine the black-eyed peas, ham hocks, and 6 cups water. Add the onion halves, garlic, and bay leaf. Place the pot over medium-low heat and bring to a boil. Reduce the heat to a simmer and cook gently for about 2 ½ hours or until the beans are tender,.

2. Transfer the ham hocks from the pot to

a cutting board. Trim off the meat, dice, and set aside. Drain the peas and reserve both peas and liquid. Remove and discard the bay leaf, onion halves, and garlic.

3. Add 2½ cups of liquid to the pot and bring to a boil. Add the rice, cover, and reduce the heat to a simmer. Cook until the rice is nearly tender, about 30 minutes.

4. Add the minced onion, the reserved peas, the tomatoes and their juices, red and green bell peppers, celery, jalapeño, Creole seasoning, thyme, cumin, and salt to the

SUMMER MEMORY: **eating at the fair**

The highlights of summer in many communities across America are the state and local fairs. And the highlights of the fairs are the foods served there. These foods tend to have a regional character, so it's fun to do some culinary exploring while you're traveling through regions when their fairs are being held.

In my boyhood home of Monroe County, Pennsylvania, we had two fairs: the big county fair and the smaller West End Fair. The latter was right in the middle of Pennsylvania Dutch country, and there was a food hall serving huge plates of roast pork and mashed potatoes to the farmers who flocked to it.

I was lucky enough to visit Milwaukee while the Wisconsin State Fair was going on a few years ago, and got to sample real Milwaukee gastronomy. There were bratwursts galore, kielbasa, and Polish sausage, too. The beer halls served Pabst Blue Ribbon and Miller's. Corn-roasting stands served golden-brown roast corn on the cob dripping with butter. You could sample the state's renowned cheeses. And the featured food of the whole fair was the cream puff.

People by the thousands formed long queues and shuffled past counters where cream puffs by the multi-thousands were made and handed out. These simple confections—basically popovers filled with whipped cream—seemed to satisfy something peculiarly chauvinistic in the crowds. Eating one of those cream puffs somehow validated your status as a resident for another year. It made you a certified Wisconsinite. And it tasted great.

Or maybe it was the shared tedium of standing in line for a half hour as you made your way toward the cream puff that made you a Wisconsinite.

rice. Cook for about 10 minutes, or until the rice is tender. Stir in the scallions and the reserved diced ham. Allow the pot to cool, then freeze meal-size portions.

summer garden medley

MAKES 4 SERVINGS

The best time to make this delicious dish is when summer vegetables are at their finest and most available. It has a more refined flavor than ratatouille and an interesting mix of textures. Plump those pillows on the back deck furniture, pour some long drinks made with lemonade, ice, and mint, and enjoy this sumptuous dish.

WINE SUGGESTION: SERVE WITH SAME WINE USED IN THE RECIPE, SUCH AS AN AUSTRALIAN SEMILLON.

8 artichokes
Juice of 1 lemon
2 medium onions
¼ cup extra virgin olive oil
12 cloves garlic, peeled and halved lengthwise
6 sprigs summer savory or thyme and
    parsley, tied into a bouquet
¼ teaspoon salt
1 cup baby lima beans
2 cups shelled garden peas
2 dozen asparagus tips
3 tomatoes, peeled, seeded, and chopped
1½ cups white wine
1 tablespoon unsalted butter

1. Trim the artichokes to their hearts. Quarter the hearts and place them in a large bowl of acidulated water—water with the juice of a lemon added. This prevents the artichokes from discoloring. Set aside.

2. Peel and quarter the onions. Thinly slice the quarters. Place a large skillet over medium-high heat and add the oil, garlic, herb bouquet, and the onions. Stir to coat. Cover the skillet and reduce the heat to low. Cook, stirring occasionally, about 10 minutes.

3. Meanwhile, place a large pot over medium-high heat and bring water to a boil. Working in batches, if necessary, and keeping them separate from one another, blanch the lima beans, peas, and asparagus tips for 1 minute, then plunge into ice water to stop the cooking.

4. Add the artichokes, limas, tomatoes, and wine to the skillet and simmer for 10 minutes, or until the alcohol has evaporated. Add the peas and asparagus tips and simmer for 10 minutes more. Remove the pan from the heat and stir in the butter. Remove and discard the bouquet of herbs. Adjust the seasoning as needed and serve immediately.

stir-fry of summer vegetables

MAKES 4 TO 6 SERVINGS

The goal of stir-frying vegetables is to preserve their fresh taste and good color, while rendering them tender. It requires knowing how long it takes different vegetables to reach this moment of perfection, but that's not hard. Solid, stringy vegetables like green beans, cabbage, okra, and snap peas take longer than tender, leafy vegetables like spinach, chard, and kale. When using celery, break back the large ends and zip the broken piece up the stalk

to remove many of the strings. Cut solid pieces on the diagonal. Use 1 or 2 tablespoons of vegetable oil per pound of vegetables. Canola oil is good because it reaches the desired temperature of 375°F before reaching its smoke point. Serve over warm rice.

WINE SUGGESTION: SAUVIGNON BLANC

3 pounds mixed summer vegetables of your choice (see the headnote for options)
3 to 6 tablespoons vegetable oil
Salt and freshly ground black pepper to taste
½ teaspoon soy sauce
¼ cup chicken stock
1 teaspoon garlic, minced
1 teaspoon fresh ginger, minced

1. Prepare the solid and stringy vegetables so that the pieces are all approximately equal size. Set them aside. Cut leafy vegetables into pieces about 3 x 3 inches. If there are thick, meaty mid-ribs, such as with kale or chard, cut them separately and add them to the solid vegetables.

2. Place wok or skillet (with a lid) over medium-high heat and add the oil. Add the solid and stringy vegetables and stir until they are wilted and coated lightly with oil. They should be crisp, not quite tender, with a brighter color.

3. Add the leafy vegetables and stir until the leaves are wilted. Stir in the salt, pepper, soy sauce, chicken stock, garlic, and ginger and cover. Reduce the heat to medium low and cook, stirring once or twice, for about 5 minutes, or until the vegetables are just tender. Serve immediately.

fried fennel

MAKES 4 SERVINGS

One of the choicest bounties of late summer is the fresh fennel bulbs that show up in the markets. Here's an Italian way of presenting them as a side dish for dinner. Note that the batter needs a 2-hour rest in the fridge, so plan accordingly.

1 cup all-purpose flour, plus more
    for dredging
¼ teaspoon salt
¼ teaspoon freshly ground black pepper
1 egg, separated
1 tablespoon extra virgin olive oil
1 tablespoon white wine
6 tablespoons cold water
2 fennel bulbs
1½ cups canola oil for frying
Kosher salt to taste

1. In a large bowl, place the 1 cup flour, salt, and black pepper. Mix thoroughly and make a depression in the center of the ingredients. In a small bowl, beat together the egg yolk, olive oil, and wine.

2. Slowly pour the egg mixture into the well made in the flour mixture. Stir slowly to mix the flour mixture into the egg mixture. When the mixture is smooth, add the water, 1 tablespoon at a time, slowly beating it into the batter, until well incorporated. Cover the bowl with plastic wrap and refrigerate for 2 hours.

3. Cut the fennel bulb into eighths by trimming ¼ inch off the root end and trimming away the stalk ends, then cutting the bulb from stalk end to root end, being careful not to remove the white core.

4. Place a large stockpot over medium-high heat and add water and salt. Bring to a boil, then add the fennel. Cook 5 to 7 minutes, or until fork tender. Using a slotted spoon, remove the fennel and drain on a dish lined with paper towels.

5. Remove the batter from the fridge. In a small bowl, whip the egg white until stiff peaks form. Fold it into the batter. In a dish, add flour for dredging. Coat the fennel wedges with the flour, shaking off the excess.

6. Place a large skillet over medium-high heat and add the canola oil. When hot (not smoking), dip the flour-coated fennel into the batter, twisting until well coated. Working in batches, place the battered pieces in the hot oil and fry them for 3 to 4 minutes, turning several times, or until they are golden and crispy. Place them on paper towels to drain, then on a warmed tray. Sprinkle with kosher salt, and serve hot.

chiles rellenos

MAKES 4 TO 6 SERVINGS

Classic stuffed peppers usually means green bell peppers stuffed with a mixture of hamburger and rice, then baked. But today, summertime brings us fresh poblano chiles to markets, especially Mexican markets, across the country. These dark green, almost black, chiles have a wonderful pepper flavor. Now, finally, we can make authentic *chiles rellenos*, a Spanish term meaning "stuffed peppers." Serve them along with Spanish rice and grilled, thinly sliced flank steak. You may substitute Anaheim chiles if poblanos are unavailable.

6 poblano chiles
8 ounces Jack cheese, at room temperature
   or slightly chilled, sliced into 6 pieces
6 eggs, separated
½ cup all-purpose flour
1 teaspoon salt
1 cup canola oil
1 cup salsa verde

1. Preheat the grill on high, or preheat the broiler. Clean the grates with a wire brush, and wipe them down with oil. Place the chiles on the grill and cook, turning until all sides are blistered with black patches of charring. If using a broiler, turn the chiles regularly so all sides are close to the broiling element, until at least half the entire surface is charred black.

2. Remove the chiles from the fire, place them in a brown paper bag, and tie with string so they cook some more in their own steam. After 10 to 15 minutes, open the bag.

3. Slowly peel the skin off the chiles, then make a slit in each chile from the top by the stem to about 1 inch from the tip. Form a T by making a horizontal slit across the top of the chile by the stem. Gently open the chile and remove the core and seeds, leaving the stem intact. Place a piece of the cheese into the interior of the chile—not so much cheese that the slit won't close. Set the chiles aside.

4. In a small bowl, beat the egg whites until stiff peaks form. In a separate bowl, beat the yolks with 1 tablespoon of the flour and the salt. Add the yolks to the egg whites and stir until a thick paste forms. On a plate, place the remaining flour and dredge each chile in the flour until all sides are coated lightly.

5. Place a skillet over medium heat and add the oil. When hot (not smoking), begin coating all sides of each chile in the egg batter. Working in batches, add the chiles to the pan, seam side down. This seals the slit so the melting cheese doesn't run out into the pan. Cook for 3 to 4 minutes, or until golden brown. When the seam side is done, turn the chiles so all sides fry to a pretty golden brown. Drain on a plate lined with paper towels.

6. Place the salsa verde in a microwave-safe bowl and heat for 40 seconds. Swirl a large spoonful of salsa onto each plate, then add 1 or 2 chiles rellenos on top of the salsa. Serve hot.

hash brown potatoes
MAKES 4 TO 6 SERVINGS

These potatoes are the best possible side dish for a flavorful grilled sirloin steak. Here's my mom's recipe, and she made the best hash browns imaginable. If you're feeding the masses, double this recipe. They're sure to disappear quickly.

3 strips bacon
3 pounds waxy (red) potatoes, peeled and
   cut in half
4 tablespoons canola oil
3 tablespoons extra virgin olive oil or
   butter, as you prefer
1 large onion, chopped
6 cloves garlic, chopped
Salt and freshly ground black pepper
   to taste

1. Place a large skillet over medium-high heat. When hot, add the bacon and cook until crispy and the fat has been rendered. Remove the bacon strips and save for another use. Set the pan with the bacon fat in it aside.

2. Place a large stockpot over medium high heat and add water and salt. Bring to a boil, then add the potatoes. Parboil about 10 minutes, or until barely tender. Drain the potatoes into a colander and run cold water over them to stop the cooking.

3. Take each potato half and cut it into three ½-inch-thick slices crosswise. Then lay them flat side down and slice them into ½-inch strips across the stack. Turn the stack 45 degrees and cut the stack into ½-inch dice.

4. Add the canola oil and olive oil (or butter) to the bacon fat in the skillet and set over medium heat. Add the potatoes and stir with a spatula every few minutes, until the surfaces of the dice are browned, about 15 minutes.

5. Reduce the heat to medium low and continue cooking for 20 minutes, turning every 4 to 5 minutes. Add the onion and turn the potatoes and onions every 5 minutes, for another 20 minutes. Add the garlic, salt, and black pepper and cook for another 15 minutes, turning every 5 minutes, until the hash browns are well browned and the onions and garlic slightly caramelized. Serve hot.

summer squash au gratin

MAKES 4 SERVINGS

In midsummer, the summer squash comes fast and furious because farmers or gardeners have to pick the young fruits (as the squashes are called) daily, or they grow too large and the plant slows or even stops production. A perfect excuse to enjoy their delicious flavors and textures on a regular basis! Their mild flavor gets a royal bump from the cheese in this recipe. You can use just about any mild cheese you prefer. Any of the summer squashes will do, as long as they are small: 6 to 7 inches for zucchini, 3-inch diameter for patty pan, 7 to 8 inches for crooknecks see sidebar on page 226 for information on how to prepare summer squash.

WINE SUGGESTION: WASHINGTON STATE RIESLING

1 pound summer squash, cut into ½-inch dice
1 tablespoon olive oil
½ small onion, diced
½ cup finely diced Jack cheese
4 tablespoons freshly grated Parmesan
   cheese
¼ cup sour cream or plain yogurt
1 tablespoon dry white wine
1 tablespoon ground coriander
Salt and freshly ground black pepper
   to taste
1 cup breadcrumbs
½ teaspoon paprika
2 tablespoons unsalted butter, cut into
   pieces, plus more for the baking dish

1. Preheat the oven to 350°F. Grease a 9-inch-square baking dish with butter and set aside.

2. Add 1 or 2 inches of water to a large stockpot with a steaming basket in the

bottom and set over medium heat until water boils. Add the squash and steam for about 8 minutes, or until tender. Transfer into a large bowl and set aside.

3. Place a skillet over medium heat and add the oil. When hot (not smoking), add the onion and stir occasionally until the onions are soft and translucent. Add the onion to the bowl with squash.

4. Add the Jack and 2 tablespoons of the Parmesan to the squash. Mix in the sour cream or yogurt, wine, coriander, salt, and black pepper and toss to coat well. Transfer the mixture to the prepared baking dish.

5. In a small bowl, toss the breadcrumbs, paprika, and the remaining 2 tablespoons

Parmesan and spread evenly over the squash. Dot the surface with butter and bake for 30 to 35 minutes, or until the dish is bubbling and the crust is golden brown, being careful not to let the breadcrumb mixture scorch. Serve immediately.

jalapeño cornbread
MAKES 8 SERVINGS

Around the end of July or the beginning of August, the chiles pour into our stores, including serranos, habañeros, jalapeños, and more. Sure, we use them in salsa and Mexican-inspired dishes, but how about adding some peppery heat to good old-fashioned cornbread, served up with Southern fried chicken, collards, smashed taters, and milk gravy? Sounds delicious!

2 tablespoons butter
1 ½ cups buttermilk
1 cup fresh corn kernels (from 1 ear)
½ tablespoon kosher salt
3 tablespoons minced red bell pepper
3 tablespoons minced seeded jalapeños
2 tablespoons sugar
1 cup yellow cornmeal
1 cup all-purpose flour
2 teaspoons baking powder
¼ cup peanut oil
2 large eggs

1. Preheat the oven to 425°F. Grease a 7 x 11-inch Pyrex baking dish with the butter. Set aside.

2. Place a saucepan over medium-high heat and add 1 cup of the buttermilk, the

---

GOOD TO KNOW: PREPARING SQUASH FOR COOKING

Summer squash is over 90 percent water. When cooked, it yields this water to the dish you're making, and can make for a soggy mess. It's not imperative to remove excess water, but the consistency of the squash will be improved. It will be a little firmer and not fall to mush so easily. It's simple to do this: Place the diced squash in a bowl and throw in a handful of kosher salt. Toss to coat. Set aside for 20 minutes. Turn the diced squash into a colander and rinse off the salt. Keeping the colander in the sink, use the heel of your hand to press the squash firmly. You'll find quite a bit of water running out of the colander. After a couple of minutes of pressure, the squash will be ready to use.

corn kernels, and salt. Bring to a boil and immediately reduce the heat to medium low. Cook, stirring occasionally so the milk doesn't scorch on the bottom of the pan, for about 15 minutes. Take the pan off the heat and add the minced peppers.

3. In a mixing bowl, add the sugar, cornmeal, flour, and baking powder. Mix well, then add the oil, the remaining ½ cup buttermilk, the eggs, and the corn kernel mixture. Stir until well mixed.

4. With a rubber spatula, scrape the batter into the baking dish and place on the center rack. Bake 25 to 30 minutes, until golden brown and a toothpick inserted in the center of the cornbread comes out clean.

5. Remove the cornbread from the oven and let it cool for 5 minutes. Using 2 spatulas so you don't break the bread, lift it out of the dish and onto a serving plate—or serve from the dish.

SUMMER MEMORY: **bikes**

Bicycles are a central part of just about every kid's life during the "wonder years," before getting a driver's license and a car. And never more so than during the summer.

As the years go by, your bike becomes an extension of your legs and body. You finally learn to ride with "no hands." The free hands allow you to eat and drink while you make your way down the road. You might have eaten a MoonPie or a Goo Goo Cluster if you were from the South. It could have been a bag of Fairy Food if you were from Milwaukee. Kids in New England loved their Sky Bars. Peanut Chews ruled in Pennsylvania, along with Mallo Cups. Kansas kids had their Valomilks. It may have been an ice-cream sandwich if you were from just about anywhere. In my case, it may have been an American cheese sandwich and an A-Treat soda.

Nowadays, kids are more likely to be texting than eating while they ride hands-free.

Summer is still the time for riding your bike, coasting down a hill with the wind in your face—your hair blowing, the sweat evaporating from you and cooling you—off, and finding yourself going fast enough to scare yourself silly.

ICE CREAMS, SORBETS, & FROZEN TREATS

Watermelon Water Ice

Cucumber Sorbet

Litchi Sorbet

Blueberry-Yogurt Popsicles

Super-Fast Homemade Ice Cream

CLASSIC DELIGHTS

Traditional Berry Summer
  Pudding

Cold Lemon Soufflé

Summer Fruit Coulis

Ambrosia

Peach Delight

Apple Fritters

Crêpes Suzette

Sweet Fruit Crêpes

Grilled Apricots in Caramel Sauce

Cherries Jubilee

Brandied Peaches

Strawberry Shortcake

Genoise Cake with Apricot Glaze

Carrot Cake

PIES, TARTS, & COBBLERS

All-American Apple Pie

Blueberry Pie

Cherry Pie

Summertime Pie

No-Cook Blackberry Pie

Summer Stone Fruit Tart

Tarte Tatin

Peachberry Almond Galette

Plum Crisp

Plum and Nectarine Crisp

Nectarine-Blueberry Crisp

Summer Stone Fruit Cobbler

DESSERTS

The best way to eat is organic, local, and seasonal. And that makes locally grown, organic, summer fruits the sweetest, as well as the best, way to eat.

You can find locally grown summer fruits at pick-your-own farms, at roadside farm stands, at farmers' markets, and increasingly, at supermarkets. In summer, these fruits are in season, at their peak of ripeness and flavor, and—bonus!—at their cheapest. These days, we see summer fruits in our markets at all times of the year. They come from the temperate climates below the equator, where it's summer when it's winter here. But it's a long, long way from Buenos Aires, Argentina, and Valparaiso, Chile, to our ports. And it's even farther from Australia and New Zealand. So growers there choose varieties that travel well and they pick them while still firm. It takes an enormous amount of fuel to power the boats or planes that carry them to us, and despite their appearance, they aren't fresh as we know fresh can be when local fruits come to nearby farmers' markets ripe in June through September.

I'll choose my own summer fruits from the freezer any day over fruits hauled up from South America or the Antipodes. I can put them up at their absolute best, and I know for sure they're organic and that nothing has been added to them except what I use to pack them—and that's just a light syrup of water, lemon juice, and a touch of honey.

What a bounty! Strawberries, black currants, cherries, apricots, plums, blueberries, huckleberries, gooseberries, elderberries, red currants, peaches, nectarines, plumcots, red and black raspberries, blackberries, grapes, dewberries, pears, melons, early apples, and more. Eat them fresh out of hand. Cook them into pies and pastries, cobblers and crisps. Toss them in fruit medleys. The possibilities are endless.

ICE CREAMS, SORBETS, & FROZEN TREATS

watermelon water ice

MAKES ABOUT ½ GALLON

Here's a fun job for the kids. Have them wash their grubby hands scrupulously and scrub their fingernails. Set your largest strainer over a bowl. Give them chunks of fresh, sweet watermelon and let them squish the chunks so the juice runs through the strainer but the seeds and flesh stay behind. Then make this simple water ice.

½ cup Simple Syrup (page 266)
1 large watermelon
Plenty of ice
Mint sprigs, for garnish (optional)

1. Chill the syrup.

2. Separate the sweet flesh from the watermelon rind and cut into chunks. Set a strainer over a bowl and add the watermelon chunks, several at a time, pressing down to release the juices. Discard the seeds.

3. Add the syrup to the watermelon juice. Taste and add more if you wish, but the water ice should be refreshing, not overly sweet.

4. Pour the liquid into glasses filled with ice, or into a pitcher half filled with ice. The watermelon juice is good the day you make it, but falls in quality by the next day, so serve immediately.

cucumber sorbet

MAKES ABOUT 1½ PINTS

There isn't a more refreshing palate cleanser than this crisp sorbet. Serve it between the starter and the main dish.

3 medium cucumbers
Juice of 1 lime
2 tablespoons quick-dissolving (superfine) sugar
¼ teaspoon coarsely cracked black peppercorns

1. Peel two of the cucumbers but leave the peel on the third, which gives this sorbet a pleasant green color. Wash the cucumbers, trim off the ends, and slice them in half lengthwise. With a teaspoon, scoop out the seeds.

2. Cut the cucumbers into 2-inch chunks. Place them in a blender with a quarter cup of water and blend to a smooth puree.

3. Add the lime juice, sugar, and pepper and pulse a few times to incorporate.

4. Pour the mixture into an ice-cream maker and process according to the manufacturer's instructions. When the mixture has become thick and frozen, turn it into a freezer-chilled container, cover, and place in the freezer until it hardens, or serve scoops immediately in small chilled cups.

Melon with Sorbet

An icy slice of sweet melon that holds a scoop of sorbet is a perfect hot-weather re-fresher. Chill the melon in the fridge or the ice cooler for at least an hour. As for the sor-bet, the colder the better.

The question is, really, which fruit sorbets go with which melons. Well, melon pairs well with melon, so a yellow or salmon-fleshed melon sorbet would go well with a green-fleshed melon, and vice versa. Always try to use contrasting colors. Sorbets are for sale everywhere, including the gelaterias, but if you have a glacière, it's simpler to make some of your own ahead of time and have it waiting in the freezer.

Here are some suggestions for pairings:

CANTALOUPE MELON
Charentais are the true cantaloupes, although the name is often misapplied to muskmelons. Charentais have a rough skin, but no netting, such as you see on muskmelons. They are considered among the finest flavored melons in the world. They have very sweet, orange flesh. Partners might be these sorbets:

Mandarin	Lemon
Strawberry	Lime
Raspberry	Litchi
Orange	

MUSKMELONS (GREEN FLESHED)
You can tell the common muskmelon by the netting on its skin. The green-fleshed types such as Galia have a mild, very sweet flavor. Try them with these sorbets:

Strawberry	Cucumber
Raspberry	Ginger
Lime	

MUSKMELONS (SALMON FLESHED)
Ambrosia, Burpee Hybrid, and Persian melons are three popular types of salmon-fleshed muskmelons with reticulated (netted) skin. All have deeply colored, very sweet, juicy flesh. They all pair well with these sorbets:

Lime	Blackberry
Orange	Grapefruit
Strawberry	

HONEYDEW MELONS (GREEN FLESHED)

Honeydews have smooth, white to light-gold skins. The emerald green–fleshed kinds are the most popular and most frequently found in markets, and they have a sweet, juicy, and spicy flavor that pairs well with tropical and semitropical fruits:

Mango	Cherimoya
Pineapple	Lime-mint
Kiwi	Pear

HONEYDEW MELONS (YELLOW/GOLD FLESHED)

Many honeydews have salmon, orange, gold, or white flesh. They tend to have rich, aromatic flavor and meltingly sweet texture. Pair them with these sorbets:

Lime	Raspberry
Lemon	Strawberry
Mango	

CRENSHAW MELON

Crenshaws are large melons with yellow skin with crinkled striations when ripe. Their salmon-colored, juicy, sweet flesh carries a unique flavor that pairs with these:

Strawberry	Blackberry
Black raspberry	

WATERMELON

Watermelon makes a fine sorbet when pureed to smoothness in a blender with the following fruits. Use the pulp from a baby seedless watermelon, and puree with 3 cups of superfine sugar, 1 pound of hulled strawberries, $\frac{1}{3}$ pound of raspberries, and $\frac{1}{2}$ pound of cherry preserves. Freeze in an ice-cream maker according to the manufacturer's instructions.

Strawberry	Cherry
Raspberry	

litchi sorbet

MAKES 1 PINT

Here's a refreshing sorbet with an intriguing aromatic flavor. Serve it with fresh seasonal fruits, which in high summer might mean apricots, peaches, or nectarines. Litchis have the interesting quality of tasting and smelling just about as good when canned as when fresh. They can be found in most large supermarkets and certainly in any Asian market. If you don't have an ice-cream maker, you can use an ice cube tray with the cube chambers removed, or a simple shallow bowl covered with plastic wrap.

One 15-ounce can litchis in syrup
1 ½ teaspoons unflavored gelatin
½ cup sugar
¼ cup water

1. Strain the litchi syrup and pour ½ cup of it into a small bowl. Sprinkle the gelatin over the syrup and set aside for a few minutes to allow the gelatin to soften.

2. Place a small saucepan over medium-high heat and add the sugar and water. Heat until the sugar melts, remove from the heat, and stir in the gelatin mixture. Set aside.

3. Place the litchis and remaining syrup in a food processor or blender, making sure the litchis' large seeds are all removed. Puree until smooth. Add the sugar-gelatin mixture and blend until smooth.

4. Pour the mixture into an ice-cream maker and freeze according to manufacturer's instructions. Scrape and stir the mixture occasionally as it freezes so that a granite-like sorbet is formed. Serve with fresh summer fruits.

blueberry-yogurt popsicles

MAKES 8 TO 10 SERVINGS

Instead of buying those sugary, unnaturally flavored and colored popsicles, make these, using plastic popsicle trays and wooden sticks. The set-up is inexpensive to buy and the popsicles are full of great nutrition and so are well worth the cost. This is a great summer activity that your kids are sure to enjoy.

4 cups fresh blueberries, picked over
2 cups water
⅔ cup sugar
¼ teaspoon ground allspice
16 ounces plain yogurt

1. Place a saucepan over medium-low heat and add the blueberries, water, sugar, and allspice. Bring the mixture to a boil, stirring frequently. When the sugar has dissolved and the blueberries are soft, remove from the heat and let cool to room temperature.

2. Add the yogurt to the cooled blueberry mixture and stir well. Working in 2 batches, add the yogurt mixture to a blender and puree until smooth.

3. Insert wooden sticks in the popsicle trays and fill the trays. Place in the freezer until frozen solid. Wrap each frozen popsicle in plastic wrap and return to the freezer.

super-fast homemade ice cream

MAKES ABOUT 1 PINT

Food science writer Harold McGee, writing in the *New York Times*, suggested the following fast method of making ice cream at home without using an ice-cream maker. I tried it. It works, not only with ice creams, but with fruit sorbets, too. It's perfect for a hot summer afternoon—you'll have a refreshing summer treat in less than an hour!

This recipe makes chocolate ice cream. Note that the bags of salted ice water are made at least a day ahead and can be refrozen and reused.

3 gallon-size food storage freezer bags
3 quarts water
1 pound kosher salt
2 cups half-and-half
½ cup cocoa powder
½ cup granulated sugar
½ teaspoon vanilla extract

1. In a large bowl, add the water and salt and stir until the salt has dissolved. A saturated salt solution won't freeze until the temperature drops to about 22°F. Place half the liquid into each of 2 of the food storage freezer bags. Seal bags, leaving a little air to allow for expansion after freezing. Lay the bags flat in the freezer. Freeze overnight, until frozen solid. These super-cold bags will be used to freeze your ice-cream mixture.

2. Place 3 small serving bowls in the freezer. In a saucepan, mix the half-and-half and cocoa over low heat, stirring until a chocolatey liquid forms. Don't boil. Add the sugar and stir until it dissolves.

3. Remove from the heat, stir in the vanilla

extract, and set aside to cool. When the mixture reaches room temperature, pour into the third gallon-size food storage freezer bag, exclude as much air as possible, and seal.

4. Lay two fully open bath towels over each other on a table. Place one bag of frozen brine in the center of the towels. Lay the bag with the chocolatey mixture on top of the frozen brine bag, then place the second bag of frozen brine on the chocolatey bag. Fold the towels over the stack of bags so they are covered and insulated. The towels keep the supercooled brine's coolth (a real word and the opposite of *warmth*) focused on the ice cream mix.

5. After 20 minutes, open the towels and remove the ice cream bag. It will be partially frozen. Gently knead the bag to mix the frozen part with the liquid, then reassemble the stack and fold up the towels again. Allow to freeze for another 20 to 25 minutes. Open the ice cream bag and spoon the ice cream into the bowls taken from the freezer. Serve immediately.

CLASSIC DELIGHTS

traditional berry summer pudding

MAKES 8 SERVINGS

Use the fruits of high summer—cherries, blueberries, raspberries, blackberries, red currants, plums, apricots, peaches, nectarines, and strawberries—to make this

yummy no-cook dessert. It's a showstopper. Note that this dish is made the day before it's to be served.

2 loaves of egg bread (challah, brioche), crusts removed
8 cups mixed summer fruits, pitted, peeled, or hulled as appropriate
1 cup sugar
2 tablespoons brandy
1 pint heavy cream

1. Line a large bowl with plastic wrap. Cut ½-inch-thick slices from the bread into triangles as large as possible, removing crusts. Cover the bottom and sides of the bowl completely with the triangles. Reserve unused triangles.

2. Place a large saucepan over medium heat and add all the fruit. Add ½ cup of the sugar and brandy and cook for about 5 minutes, or until the juices just begin to run but the fruit still holds its shape. Set aside to cool slightly.

3. Using a slotted spoon, place the fruit in the bread-lined bowl, leaving the juices behind. Pour about three-quarters of the juices from the saucepan over the fruit. Completely cover the top of the fruit with the remaining bread triangles. Cover with plastic wrap and set a plate on top to add pressure to the pudding. Set about 2 pounds of weight on the plate (butter, a sack of sugar, etc.). Place the bowl in the fridge for at least 8 hours, but preferably overnight.

4. In a small bowl, whip the cream to soft peaks, add the remaining ½ cup of sugar, and continue to whip until stiff peaks form.

5. Remove the pudding from the fridge and remove the weights, plate, and plastic

wrap. Place a serving platter upside down over the top of the bowl and quickly but gently invert the pudding and serving platter. Lift the bowl and remove the bottom layer of plastic wrap. Pour the reserved juices over the top of the pudding and serve with whipped cream.

cold lemon soufflé
MAKES ABOUT 1 QUART

Light and airy, cold and refreshing, sweet and tangy—that's this easy cold soufflé. Make it a day ahead so it gets plenty of refrigerator time, which will help it set and its flavors to marry. Have some extra sweetened whipped cream on hand—it's delicious on top of this soufflé. You may substitute limes or oranges for the lemon in this recipe.

¼ cup cold water
1 tablespoon unflavored gelatin
3 eggs, separated
1 cup sugar
2 organic (or well-washed) lemons, zest removed and juiced
1 cup heavy cream, beaten to stiff peaks

1. Place the cold water in a cup, sprinkle the gelatin over, and set aside for a few minutes to allow the gelatin to soften. In a small bowl, place the egg yolks and the sugar. Beat until smooth, thick, and light yellow in color. Whisk in the lemon zest and juice until well combined. Set aside.

2. Beat the egg whites until they form stiff peaks, but not to dryness. Set aside.

3. Heat the gelatin mixture in the microwave at full power for 15 seconds, then stir. If not completely dissolved, heat for an additional 15 seconds.

4. Mix the gelatin into the lemon mixture, then fold in the egg whites and whipped cream until well combined. Transfer the mixture to a serving dish, such as a large, round ramekin. Cover and refrigerate overnight.

summer fruit coulis

MAKES 2 TO 4 SERVINGS

Though the term *coulis* can refer to everything from meat juices to thick purees and soups, it most often refers to uncooked fruit juices. Nab the summer fruits in their high season and steal their essence. Use them now in spritzers and over desserts or under grilled meats, or freeze them in half-pint freezer bags for use in other seasons.

1 quart fresh summer fruit (raspberries, strawberries, blackberries, blueberries, boysenberries, black raspberries, cherries, apricots, peaches)
¼ cup seedless fruit jam (of one of the fruits used)
½ cup sugar
2 tablespoons water

1. Wash and pit stone fruits. Don't wash berries. Place the fruit in a blender or food processor and pulse just until the fruit releases its juices. Strain through a strainer, sieve, or through two layers of cheesecloth, catching the juice in a bowl.

2. Place a small saucepan over medium-low heat. Add the jam, sugar, and water and cook, stirring occasionally, until mixture is melted. Add the melted sugar and jam to the juice and stir well to incorporate. The coulis will keep for a week in the fridge. For unused coulis, pour ½ cupfuls into small freezer bags, seal, and freeze.

ambrosia

MAKES 6 TO 8 SERVINGS

There used to be a little shop on West Third Street near Sixth Avenue in Greenwich Village in the 1960s that served this fruit salad to legions of musicians, hippies, and other denizens of the demimonde. On hot summer days, with "Summer in the City" as background music, ambrosia was just the fortification we needed to get back on the streets and fight the culture wars. It is still delicious. Here is that same ambrosia, right down to the Cool Whip.

6 navel oranges, peeled and segments separated
½ pineapple, peeled and cut into 1-inch cubes
3 mangos, cut into ½-inch cubes
1 pint strawberries, trimmed, hulled, and cut into ¼-inch slices
4 ounces sour cream
16 ounces Cool Whip

1. Prepare the oranges: Working over a large bowl, use a grapefruit spoon to dislodge the flesh from segments of the navels, leaving the membranes behind.

Keep as much of the juice with the orange flesh as possible. Add the pineapple, mangos, and strawberries, and toss to combine.

2. Add the sour cream and Cool Whip and fold all the ingredients together. Cover the bowl and refrigerate until cold, at least 1 hour. Serve in bowls or sundae glasses.

✱ **VARIATION**
Add 3 tablespoons Cointreau or Grand Marnier to the bowl before stirring in the sour cream and Cool Whip.

 WATERMELON BASKET FOR SUMMER FRUITS
MAKES 8 TO 10 SERVINGS

This is a delightful way to present a medley of summer fruits when entertaining. If using peaches and nectarines, peel and slice them into a bowl of acidulated water (the juice of 1 lemon to every 4 cups of water). This keeps them from browning when exposed to air. Drain and add them to the fruit mixture just before serving. You'll need a melon baller for this dish, but you can also use a teaspoon.

1 large seedless watermelon
1 ripe muskmelon
2 large bunches seedless grapes
1 pint blueberries
Large bowl acidulated water
5 ripe peaches, peeled and sliced
3 ripe nectarines, peeled and sliced

1. Place the watermelon on a work surface, yellow side down (the side with the yellow oval where the watermelon lay on the ground as it grew). Using a serrated knife, make 2 vertical cuts halfway through the melon, about 3 inches apart, each cut about 1½ inches from the center point of the top of the melon. Now cut horizontally from the middle of each end toward the vertical cuts, stopping when you reach them. Remove the 2 freed pieces from the melon and set aside. Using a sharp, pointed knife, and working very carefully so as not to break the rind, cut the flesh from under the "handle" you've just created. Set the flesh aside. Using the melon baller's large end, make melon balls from the flesh of the 2 large pieces and the flesh under the handle, and place them in the large bowl. Use the melon baller to scoop out the flesh from the watermelon and smooth the inner surface with the edge of a tablespoon when you reach the whitish material closest to the rind.

2. Cut the muskmelon in half, seed it, and use the melon baller to make melon balls to add to the watermelon bowl. Wash the grapes and shake them dry, then pull the grapes from their stems and add them to the melon bowl. Add the blueberries to the melon bowl.

3. Blanch the peaches in boiling water for 90 seconds, then plunge into cold water. Remove the skins and, using a butter knife, cut slices about ½-inch wide and drop them into the acidulated water. Slice the nectarines with their skins on and add them to the peaches. Pour out the peaches and nectarines into a colander and let drain, giving the colander a good shake once or twice over 1 or 2 minutes. Add the peaches and nectarines to the melons and, using a large wooden spoon or your hands, very gently stir up the fruit to mix well.

4. Transfer the fruit to the melon basket and serve, or refrigerate with the fruit medley covered with cling wrap until you're ready to serve. If there's leftover fruit, place in a bowl, cover with cling wrap, and refrigerate for use later. The colder the fruit, the better.

✱ VARIATIONS

If using the basket right away, add strawberry slices. If you want to use raspberries or blackberries, sprinkle them on top of the medley, rather than stirring them in, as they are tender and will break and squish.

peach delight
MAKES 4 TO 6 SERVINGS

The best quality, tree-ripened, and locally grown peaches are only available for a month or so in high summer, so enjoy them while you can. Make extra batches of this salad and keep them stored in sealed plastic bags in the freezer. Then gently thaw a bag in a bowl of water hot from the tap so the fruit is still cold but almost all thawed.

Juice of 1 lemon
6 ripe peaches
½ pint blueberries
½ pint red raspberries
½ pint blackberries
½ cup orange juice
3 tablespoons Cointreau

1. Fill a large bowl with ice water. In another bowl, add the lemon juice and ½ cup water. Set aside.

2. Blanch the peaches in boiling water for 90 seconds. Plunge into the ice water. Remove the skins.

3. Use a sharp knife to cut the peaches into ½-inch-wide slices, dropping them into the bowl with the lemon juice. Stir the slices occasionally as you work so they are coated all over with the lemon juice, which prevents browning. Discard the pits.

4. Add the other fruits to the bowl with the peaches. Don't stir yet, as the blackberries and raspberries rupture easily. Add the orange juice and the Cointreau. Now stir gently to mix and serve in individual bowls.

✱ WILD BERRY DELIGHT
Add wild berries you gather from the fields and meadows, such as wineberries and

black raspberries (black caps). Top each bowl with a dollop of whipped cream and a mint sprig.

To freeze this dessert: The following assemblage can be mixed with 2 cups of lightly sweetened and acidified water (juice of 1 lemon and a tablespoon of honey added; in which case, omit the first ingredient in the recipe), put up in freezer bags, and frozen for further delights after summer ends. If you do put some up, thaw bags as needed in a bowl of hot tap water so the fruit is still cold but the sweetened, acidified water is almost all thawed.

apple fritters
MAKES 4 SERVINGS

We have the benefit of having easy access to good apples all year round thanks to controlled atmosphere storage here in the United States. But the first local apples of the new season, which arrive in midsummer, always give cause for rejoicing. No

✳ GOOD TO KNOW: FORAGING FOR WILD SUMMER FRUITS

When making summer fruit coulis, don't forget the wild fruits of summer. If you live in an urban or suburban area, it's a good excuse to make a foraging expedition into the country. You'll be surprised how close the wilderness is to even our largest cities. Pike County, Pennsylvania, for instance, is only 100 miles from Times Square, but has the greatest concentration of black bear of any county in the country. And those bears just love wild summer fruits. Here's what you can find growing wild in the mid-Atlantic states and parts of New England.

✳ HUCKLEBERRIES AND BLUEBERRIES. You'll find them ripe and in abundance on the Pocono Plateau and Appalachian Mountains in mid-July.

✳ WINEBERRIES. They look like red raspberries but taste better. They were brought to the United States over 100 years ago and escaped into the wild, where they have proliferated in shady, east-facing locations. They ripen in mid-July.

✳ DEWBERRIES. These small blackberries grow on low, trailing stems and are ripe in late July and early August.

✳ BLACKBERRIES. They ripen at the same time as dewberries but grow on four- to six-foot-tall canes.

✳ BLACK RASPBERRIES. Also called black caps, these beautiful bramble fruits are ripe on the Fourth of July through much of their range. Finding a stand where they've access to enough water to make plump berries is a cause for rejoicing.

✳ WILD STRAWBERRIES. Probably the best-tasting fruit of them all. They grow in poor, clay and shale soils and are ripe just as summer begins.

✳ ELDERBERRIES. Also called shadblow, their large panicles of berries weigh down the branches. The fruit is edible but the wood and stems are poisonous, so pick carefully.

✳ WILD CHERRIES. Part of the mixed hardwood forests of the East Coast with small, intensely flavored fruits.

There may be other, local wild fruits in your area, such as pawpaws, jujubes, and persimmons. For more information, check with the North American Fruit Explorers (www.nafex.org).

other apples beat their fresh flavor or just-off-the-tree goodness. We don't start many breakfasts with apple fritters, but these tasty sweets can signal the start of apple season in a celebratory way. They also make a delightful end to any casual summer meal.

3 large apples, peeled and cored
Juice of 1 lemon
¾ cup all-purpose flour
1½ tablespoons sugar
1½ teaspoons baking powder
Pinch salt
½ cup milk
1 egg, separated, plus 1 egg white
1 tablespoon canola oil
Peanut oil for deep frying
Powdered sugar, for serving
Maple syrup (optional)

1. Cut the apples into ¼-inch slices. In a bowl, place the apples and lemon juice and toss to coat. Set aside.

2. In a mixing bowl, mix together the flour, sugar, baking powder, and salt. In a separate bowl, add the milk, the egg yolk, and the canola oil. Beat to mix well. Add the milk mixture to the flour mixture and stir to mix.

3. Place a heavy pot or deep fryer over medium (375°F) heat and add 3 inches of the peanut oil. Beat the 2 egg whites until they form stiff peaks. Fold the whites into the batter.

4. Take one apple slice at a time and shake off any excess lemon juice. Dip the slice into the batter and let excess fall off, then slide the slice into the hot oil. Continue with more slices. Turn each slice when the color reaches a light gold, and continue

GOOD TO KNOW: MAKING SUMMER FRUIT SAUCES

Now that the summer fruits are here, it's time to make sweet fruit sauces to pour over vanilla ice cream, drizzle over pancakes, mix with icing to cover cakes, pair with lemon Bavarians and custards, make sorbets, and as many other uses as you can think of.

The berries make quick and easy sauces. Use black and red raspberries, blackberries, blueberries, and wild berries like the wineberries you pick yourself from the hedgerows and meadow edges. Place the berries in a saucepan and mash them until some juices flow, then turn the heat to medium. Add sugar and lemon juice to taste and cook, stirring frequently, until the berries have released their juices. Strain the liquid to remove the seeds and solids. Let cool to room temperature, then store covered in the fridge.

Make sauce from other fruits, like cherries, apricots, plums, and peaches. Simply pit the fruits and chop them coarsely, then cook them with a little lemon juice and sugar to taste.

Be creative. Try a little vanilla and orange in a peach sauce, add a lavender flower spike to a strawberries-and-orange mixture, try some grated ginger and sugar with blackberries.

These fruit sauces freeze well in zipper lock freezer bags. Thaw them quickly by placing a bag in a bowl of hot water. They bring the refreshing taste of summer to meals later in the year.

frying until it's golden brown and puffed, about 4 minutes.

5. Using a slotted spoon, remove the fritters from the oil and let drain on paper towels. Transfer the drained fritters to a platter in a low oven to keep them warm. Serve them dusted with powdered sugar and warm maple syrup on the side, if desired.

crêpes suzette

MAKES 4 SERVINGS

Crêpes suzette are marvelous any time of the year and classically call for orange butter. But this variation combines strawberries and black currants, both of which ripen at the very beginning of summer. It's the perfect dessert (or sweet lunch) to celebrate the summer solstice. If you can't find a source of fresh black currants, substitute cassis or red currant jelly as noted in the recipe. Yes, there's a lot of butter, but this is celebratory food, eaten at the solstice to welcome in the glorious summertime.

CRÊPES
1 cup white or whole wheat pastry flour
2 whole eggs, plus two egg yolks
8 tablespoons canola oil
1 ½ cups whole milk

BLACK CURRANT SYRUP
2 cups black currant berries
2 tablespoons sugar

CURRANT BUTTER
3 tablespoons Black Currant Syrup (or same amount of cassis or red currant jelly)

6 tablespoons unsalted butter
1 teaspoon organic lemon zest

SAUCE
½ cup unsalted butter
¼ cup Black Currant Syrup (or cassis)
⅓ cup red currant jelly
1 tablespoon organic lemon zest

2 cups strawberries (whole if wild berries, quartered if large)
Powdered or superfine sugar for sprinkling
⅓ cup Cognac or brandy

1. Make the crêpes: In a large mixing bowl, add the flour, eggs, extra yolks, 6 tablespoons of the oil, and ½ cup of the milk. Whisk until thoroughly mixed, then slowly drizzle in the rest of the milk as you whisk, until the batter becomes as thick as cream and coats a metal spoon. Cover the bowl and place in the fridge for at least 1 hour or up to a day.

2. If the batter is too thick after resting, add a little milk until it reaches the consistency of heavy cream. Place a 7- to 10-inch saucepan with sloping sides over medium-high heat and wipe with some of the remaining 2 tablespoons oil. When the pan is hot, add about ⅓ cup of batter, lift the pan, and tilt and swirl it so the batter spreads out evenly and thinly to about a 6- or 7-inch crepe. Return pan to heat until the crêpe is lightly browned on one side, then flip with a spatula and lightly brown the other side.

3. Continue until all the batter is used and you have a stack of about 8 crêpes. Stack the crêpes on a plate with pieces of wax paper between them. You can freeze these for later use or proceed with making the crêpes suzette. If you freeze them, have them completely thawed before proceeding with the dessert.

4. Make the syrup: Place a saucepan over medium-low heat and cook the black currants until their juices flow. Mash the fruit with a wooden spoon and strain through a fine-mesh sieve into a bowl. Discard the solids. Add the sugar and stir until it has dissolved. If using cassis or red currant jelly as an alternative to fresh black currants, omit the sugar and use them as is.

5. Make the butter: In a medium bowl, add 3 tablespoons of the Black Currant Syrup. Reserve the rest of the syrup. In a medium bowl, beat the butter until it's soft and creamy. Add the lemon zest and beat until thoroughly mixed. Add the Black Currant Syrup or one of the alternatives and beat to incorporate.

6. Make the sauce: Place a large saucepan over low heat and add the butter, syrup, jelly, and lemon zest. Bring to a simmer, cook for 3 to 4 minutes, and remove from the heat.

7. Assemble the dessert: Place the crêpes on the work surface with the underside of each crêpe (the side cooked last) facing up. Spread with a bit of the currant butter, then fold in half, and in half again to make quarter-round wedges. Place in the pan with the sauce.

8. Scatter the strawberries over the crêpes, cover the saucepan and place the pan over low heat until the dessert is warm. Uncover, sprinkle the crêpes with a little powdered or superfine sugar, and pour the Cognac or brandy over.

9. Being careful not to singe off your eyelashes, ignite the Cognac with a match, let the flame die, then spoon some of the sauce in the pan over the crêpes and fruit.* Serve

each person two crêpes with berries and sauce.

*Take extra precautions with open flames while cooking. Keep the children away from the kitchen.

sweet fruit crêpes
MAKES 3 TO 4 SERVINGS

The secret of good fruit crêpes is to make them as thin as possible. This recipe will make slightly puffy crêpes, so starting with a thin batter is essential. You'll notice that the batter must rest for a good 2 hours or overnight after it's made and the filling needs 1 hour's rest, too.

CRÊPES
1½ cups fat-free milk
3 large eggs, separated
1 tablespoon sugar
3 tablespoons orange liqueur, rum, or brandy
1½ cups all-purpose flour, sifted
5 tablespoons melted unsalted butter
⅛ teaspoon salt
Nonstick cooking spray

FILLING
2 pints strawberries, hulled and sliced
½ pint red raspberries
½ cup sliced bananas
¼ cup granulated sugar
¼ cup orange liqueur or brandy

Powdered sugar

1. Make the crêpes: Place the milk, egg yolks, sugar, liqueur, flour, and butter in a blender. Blend on highest speed for 1 minute. Pour the batter into a pitcher with a spout.

Whip the egg whites and salt until they form stiff peaks. Fold the whites into the batter.

2. Spray a skillet (or crêpe pan) with a light coating of nonstick cooking spray and place over medium heat. When the pan is hot, add a scant ¼ cup of batter, lift the pan, and tilt and swirl it so the batter spreads out evenly and thinly. Return pan to heat until the crêpe is a light nutmeg brown on one side, about 1 minute, then flip, gently lifting with your fingers, and cook for an additional 30 seconds on the other side.

3. Continue until all the batter is used and you have a stack of about 15 to 20 crepes. Stack the crêpes on a plate in a warm oven with the pretty side up (the side you cooked first). Place squares of wax paper between the crêpes. Cover with a bowl so they don't dry out.

4. Make the filling: In a bowl, gently mix together the fruit, sugar, and liqueur to coat. Let stand for 1 hour.

5. Place 2 tablespoons filling across the crêpe about one-third of the way from the side, then roll it up starting from the short side, gently exerting a little pressure as you roll so the filling travels out toward the edges of the crêpe. Place the crêpe on a warm plate and sprinkle powdered sugar over lightly.

grilled apricots in caramel sauce

MAKES 4 SERVINGS

When you're planning to fire up your grill in early summer when apricots are ripe, consider making this superb dessert. Just make sure you use a fine mesh cooking plate on the grill so the apricots don't fall through. You can use the oven's broiler too—just be careful not to let them burn.

12 ripe apricots
⅔ cup superfine granulated sugar
1 pint vanilla ice cream
4 tablespoons caramel sauce
½ cup slivered, toasted almonds

1. Cut apricots in half and remove the pits. Place the fruit halves in a plastic bag with the sugar and shake until the apricots are coated. Grill them over medium heat, turning frequently until the sugar melts and caramelizes and the apricots are heated through.

2. Divide the apricots among 4 serving bowls, top with 1 scoop of vanilla ice cream, 1 tablespoon of warmed caramel sauce, and 1 tablespoon of toasted almonds. Serve immediately, before the ice cream melts.

cherries jubilee
MAKES 4 SERVINGS

It's the Fourth of July and the Bing cherries are arriving in the stores, so why not make this wonderfully delicious and traditional dessert for the Fourth of July barbecue or dinner? There are many brands of cherry brandy, but Bols, DeKuyper, Kirschwasser, and Seagram's are among the most popular. This cherry-flavored brandy is only 50 proof, so to make sure it flames during the flambé step, gently warm it in a saucepan before igniting.

½ cup (1 stick) butter
1 cup sugar
1 pound sweet cherries, pitted
1 organic (or well-washed) orange, zest removed and juiced
1 cup cherry brandy
1 tablespoon cornstarch
1 tablespoon cold water
1 pint vanilla ice cream

1. Set a saucepan over medium heat and add the butter. When the butter has melted, add the sugar and cook about 2 minutes, until the sugar has dissolved. Add the cherries and orange zest and juice and cook, stirring often, for 3 minutes.

2. In a separate saucepan over low heat, warm the brandy (see headnote).

3. In a cup, stir together the cornstarch and water, then pour the mixture into the saucepan with the cherries and stir to mix. Pour the warmed brandy over the cherries. Use a match or lighter to flame the brandy.* Set the saucepan off the heat and let the alcohol burn off.

4. Spoon ¼ pint of the ice cream into each of 4 bowls, and spoon the cherry mixture over. Serve at once.

*Take extra precautions with open flames while cooking. Keep the children away from the kitchen.

brandied peaches
MAKES 4 QUARTS

Now, in midsummer when the peaches are perfect, is the time to make several jars of brandied peaches for Thanksgiving and the Christmas and New Year's holidays. It's fun and easy to do and the result will be welcome indeed when the snow is blowing. I have a lidded stoneware crock that I use to make the peaches, but you can use Mason jars with lids and rings. Sterilize them for 5 minutes in a boiling water bath before filling them. Store the jars in a cool, dark place.

4 sterilized Mason jars, lids, and rings
9 pounds whole ripe peaches
2 sticks cinnamon
2 tablespoons whole cloves
1 quart water
5 pounds granulated sugar
6 cups brandy

1. Fill a clean kitchen sink with cold water. In a large pot over high heat, bring water to boil. Blanch 7 to 9 peaches in the boiling water for 2 minutes. Plunge into the cold water. Remove the skins and put them in a colander set over a pot to catch any juices. Process the rest of the peaches until they're all peeled.

2. Tightly tie up the cinnamon and cloves in a cheesecloth bag.

3. In a large pot over high heat, add the water, sugar, and spice bag. Boil until the liquid turns clear, about 5 minutes. Add the peaches and continue boiling until the peaches are tender but not soft, just 1 to 2 minutes. Remove the peaches and set aside. Continue boiling the liquid until it reaches the syrup stage (220°F or 105°C.), checking the temperature with a candy thermometer. Allow the syrup to cool to room temperature.

4. Add the brandy to the cooled syrup, stirring to mix.

5. Add the peaches to the sterilized jars. Discard the spice bag and ladle the brandy syrup into the jars, leaving about ½-inch headroom. Put on the lids and rings and process the jars according to the manufacturer's instructions to seal.

strawberry shortcake

MAKES 8 SERVINGS

Strawberry shortcake is derived from the Native American practice of mixing wild strawberries with corn cakes. You'll find shortcake biscuits in the supermarket, but they can't compare to homemade. At the height of the strawberry season, it's worth it to make the biscuits yourself.

STRAWBERRIES

3 pints strawberries, washed, dried, and hulled
⅓ cup superfine sugar

BISCUITS

1½ cups all-purpose flour
½ cup cornmeal
2 teaspoons baking powder
½ teaspoon baking soda
2 tablespoons sugar
6 tablespoons cold unsalted butter
¾ cup buttermilk

WHIPPED CREAM

1½ cups cold whipping or heavy cream
2 teaspoons superfine sugar
¼ teaspoon vanilla extract

1. Make the strawberry mixture: With a potato masher, crush one quarter of the berries. Slice the rest into thin slices. In a bowl, mix the crushed and sliced berries with the sugar until it dissolves.

2. Make the biscuits: Preheat the oven to 450°F. In a large mixing bowl, combine the flour, cornmeal, baking powder, baking soda, and sugar. Place the mixed dry ingredients in their mixing bowl in the freezer or refrigerator for 1 hour before proceeding to help to keep the butter solid. Cut the cold butter into small pieces and drop into the bowl. Using 2 knives, cut it into the flour mixture until the mixture has the consistency of coarse meal. This will take about 200 crosscuts.

3. Add the buttermilk and stir until the dry ingredients are moist. Lightly flour your hands, form the dough into a ball, and knead it against the bottom of the bowl about 10 times, turning it with each kneading.

4. On a lightly floured board, roll out the

dough about ¾ inch thick and cut into 3-inch squares, or, alternatively, cut 3-inch rounds with a biscuit cutter. Reroll any scraps and make further squares or rounds. This makes 8 biscuits. Place them on an ungreased baking sheet. Brush the tops of the biscuits with buttermilk and bake 10 to 12 minutes, or until they have risen and are golden brown on top.

5. Make the whipped cream: In a chilled bowl, whip together all the ingredients until they form fluffy mounds.

6. To assemble the dessert: Remove the biscuits from the oven, and let rest 1 to 2 minutes. Using a fork, split them in half horizontally, as you would an English muffin.

7. Place each bottom on its own dessert plate. Spoon some of the strawberry mixture over each bottom, and then place the biscuit tops over. Top each dessert with a large dollop of whipped cream and serve at once. If you are serving fewer than 8 people, save the unsplit biscuits and strawberry mixture separately in the fridge. Rewarm the biscuits in a 200°F oven before assembling the desserts. Only make as much whipped cream as you'll need.

genoise cake with apricot glaze
MAKES 8 SERVINGS

Summer isn't a time for heavy cakes, but it *is* a time for cakes so light they might float away on a warm breeze. Here's one example. A Genoise depends more on eggs than flour for its light and lovely texture. Just be patient when whipping the eggs with a handheld electric mixer—it will take at least 15 minutes for the eggs to have enough air whipped into

them. The result, however, is the fluffiest cake imaginable, one just begging to be given an apricot glaze. It really helps to have two 9-inch cake pans with removable bottoms.

CAKE
1¼ cups pastry flour
1 cup sugar
⅓ cup unsalted butter, melted
6 large eggs
1 teaspoon vanilla extract

GLAZE
3 cups fresh, ripe, pitted apricots*
1 cup sugar
1 cup light corn syrup
2 teaspoons unflavored gelatin

1. Make the cake: Preheat the oven to 350°F. Remove the bottoms of the cake pans and set them on wax paper. With a sharp knife, use the pan bottoms as a template and cut out wax paper rounds to fit them exactly. Place the bottoms back in the pans, cover each with a round of wax paper, and grease the inside and bottom of the pans with a thin coating of butter, then lightly flour them.

2. Into a bowl, sift together the flour and ¼ cup of the sugar and set aside. In a saucepan, gently heat the butter just until it melts, then remove from the heat. In a large warmed bowl, whisk together the eggs and the remaining ¾ cup of sugar until smooth.

3. Using a handheld electric mixer on high speed, mix the egg-sugar mixture briskly for about 15 minutes, until the batter turns a light lemon yellow, triples in bulk, and forms a continuous ribbon when allowed to drip from the edge of a spoon. Dust ½ cup of the flour mixture over the batter and gently fold it in until mixed.

Repeat with the rest of the flour mixture in ½-cup additions until all is incorporated.

4. Rewarm the butter and add 1 ½ cups of the batter and the vanilla extract to the butter in the pan, stirring until well mixed. Add the butter mixture back into the egg batter and mix gently until smooth.

5. Pour the batter into the cake pans and bake for 15 to 17 minutes, or until the cake begins to pull away from the sides of the pans. Remove to the kitchen counter and let cool on racks for 10 minutes. Slide a knife around the sides of the pans, then invert the first pan onto a serving dish. Remove the pan and wax paper. Invert the second pan onto a smooth plate (so this layer can be slid or lifted onto the first layer), and remove the pan and the wax paper. Let the layers cool to room temperature.

6. Make the glaze: In a saucepan over low heat add the apricots, sugar, and corn syrup and cook until the apricots are very tender and the sugar is dissolved, about 20 minutes. Stir frequently so that the fruit and sugar don't scorch. Set a strainer over a bowl and press the cooked apricots and syrup through.

7. In a saucepan, warm 1 cup water and sprinkle the gelatin over. Allow to sit for 3 minutes, then heat on low heat until the gelatin has dissolved. Mix into the apricots. Cool until thickened into syrup.

8. Make sure the Genoise is room temperature before glazing. Pour the glaze onto the center of the cake on the serving dish and spread it out evenly to the edges. Gently lift or slide the top layer onto the bottom layer. Glaze the surface of the top layer and the sides of both.

---

* If apricots are in season, use the homemade recipe above. If they are out of season, simply melt ½ cup of apricot preserves in a saucepan and mash until smooth, strain, and let cool. Then skip steps 6 and 7 of the recipe.

carrot cake

MAKES 8 SERVINGS

Carrot cake is especially good when summer's fresh local carrots are in the markets. If you grow them in your garden, pull them young and tender, wash them, and make this cake immediately. You have never tasted carrot cake as good as one made with plucked-from-the-garden carrots.

2 cups all-purpose flour
2 teaspoons baking powder
2 teaspoons baking soda
1 teaspoon cinnamon
1 teaspoon salt
¼ teaspoon ground mace
1 ½ cups sugar
½ pound room temperature unsalted butter
4 eggs
3 cups finely shredded carrots
1 tablespoon plus 1 teaspoon lemon zest
    from an organic lemon
¾ cup chopped walnuts
½ cup freshly squeezed lemon juice
1 ½ cups powdered sugar

1. In a medium bowl, sift together the flour, baking powder, baking soda, cinnamon, salt, and mace.

2. In a separate bowl, beat the sugar and butter together until smooth. Beat in the eggs until smooth, then beat in the flour and spice mixture. Fold in the carrots, 1 tablespoon lemon zest, and nuts.

3. Preheat the oven to 350°F. Grease a deep, 10-inch cake pan. Pour the batter into the pan and bake for 50 to 60 minutes, until a toothpick inserted in the center comes out clean. Allow the cake to cool on a rack for 15 minutes.

4. In a bowl, beat together the lemon juice, 1 teaspoon of lemon zest, and powdered sugar until smooth. When the cake has cooled, slide a knife around the sides of the pan to release the cake. Invert it onto a serving plate. Warm the lemon glaze in a microwave for 30 seconds. Pour the warmed lemon glaze over the cake in an artful drizzle. Allow to cool to room temperature before serving.

✳ CARROT CAKE WITH RAISINS AND CREAM CHEESE FROSTING

Add ½ cup raisins to the cake batter. Substitute grated nutmeg for the mace. Instead of the lemon glaze, make cream cheese frosting by beating together until smooth 8 ounces cream cheese, 5 tablespoons unsalted butter, 1 teaspoon vanilla extract, and 2 cups powdered sugar.

PIES, TARTS, & COBBLERS

all-american apple pie

MAKES 6 TO 8 SERVINGS

Just the other day, I heard someone say, "Apple pie isn't all-American anymore. Nobody makes apple pie." I say let's defeat that notion, especially since we have so many different varieties of apples available. The season's first local apples—Gravenstein, Pink Lady, and Paulared—start arriving in August and make excellent pies. A slice of pie with a scoop of vanilla is the perfect end to a summer barbecue after the softball game. Or maybe nobody plays softball anymore, either.

6 medium apples, peeled, cored, quartered, and cut into thin slices
½ cup brown sugar
1 tablespoon cornstarch
⅛ teaspoon salt
½ teaspoon cinnamon
⅛ teaspoon nutmeg
Dough for 2 Flaky Pie Crusts (page 251)
1 tablespoon lemon juice
1½ tablespoons butter
1 tablespoon milk
1½ teaspoons granulated sugar
1½ teaspoons cinnamon

1. Preheat the oven to 450°F. In a bowl, add the apples. In another bowl, mix together the brown sugar, cornstarch, salt, cinnamon, and nutmeg. Add them to the apples and toss gently until the apples are evenly coated.

2. Line a 9-inch pie pan with one of the pie crusts. Place the apple mixture in the shell and sprinkle it with the lemon juice, then dot with the butter. Place the second pie crust over and trim off any excess. Crimp the top and bottom crusts together along the rim of the pie pan with the back of a fork. Brush the top crust with milk. Mix together the sugar and cinnamon, then very lightly sprinkle the top of the crust with it. Prick the pie crust in five places with a fork.

3. Place a sheet of aluminum foil on the oven rack to catch any juices and set the pie on it. Bake for 10 minutes, then reduce

the heat to 350°F and bake for 45 to 60 minutes more, or until the crust is golden brown and the juices are running.

4. Allow the pie to cool until just warm. Serve slices plain, à la mode, or with a wedge of cheddar cheese.

blueberry pie

MAKES 8 SERVINGS

Blueberry season hits its peak in July in the mid-Atlantic states and later in northern New England, Maine, and Alaska where tiny, flavorful wild blueberries grow on short bushes. Whether you have access to the wildings or commercial blueberries at the store, don't let the high summer season go by without making at least one blueberry pie. It's the traditional ending to a Maine clambake, but it's worth fighting your way through any dinner to get to that piece of blueberry pie.

Dough for 2 Flaky Pie Crusts (page 251)
5 cups blueberries
1 tablespoon freshly squeezed lemon juice
¾ cup sugar
Generous pinch of salt
¼ cup cornstarch
2 tablespoons butter, cut into ¼-inch pieces

1. Preheat the oven to 425°F. Set the oven rack in the middle of the oven and place a baking sheet on it. Roll half the dough into a 12-inch round. Line a 9-inch pie pan with the dough. Fold the edge of the overhang back on itself to slightly overlap the rim of the pie pan.

2. In a bowl, mix together the blueberries, lemon juice, sugar, salt, and cornstarch, and set it aside. Stir the mixture occasionally over the next 10 minutes. Stir one last time before adding to shell.

3. Pour the blueberry mixture into the shell, then dot with the butter.

4. Roll out the other half of the pie crust to a 12-inch round. Moisten the edge of the bottom crust with milk and fit the top crust over the pan. Pinch the edges of the crust together to seal. With a sharp knife, make five 2-inch slits in the top crust about halfway between the center of the pie and the edge, following an imaginary line from the center to the edge.

Blueberries

When blueberries are in season—in July and August throughout most of the country—they are at their cheapest and best. Blueberries are wonderfully easy to preserve. Simply pour onto a cookie sheet and place in the freezer until they freeze solid, then add them to freezer bags and store in the freezer. Blueberries out of season are delightful, but terribly expensive and often shipped in from as far away as Chile.

When frozen blueberries thaw out, they are soft and lose their textural snap, but don't let that stop you. They still make wonderful blueberry pies, pancakes, and muffins, and can be added to morning cereals.

So freeze enough to last the entire year and avoid the high price of out-of-season blueberries. Eat them locally in every season, straight from your freezer.

5. Bake for 30 minutes, then reduce the heat to 350°F and bake 30 to 35 minutes more, or until the blueberry juices come bubbling through the steam vents. Cool on a rack at room temperature. Serve when completely cooled, which allows the filling to congeal and avoids runniness.

✳ HUCKLEBERRY PIE
Substitute huckleberries for the blueberries, if you're lucky enough to find them. Follow the same recipe for blueberry pie, substituting 5 cups of huckleberries for the blueberries, and brushing the top crust with milk and sprinkling it with 2 teaspoons sugar before cutting vents.

FLAKY PIE CRUST
MAKES 2 CRUSTS

I've heard many ideas about how to make a flaky pie crust but none are as simple and effective as this recipe. This simple recipe represents about ten years of my fiddling around before hitting on just the right way to make a flaky crust.

2 cups all-purpose flour
½ teaspoon kosher salt
½ cup (1 stick) cold butter
1½ tablespoons canola oil
⅓ cup ice water plus more as needed

1. All ingredients should be as cold as possible. Sift the flour and salt together in a mixing bowl. Add the butter and canola oil and cut it into the flour using 2 knives, until it resembles a coarse meal. Add the water, quickly tossing it through the dough with 2 forks.

2. Press the damp dough together. It's a good idea to use a spatula between your hand and the dough, so you don't transfer the heat of your hand to the dough. If the butter melts, it soaks into the flour and loses the ability to make a flaky crust. If the dough forms a ball that doesn't fall apart, you've added enough water. If it's still crumbly, add ice water one tablespoon at a time until a ball forms. When the dough holds together, cut it in half, press each piece down into a 6-inch round, like a hamburger patty, wrap each in wax paper, then refrigerate.

3. Refrigerate for an hour before rolling the pieces out on a floured board to make a bottom crust that's 12 inches in diameter and a top crust that's 10 inches in diameter.

cherry pie

MAKES 8 SERVINGS

Cherries start coming in during June, but the best pie cherries arrive in July when the tart cherries are ripe. Sweet cherries just don't have the tart snap to make a succulent pie. Cherry pie demands a scoop of vanilla ice cream, so who are we to argue? Kirsch is available at most markets or liquor stores.

1 1/4 cups sugar
1/3 cup cornstarch
1/2 cup Kirsch
4 cups pitted fresh pie (tart) cherries (or frozen if fresh are unavailable)
1/2 teaspoon ground cinnamon
1/4 teaspoon ground allspice
1/4 teaspoon almond extract
2 cups all-purpose flour
1/2 teaspoon salt
2/3 cup butter
Cold water

1. Preheat the oven to 425°F. Mix the sugar and cornstarch in a saucepan, then add the Kirsch and enough water to make a smooth batter, about 1/2 cup. Set the pan over medium heat and bring to a boil. Continue to boil until the mixture thickens, about 2 to 3 minutes. Add the cherries, cinnamon, allspice, and almond extract, and mix well.

2. In another bowl, mix together the flour and salt. Add the butter and, using 2 knives, cut it into the flour until the flour has a mealy texture. Add cold water a tablespoon at a time and toss it through the dough with 2 forks until the dough forms a ball.

3. Divide the dough in half, making one half slightly larger than the other. Lightly flour a board or smooth surface and roll out the larger half into a 12-inch circle.

4. Line a 9-inch pie pan with the 12-inch crust. Fill the pie pan with the cherry mixture. Make a lattice top from the second ball of dough (see sidebar page 253). Bake for 10 minutes, then reduce the heat to 375°F and bake for 50 minutes, or until the crust is golden brown. Remove from the oven to cool on a rack.

5. Serve at room temperature so filling sets.

summertime pie

MAKES 8 SERVINGS

It's high summer and the berries are at their cheapest and best—or they're free if you know where to look. If you know a wild blackberry patch, snag some. Ditto with wineberries. Or seek some fresh berries at the farmers' market. The point is that the window of opportunity to make summertime pie will close quickly. And he or she who hesitates will have to wait another year.

Parchment paper and pie weights (or dry beans)
Dough for 2 Flaky Pie Crusts (page 251)
3 cups fresh blueberries
2 cups fresh blackberries
1 cup wineberries (or red raspberries)
2 tablespoons honey
1 tablespoon real maple syrup
1 cup granulated sugar
3 tablespoons cornstarch

½ teaspoon ground cinnamon
¼ teaspoon kosher salt
3 tablespoons cold butter, cut into small bits
1 tablespoon freshly squeezed lemon juice
¼ cup whipping cream

1. Preheat the oven to 350°F. Roll out half the pie dough into a 12-inch round. Line a 9-inch pie pan with the dough. With scissors, trim the dough to leave about ½-inch overhang over the rim of the pie pan. Fold this under the rim and crimp the crust all the way around with your thumb.

2. Line the dough with parchment paper and fill the pan with pie weights or dry beans. Bake the dough for 20 minutes, then remove the weights and the paper and bake for 5 minutes more. Set the pan to cool.

3. In a large bowl, place the blueberries, blackberries, and wineberries. Add the honey and maple syrup and very gently toss to coat.

4. In another bowl, stir together the sugar, cornstarch, cinnamon, and salt. Add to the fruit mixture and very gently toss to coat.

5. Fill the par-baked crust with the berry mixture, sprinkle on the lemon juice, and dot the tops with bits of the butter. Roll out the remaining pie crust into a 12-inch round and fit the top crust over the pan. Trim the excess to leave ½-inch overhang and gently lay this on the pie, being careful not to break the bottom crust. Crimp gently with the back of a fork. Brush the crust with the whipping cream. With a sharp knife, make three evenly spaced 3-inch slits in the top crust.

6. Place a sheet of aluminum foil on the oven rack to catch any juices and set the pie on it. Bake for 40 minutes, until some juice runs and the crust is a golden brown.

7. Allow to cool to room temperature and serve.

GOOD TO KNOW: MAKING A LATTICE-TOP CRUST

Like making braids, it's not difficult once you get the hang of it. But getting the hang of it may take a little bit of practice. You have 2 balls of dough, one slightly larger than the other. Roll out the large ball so it fits in a pie pan and fill it with pie filling. Roll the smaller ball of dough into a 13 ½-inch round, then cut it into 18 strips each about ⅔-inch wide. Cut the first, longest strip from the center and work out toward the edges. Seventeen equally-spaced cuts will make 18 strips.

Brush the edge of the bottom crust with water. Lay the first layer of strips across the pie spaced ½-inch apart, with the shortest pieces at the edges and longer pieces toward the center. Fold back *every other* strip of the first layer, but don't pinch them. Now lay down the first strip of the second layer and unfold the strips of the first layer, laying them flat. Now take the strips of the first layer *that were not* folded back on the first go-round and fold them back. Lay the second strip of the second layer and lay everything out flat again. Now fold back the first layer's strips that you originally folded and lay the third strip of the second layer, then lay everything out flat again. Repeat until the woven lattice is formed across the whole pie.

Trim the excess, seal the lattice ends to the bottom crust, and flute with the back of a fork around the entire pie. Voilà!

no-cook blackberry pie

MAKES 8 SERVINGS

Blackberries combine deliciously with the sweet, lemony flavor of the filling, but you can use any summer fruit: apricots, peach or nectarine slices, blueberries, raspberries, strawberries, or pitted cherry halves.

8 whole graham crackers, crushed
3 tablespoons butter at room temperature
8 ounces cream cheese
1 cup drained ricotta cheese
¼ cup sugar
Zest of 1 organic lemon
¼ teaspoon kosher salt
1½ cups fresh fruit

1. Pour the crackers into a bowl and add the butter. Mix well, then spoon the mixture into a 9-inch pie pan and press down hard to line the pan with the graham cracker crust.

2. In a bowl, mix the cream cheese, ricotta, sugar, lemon zest, and salt until thick and creamy. Spoon this into the pie pan and gently smooth it out evenly.

3. Arrange the fruit in an attractive pattern, covering the top of the pie. Place the pie in a plastic bag and transfer to the refrigerator for at least an hour, or until well chilled. Serve cold.

summer stone fruit tart

MAKES 8 SERVINGS

When the summer stone fruits are in season, it's tempting to make fruit tarts for eating right away or for freezing for when the summer fruits are gone. Apricots, peaches, nectarines, plums, and cherries can all be used to make tarts. Most of us think of tarts as small fruit pastries about 4 inches in diameter, but you can also make a larger tart in a false-bottomed cake pan, as you do in this recipe, then cut slices like wedges of pie. For the smaller tarts, it helps to have small metal tart cups in which to mold the shell. In all cases, the buttery, sugary dough will soften and collapse in the oven if not held firmly to shape with a lining of foil filled with beans.

Note that the dough requires a 2-hour resting period in the fridge. Use slivered almonds in an attractive sunburst pattern to decorate the fruit after baking and before glazing.

TART SHELL
2½ cups pastry flour
¼ teaspoon kosher salt
3 tablespoons granulated sugar
½ cup (1 stick) cold butter
3 tablespoons canola oil, chilled
½ cup ice water plus more as needed

FILLING
1 cup sugar
4 cups pitted, peeled, and sliced ripe apricots, peaches, or nectarines; pitted and sliced plums; pitted and halved cherries
2 tablespoons cold butter, cut into ¼-inch dice
½ cup apricot preserves

1. Make the tart shell: In a bowl, mix the flour, salt, and sugar. Add the butter and, using 2 knives, cut it into the flour until the pieces of butter are about half the size of peas. Sprinkle the dough with the canola oil and enough ice water that the dough forms a ball that holds together.

2. Place the dough on a lightly floured board and, using the heel of your hand, smear it over the board a little at a time to further incorporate and flatten the butter, then gather it up into a ball again. Wrap it in wax paper and refrigerate for 2 hours.

3. Preheat the oven to 400°F. Butter the sides and bottom of a 9-inch removable-bottom cake pan. Lightly flour the dough. On a lightly floured board, roll out the dough into a circle about ⅛ inch thick and 2 inches larger all around than the diameter of your cake pan. Fold the rolled dough in half, and then in half again. Lift it and lay it on the cake pan with the center point of the dough at the center of the cake pan. Now unfold the dough.

4. Gently work the dough down the sides of the pan so the bottom and sides are completely covered and the sides are about ½-inch thick. Trim off the excess. With your thumbs, press the dough on the sides of the pan so it rises just slightly above the edge of the pan. You can make a milled edge by pressing the raised edge with the back of a fork. Prick the bottom of the dough at ½-inch intervals with a fork.

5. Butter a sheet of aluminum foil and line the dough in the pan with it, butter side on the dough. Fill the foil with dry beans. Bake the pan for 8 to 9 minutes, until dough is set. Remove from the oven and lift out the foil and beans. Prick the bottom of the dough with a fork again, which will keep it from rising and becoming too fragile. Return the pan to the oven for 2 to 3 minutes more, or until the dough just begins to color. Remove from the oven.

6. Make the filling: Reduce the oven to 375°F.

GOOD TO KNOW: STORING AND FREEZING SUMMER FRUITS

Stone fruits need to be freed from their stones before freezing or canning, so I always choose freestone peaches. Cherries, apricots, and most nectarines easily come free from their pits. I freeze cherries and apricots as halves, packed in light syrup made from 2 cups of water, the juice of 1 lemon, and 1 tablespoon of honey. For peaches, I blanch them for a minute or two in boiling water to make them easy to peel, then cut them into slices and add them to light syrup. I see no need to peel nectarines. The slices go into freezer bags that twist-tie shut, so I only need a minimum amount of syrup for each bag. Use bags that will provide your family with a single night's serving.

To thaw the peaches, drop the bag into a bowl of hot water from the kitchen tap about 45 minutes before you plan to serve them. They'll gently thaw out by then and give back all that summer sunshine and goodness while the snow flies outside.

I freeze berries like blueberries, raspberries, blackberries, and black currants in a single layer on baking sheets, and when they're frozen hard, pour them into freezer bags and twist-tie them shut, then put them back in the freezer to store.

It's a great feeling knowing that summer's ripe goodness is near at hand throughout the year.

Sprinkle 2 tablespoons of the sugar evenly over the bottom of the pastry shell. Arrange the fruit in a series of overlapping slices forming concentric rings from the center to the edge of the pastry shell. If using cherries, place them convex side up and pack them closely in the shell. Rings of cherries alternating with peaches make an attractive pattern.

7. Pour ¾ cup of the sugar evenly over the fruit and dot with the butter. Bake for 35 to 40 minutes, or until the fruit's juices are bubbling and have thickened slightly.

8. Push the apricot preserves and the remaining 2 tablespoons of sugar through a sieve into a saucepan and cook over medium-high heat for 2 to 3 minutes, or until the glaze becomes sticky (if you have a candy thermometer, between 225° and 228°F). Don't overcook or the glaze will harden when cool.

9. Remove the tart from the oven and gently brush on the apricot glaze. Let rest for 5 minutes. Set the metal pan on a jar with a flat top so the bottom is supported but the metal sides of the pan fall to the surface of the counter. If the pan sides are sticking in any place, gently loosen with a knife. Loosen the tart from the bottom and slide it gently onto a serving plate.

tarte tatin

MAKES 4 SERVINGS

This upside-down apple tart is at its best served hot from the oven. Use very flavorful, sweet, end-of-summer apples that cook well, such as Cortland, Jonagold, or Empire.

½ cup all-purpose flour
1 teaspoon sugar
Pinch salt
2 tablespoons cold butter
2 teaspoons cold canola oil
1 to 2 tablespoons cold water
2 pounds crisp apples
½ cup sugar
½ teaspoon cinnamon
3 tablespoons melted butter

1. In a bowl, combine the flour, sugar, and salt. Add the butter and, using 2 knives, cut it into the flour until the flour looks grainy. Sprinkle in the canola oil and the water and quickly toss it through the dough with 2 forks until the dough forms a ball. It should just stick together. Wrap the dough in wax paper and place it in the refrigerator for 1 hour.

2. Preheat the oven to 375°F. Cut the apples into quarters, then core and peel them. Cut them into slices about ⅛ inch thick and place in a bowl. Add ¼ cup of the sugar and the cinnamon and toss to coat. Butter a 7-inch ramekin, making sure the bottom is well coated.

3. Sprinkle half the remaining sugar into the bottom of the ramekin. Place one-third of the apple slices in the bottom, and drizzle with one-third of the melted butter. Repeat with two more layers and sprinkle the remaining sugar on top.

4. On a lightly floured board, roll out the dough to about ⅛ inch thick and cut it into a circle that will cover the ramekin. Place it over the apples and cut 5 small vents in the dough so steam can escape.

5. Bake in the lower third of your oven for 50 to 60 minutes. If the dough seems to be browning too quickly, cover lightly with aluminum foil. Tilt the tart slightly so you can see the liquid that has formed. When it's caramelized brown rather than lightly colored, the tart is done.

6. Remove it from the oven, run a knife around the inside wall of the ramekin, place a serving plate upside down on top of it and quickly turn it upside down, then remove the ramekin. Be careful not to let any hot sugar spill onto your skin when you flip it.

peachberry almond galette

MAKES 8 SERVINGS

Galettes are like pie without the pie pan. In this recipe, fresh summer peaches and raspberries team up with ground almonds to make a super-nutritious dessert. By freezing summer fruits and the ground almond mixture, you can make galettes any time of the year.

Parchment paper.
Dough for 1 Flaky Pie Crust recipe (page 251) (half recipe)
½ cup plus 2 tablespoons sugar
½ cup whole almonds, skins on
½ cup butter at room temperature
1 large egg
4 large, ripe freestone peaches, skins removed
2 tablespoons freshly squeezed lemon juice
1 cup fresh red raspberries
2 tablespoons whipping cream

1. Preheat the oven to 325°F. Place the ball of pie crust dough in the fridge for ½ hour. Roll it on a lightly floured board into a 12-inch circle. Place the dough onto a baking sheet lined with parchment paper.

2. Place the ½ cup sugar and almonds in a blender or food processor and grind until the almonds are in coarse chunks. Add the butter and pulse a few times to combine. Add the egg and blend until well combined and the almonds are a coarse meal, about 30 seconds.

3. Working over a bowl, cut the peaches into ½-inch slices, dropping them into the bowl as you slice around the pits. Discard the pits. Sprinkle the peach slices with the lemon juice to prevent browning.

4. Place about ½ cup of the almond mixture in the center of the dough and smooth it out, leaving a 2-inch border of dough uncovered all around. Freeze the remaining almond mixture for use the next time you make a galette. Top the almond mixture with peach slices artfully arranged into a spiral, each slice slightly overlapping the one before, starting in the center and spiraling outward to the edge of the ground nut mixture, again leaving the outer 2 inches of dough empty. Dot with the raspberries in an evenly spaced polka dot pattern.

5. Fold up the edge of the pie dough all around, making pleats when necessary, so that it partially covers the outer edge of the almond mixture and fruit topping. Sprinkle the 2 tablespoons of sugar over the fruit. Brush the folded pie dough edge with whipping cream. Bake for about 25 to 30 minutes on a middle rack, until the crust turns golden brown.

6. Serve the galette on a platter brought to the table. Make portions by cutting across the galette and serve on individual plates.

plum crisp

MAKES 6 SERVINGS

When the window opens on Santa Rosa plum season, try this easy dessert. It takes advantage of the plums' sweet yet tart flavor. And don't forget the scoop of vanilla ice cream.

2 pounds firm, ripe plums
½ cup brown sugar
2 teaspoons ground cinnamon

> ### ❋ GOOD TO KNOW: TRANSFERRING PIE DOUGH
>
> Recipes often call for transferring pie crust dough from one place to another, as in the recipe for Peachberry Almond Galette, which calls for rolling out the dough, then placing it on a baking sheet lined with parchment. There's an easy way to do this without tearing the dough or bending it completely out of shape.
>
> Make sure the rolled-out dough is lightly floured, then flour up your rolling pin. Place the pin at about 3 or 4 inches from the far edge of the circular dough. Gently pull the far edge of the dough up and onto the rolling pin. Holding the dough to the pin, roll the pin toward you slowly, until you've gently rolled at least half the dough onto the pin. Take the rolled-up dough to the baking sheet or pie pan, place the dangling edge of the dough so it's at the edge of the parchment or slightly overhangs the near edge of the pie pan, and then carefully unroll the dough off the pin onto the sheet or pan.

Pinch ground cloves
Zest of ½ an organic orange
¾ cup flour
½ cup white sugar
¼ cup butter
Pinch salt

1. Preheat the oven to 375°F.
2. Rinse the plums and pat dry. Cut each into sixths and drop the pieces into a bowl. Add the brown sugar, 1 teaspoon of the cinnamon cloves, and the orange zest to the bowl and mix to combine. Set aside.
3. In a separate bowl, add the flour, sugar, butter, the remaining 1 teaspoon cinnamon, and the salt. Cut the butter into the dry ingredients using 2 knives until you have a coarse meal.
4. Place the plum mixture in a pie plate and crumble the coarse meal lightly over the top. Bake for about 30 minutes until the top is lightly browned and the fruit soft and bubbling. Allow to cool to room temperature or serve warm, not hot.

plum and nectarine crisp

MAKES 4 TO 6 SERVINGS

Plums and nectarines are relatives—both are in the genus *Prunus*. Their flavors make a harmonious pairing, too, in this midsummer classic. When the fresh plums and nectarines are in the stores in July, this one's a must. Use just-ripe fruit. And of course, top with vanilla ice cream.

3 cups pitted and sliced plums
2 cups pitted and sliced nectarines
Juice of ½ lemon

½ teaspoon vanilla extract
Pinch ground cinnamon
1 cup rolled (5-minute) oats
¾ cup all-purpose flour
¾ cup brown sugar
5 tablespoons unsalted butter, melted

1. Preheat oven to 350°F. Grease a 9 x 9-inch baking dish.

2. Place the plums and nectarines in the dish, sprinkle the lemon juice and vanilla extract over them, and rub the pinch of cinnamon between your fingers so the powder falls evenly over the dish.

3. In a separate bowl, mix together the oats, flour, and sugar. Add the melted butter by drizzling it over the dry ingredients, then work the mixture with your fingers to form small lumps. Shake the lumps on top of the fruit mixture, making sure some falls near the edges. You should see some fruit between the lumps.

4. Bake for 40 to 45 minutes, or until browned and bubbling. You may need to cover loosely with a sheet of aluminum foil if browning too quickly before the fruit is completely cooked. Serve warm with a scoop of vanilla ice cream on top.

✳ VARIATION

Substitute peaches for nectarines. Substitute blueberries for plums.

nectarine-blueberry crisp
SERVES 4 TO 6

The secret to this luscious dessert is to make sure the nectarines are ripe—that is, the shoulder of the nectarine (the raised part around where the stem attached) yields to a little gentle thumb pressure. The combination of nectarines and blueberries is profoundly tasty.

4 cups nectarines, cut into slices
Juice of ½ lemon
2 cups blueberries
1 cup white sugar
½ cup packed brown sugar
½ cup pastry flour
½ cup crushed vanilla wafers
¼ cup chopped pecans
¼ cup melted but not browned butter

1. Preheat the oven to 400°F. Toss the nectarines with the lemon juice.

2. In a saucepan over medium heat add the blueberries, white sugar, and ¼ cup water, stirring until the mixture boils, then reducing the heat and cooking to a sweet sauce, about 10 minutes. In another bowl, combine the brown sugar, flour, cookies, and pecans.

3. Grease a 9 x 13-inch baking dish and pour the nectarine slices and any juice into it. Pour the blueberry sauce over the nectarines. Crumble the dry ingredients over the blueberry sauce and drizzle with the butter.

4. Bake uncovered for about 20 minutes, until the crisp is bubbling.

5. Allow to cool to room temperature or serve slightly warm.

summer stone fruit cobbler

MAKES 6 TO 8 SERVINGS

Cobblers combine sweetened dough with luscious fruit, and summer's stone fruits make the best cobblers. Use the fruit singly or mix 2 or more than one of these fresh fruits together: cherries, plums, apricots, peaches, or nectarines. And add a handful of summer berries to the combo. You can't go wrong—especially with a scoop of vanilla ice cream on top.

3 cups pitted, sliced ripe plums
2 cups pitted, halved ripe cherries

SUMMER MEMORY: **discovering tree-ripened peaches**

I can still remember the first time I plucked a ripe peach from a tree and ate it. Peaches to me until that day had been slippery yellow slices packed in sugar water that came in a can. But when I was about 10, my dad moved our family from the very suburban setting of Long Island's North Shore to the Pocono Mountains, and suburban boy Jeff was launched, to my terror, into the country—real country, complete with bear and bobcat. And, to my subsequent delight, trout in the streams, wild berries on the bushes, and fruit on the trees. The neighbor boys and I had the run of the place—and the place was the whole region as far as we wanted to wander.

One day, wandering with my friend, we encountered a peach tree ripe with sunny fruit. We figured the property owners wouldn't miss a couple of peaches, and took one for each of us. They were warm from the sun. The juice ran down our faces. The flavor was wonderful good, as the local Pennsylvania Dutch would say. At that moment, I understood what peaches were all about.

So when peaches are summer ripe, find an orchard that's growing them and arrange to go pick a basket all your own when they're really ready to eat. Check www.localharvest.org in early July for the nearest source of tree-ripened peaches. They bear little resemblance to peaches that are shipped nearly unripe to the markets, and no resemblance at all to canned peaches.

³⁄₄ cup sugar

2 ½ tablespoons freshly squeezed
   lemon juice

3 tablespoons cornstarch

1 teaspoon lemon zest

1 cup all-purpose flour

1 ½ teaspoon baking powder

½ teaspoon salt

4 tablespoons (½ stick) chilled butter, cut
   into ¼-inch bits

½ cup milk

1 large egg

½ teaspoon vanilla extract

Vanilla ice cream, for serving

1. Preheat the oven to 400°F. Butter a 9 x 12-inch baking dish.

2. In a saucepan over low heat, mix together the fruit, ½ cup of the sugar, the lemon juice, cornstarch, and lemon zest, and cook, stirring occasionally, until the mixture simmers, 4 to 5 minutes. Pour the fruit mixture into the baking dish.

3. In a bowl, combine the flour, the remaining ¼ cup sugar, baking powder, and salt and stir until well mixed. Add the butter and stir until the ingredients are just combined but still crumbly. Add the milk, egg, and vanilla extract and beat to form a smooth batter.

4. Drop the batter by heaping teaspoons all over the fruit mixture, leaving open spaces. Bake for 20 minutes, or until the cobbler is lightly browned and the fruit mixture is bubbling. Serve warm, not hot, with a scoop of vanilla ice cream.

FREE ICE CREAM

To thank all the folks who buy their dairy products throughout the year, the Clover-Stornetta Dairy here in Sonoma County sets up a booth at each summer's Sonoma County Fair and gives away free ice cream cones.

The weather is invariably hot, it takes a while standing in long lines to get your free cone, and the flavor is always vanilla—but nobody seems to mind. After receiving their free ice cream, fairgoers drift off to see the farm animals—horses, cows, hogs, goats, chickens, ducks, and rabbits—and even a great horned owl who presides over the Sonoma County Humane Society's stand.

As I watch the kids eating their ice cream as they wander among the animals, I realize that they are storing up memories that will last a lifetime. They may forget the animals, but they'll never forget free ice cream.

JUICE, SMOOTHIES, TEA, & COFFEE

Super Carrot Juice

Fruity Agua Fresca

Orangeade

Lemonade or Limeade

Frozen Berry Smoothie

Berry-Banana Smoothie

Fruity Protein Smoothie

Mango Lassi

Strawberry Ice-Cream Soda

Black-and-White Soda

Herbal Iced Teas

Anise-Lemongrass Iced Tea

Cold-Brewed Coffee

ALCOHOLIC DRINKS

Gin and Tonic

Tom Collins

Wine Spritzer

Mimosa

Bellini

Mojito

Tequila Refresher

Ramos Fizz

Margarita

Ratafias

Daiquiri

Strawberry Slush

SIPPERS

Of course, the best summer sipper—the one that really keeps you hydrated without calories or alcohol—is water. Last year I installed a high-quality water filter system under my kitchen sink, and now the water I draw from its tap is as pure and sweet as spring water that bubbles cold from the earth. I keep a bottle of it filled and in the fridge at all times.

But sometimes you want something with flavor, or a relaxing highball, or an ice cream soda as a treat. At those times, check out the recipes in this chapter. I guarantee that any of them will more than adequately cool you down and tease your palate with goodness.

JUICE, SMOOTHIES, TEA, & COFFEE

super carrot juice
MAKES ABOUT 1 QUART

Summer is the most active time of the year for most of us—sports, swimming, gardening, and in other ways expending energy. Here's a revitalizing drink that will keep you on the go and your body stoked with the living juices of fresh vegetables. You'll need a vegetable juicer to make this treat, but if you invest in one, you'll be glad you did. A pint of this sweet, power-packed concoction will rejuvenate your body and clear your mind.

Aim for all organic vegetables. And drink it right away, as enzymes start to work on the juice as soon as it's made and reduce its nutritional power.

2 pounds fresh carrots, washed, tops and
    tips trimmed
½ bunch Italian flat-leaf parsley
3 stalks celery
4 leaves kale
4 leaves red chard
1 small beet, quartered

1. Split the carrots lengthwise if they are too large to fit in the juicer's feeding slot.
2. Begin adding the ingredients to the juicer, one at a time, starting with the parsley and ending with the carrots. Some vegetables won't have as much juice as others. The resulting drink will be a murky green color, but it will taste sweet, cool, and delicious.

fruity agua fresca
MAKES 4 SERVINGS

Most Mexican restaurants have large jars of agua frescas sitting up on the counter. When you order one, the counterperson will ladle it into a glass for you. There are many kinds, made from many fruits and even grains like rice, barley, or oatmeal, but this one is perhaps the most popular. It's a cooling drink on a hot summer day.

4 cups water
1 cup sugar
2 cups red grape juice
⅓ cup freshly squeezed lemon juice
⅓ cup freshly squeezed orange juice

1. Place a small saucepan over medium-low heat and add the water and sugar. Heat until sugar has dissolved and the water is clear. Remove from the heat and set aside to cool.
2. Pour the sugar water into a large pitcher, then add the grape, lemon, and orange juices. Keep cool in the refrigerator. Serve in glasses that have been chilled in the freezer.

orangeade
MAKES 2 SERVINGS

There was a time, before the domination of unhealthy high-fructose corn syrup soft drinks with brand names and high marketing costs, when kids, heated from their play, would be given orangeade, lemonade, or limeade coolers made in the kitchen and

served over ice—nothing but pure citrus juices, Simple Syrup, and water. And the kids loved it. You will too, when you try this refreshing drink.

SIMPLE SYRUP
1 cup granulated sugar
1½ cups water

JUICE
2 tablespoons Simple Syrup
2 cups orange juice
½ cup water
1 tablespoon freshly squeezed lemon juice

  1. Make the Simple Syrup: Place a small saucepan over medium-low heat and add the sugar and water. Bring to a boil and boil, stirring occasionally, for about 2 minutes. Remove from heat and refrigerate.
  2. Place 2 tablespoons Simple Syrup, the orange juice, water, and lemon juice in a glass and stir to mix. Add ice to fill glass.

  ✻ FIZZY ORANGEADE
Substitute ½ cup of club soda for the ½ cup of water.

lemonade or limeade
MAKES 1 SERVING

This recipe is for a glass of fresh lemonade, or limeade if using limes. Ice works fine if you're making one glass of lemonade at a time and expect to drink it fairly quickly.

  If the kids want to operate a lemonade stand or you're preparing for a crowd, a recipe for a large quantity of lemonade

syrup is given in the variation. Be sure to chill the syrup if you prefer not to dilute the lemonade by adding ice.

SIMPLE SYRUP
1 cup granulated sugar
1½ cups water

JUICE
2 tablespoons Simple Syrup
1½ tablespoons freshly squeezed lemon or lime juice
Small pinch salt
Ice cubes

  1. Make the Simple Syrup as directed in the orangeade recipe. Place in the refrigerator to chill.
  2. When the Simple Syrup is cold, pour the 2 tablespoons into a tall glass and add the citrus juice and just a few grains of salt. Fill with ice cubes. Stir to mix and serve.

  ✻ LEMONADE SYRUP
For 5 minutes, boil together 2 cups sugar, 1 cup water, the rind of 2 lemons cut into thin strips, and a pinch of salt. Strain and chill for several hours. When cold, add the juice of 6 lemons. Pour into a jar with a tight-fitting lid and store in the fridge for up to 2 weeks. To make a glass of lemonade from this syrup, add 2 tablespoons to a tall glass full of ice and fill with water or club soda. Stir and serve.

frozen berry smoothie
MAKES 4 SERVINGS

This smoothie might make a fine breakfast all by itself. It'll surely make a cooling drink any time of the day. Freeze quantities of red raspberries and pitted Bing cherries in summer when they're plentiful and inexpensive and you can make this treat at any time of the year. Note that the fruits are frozen, so freeze them the night before if you're making just one batch.

1½ cups fat-free milk
1 cup frozen red raspberries
1 cup frozen halved, pitted Bing cherries
½ frozen banana
1½ cups raspberry sorbet

Place all ingredients in a blender and blend until smooth. Serve in tall glasses.

berry-banana smoothie
MAKES 4 SERVINGS

Forget what used to be said about never putting bananas in the fridge. That was just so your bananas would go bad faster and you'd have to buy more bananas. Peel and freeze some fully ripe bananas (lightly flecked with brown spots) for the base of this incomparable summer smoothie. Tip: Have all the ingredients, other than the bananas and honey, refrigerator cold.

2 ripe, peeled bananas, frozen
1 cup orange juice
2 cups plain, low-fat yogurt
¾ cup red raspberries, washed and drained
¾ cup blackberries, washed and drained
¾ cup blueberries, washed and drained
Honey to taste

Cut the fully frozen bananas into 2-inch pieces and place them in a blender. Add the orange juice, yogurt, and berries and blend into a smooth puree (2 to 3 minutes). Taste and adjust sweetness to your taste using small increments of honey, and blending to mix. Serve in tall glasses.

fruity protein smoothie
MAKES 4 SERVINGS

Don't throw out bananas ever again. Unless they are mushy and brown, peel them and freeze them to make the best and sweetest smoothies. Freeze plenty of strawberries and blueberries in their summer season, and you can make fresh-tasting smoothies any time.

This smoothie lives up to its name and packs a protein punch, and the whey powder gives the drink a rich, creamy texture and a slight nutty flavor to balance the fruit.

1½ ripe, peeled bananas, frozen
1 cup frozen destemmed whole strawberries
½ cup frozen blueberries
2 cups cold orange juice
4 tablespoons whey protein powder

Place all the ingredients in a blender and blend until thick and smooth.

✱ VARIATIONS
For the frozen bananas, substitute frozen vanilla yogurt or vanilla ice cream.

mango lassi

Much of India is known for its intense heat, but it's no surprise that this cooling yogurt drink works just as well in middle-of-summer Indiana. It is also effective in reducing the burn from very spicy-hot foods.

1 ripe mango
2 cups plain yogurt
2 tablespoons sugar
10 ice cubes

Peel and pit the mango and place the flesh into a blender. Add the yogurt, sugar, and ice cubes and blend until fairly smooth, but with small crystals of ice still detectable. Serve immediately.

strawberry ice-cream soda

MAKES 4 TO 6 SERVINGS

This recipe is for a strawberry ice-cream soda completely from scratch, but you could cheat and use good-quality strawberry sorbet and vanilla ice cream. When it's made from scratch with your best ingredients, though, this strawberry soda reaches empyrean heights.

Make the ingredients ahead of time and blow your guests away with this throwback drink. You'll need a candy thermometer and an ice-cream maker. The recipe is from the very talented Joseph Humphrey, chef at Murray Circle restaurant in Sausalito, California.

STRAWBERRY SORBET
4 cups strawberries, hulled and
    quartered
$\frac{1}{4}$ cup sugar
$\frac{3}{4}$ cup water
1 $\frac{1}{4}$ cups Simple Syrup (page 266)
1 teaspoon freshly squeezed lemon juice

VANILLA ICE CREAM
1 cup whole milk
2 cups heavy cream
2 vanilla beans, split and cut into
    2-inch lengths
5 egg yolks
$\frac{3}{4}$ cup sugar

GOOD TO KNOW: PREPARING A MANGO

Without a plan, getting the sweet flesh from a mango can yield a mess of mush. So, here's the plan:

Stand the mango straight up, stem end on the cutting surface and thin edge toward you. With a sharp serrated knife, slice off the "cheeks" on either side of the fruit, being careful not to cut into the fibrous seed housed in the center of the fruit. When the flat sides are cut off, turn the mango a quarter turn and slice off the thin edges.

Lay the cheeks on the cutting surface, flesh side up. With a knife, score the flesh into $\frac{3}{4}$-inch cubes. Hold each flat side with both hands and turn it inside out. With the knife, cut off the cubes of projecting mango flesh. Repeat with the thin edges.

STRAWBERRY SYRUP
2 cups strawberries, hulled and cut in half
½ cup sugar

TOPPING
Club soda
Several sprigs of fresh mint

1. Make the sorbet: In a bowl, toss the strawberries with the sugar. Let sit at room temperature, covered with a plate, for 2 hours.

2. Place the mixture in a blender with the water and puree until smooth. Strain the puree through a fine-mesh sieve, then add the Simple Syrup and lemon juice. Mix well and place the mixture in your ice-cream maker. Freeze according to the manufacturer's instructions.

3. Make the ice cream: Heat the milk, cream, and vanilla beans in a saucepan just to a simmer. Turn off the heat, cover, and let steep for 15 minutes.

4. In a bowl, beat together the egg yolks and sugar. Slowly drizzle the cream mixture into the egg yolk bowl, vanilla beans and all, stirring constantly. Place the mixture into a saucepan and heat gently over low to 175°F—no hotter or the yolks will cook and curdle. Use a candy thermometer to gauge. You should see a little steam rising from the mixture, but no bubbles. Stir frequently.

5. Remove from the heat and refrigerate until cool. Remove the vanilla beans and strain the mixture through a fine-mesh sieve. Place the mixture in the ice-cream maker and freeze according to the manufacturer's instructions.

6. Make the syrup: Combine the strawberries and sugar in a saucepan. Add just enough water to cover and bring to a boil.

Reduce heat and simmer for 10 minutes. Transfer to a blender and puree until smooth. Strain through a fine-mesh sieve and chill.

7. Place 2 scoops each of the sorbet and ice cream in a tall, chilled glass. Add 3 tablespoons of the strawberry syrup to each glass and top with club soda. Garnish the top with a little sprig of mint and serve.

black-and-white soda
MAKES 1 SERVING

I remember the first black-and-white soda I ever had. I must have been about three years old. It was cold and delicious. It was frothy and bubbly. You could drink it through a straw and eat it with a spoon. The ice cream was smooth but acquired little crunchy crystals from the club soda that poured from a spout with a black handle behind the counter. It tasted of chocolate and vanilla. And best of all, when you got to the bottom, you could make a wondrously annoying crackling sound as you took the last sip.

New Yorkers will make this soda with Fox's U-Bet, others may use Hershey's syrup. But the best flavor comes by making your own chocolate syrup (see below).

2 tablespoons Homemade Chocolate
    Syrup (page 270)
2 tablespoons club soda, plus more as
    needed
2 scoops vanilla ice cream

1. In a tall glass, pour in the chocolate syrup, followed by the club soda. Mix with a spoon until smooth, then add the ice cream.

2. Top the glass with club soda and stir with a long spoon just until the chocolate syrup permeates the club soda. Add a straw and serve.

✱ **VARIATIONS**

Add 1 tablespoon of malted milk powder to the chocolate syrup before adding the club soda. Or, if you make your own syrup from cocoa powder, add ½ cup of malted milk powder to the dry ingredients before adding ¾ cup water.

HOMEMADE CHOCOLATE SYRUP

1 cup unsweetened cocoa powder (not Dutch cocoa)
¾ cup sugar
½ cup water

1. Place a small saucepan over medium-low heat. Add the cocoa powder and sugar and mix well. Add the water and stir constantly until it begins to boil.

2. Reduce heat to low and simmer, continuing to stir, for about 4 minutes. Pour into a container with a cover and let cool. Store the syrup, covered in the fridge, for up to 3 weeks. It will thicken when cold. Turn it back into a liquid with 30 seconds in the microwave.

herbal iced teas

MAKES 1 SERVING

If you live in the city, you must visit the herb shop for your herbs, but if you live in the country, they may be growing in your herb garden or wild along country paths. Mint— but not pennyroyal as it is an abortifacient—chamomile, wild bergamot, elderberry blossoms, wintergreen, and clover blossoms all can be found wild throughout the East and make excellent teas. In your herb garden, angelica, anise hyssop, lemon verbena, sage, thyme, and fennel blossoms are also used for tea.

Use 1 tablespoon of fresh herb or ½ teaspoon dried herbs if they are strongly flavored, such as wild bergamot, mint, lemon verbena, and thyme, or twice those amounts if they are mildly flavored like chamomile, elderberry flowers, and clover blossoms. Let your taste be your guide. This recipe calls for chamomile blossoms, but any of the edible herbs can be substituted or combined. Don't use any herb for tea unless you know for certain it is safe to ingest.

1 tablespoon fresh chamomile flowers or other edible herbs
⅛ teaspoon honey
¼ teaspoon lemon juice

Place a saucepan on high heat, add 1 cup of water, and bring to a rolling boil. In a cup, place the chamomile blossoms, honey, and lemon juice, then add the boiling water. Steep for 8 to 10 minutes, then strain into a second cup. Cool to room temperature, then chill in the fridge. Fill a tall glass with ice cubes and pour in the chilled chamomile tea. Or better, to prevent dilution, make ice cubes from a second batch of chamomile.

anise-lemongrass iced tea

MAKES 4 SERVINGS

You can make this tea as a sun tea or use boiling water. Either way, the chilled result is a refreshing break from the usual black tea from teabags.

5 pieces whole star anise pods
3 stalks of lemongrass, chopped into
   ½-inch pieces
Honey (optional)

Crush the anise pods in a mortar with a pestle. Place the anise and lemongrass in a teapot and add 4 cups boiling water. Add honey, if desired, to taste. Let steep for 10 minutes, then cool. Fill 4 glasses with ice and pour the tea over.

GOOD TO KNOW: BREWING TEA WHILE YOU HIKE

Pacific-Cornetta Company makes a terrific tea infuser that brews tea while you hike—perfect for all your outdoor summer activities. Unscrew the top and you'll find a perforated stainless steel compartment screwed upside down into the top. Fill this with your favorite tea—or ground coffee—then fill the canister almost full of clean water. There's a D-ring so you can hook it to your belt or backpack. As you walk, the water sloshes through and around the perforated compartment, and when you get where you're going, your tea or coffee will be served. Read about it at www.active-gear.com—click on Coffee and Tea Products and you'll find the Tea-Zer.

cold-brewed coffee

MAKES ABOUT ½ GALLON

Cold-brewed coffee is all the rage among coffee aficionados these days, and it could hardly be simpler to make. The following recipe makes a coffee concentrate, but one with less acid and less caffeine than coffee brewed with hot water.

When using, try it mixed 50/50 with cold nonfat milk, then heated in a microwave for 2½ minutes. For black coffee, dilute the concentrate with an equal amount of water or even twice the water. Freeze some of the concentrate into ice cubes and use them with an equal number of regular water ice cubes to make iced coffee. Ah, iced coffee—it could be the most refreshingly cooling summer drink of all. Reduce this recipe by half if using a Mason jar.

1 pound coffee beans, finely ground
9 cups water

1. In a large jar with a screw-on lid, place the coffee grounds and add the water. Screw on the lid. Let stand on the kitchen counter out of direct sunlight overnight.

2. Strain the coffee into a pitcher through a fine sieve, several layers of cheesecloth, or cloth tea-brewing bag, then through a paper coffee filter to catch any hazy sediment.

3. Store the concentrate as ice cubes or covered in the fridge for 4 to 5 days.

ALCOHOLIC DRINKS

gin and tonic
MAKES 1 SERVING

Few drinks are simpler to make or more refreshing to drink in hot weather.

2 ounces gin
¼ whole lime
Tonic water

Pour the gin into a highball glass and fill with ice cubes. Squeeze the lime wedge into the glass and drop the squeezed rind in. Top with tonic water. Stir.

✳ VARIATION
Many people like this drink made with unflavored vodka.

tom collins
MAKES 1 SERVING

Rediscover the drink that cooled America before air conditioning.

2 ounces gin
Juice of ½ lemon
1 teaspoon powdered sugar
Club soda

Place the gin, lemon juice, and powdered sugar in a cocktail shaker filled with ice and shake. Strain into a tall highball glass. Add ice to the top of the glass and fill with club soda. Stir before serving. Traditionally served with slices of lemon and orange, and a maraschino cherry, but the fruit salad isn't necessary.

✳ JOHN COLLINS
A John Collins is made exactly the same way, but with blended whiskey instead of gin. Vodka can also be used.

wine spritzer
MAKES 1 SERVING

The ancients used to dilute their wine with water—even with sea water. I think club soda is far superior, and it's certainly thirst quenching. Any wine can be used, but on a summery day, a Gewurztraminer, Riesling, off-dry Chenin Blanc, or Albariño would be a fine choice. Make sure the wine and the club soda are well chilled.

Ice cubes
6 ounces wine of your choice
4 ounces club soda

Place ice cubes in a tall glass, add the wine, and top with the club soda.

mimosa
MAKES 1 SERVING

For the adventurous or for the rare morning cocktail with breakfast, nothing beats a mimosa. It's simple to make and divine to drink.

2 ounces cold orange juice
Cold sparkling wine

Pour the orange juice into a Champagne flute, then top with sparkling wine.

✱ ORIOLE
The Oriole is 1 ounce of Grand Marnier in the flute instead of orange juice, topped with sparkling wine.

bellini
MAKES 1 SERVING

In late summer, the white peaches ripen. Then it's time for a Bellini, a drink popularized at Harry's Bar in Venice, Italy.

1 very ripe white peach
1 tablespoon chilled Simple Syrup
   (page 266)
Prosecco, chilled

1. Pit the peach and mash the flesh in a bowl. Set a strainer or fine-mesh sieve atop another bowl and scoop the peach pulp into the strainer. Push the pulp around until you have 2 tablespoons of peach juice. Pour the juice into a Champagne flute.
2. Add the Simple Syrup. Top the flute with chilled Prosecco and serve.

mojito
MAKES 1 SERVING

The mojito may be the ultimate summer cooler. It originated in La Bodeguito del Medio in Havana, Cuba, and this is the original recipe. It's a ubiquitous long drink these days. It requires muddling the mint; that is, smashing it against the side of the glass. I once asked a bartender what made her mojito so good. "Muddle like you mean it," she said.

3 sprigs fresh mint
2 ounces freshly squeezed lime juice
1 teaspoon powdered sugar
2 ounces light rum
Club soda

1. Place 2 of the mint sprigs into a tall highball glass and add the lime juice and powdered sugar. Mix and muddle the sprigs, using a wooden muddler or the back of a fork or tablespoon.
2. Add ice cubes or coarsely crushed ice, pour in the rum, and stir. Top with club soda and garnish with the remaining 1 mint sprig.

tequila refresher
MAKES 1 SERVING

Man—or woman—doesn't live by mojitos or margaritas alone. Sometimes hot summer days require something that combines fruits of the tropics with fruits of the North and a little good tequila to add that subtle agave flavor.

1¼ ounces agave tequila (such as Patron
    or Herradura)
2 ounces pineapple juice
2 ounces cranberry juice
Lemon-lime soda

   Place all the ingredients in cocktail shaker
filled with ice and shake. Strain into a glass
filled with ice and serve.

ramos fizz

MAKES 1 SERVING

You get some high-energy protein with a
Ramos Fizz, thanks to the egg white.

1 egg white
2 ounces gin
½ teaspoon triple sec
Juice of ½ lemon
½ tablespoon half-and-half
1 teaspoon powdered sugar
Club soda

   1. Place the egg white in a cocktail shaker
and inspect it. Pick out any opaque material
or blood spot.
   2. Add the gin, triple sec, lemon juice,
half-and-half, and powdered sugar. Fill the
shaker with ice and shake vigorously until
well mixed.
   3. Place two ice cubes in a highball glass
and strain the shaken ingredients into the
glass. Top with club soda and serve.

margarita

MAKES 1 SERVING

The best margaritas are made with good-
quality tequila. Some rub the rim of the
glass with a lemon or lime peel and then dip
it into salt, but that's too much salt for my
taste, so I omit it. Always make your margaritas with fresh ingredients, not prepared
margarita mixes. Yuck.

1 ½ ounces tequila
½ ounce triple sec
1 ounce freshly squeezed lime juice

   Place all the ingredients in a cocktail
shaker and fill with ice. Shake well and strain
into a martini glass.

✱ **FROZEN MARGARITA**
For a frozen margarita, pour tequila, triple
sec, and lime juice into a blender with 1 cup
of crushed ice and blend until slushy. Serve
in a martini glass.

ratafias

MAKES 1 SERVING

Ratafias are liqueurs made from spirits and
whatever fruits, vegetables, and herbs are
available in season. So in summer, everything from strawberries to late peaches,
from celery to cucumbers, from thyme to
sage, can be used. They are part tisane and
part infusion, and very easy to make. Here's
one of my favorites.

1 cup diced ripe peaches
3 whole cloves
¼ cup unflavored vodka
¼ cup sugar
¼ vanilla bean, sliced lengthwise
1 bottle white wine, especially
    Sauvignon Blanc

1. Mix everything together in a jar with a tight-fitting lid and shake until sugar dissolves. The jar should hold about 1.5 liters, so there's just a little head space.

2. Refrigerate for 1 month, then strain the liqueur through a fine-mesh sieve into a pitcher. Pour the liqueur through a funnel into empty, cleaned, screw-cap wine bottles and store the liqueur in the fridge. Serve in port glasses.

✳ **VARIATIONS**
Lemons make excellent ratafias, as Italian limoncello proves. Be creative. Use vegetables and herbs as well as fruit, and be aware that whatever combinations work on the dinner plate will also most likely work as a liqueur. Use organic produce to avoid the leaching of pesticides into your liqueur.

daiquiri
MAKES 1 SERVING

The daiquiri conjures up visions of wicker furniture overlooking Long Island Sound, lazy summer afternoons, yachting, and the good life.

1½ ounces light rum
Juice of 1 lime
1 teaspoon powdered sugar

Place all the ingredients into a cocktail shaker filled with ice and shake well. Strain into a cocktail glass and serve.

✳ **FROZEN DAIQUIRI**
Make a frozen daiquiri—an alcoholic slushie—by whizzing the ingredients for the daiquiri plus 1 tablespoon of triple sec with 1 cup of crushed ice in a blender until you reach the consistency of slush. Double or triple the recipe depending on guests, but always make frozen daiquiris to order, as the ice will melt quickly. Traditionally served in a Champagne flute.

strawberry slush
MAKES 8 SERVINGS

This refreshing slush is sweetened with a "sticky," as a sweet, late harvest after-dinner wine is called. Use a late harvest white wine made from Gewurztraminer or Riesling, or find a reasonably priced Sauternes or Beaumes-de-Venise.

1 pint fresh, destemmed strawberries
1 cup late harvest white after-dinner wine
One 6-ounce can of limeade concentrate
8 ice cubes

Place all the ingredients in a blender and blend until a smooth slush. Serve immediately in cold wine glasses.

We've entered the golden age of local, microbrewed beers, and everyone has his or her fa-vorite—try different light, medium, or dark beers and ales with your summer foods to find the ones you think are most refreshing and work well with your food. There's nothing like a couple of cold ones on a hot afternoon, especially with a burger, freshly made clams, or . . . well, pick your favorite summer foods. Just stay out of the sun unless you want to feel woozy.

Wine is another story.

Consider wine as a food, for that is what it is. It's a food that glorifies other foods. It has a catalytic effect, improving the flavor of all foods except vinegary ones like pickles and sauerkraut. That's because if you leave wine in contact with air, it becomes infected with bacteria that turn it into vinegar, and vinegar is the waste product of the metabolism of the microorganisms that turn wine into acetic acid. Nothing can live in its own waste products, and that holds true for wine. And so wine and vinegar make a repulsive duo. Lots of people who have wine with their meals make their salad dressing with lemon juice or *verjus* instead of vinegar. However, if you should have a vinaigrette on your salad while you have a glass of wine, don't worry. Both the wine and the vinaigrette are good for you, even though they may not taste like it.

In the summer heat, red wines—especially heavy reds like Cabernet Sauvignon, Amarone, and Port—take a step back out of the spotlight. Now is the time for the white wines like Riesling, Gewurztraminer, Sauvignon Blanc, Chardonnay, Viognier, Roussanne, Marsanne, Fiano, Greco di Tufo, Alberino, and others to take center stage. Rosés are having a vogue now, and chilled, they are perfect wines for summer. Rosés of Pinot Noir are especially wel-come when the weather turns close.

Sparkling wines, no matter where they are from, are wonderful summertime accompani-ments to food. Amazingly, sparklers go well with just about any food in any weather. Grilled steak and sparkling wine? Absolutely. Cheese and sparkling wine? Perfect! Why? Because the grapes for sparkling wine are picked relatively unripe, when they are low in sugar and high in acid. These unripe grapes are fermented to dryness, making a still wine with a low 10 to 11 percent alcohol level but high levels of appetite-stimulating acid. This still wine is then given a dose of yeast and sugar, which referments in the bottle, raising the alcohol level and creating the bubbles. The sparkling wine ends up with an acceptable alcohol level of around 12 to 13 percent after the refermentation, yet with an extra amount of acid that whets the appetite for almost all foods. And that's why sparkling wines go with just about anything.

All this doesn't mean you must slavishly avoid big red wines in the summer. Many restaurants are air conditioned to wintertime temperatures, and if you are having the osso bucco or the duck breast with foie gras, and the room and the wine are chilled, by all means go for the wine that seems appropriate. But for casual gatherings like picnics, backyard barbecues, deck parties at the ocean, soirees on the lake, or other events where summer weather is present in all its warmth and beauty, think light wine.

 **SUMMER COCKTAILS**

Darrell Corti, the ultimate foodie's foodie who owns Corti Brothers emporium of fine foods and wines in Sacramento, taught me that summer cocktails are more properly called "long drinks."

I suppose that's because they are served in tall glasses with lots of ice. Mojitos are the current rage, but in past years famous long drinks might have included gin and tonic, rum and Coke, Bloody Mary, Campari and soda, limon sunrise, Tom Collins and his brother John, scotch and soda, mint julep, and many others.

But here's a summer cocktail you may not have heard of. It's just right for cooling you off when you're working hard—on your tan.

CRIMSON GREYHOUND

> $^2/_3$ cup freshly squeezed pink grapefruit juice
> $^2/_3$ cup vodka
> 2 tablespoons pomegranate juice

Mix the ingredients and pour half into each of 2 tall glasses. Fill with ice and garnish with a twist of grapefruit peel. Makes 2 drinks.

SPREADS & CONDIMENTS

Pesto

Pistou

Persillade

SALAD BASICS

Classic Vinaigrette

Asian Soy-Ginger Dressing

Sesame-Citrus Dressing

Carrot-Ginger Dressing

Ginger-Soy Dressing

Creamy Blue Cheese Dressing

Creamy Buttermilk Dressing

Russian Dressing

Garlic-Parmesan Dressing

Walnut-Lemon Dressing

Cobb Salad Dressing

Summer Berry Dressing

Verjus Salad Dressing

Candied Walnuts

Croutons

MARINADES & SEASONINGS

Red Wine Marinade

Citrus Marinade

Lemon-Herb Marinade

Soy-Sherry Marinade

Bourbon Marinade

Jamaican Jerk-Style Marinade

Jamaican Jerk Spice Rub

Homemade Cajun Seasoning

Fines Herbes

SAUCES

Raw Tomato Sauce

Heirloom Tomato Sauce

Lime-Chile Sauce

Homemade Barbecue Sauce

Spicy Barbecue Sauce

Chimichurri Sauce

Homemade Indian Curry Sauce

HOMEMADE SUMMER STAPLES

These recipes are the summer's great flavorings, ranging from dressings to sauces to marinades and more that bring your meals to life. Here's where the intense flavors of spices, juices, and fermented liquids meet the staples of meat, fish, and vegetables and turn the ordinary into the extraordinary. The best part is that they are homemade from natural ingredients, not factory-produced versions that contain a list of chemical analogs of the real thing. The quality will show up in the flavors they impart to your cooking.

SPREADS & CONDIMENTS

pesto

MAKES ABOUT 4 CUPS

I first learned to make basil pesto several decades ago from a recipe a reader submitted to *Organic Gardening* magazine, where I was working at the time. The recipe was a good one, and I don't think the freezer compartment of my refrigerator has been without a tub or three since. I make a year's worth of pesto all at once, since it freezes beautifully, thus capturing the intensely fragrant cinnamon-clove spiciness of fresh summer basil to use in all seasons.

For the quickest of summer dinners, just grill up a few sausages, then thaw a few tablespoons of pesto in the microwave, boil up your favorite pasta, and serve. The pesto is ideally made in a mortar with a pestle. If you don't have one handy, use a metal bowl or small pot and a wooden mallet.

Consider substituting other nuts such as almonds or walnuts for the pine nuts if you like (but pine nuts give it that ineffable quality; just taste a few first to make sure they taste resinous and fresh and aren't rancid).

3 cups packed basil leaves, preferably the Genovese variety, destemmed
5 tablespoons pine nuts
4 cloves garlic
1 tablespoon kosher salt
1 cup grated Parmigiano-Reggiano cheese
4 tablespoons grated Pecorino-Romano cheese
1 cup extra virgin olive oil
4 tablespoons butter, softened

1. Place the basil, pine nuts, garlic, and salt in a mortar and grind to a thick paste with the pestle, or use a blender.

2. Add the cheeses and grind into the paste until they're well incorporated.

3. Add the oil a little at a time, beating it into the paste with a spoon.

4. Add the butter and beat it into the paste. Spoon the mixture into a food-grade plastic container with a lid and store in the freezer for up to 1 year. Even when frozen it will yield chunks of pesto easily.

pistou

MAKES 1 CUP

As you can probably tell by the name, French pistou and Italian pesto are cousins, but they are definitely not the same thing. Pistou is lighter and no pine nuts are used. It's a fine spread for sandwiches. Add it to soup made from summer-fresh vegetables. Spread some on fish. Or spoon some over pasta.

2 cups fresh basil leaves, destemmed
3 cloves garlic, chopped
½ cup extra virgin olive oil
½ teaspoon kosher salt
½ cup finely grated Parmesan cheese
¼ teaspoon freshly ground black pepper

1. Place basil, garlic, oil, and salt in a blender and puree until smooth. Add mixture to a bowl.

2. Beat in the cheese and pepper until the mixture is smooth. Cover and refrigerate. Use within 2 days. Pistou can be frozen for 3 months.

✱ VARIATION

Add 1 peeled small tomato to the blender and puree with the other ingredients.

persillade

MAKES 1 CUP

Nothing is simpler nor more useful in adding flavor to dishes than persillade. Use on browned potatoes and on roast rack of lamb. The persillade is usually added to foods toward the end of cooking, but can also be stirred into soups and stews or, mixed with breadcrumbs, used as a crust on roast meats, especially lamb.

½ cup finely chopped Italian flat-leaf parsley
½ cup finely minced garlic

Mash both ingredients together in a small bowl. Stores in the fridge for 10 days and in the freezer for 6 months.

✱ VARIATIONS

Persillade augmented with lemon zest becomes gremolata, the traditional garnish for braised lamb shanks. With added olive oil and grated Parmesan, it becomes similar to pistou, a fine topping for pasta or garnish for summer soups.

SALAD BASICS

classic vinaigrette

MAKES ABOUT 1½ CUPS

This is my basic recipe for vinaigrette, the delicious salad dressing with a thousand uses that combines sweet and sour with rich, flavorful olive or nut oil. I like the added flavor and brightness of the lemon juice but you can leave it out to simplify it further. You can tone down the sourness by replacing the red wine vinegar with Japanese rice vinegar, or give it a caramelized depth with a good balsamic vinegar.

1 cup extra virgin olive oil or walnut oil
¼ cup red wine vinegar
1 tablespoon freshly squeezed lemon juice
Pinch of sugar
Pinch of kosher salt
Pinch of freshly ground black pepper

Place all the ingredients in a jar with a lid. Screw the lid shut and shake vigorously for a few moments. Dress the salad with a scant quarter-cup of the vinaigrette. Add more a teaspoon at a time if you think it's too lightly dressed. Serve immediately.

asian soy-ginger dressing

MAKES ABOUT 1¼ CUPS

This is especially good over finely sliced napa cabbage or other Asian slaws and salads. It makes a great marinade for fish as well.

½ cup organic canola oil
⅓ cup tamari or soy sauce
¼ cup Japanese unflavored rice vinegar
¼ medium onion, finely chopped
1 teaspoon minced garlic
1 thumb ginger root, peeled and chopped
1 teaspoon freshly squeezed lemon juice
1 teaspoon tomato paste
¼ teaspoon toasted sesame oil

Place all the ingredients in a blender and blend until smooth. Store in a covered jar. This dressing will keep in the fridge for 2 weeks.

✳ VARY YOUR VINAIGRETTE

You can give this dressing added interest by:

✳ Dribbling in a few drops of toasted sesame oil

✳ Adding 2 tablespoons of sherry

✳ Adding 2 tablespoons of sweet dessert wine

✳ Adding 1 teaspoon of dry mustard or prepared Dijon

✳ Substituting ¼ cup lime juice for the vinegar and adding a pinch of toasted cumin seeds

✳ Adding a minced shallot, red onion, or snips of chives for a nice hint of onion

✳ Plumping 2 dried figs in the vinegar, whizzing them in the blender, then adding to the vinaigrette

✳ Mashing a clove of garlic through a garlic press

✳ Mincing French tarragon, mint, basil, parsley, chives, or thyme until you have about ¼ cup, then add to the vinaigrette

✳ Reducing the vinegar to 1 or 2 tablespoons and adding ¼ cup lime juice along with the lemon juice

✳ Making a honey-mustard vinaigrette, by adding 1 teaspoon each of honey and Dijon mustard to the basic recipe

✳ Adding chopped basil and snips of chives to the dressing

sesame-citrus dressing

MAKES ABOUT ⅔ CUP

This is an excellent dressing for any Asian-themed salad, or any salad of mixed greens for that matter, especially if it contains peeled segments of orange or mandarins.

1 tablespoon sesame seeds
2 cloves garlic, minced
2 tablespoons peanut oil
2 tablespoons plain rice vinegar
2 tablespoons freshly squeezed
    orange juice
1 teaspoon honey
1 teaspoon tamari
½ teaspoon freshly grated ginger
½ teaspoon toasted sesame oil
Salt and freshly ground black pepper
    to taste

1. Place a small skillet over medium heat and add the sesame seeds. Shake the pan frequently for 2 to 3 minutes, or until the seeds turn golden brown (not dark brown). Remove from the heat.

2. In a bowl, combine the remaining ingredients and whisk until well mixed. Add the sesame seeds, whisk again and use immediately. The oils will separate out fairly quickly, so whisk it just before each use. It will keep in the fridge for 2 weeks.

carrot-ginger dressing

MAKES ABOUT 1 CUP

This simple but delicious dressing can be used on a cucumber salad, on field greens, on lettuces, even on Asian greens. It makes friends with all sorts of ingredients because of its lightness and touch of sweetness.

½ cup finely shredded carrot
3 ounces soft tofu
2 tablespoons mirin
2 tablespoons plain rice vinegar
1 tablespoon soy sauce
1 teaspoon freshly grated ginger
½ teaspoon toasted sesame oil

Place all the ingredients in a blender and blend until smooth. Refrigerate until ready to use. Store the excess in the fridge for 1 week.

ginger-soy dressing

MAKES ABOUT ⅔ CUP

Make a dressing for steamed greens from these ingredients.

¼ cup vegetable oil, preferably canola
¼ cup Japanese rice vinegar or red
    wine vinegar
2 tablespoons soy sauce
1 tablespoon freshly squeezed lemon juice
1 tablespoon finely chopped peeled
    fresh ginger
1 clove garlic, minced
Freshly ground black pepper to taste

Place all the ingredients in a jar with a lid. Screw the lid shut and shake vigorously for a few moments. Use as much dressing as appropriate for the amount of greens.

creamy blue cheese dressing

MAKES ABOUT 1 CUP

I usually use Point Reyes Blue Cheese, but Roquefort, Stilton, Gorgonzola, Maytag, or any fine blue cheese will do.

½ cup full or reduced-fat mayonnaise
¼ cup sour cream
1 tablespoon red wine vinegar
½ teaspoon Worcestershire sauce
2 tablespoons minced flat-leaf parsley
½ teaspoon minced garlic
Freshly ground black pepper to taste
2 ounces blue cheese

Place all the ingredients except the blue cheese in a blender and puree until smooth. Add the cheese and pulse until desired consistency is reached. You may want it creamy, or with some small lumps of blue cheese remaining. Refrigerate covered until needed for up to 10 days.

creamy buttermilk dressing

MAKES ABOUT 1¼ CUPS

This salad dressing is especially good on vegetable salads, and on salads of endive, arugula, dandelion greens, and other bitter herbs.

¼ cup Japanese unflavored rice vinegar
¼ cup plain nonfat yogurt
¼ cup buttermilk
3 tablespoons wildflower honey
1 teaspoon minced garlic
1 scallion, minced
Salt and freshly ground black pepper
    to taste
½ cup extra virgin olive oil

Place all ingredients except the oil in a bowl and whisk until well mixed. Add the oil in a slow, steady stream, whisking constantly, until well incorporated. Store in a jar with a tight lid in the fridge, shaking well before each use. This dressing will keep in the fridge for 1 week.

russian dressing

MAKES 1 GENEROUS CUP

I love Russian dressing. But for years I felt a little guilty about it because it was served to me as a kid and ubiquitously offered for kids—so it seemed like something for an "undeveloped" palate. When I got old enough, I stopped caring about whether or not it's for kids. (After all, I like ice cream, and that's not just for kids.) Now I simply enjoy it on salads and on deli-style sandwiches where it joins roast beef and sauerkraut on toasted rye bread. Thousand Island dressing is very similar to Russian dressing. Use this recipe and add 2 tablespoons of pickle relish, a tablespoon of snipped chives, and a tablespoon of minced parsley. Many cooks chop a hardboiled egg

to coarse crumbles and add it to Thousand Island, but many don't.

1 cup mayonnaise
¼ cup chili sauce
1 tablespoon freshly grated horseradish
1 tablespoon minced parsley
1 teaspoon grated onion
1 teaspoon Worcestershire sauce
Salt and freshly ground black pepper
    to taste

Place all the ingredients in a bowl and mix well. Store in a covered jar. This dressing will keep in the fridge for 1 week.

garlic-parmesan dressing
MAKES ½ CUP

Here's a simple dressing for a simple salad of mixed lettuces. The garlic, vinegar, and cheese boost the flavors, while the olive oil gives it a mouth-coating texture. This variation of a classic vinaigrette is useful for most salads.

2 cloves garlic, minced
2 tablespoons balsamic vinegar
2 tablespoons grated Parmigiano-Reggiano
    cheese
1 teaspoon minced parsley
¼ cup extra virgin olive oil

In a small bowl, mix together the garlic, vinegar, cheese, chicken broth, and parsley. Add the oil in a slow, steady stream, whisking constantly, until well incorporated. Refrigerate until cold. Whisk just before using.

walnut-lemon dressing
MAKES A LITTLE MORE THAN 1 CUP

Fine wine doesn't like to compete with sour vinegar at the dinner table—after all, vinegar is what happens if wine turns bad. This salad dressing avoids vinegar altogether, showcasing the richness of walnut oil and tartness of lemon. The after-dinner wine can be Port, late harvest red wine from California, Muscat, Beaumes-de-Venise, or Sauternes.

Be sure to use good-quality walnut oil from a store you trust; it can turn rancid quickly. If you smell it or taste it, the impression may be strong, but it blends beautifully with the balancing flavors in this dressing.

1 cup walnut oil
¼ cup lemon juice
2 tablespoons sweet after-dinner wine
½ teaspoon minced thyme
¼ teaspoon Coleman's mustard
Pinch salt

Place all the ingredients in a jar with a lid. Screw the lid shut and shake vigorously for a few moments, or until the mustard and salt have dissolved and are well incorporated. Stir with a fork to keep it mixed as you drizzle it on a salad.

✳ VARIATION
Substitute *verjus* for the lemon juice.

cobb salad dressing

MAKES ABOUT 2 CUPS

There is no required dressing for a Cobb Salad, but this one is purported to be the one originally used at the Brown Derby in the 1920s and can be used on a variety of salads.

¾ cup salad oil
¼ cup full-flavored olive oil
¼ cup cold water
¼ cup red wine vinegar
2 teaspoons salt
1 teaspoon freshly squeezed lemon juice
¾ teaspoon Worcestershire sauce
¼ teaspoon freshly ground black pepper
¼ teaspoon sugar
¼ teaspoon dry English mustard
1 small clove garlic, chopped

Place all ingredients in a blender and blend until the sugar is dissolved and the garlic is finely minced.

summer berry dressing

MAKES 3 CUPS

Raspberries probably make the best version of this fruity, light dressing, but it works well with other brambleberries as well. If you live in an area where the wineberries grow wild, use them in the recipe for a special treat. Use the dressing on a mixture of sweet lettuces and bitter or spicy field greens like endives and mustards. Note: This dressing comes together slowly; you'll need to let it rest in the fridge for 3 weeks.

> ### GOOD TO KNOW: ADDING BROTH TO DRESSINGS
>
> Years ago, when visiting my aunt in Kentucky, we made dinner together. She made the salad dressing and I noticed that she added a splash of chicken broth to the dressing. "What does that do?" I asked.
>
> "It warms the flavor," she said. "The broth adds substance. Otherwise, the salad dressing tastes a little thin to me." Later, I tried it and discovered that for dressings for light salads, such as vinaigrettes or "the perfect dressing for an all-lettuce salad (page 87);" just 4 tablespoons of chicken broth per cup of dressing smoothes, balances, and warms the dressing with a savory note.

3 cups fresh brambleberries (raspberries, blackberries, or black raspberries)
2 cups plain rice vinegar
¼ cup sugar

1. Place the berries in a large bowl that has a cover. In a saucepan over high heat, bring the vinegar and sugar to a boil and pour the boiling liquid over the raspberries. Stir, then cover the bowl. When completely cool, place the bowl in a plastic bag and twist-tie it shut, then put in the fridge for 3 weeks. This draws the berry flavor into the liquid gently.

2. After 3 weeks, line a colander with a double thickness of cheesecloth and set the colander into a bowl or pot. Pour the liquid into the colander to remove the solids. Transfer the liquid to a saucepan over high heat, bring to a boil, reduce heat, and simmer for 5 minutes. Remove from heat and let cool. Either use plain as a light dressing for greens, or add a few table-spoons of canola oil to ½ cup of the dressing and shake to emulsify, and then use immediately on your salad. Freeze the rest of the berry liquid in half-cup containers (I use clean yogurt containers wrapped in cling wrap) for later use. This will keep in the freezer for 6 months.

verjus salad dressing

MAKES ¾ CUP

Verjus—the juice of unripe grapes—has all the acid tang of vinegar, but unlike vinegar, it complements rather than competes with wine at the dinner table. *Verjus* signals the good flavors to come when the grapes mature.

The tangy juice is used to deglaze pans used for cooking fowl or fish to make sauces. It has a tart apple taste that brightens flavors it's paired with. It sings soprano to other flavors' bass notes.

One of its chief uses is as an ingredient in salad dressings where wine is being served. Instead of curdling the nuanced flavors of wine the harsh way vinegar does, it complements rather than competes. In the Middle Ages, it was often preferred over vinegar and used as an ingredient in sauces and as a meat-tenderizing marinade.

Terra Sonoma makes an organic *verjus* and suggests reducing it until it becomes thick and creamy and pouring a little over fresh fruits like strawberries. It can replace

vinegar and lemon juice in recipes calling for those ingredients.

My favorite *verjus* (pronounced vair-zjoo) is produced by Navarro Vineyards in Mendocino County's Anderson Valley. Here's a recipe for *verjus* salad dressing that Navarro suggests:

⅓ cup *verjus*
⅓ cup grapeseed oil
1 large shallot, finely chopped
2 teaspoons fresh thyme leaves, chopped

In a medium bowl, whisk all the ingredients together just before using.

candied walnuts

MAKES ABOUT 1½ CUPS

Candied walnuts have a sweet crunch that raw walnuts don't have and are very tooth-some and texturally interesting in a salad. They're simple to make, but there are some tricks. Once the sugar starts to melt, work fast. Once the sugar hardens, the walnut pieces will become a solid, glued-together mess if not quickly separated.

1 ½ cups raw walnut halves or pieces
½ cup sugar
⅛ teaspoon coarse salt

1. Preheat the oven to 350°F. Line a baking sheet with wax paper and set aside. Spread the walnuts on another baking sheet and bake for 5 minutes. Test for doneness (they'll be crunchy and slightly browned, but not bitter or burnt). If necessary, bake for 1 minute longer until baked through. Be careful not to burn the nuts. When they're done, place them in a bowl to cool.

2. Place a saucepan over medium heat and add the sugar. Stir with a wooden spoon until all the sugar has melted and its color is a medium amber. Remove the saucepan from the heat, immediately add the walnuts, and stir to coat each nut thoroughly.

3. Working quickly, turn the nuts onto the prepared wax paper–lined baking sheet and, using 2 forks, separate the pieces so they're not touching, removing any thick gobs of sugar. Sprinkle with the salt and set aside to cool. When thoroughly cool, store in a closed jar for up to 6 months.

croutons

MAKES 2 CUPS

To make croutons, you can use any kind of bread, including rye and cornbread, but for inclusion in a salad, an herbed whole wheat bread is the best choice. For an extra flavor kick, mix the oil with 1 crushed clove of garlic before pouring the oil into the skillet.

2 tablespoons extra virgin olive oil
2 cups ½-inch diced bread

1. Preheat the oven to 350°F. Place the oil in a large ovenproof skillet and add the bread. Stir and toss to coat the bread with the oil. Bake for 8 to 10 minutes, shaking the skillet once or twice. With a spatula, loosen any croutons that stick.

2. When the croutons are golden brown, transfer them to a plate covered with paper towels and allow them to cool. Store in a plastic container in the fridge for up to 2 weeks, using as needed, or use immediately. Let refrigerated croutons warm to room temperature before incorporating. If they are at all soggy, refresh them in a 350°F. oven for 8 minutes.

MARINADES & SEASONINGS

red wine marinade

MAKES ABOUT 1 CUP

This marinade gives a sweet-sour effect to your burgers.

½ cup good red wine
⅓ cup red wine vinegar
2 tablespoons olive oil
1 tablespoon Dijon mustard
2 cloves garlic, minced
1 tablespoon chopped fresh thyme, or
    1 teaspoon dried
1 tablespoon chopped fresh oregano, or
    1 teaspoon dried
¼ teaspoon freshly ground black pepper
Pinch of salt

Place all the ingredients in a jar with a lid. Screw the lid shut and shake vigorously for a few moments. Use immediately, before the marinade has time to separate.

citrus marinade

MAKES ABOUT 1¼ CUPS

This simple marinade will add enormous amounts of flavor to ordinary ground meat or poultry. Feel free to leave out the vodka, although it does give the marinade a nice kick.

½ cup freshly squeezed orange juice or
    lemon juice
¼ cup soy sauce
1 clove garlic crushed through a garlic press
2 dashes (about ¼ teaspoon or less)
    ground cloves
½ cup vodka (optional)

Place all the ingredients in a jar with a lid. Screw the lid shut and shake vigorously for a few moments. Use immediately, before the marinade has time to separate.

lemon-herb marinade

MAKES ABOUT 1 CUP

Here's an all-purpose marinade for all kinds of meat and fish.

½ cup loosely packed chopped Italian
    flat-leaf parsley
¼ cup extra virgin olive oil
Juice of ½ fresh lemon
2 tablespoons dry white wine
2 teaspoons chopped fresh oregano
2 cloves garlic, minced
1 teaspoon chopped fresh thyme
½ teaspoon salt
Freshly ground black pepper to taste

Place all the ingredients in a bowl and whisk to incorporate. Use immediately.

soy-sherry marinade

MAKES ABOUT 1¼ CUPS

Soy and sherry have a natural affinity of flavors and aromas. Try this for mild fish like catfish or tilapia filets, or for chicken to be grilled.

½ cup dry sherry (such as fino, manzanilla,
    or amontillado, but for goodness, sake,
    not salt-infused "cooking sherry")
½ cup tamari soy sauce
¼ cup canola oil
2 tablespoons Dijon-style mustard
1 tablespoon Tabasco or other hot sauce

Place all the ingredients in a bowl and whisk to incorporate. This marinade can be stored in the fridge for up to 2 weeks.

bourbon marinade

MAKES 3 CUPS

Marinate beef steaks and roasts, pork chops, and beef or pork ribs in this whoopee-style Southern sauce. Then grill.

1 cup bourbon
½ cup chili sauce
½ cup red wine vinegar
½ cup canola oil
¼ cup molasses
3 tablespoons fresh lemon juice
1 tablespoon ground cloves

1 tablespoon ground nutmeg
1 tablespoon salt
1 tablespoon Tabasco or other hot sauce

1. Place a saucepan over medium heat and add the bourbon, chili sauce, vinegar, oil, molasses, and lemon juice, stirring together for 1 to 2 minutes. Don't let the mixture scorch.

2. Add the cloves, nutmeg, salt, and Tabasco, and cook for 1 minute more. Reduce the heat to low and simmer gently for 5 minutes. Remove from the heat and allow to cool to room temperature before using.

jamaican jerk-style marinade
MAKES ABOUT 1½ CUPS

This marinade may become your all-time favorite for pumping up the flavor of your hamburger and spicing it up. It has become mine.

³⁄₄ cup commercial Italian salad dressing, such as Newman's Own
½ cup vodka
1 tablespoon Worcestershire sauce
1 heaping tablespoon brown sugar
1 large jalapeño pepper, halved, seeded, and finely chopped
1 teaspoon ground allspice
1 teaspoon ground dry ginger

Place all the ingredients in a jar with a lid. Screw the lid shut and shake vigorously for a few moments. Use immediately, before the marinade has time to separate.

jamaican jerk spice rub
MAKES ½ CUP

The rubs you buy in the store may or may not be potent. This one, which you make yourself, will be if you start with fresh spices. Use it on pork or beefsteak before grilling to punch up the flavor and create a nice crust. Cook rubbed meat over medium heat to avoid burning the rub ingredients, which turns them bitter.

STAGE ONE
1 tablespoon sugar
1 tablespoon kosher salt
1 tablespoon allspice
1 tablespoon paprika
2 teaspoons dried thyme
1 teaspoon freshly ground black pepper
1 teaspoon ground cayenne
¼ teaspoon ground nutmeg

Mix all dry ingredients thoroughly and store in the spice cabinet in a closed jar or plastic baggie twist-tied shut until needed.

STAGE TWO
2 teaspoons minced garlic
2 teaspoons peeled, minced fresh ginger

Mince the garlic and ginger and add to the dry spice mixture, mixing in thoroughly, just before using.

homemade cajun seasoning

MAKES A GENEROUS ¼ CUP

1 tablespoon paprika
2 ½ teaspoons kosher salt
1 ½ teaspoons freshly ground black pepper
1 teaspoon onion powder
1 teaspoon garlic powder
1 teaspoon ground cayenne
½ teaspoon dried thyme

In a large bowl add all the ingredients and mix well. Store in a sealed container for up to 6 months.

fines herbes

MAKES ½ CUP

Chives, tarragon, parsley, and chervil are the fines herbes, pronounced "feenz airb," of French cooking. The fresh herbs are finely chopped and added to savory dishes just before serving, because they lose their evanescent charm if cooked. The herbs are at their best and freshest in midsummer. Try fines herbes with mild cheese, such as Jarlsberg or Jack, in your morning omelet. Add them to sauces, soups, and stews. Sprinkle them over a steak or grilled chicken breast. If you're a traditionalist, use these four herbs, but if you like to make up your own mind about these things, you can add watercress, summer savory, or salad burnet to the mix.

3 sprigs tarragon
3 sprigs parsley
5 sprigs chervil
5 spears chives

Destem the tarragon, parsley, and chervil and mince all four herbs together. Use immediately at the end of cooking.

SAUCES

raw tomato sauce

MAKES 2 TO 4 SERVINGS

Summertime is tomato-time. And tomato lovers know that raw tomatoes have a distinctive, estery flavor all their own. So when you spy some particularly good-looking fresh tomatoes for sale, abjure the jar of commercial pasta sauce and try this simple and oh-so-delicious sauce on your favorite pasta. It goes particularly well with cappellini.

WINE SUGGESTION: ITALIAN SANGIOVESE (CHIANTI)

5 medium tomatoes, peeled, seeded, and chopped into lumpy pulp
3 tablespoons minced shallots
1 teaspoon red wine vinegar
¼ teaspoon salt
Freshly ground black pepper to taste
3 tablespoons finely chopped basil
3 tablespoons extra virgin olive oil

1. Place the tomatoes, shallots, vinegar, salt, and pepper in a bowl and mix well. Set aside for 10 minutes, then put into a large sieve and let drain. Add the drained mixture back to the bowl.
2. Add the basil and oil and stir to mix.

Serve at room temperature over steaming hot pasta.

✳ VARIATION

Serve with grated Parmesan cheese and dried cayenne pepper flakes. Serve with grilled Italian chicken sausages.

heirloom tomato sauce

MAKES ABOUT 1½ QUARTS

We wait all year for the heirloom tomatoes to show up in midsummer. When they do, why not make lots of sauce and can or freeze some for those months to come? Then you can cherish the flavors of summer even in the cooler months.

WINE SUGGESTION: ITALIAN SANGIOVESE (CHIANTI)

3 tablespoons olive oil
1 head garlic, cloves peeled and
    coarsely chopped
1 yellow onion, diced
4 pounds heirloom tomatoes
½ teaspoon salt, or to taste
5 leaves of basil
Leaves from 5 stems of oregano
Leaves from 2 stems of thyme

1. Place a skillet over medium-low heat and add the oil. When hot, add the garlic and onion. Allow to simmer in the oil until the onion is clear and the garlic just begins to show a little brown color. Don't let garlic brown. Remove from the heat and reserve.

2. Heat a large pot of water and bring to a boil. Add tomatoes and blanch for 3 to 4 minutes. Run the tomatoes under cold water to stop the cooking. Place the tomatoes in a large bowl. Peel and core the tomatoes, discarding skins and cores. Using 2 knives, cut the tomatoes into small pieces. Place into a sieve to separate the juice from the pulp. Return the pulp to the bowl. Place a saucepan over medium heat and add the collected tomato juice. Allow the juice to come to a slow boil, stirring frequently. When the juice is reduced to a thick sauce, about 20 minutes, add it back to the tomatoes. Be careful not to let sauce scorch. Add the salt.

3. Coarsely chop the basil. Add the basil, oregano, and thyme to the tomatoes. Pour off any excess oil from the reserved onion and garlic mixture and add to the tomatoes. Stir to mix well. Place the tomato mixture in a saucepan and simmer, stirring occasionally to prevent scorching, for about 15 minutes more.

4. Serve the sauce over freshly made, hot pasta with a bowl of grated parmesan cheese and crushed red pepper available.

GOOD TO KNOW: PEELING TOMATOES

Set a pot of water to boil on the stove, large enough to accommodate the tomatoes you want to peel so that water covers them. Cut out the stem ends and a small cone of the tough material that descends toward the center of the fruit. When the pot is at a rolling boil, drop in the tomatoes and cook for 2 minutes, until you see the skins splitting. Keep the hot water on the stove. Using a large spoon, transfer the tomatoes to a bowl of cold water or ice water to stop the cooking. The skins will pull off easily. If one sticks, simply return it to the pot of water for 30 more seconds, then try again.

lime-chile sauce

MAKES ABOUT ½ CUP

This traditional Thai dipping sauce—hot and tangy—enlivens summer vegetables, battered and fried items, satays, and pan-fried beef with noodles. Sprinkle some over just about any dish to fire it up. I like to dip peeled steamed shrimp in it instead of cold cocktail sauce. After all, Thailand is a tropical country—they know how to stay cool. And by the way, not many Thai restaurants in America serve this spicy sauce, but it is as common in Thailand as *chimichurri* is in Argentina.

6 flat anchovy fillets, plus some of their
    packing oil
Juice of 3 limes
2 cloves garlic, finely minced
6 serrano chiles, finely chopped
1 tablespoon light brown sugar
1 teaspoon finely chopped cilantro

1. Heat a small skillet over medium-low heat and add the anchovy fillets and a few drops of the packing oil. Mash into a paste with the back of a fork. Remove the pan from the heat as soon as the fillets liquefy.

2. Add the other ingredients and stir to mix well. Refrigerate before serving.

✳ VARIATION
Substitute ¼ cup Thai fish sauce (*nam pla*) for the anchovies.

homemade barbecue sauce

MAKES 4 CUPS

The number of ready-made barbecue sauces at the market (many trying to grab you with clever marketing: "Rasta Melvin's Jamaican Disco Inferno Sauce!") has grown dramatically—but who wants to spend so much money trying one after the other to find the one you like? It's easy and much cheaper to make your own. Try my version, then adapt it to your taste. Keep one small bottle in the fridge for current use and freeze the rest indefinitely.

1 quart apple cider vinegar
One 20-ounce bottle ketchup
2¼ cups dark brown sugar
½ cup freshly squeezed lemon juice
¼ cup Worcestershire sauce
¼ cup paprika
¼ cup kosher salt
2 tablespoons crushed red pepper flakes
1 tablespoon freshly ground black pepper
1 tablespoon garlic powder

In a large bowl, mix together all the ingredients until thoroughly combined. Place into clean, empty ketchup (or other) bottles. Store in the fridge for 1 month or in the freezer indefinitely.

spicy barbecue sauce

MAKES ABOUT 2 CUPS

Here's a BBQ recipe with kick to impress your neighbors.

2 tablespoons peanut oil
1 small onion, chopped
2 cloves garlic, chopped
½ cup tomato paste
⅓ cup red wine vinegar
3 tablespoons brown sugar
1 tablespoon molasses
2 teaspoons chili powder
2 teaspoons paprika
1 teaspoon ground cayenne
1 teaspoon freshly ground black pepper
½ teaspoon salt
One 14-ounce can crushed Italian plum
   tomatoes

1. Place a a skillet over medium heat and add the oil. When hot, add the onion and sauté for 4 to 5 minutes, or until soft. Add the garlic and cook for 1 minute more.

2. While the onion and garlic are cooking, in a bowl, whisk together the tomato paste, vinegar, brown sugar, molasses, chili powder, paprika, cayenne, black pepper and salt.

3. In a large saucepan over medium-high heat, combine the onion and garlic, the tomato paste mixture, and the canned tomatoes. Stir and bring to a boil. Reduce the heat to low and simmer, stirring occasionally, for about 2 hours, or until the sauce reaches the consistency of a thick barbecue sauce. Be especially watchful toward the end that it doesn't scorch.

4. Add the cooked sauce to a blender and puree until smooth. It will keep in the fridge for 2 weeks. Or, use some right away and freeze the rest.

✳ VARIATIONS
Use smoked paprika to give a smoky flavor. Chipotles (dried, smoked jalapeños) ground

to a fine powder in a blender can be added during the 2-hour cooking to give spicy heat and a smoky flavor. Use more cayenne if you like it very spicy, or add a few dashes of commercial habañero pepper sauce after cooking and stir it in well. Add a generous splash of bourbon before cooking. Add a squeeze of lime juice or a splash of orange juice before cooking.

chimichurri sauce

MAKES ¾ CUP

In Argentina, where the beef is doubly delicious and cooked on huge grills over dried chaparral, you will invariably find it accompanied by *chimichurri* sauce. But that's not the only use for this versatile dip. Anything from empanadas to plain bread tastes that much better when a spoonful of *chimichurri* is applied.

½ cup extra virgin olive oil
2 tablespoons freshly squeezed
   lemon juice
⅓ cup minced flat-leaf parsley
1 clove garlic, minced
2 shallots, minced
1 teaspoon fresh thyme, minced
Salt and freshly ground black pepper
   to taste

In a bowl, mix together all the ingredients. Set aside for at least 2 hours so flavors marry before serving.

homemade indian curry sauce

MAKES ABOUT 1 CUP

With this easy-to-make sauce at hand, you won't have to do a lot of work to make an authentic Indian curry—a saucy, spicy meal that satisfies (and makes you sweat to cool off) in the hot weather, especially when combined with a glass of Mango Lassi (page 268). Summer's a time when folks on the move can just drop in around mealtime. Snag a rotisserie chicken at the store and deconstruct it, putting the meat in one bowl and skin and bones and gristle in another (to save to make chicken broth).

Cook up a big pot of basmati rice, crush some peanuts, add a handful of chopped dried fruit and some shredded coconut, and mix it all together with a few tablespoons of this curry sauce and some plain yogurt. Add the remaining curry sauce to the chicken meat and toss to coat. Spoon the sauced meat over the rice mixture and serve hot.

5 tablespoons coriander seeds
2 tablespoons cumin seeds
2 teaspoons whole mustard seeds
4 teaspoons peeled and grated
    fresh ginger
4 cloves garlic, crushed through a
    garlic press
2 teaspoons turmeric
2 teaspoons chili powder
1 teaspoon coarsely cracked black
    peppercorns
7 tablespoons white vinegar

1. Start with fresh spices, not the spices of indeterminate age in your spice cabinet. Roast the coriander and cumin seeds in a skillet in a 350°F oven for 3 to 4 minutes, until fragrant and slightly browned. Grind to powder in a blender, spice mill, or with a mortar and pestle.

2. In a mixing bowl, add the ground coriander and cumin, and the remaining ingredients, except the vinegar, and mash together. Add the vinegar and mix to form a smooth paste. Spoon into a container with a lid and seal. The sauce will keep in the fridge for 2 to 3 weeks.

Menus

BREAKFAST ON THE DECK

LEMON PANCAKES (PAGE 29)

SOUR CREAM BREAKFAST CAKE (PAGE 34)

SIMPLE FRUIT SALAD (PAGE 105)

FRESHLY SQUEEZED ORANGE JUICE

FRESHLY BREWED COFFEE

WEEKEND BRUNCH

LEMON PANCAKES (PAGE 29)

ZUCCHINI QUICHE (PAGE 33)

APRICOT-LEMON PRESERVES (PAGE 27)

BRIOCHE (PAGE 28)

SIMPLE FRUIT SALAD (PAGE 105)

COLD SIMPLEST GRILLED STEAK (PAGE 177)

FRESHLY BREWED COFFEE

WARM SUMMER BREAKFAST

BRIOCHE FRENCH TOAST (PAGE 29)

SIMPLE FRUIT SALAD (PAGE 105)

CARROT-CURRANT MUFFINS (PAGE 31)

COLD-BREWED COFFEE (PAGE 271)

ITALIAN LUNCH (PRANZO)

BRUSCHETTA WITH GARLIC, TOMATOES, AND BASIL (PAGE 50)

CLASSIC ITALIAN HOAGIE (PAGE 70)

BELLINIS (PAGE 273)

VACATION HOUSE LUNCH

CHILLED FRESH TOMATO SOUP (PAGE 135)

GREEK SALAD (PAGE 93) WITH OLIVE BREAD (PAGE 75)

FRIED SHRIMP AND MANGO WRAP (PAGE 73)

HERBAL ICED TEAS (PAGE 270)

PICNIC IN THE PARK

SOUTHERN FRIED CHICKEN (PAGE 163)

CHICORY AND WALNUT SALAD (PAGE 91)

HUMMUS (PAGE 42) WITH PITA BREAD

SIMPLE FRUIT SALAD (PAGE 105)

CHILLED WHITE WINE

BACKYARD FIESTA

FRUITY AGUA FRESCA (PAGE 265)

TACOS AL CARNE ASADA (PAGE 73)

PICO DE GALLO (PAGE 42)

TORTILLA CHIPS

SUMMER FRUIT SLAW (PAGE 113)

POOLSIDE LUNCH

HERBAL ICED TEAS (PAGE 270)

SWEET-AND-TART GAZPACHO (PAGE 135)

SPICY PASTA SALAD WITH OLIVES
AND FETA (PAGE 115)

MULTIGRAIN CLUB SANDWICH (PAGE 70)

STRAWBERRY ICE-CREAM SODA (PAGE 268)

LUNCH BUFFET

SUMMERY TAPAS (PAGE 52)

ARGENTINE EMPANADAS (PAGE 58)

CHEDDAR AND SARDINE CANAPÉS (PAGE 49)

CHEF'S SALAD (PAGE 94)

PROSCIUTTO AND MELON (PAGE 50)

MEDITERRANEAN DINNER

GRILLED BUTTERFLIED LEG OF LAMB
(PAGE 183)

NORTH AFRICAN-STYLE CARROTS (PAGE 203)

CORN RISOTTO WITH LIME (PAGE 216)

CAPRESE SALAD (PAGE 96)

MELON WITH SORBET (PAGE 232)

PINOT NOIR

SUPPER, SOUTHERN STYLE

SOUTHERN FRIED CHICKEN (PAGE 163)

POLENTA WITH MUSHROOMS AND CHEESE
(PAGE 215)

SIMPLE STEAMED GREENS (PAGE 213)

STRAWBERRY SHORTCAKE (PAGE 246)

CHILLED PROSECCO

MIDSUMMER BACKYARD BARBECUE

GRILLED BEEFSTEAK (PAGE 176)

HASH BROWN POTATOES (PAGE 224)

GRILLED EGGPLANT AND TOMATO
CAPONATA (PAGE 210)

CHICORY AND WALNUT SALAD (PAGE 91)

SIMPLE FRUIT SALAD (PAGE 105)

CABERNET SAUVIGNON

SEAFOOD DINNER

MESCLUN SALAD (PAGE 88)

BAKED SALMON WITH CHILES (PAGE 192)

QUINOA

GREEN BEAN AND TOMATO MEDLEY
(PAGE 211)

LITCHI SORBET (PAGE 234)

SAUVIGNON BLANC

TRADITIONAL NEW ENGLAND CLAMBAKE

NEW ENGLAND CLAM CHOWDER
(PAGE 141)

SOFT SHELL CLAMS (PAGE 193)

BOILED LOBSTER (PAGE 194)

GRILL-ROASTED CORN ON THE COB
(PAGE 206)

BLUEBERRY PIE (PAGE 250)

CHARDONNAY

15-MINUTE GOURMET FEAST

CRUDITÉS (PAGE 48)

SHRIMP WITH GARLIC AND WHITE WINE
(PAGE 187)

EGG NOODLES

SPINACH AND BACON SALAD (PAGE 90)

ALSATIAN GEWURZTRAMINER

FOURTH OF JULY BBQ

GRILLED BEEFSTEAK (PAGE 176)

HAMBURGER FROM SCRATCH (PAGE 170)

PASTA WITH RAW TOMATO SAUCE (PAGE 292)

CLASSIC AMERICAN POTATO SALAD (PAGE 110)

TABBOULEH (PAGE 117)

FRESH STONE FRUITS

ALL-AMERICAN APPLE PIE (PAGE 249)

MOJITOS (PAGE 273), BEER, WINE,
SOFT DRINKS

MEXICAN FISH FEST

COLD SUMMER SQUASH SOUP (PAGE 137)

FISH TACOS (PAGE 69)

GUACAMOLE (PAGE 41) AND CHIPS

APPLE FRITTERS (PAGE 240)

WATERMELON WATER ICE (PAGE 231)

MEXICAN BEER WITH LIMES

DOWNTOWN DELIGHTS

MOJITOS (PAGE 273)

GRILLED VEAL CHOPS (PAGE 183)

POLENTA WITH MUSHROOMS AND CHEESE
(PAGE 215)

STIR-FRY OF SUMMER VEGETABLES
(PAGE 221)

CLASSIC CAESAR SALAD (PAGE 92)

TARTE TATIN (PAGE 256)

MERLOT

RIBS-'N'-ZIN DINNER

BOURBON-HOISIN BABY BACK RIBS
(PAGE 181)

SUMMER SQUASH AU GRATIN (PAGE 225)

CORN AND BABY LIMA BEAN SUCCOTASH
(PAGE 205)

CHICORY AND WALNUT SALAD (PAGE 91)

SUPER-FAST HOMEMADE ICE CREAM
(PAGE 235)

ZINFANDEL

Farmers' Market Picks: Fruits & Vegetables

With summer come more choices for locally grown produce. Look for the best-tasting varieties for current eating as well as for putting up for later in the year. Here's a rundown of some of the highest-quality fruit and vegetable variety names to look for and when each is at its ripest. Whichever you find will be a delicious discovery.

FRUITS

APPLES

Early Joe—A greenish-yellow striped apple with a sprightly flavor that ripens in August

Gravenstein—A high-quality dessert apple from Northern California that ripens in August

Primate—A pale-yellow apple with reddish blush; its flavor is excellent for an early apple that ripens in late August or early September.

Summer Pearmain—A greenish-yellow apple with blotches of purplish-red, it's perhaps the most excellent summer apple that ripens in August.

Williams' Pride—A relatively new introduction that ripens in late July/early August. It's dark red with excellent flavor and juicy flesh.

APRICOT

Golden Amber—A light orange apricot with a superbly sweet flavor that ripens in early July

Moorpark—An apricot with yellow skin and a dark red blush and rich, juicy, sweet flesh that sets the standard of excellence in apricots

Ram Roc—It has very juicy orange flesh and is rated among the best tasting of all apricots.

ASIAN PEAR

Hosui—Its skin is a russet greenish brown, and its delicate sweet flesh is crisp and white with an excellent flavor. It ripens from July into August.

Kosui—A small Asian pear with high-quality, extra sweet, and crisp flesh that ripens in August

Shinko—With its golden bronze skin and flesh and its rich, very sweet, juicy, and distinct flavor, it is rated the best Asian pear in taste tests. It ripens in late summer.

AVOCADO

Hass—This is the summer-ripening avocado and the best tasting and richest of them all.

BLACKBERRY

Arapaho—These delicious blackberries ripen in early summer.

Cheyenne—These berries are large, up to an inch long, with superb blackberry flavor. They ripen in late July and early August.

Marionberry—A cross between blackberries and raspberries with a delightful, inimitable flavor

BLUEBERRY

Bluehaven—Large berries with highly flavored, firm flesh. They ripen in mid-July in most areas.

Elizabeth—One of the very best-tasting blueberries ripening in August

Sierra—An excellent blueberry that hits the stores in late July

Spartan—Large fruits of excellent quality that ripen in early July

CHERRY

Bing—Yes, Bing cherries are common in July and are unsurpassed for their rich cherry flavor and sweet meatiness.

Black Tartarian—A dark red to black cherry

with very fine flavor that ripens in early
summer

Merton Bigarreau—The skin of this cherry
is dark red, and the flesh is uncommonly
sweet and rich. It ripens in mid-July.

Rainier—A yellow-skinned variety with a
red blush and of excellent quality

BLACK CURRANT

Blackdown—Its real black currant flavor
with a slight muskiness make it great for
jams, jellies, and cassis.

GOOSEBERRY

Leveller—A light-skinned, European gooseberry of exceedingly fine flavor

GRAPE

Catawba—One of the finest-flavored
seeded American grapes

Delaware—Another high-quality seeded
American grape with a sprightly and
refreshing flavor

Einset—A red-skinned, seedless grape with
a lovely sweet flavor developed by
grape specialists in Geneva, New York

Interlaken—A green seedless American
grape with an excellent flavor that tastes
like Concord

Muscat of Alexandria—A very sweet and
aromatic grape with a strong Muscat
flavor

MELON

Burpee Hybrid—A muskmelon type with a
netted surface and deep orange flesh
that's wonderfully sweet and delicious

Charentais—A true cantaloupe melon,
about the size of a softball, that is extremely sweet, aromatic, and flavorful

Escondido Gold—A large Crenshaw-type
melon with very sweet, tender, juicy,
yellow-orange flesh

Iroquois—A salmon-fleshed muskmelon
with extra sweet, fine-textured flesh

Venus—A hybrid honeydew-type melon
with bright green, aromatic, lusciously
sweet flesh

NECTARINE

Double Delight—A relatively new cultivar
of yellow-fleshed nectarine with a rich,
sweet flavor

Flavortop—A pretty, mostly red nectarine
with high-quality golden-yellow flesh
streaked with red

Heavenly White—It has cream-colored
skin and an attractive red blush and is
freestone, with exceptionally delicious
white flesh.

Mericrest—Its skin is solid red, and its
flesh is golden-yellow, fine textured, extra
sweet, and aromatic.

Snow Queen—The best of the white-
fleshed nectarines, period. Freestone.

PEACH

Champion—A white-fleshed, freestone
peach of juicy, fine texture with extra
sweet flavor

Flavorcrest—A yellow-fleshed peach with a
smooth texture and meltingly sweet flavor

Halehaven—A dark red peach with yellow
flesh and very sweet flavor. Freestone.

Jerseyqueen—A yellow-skin peach with a
red blush and elegantly flavored, mild,
sweet yellow flesh

Pallas—One of the so-called honey
peaches that originated in China, it has
very juicy white flesh and a honey-sweet
flavor. Freestone.

PEAR

Abbe Fetel—Large, elongated pears that have very sweet, juicy, melting flesh of excellent quality

Beierschmitt—These yellow-green pears ripen in August. Their flesh is very aromatic and delicious and is free of stone cells.

Canal Red—One of the offspring of Red Bartlett with a melting, smooth flesh of extra high quality.

Comice—The flesh of this late summer pear is yellow, very juicy, sweet, aromatic, and buttery.

Doyenne Gris—One of the best old-fashioned pears, with sweet, delicious, rich, buttery white flesh

PLUM

Coe's Golden Drop—With its yellow skin and flesh, this plum is extremely sweet and melting and its flavor is similar to apricots.

Count Althann's Gage—A purple-red skin plum with yellow dots and sweet, firm yellow flesh with excellent flavor

Elephant Heart—It has red skin, red flesh, and red juice of extreme sweetness and quality. It was introduced by Luther Burbank.

Santa Rosa—Another Burbank introduction and a Japanese-type plum of excellent flavor

RASPBERRY

August Red—A medium-sized, extra sweet red berry with luscious raspberry flavor

Black Hawk—Large black raspberries with balanced sweetness and acidity

Chilliwack—A true summer berry with outstanding flavor and extra high quality that ripens in July

Rossana—A bright red berry with excellent flavor that ripens in late summer

STRAWBERRY (SUMMER BEARING)

Ruegen Improved—An Alpine-type strawberry with a lovely scent and intensely sweet strawberry flavor. Bears all summer long.

Sparkle—Dark red, conical fruits that have a wonderful strawberry sweetness

Suwanee—Rated as the best-tasting main crop strawberry

WATERMELON

Charleston Gray—A very sweet, full-sized watermelon with crisp, fiberless flesh

Seedless Sugar Baby—A small, "icebox"-size watermelon with great-tasting red flesh

Strawberry—A watermelon with delicate texture and a superior, distinctive sweet flavor

VEGETABLES

BEET

Burpee's Golden—With excellent flavor, it is not as earthy as red beets. Buy with greens on and use greens as a separate vegetable.

Lutz Green Leaf—You can purchase this variety as a small or large beet. It never gets tough or fibrous and always retains its excellent sweet flavor.

CARROT

Berlicummer—This matures into a long, straight, perfectly-flavored carrot in late summer.

Indian Long Red—A slim carrot with an outsized taste of true carrot flavor

Nantes Half Long—Considered by many to be the best-tasting carrot of them all

Parisian Rondo—A "baby" carrot with excellent carrot flavor that grows into a small, ball-like shape

Touchon—A Nantes-type carrot with that wonderful flavor but grows to a full-carrot size

CORN

Ambrosia—A sugary-enhanced type with great flavor and sweetness

Golden Bantam—Introduced 110 years ago, it is still one of the most popular yellow-corn varieties because of its sweet, tender, fine-flavored kernels.

Honey and Cream—A bi-color corn with white and yellow kernels and a rich, sweet corn flavor

Honey 'n' Pearl—An Xtra-Sweet bi-color corn that has rated high in All-American taste tests

How Sweet It Is—One of the first Xtra-Sweet hybrids and still one of the very best

Illini Xtra-Sweet—The first Xtra-Sweet hybrid with unbelievably sweet kernels.

Iochief—Its old-time real corn flavor makes it the winner in taste trials.

Luther Hill—Because of its exceptional old-fashioned flavor, it's used by breeders to impart quality to their hybrids.

Silver Treat—Superior to Silver Queen for taste

Silverado—Another white-kernel corn with excellent flavor

CUCUMBER

Burpless—An easily digested cucumber of fine, mild flavor and nonbitter skin, so it needs no peeling

Sweet Slice—A hybrid with nonbitter skin (needs no peeling) and very sweet flesh

Telegraph Improved—A dark green, tapered vegetable that yields crisp, white, flavorful flesh

Greenhouse—These are the extra long, striated cukes you find wrapped in plastic in the stores. They are super high-quality cucumbers.

Middle Eastern—Considered by connoisseurs to be the best flavored of all cucumbers for salads. Also called Beit Alpha.

EGGPLANT

Dourga—The cylindrical eggplants are usually six inches long and have pure white skin. The flesh is also white with a sweet, delicate flavor.

Louisiana Long Green—Green eggplants with darker green stripes and excellent quality

Rosa Bianco—These eggplants are four to six inches long and three inches across, with lavender and cream skin and very fine-flavored flesh of fine texture.

Violetta Lunga—These are oblong and bulbous at the blossom end; their skin is purple-black and they have out-of-this-world flavor.

GREEN (SNAP) BEANS

Aramis—A French-style filet bean that is rated best in taste tests

Blue Lake—One of the most widely planted and best-flavored beans

Fortex—A filet pole bean with rich flavor, especially when it measures just 5 to 7 inches.

Frenchie—A gourmet mini-bean that is small in length but large in sweet flavor

Gold Crop—One of the very best golden

yellow wax beans that is an All-America Selections winner

Kentucky Blue—A bean that combines the best flavors of two pole beans, Kentucky Wonder and Blue Lake Pole, and is sweeter than both of them

Masai—A very slender filet bean of surpassing quality used in gourmet restaurants around the world

LETTUCE

Forellenschluss—Green romaine-type leaves flecked with burgundy that have gourmet-quality sweetness

Little Gem—Small- to medium-sized romaine-type heads with very sweet flavor

Merveille des Quatre Saisons—An excellent lettuce that actually does best in summer

Oakleaf—Looseleaf type of lettuce that resembles an oak leaf. Its leaves are sweet, tender, and never bitter, even in hot weather.

Sierra—Batavian-type of French lettuce with red-tinged green outer leaves and a creamy heart

Summer Bibb—Small, thick-leaved, high-quality, sweet lettuce that grows well throughout the warm months

LIMA BEANS

Fordhook 242—Same excellent flavor as Fordhook but better for hot weather and easier to shell

King of the Garden—An old-fashioned but high-quality pole lima bean

OKRA

Cajun Delight—Its pods have less fiber and stay tender longer than most other okras.

ONION (SWEET SUMMER)

Red Torpedo—Large spindle-shaped, slightly pungent bulb with a delicate, sweet flavor.

Texas 1015Y—A mild, sweet yellow onion of the same type as Walla Walla, Maui, and Vidalia; it's great when used raw in salads.

PEA

Burpeeana—Sweet, tender peas for the beginning of summer

Lincoln—Short pods, small peas, but surprisingly sweet flavored

Sugar Mel—One of the stringless, eat-all sugar snap peas and a taste-test winner to boot

Tall Telephone—An old variety that produces large pods full of exquisitely sweet, tender peas

Waverex—A petit pois type, with super-sweet small peas

PEPPER (SWEET)

California Wonder—A green bell pepper that ripens to a sweet, crunchy, thick-walled crimson color

Corno di Toro Rosso—A long, tapered pepper that is red when ripe and perfect for frying, pickling, and eating raw

Golden Summer—A golden-yellow bell pepper with thick walls, blocky shape, and prize-winning flavor

PEPPER (PUNGENT)

Ancho—Also known as poblano, this pepper is the chief pepper for chilies relleno, with its medium spiciness and delicious pepper flavor.

Chilcostle—A gourmet pepper from

Oaxaca, Mexico, it is widely planted now in the United States for the restaurant trade because of its superiority.

Guajillo—A very hot pepper that turns a pretty red at maturity

Habanero—A pepper that carries an attractive aroma and flavor, if you can stand its blistering heat

Pasilla de Oaxaca—Long, tapered peppers that turn black-brown when ripe and are prized for making mole sauce

POTATO

Bintje—These are small potatoes, but they are widely grown around the world for their fine flavor.

French and German Fingerlings—Great flavor in small, narrow potatoes with waxy texture

Kennebec—The potato for making French fries; they are not always easy to find, but worth looking for.

Rose Finn Apple—Its rosy skin, great flavor, and fine waxy texture make this fingerling-type potato perfect for roasting or pan-frying.

SEAWEED

Dulse—Its reddish purple leaves are eaten raw as a snack and have a unique, delicious flavor.

Kiwa—One of the best tasting sea vegetables, it can be eaten raw or mixed with small pieces of meat and fried.

Wakame—With its delicious, fine-textured, and sweet fronds, it is often a part of kim chi.

SQUASH (SUMMER)

Gold Rush—Straight 7– to 8-inch zucchini cylinders with golden skin and flavorful white flesh

Long Cocozelle—Long, straight, cylindrical zucchini with greenish-white, firm flesh of excellent quality

Peter Pan—A hybrid patty pan–type of summer squash with light green skin and pale green, high-quality flesh

Sunburst—Another hybrid, with golden-yellow skin and white flesh with a delicate and buttery flavor

TOMATO

Big Beef—All the old-time flavor of a beefsteak tomato in an extra-large package

Brandywine—An heirloom tomato with a fine, gourmet-quality, wine-like flavor

Costoluto Genovese—A ribbed, red, old-fashioned Italian tomato with outstanding flavor

San Marzano—An Italian paste tomato that is very meaty and exceptional for making marinara sauce

Sun Gold—A very high-quality small tomato with an orange-gold color and intense sweet flavor

Sweet 100—An extraordinarily sweet red cherry tomato with a high vitamin C content.

Recipes by Icon

Make Ahead ❄

No Cook ⊖

Recipes by
Summer Spotlight Ingredient

CORN

CUCUMBER

LETTUCE

MELON

SUMMER SQUASH AND ZUCCHINI

Index

C

Roasted Red Pepper Tapenade, 48
Rotisseried Chicken on the Grill, 167–168
rum
    Daiquiri, 275
    Mojito, 273
Russian Dressing, 285–286

S

safety
    allergy warnings, 9
    chicken, 156, 162
    chile peppers, 74
    eating outdoors, 71, 110
    heat and flames, 55, 56, 185, 214, 215, 245
    lobster, 195
    marinating, 172, 189
salad bowl, 86
salad dressings, 283, 287
    Asian Soy-Ginger Dressing, 283
    Carrot-Ginger Dressing, 284
    Classic Vinaigrette, 282
    Cobb Salad Dressing, 287
    Creamy Blue Cheese Dressing, 285
    Creamy Buttermilk Dressing, 285
    Garlic-Parmesan Dressing, 286
    Ginger-Soy Dressing, 284–285
    Russian Dressing, 285–286
    Sesame-Citrus Dressing, 284
    Summer Berry Dressing, 287–288
    Verjus Salad Dressing, 288
    Walnut-Lemon Dressing, 286
salad embellishments
    Candied Walnuts, 288–289
    Croutons, 289
salads, 84–86, 89, 91, 94, 95

Asian Steak Salad, 124
Baby Greens Salad, 87
Caprese Salad, 96–97
Ceviche, 130–131
Chef's Salad, 94–95
Chicken and Jasmine Rice Salad, 121–122
Chicory and Walnut Salad, 91
Citrusy Tofu and Rice Salad, 120
Classic American Potato Salad, 110
Classic Caesar Salad, 92–93
Cobb Salad, 96
Cold Green Bean Salad, 103
Cold Roasted Beet Salad, 102
Coleslaw, 111–112
Couscous Salad with Pine Nuts and
    Summer Fruits, 116–117
Crab and Cucumber Salad, 129
Crab Louis, 130
Creamy Polish Cucumber Salad, 100
Cucumber Salad, 97
Cucumber, Tomato, and Olive Salad, 100
French Potato Salad, 110
Fresh Herbed Salad, 91–92
German Potato Salad, 110–111
Ginger-Scallion Coleslaw, 113
Greek Salad, 93–94
Green Papaya Salad, 106–107
Grilled Corn Salad, 103
Grilled Peach and Fig Salad, 109
Heirloom Tomatoes and Prawns, 127
Lettuce Medley Salad, 87
Lobster Salad, 128–129
Mâche and Baby Arugula Salad, 90–91
Melon-Lime Salad, 107
Mesclun Salad, 88–89
Midwestern Sweet-and-Sour Coleslaw,
    112